The World We're In

The World We're In

WILL HUTTON

LITTLE, BROWN

A *Little, Brown* Book

First published in Great Britain in 2002 by Little, Brown

Copyright © 2002 by Will Hutton

The moral right of the author has been asserted.

A CIP catalogue record for this book is available from the British Library.

Typeset in Dante by M Rules
Printed and bound in Great Britain by Clays Ltd, St Ives plc

Little, Brown
An imprint of
Time Warner Books UK
Brettenham House
Lancaster Place
London WC2E 7EN

www.TimeWarnerBooks.co.uk

To

Jane, Sarah, Alice and Andrew

Contents

Acknowledgements

There are many to thank in the writing of a book this length and with this degree of perhaps foolhardy ambition. At many times over the last eighteen months I have wondered whether I had bitten off more than I could chew, and wished that I had decided on something more modest. But in the writing I became more convinced that one of the book's central contentions – that in today's world it is impossible to conceive of a national economic, political and social programme in isolation – is correct. Developments in Britain are governed to so great an extent by events and ideas outside our borders, particularly by those in the US, that the only way to capture what is happening is to offer an international context and analysis. Unless we do, we comprehend only a small fraction of the reasons why we make the choices we do and of the political and economic battles we need to fight.

The first person whom I must thank is William Davies, who has worked for me as my principal researcher for fifteen months. Research is a demanding and sometimes solitary activity, and I was lucky to find William, who is intelligent, dedicated, thorough and capable of sustained research. He understood the thesis and directed his efforts to support it. There is no chapter where his research has not been important. He offered considered feedback and honest criticism as the book unfolded, and I hope he is pleased with the result.

Charlotte Beaupère worked as an additional researcher for some eight months, largely on chapter 2 and the European chapters of the book. I hoped she would bring a distinctive French perspective on Europe, and access to a different literature. I was not disappointed. Charlotte's work was thoughtful and original. Together, she and William provided the depth of research from which the book could be written.

I was also lucky in my friends in Britain, the US and Europe who have read draft chapters or sequences of draft chapters and offered invaluable feedback, corrections and advice. Halfway through I held a seminar at the LSE on the first five chapters (excluding chapter 2), and I owe thanks to Richard Layard, Richard Sennett, Adam Swift, Nina Planck and David Held for their constructive criticism. Adam in addition read no fewer than three drafts of chapter 2, and his knowledge of political philosophy is awesome. My huge thanks to him; if there are still problems with the chapter then they are wholly mine. David Held, who helped with *The State We're In*, proved to be a no less loyal and wise supporter of this effort. By the end he had read the entire first and second drafts, and I profited enormously from his detailed comments as well as his view of the shape of the overall argument.

None of my American friends should take any responsibility for my thesis or any row that may ensue. It's all my fault. Three seminars in July 2001 on the first half of the book were invaluable. At the University of Berkeley, Jerome Kerobel put together a group who gave me intelligent feedback and counsel; my thanks to him, Issac Martin, Michael Reich, Fred Block and George Lakoff and their detailed written comments afterwards. It was Todd Gitlin who led to Jerome; thank you for the suggestion! Laura Dyson and John Zysmann at Berkeley took time out of their hectic schedules to offer comment and critical feedback.

Bob Kuttner, the editor of the American *Prospect*, organized a seminar at his wonderful summer house in Wellfleet, Cape Cod. Robert Reich, Barry Bluestone (and his father), Richard Rothstein and Bob gave me a concentrated and critical appraisal – thanks again for their comments at the time and afterwards.

In Washington, John Judis, Gene Sperling, Larry Mishel, Tom Edsall, John Schmitt, Roger Hickey and Kathleen Thelen all offered important reactions and insights. Samuel Wells, a friend of nearly twenty years, kindly organised a seminar at the Wilson Center. This was again an opportunity for constructive critical feedback and commentary, and my thanks go to Martin Albrow, Jodie Allen, Joseph Bell, Matthew Holden, Kent Hughes, Bruce Stokes, Philippa Strum, Michael van Dusen and Sam and Sherry Wells for investing so much time in putting me if not right, at least less wrong. Philippa Strum and Matthew Holden made detailed comment afterwards, and later in December I was lucky to find an insomniac Philippa who cast an eye over my second draft of the first five chapters, again to my profit. Thanks also to Sidney Blumenthal, who gave a very useful critique of the central thesis.

In October Timothy Garton Ash and David Miliband joined a small seminar on the European chapters at what was then the Industrial Society (now the Work Foundation); together with commentary from Charles Grant, this was a crucial benchmark in showing where the argument needed to be strengthened. Three of my then fellow directors at the Society – Richard Reeves, John Knell and Patrick Burns – offered important feedback and comment, as did Robin Cook, Andrew Oswald, Mary Koi, James Long, Ian McEwan, Hans-Friedrich von Ploetz and Noreena Hertz. My thanks also to the anonymous reader arranged by Little, Brown.

In early November I was privileged to have a short tour of Germany, arranged by Gero Mass, director of the London office of the Friedrich-Ebert Stiftung. My thanks to him, and to Martin Behrens, Ludiger Pries, Hagen Lesch, Wolfgang Streeck, Martin Hopner and Wolfgang Üllenberg. All provided important feedback and comment on the book, offering a German dimension on the issues raised that came at a critical juncture in my thinking. I must also include the Venice Seminar, which I attended at the invitation of the Italian ambassador to London, Luigi Amaduzzi, and the British/Italian colloquium in Potignano, in March and September of 2001, respectively, as important moments when I was able to test-run some arguments. My thanks for inclusion at both. Jim Garrison of the State of the World Forum and Marcello Palazzi – two doughty campaigners for a better world – offered important encouragement.

Then to my editors. Philippa Harrison at Little, Brown had promised to edit the book, but left the company before it was completed. However, she kept her promise and edited it as a personal favour. I was the beneficiary of a master craftswoman at work. Whether it was the chapter sequence, the structure of individual chapters, or questions of content and style, she was and is superb. And when I was fading towards the end, she and David Held combined to keep up my spirits and insist I find the energy for yet more redrafts. Richard Beswick took over her role at Little, Brown, so that in the closing months I was lucky to have a second fine editor, joined for the final copy-edit by the meticulous Gillian Bromley. My thanks to them all; and of course to that great agent and lover of books, Ed Victor, without whom this book would not have been written. My father, as for all my books, was a valued and constructive critic and adviser; many of the views expressed he, and my mother, will recognise as those we have discussed since my boyhood. Roger Alton, editor of the *Observer*, agreed to a month's leave of absence from my column and other writing obligations to help complete the book; and Sir Christopher Wates and the trustees of the Industrial Society, in allowing me to express 'time sovereignty', gave me the scope to find crucial writing time in an otherwise crowded working week.

Almost all of these 140,000 words – along with redrafts – were written in 2001 while I was simultaneously discharging my responsibilities to the Industrial Society and the *Observer*. It was physically and intellectually shattering, and inevitably my family bore some of the costs having to make do with a distracted and obsessed father – especially towards the end. Sorry. My wife, Jane, in trying times was magnificent. All I can say is a profound and intensely felt thank-you for your love and forbearance. I hope you think it's been worth it.

Will Hutton
17 March 2002

Introduction

With the launch of the euro and the hardening of self-confident American unilateralism in the defence of what the Republican party now calls 'the homeland', the relationship between the US and Europe is set to become more tense. These are two enormous power blocs with different visions of how the market economy and society should be run, and with different conceptions of how the great global public goods – peace, trade, aid, health, the environment and security – can be achieved and maintained. The relationship between the two is the fulcrum on which the world order turns. Managed skilfully, this could be a great force for good; managed badly, it could give rise to incalculable harm.

Britain is faced with a fundamental choice about whom it sides with. European integration is accelerating: the euro is in circulation, and at the Laeken summit in December 2001 agreement was reached to establish a preparatory convention to examine the outlines of a European constitution before the 2004 intergovernmental conference. The issue will come to a head if and when the referendum on the euro is held. But the question is larger than whether Britain should join the euro. It is: on which side of this argument do we want to put our weight? And that in turn is a question about what values should underpin the building of Britain's economic and social model. How much are we European – and how much do we have in common with an America increasingly in thrall to a very particular conservatism?

This question is posed as British politics drifts around a managerial centrism. There are no great political movements or inspirational causes. Voter apathy is widespread. Our political leaders are well-intentioned, but they are at a loss as to how to revive a belief in politics and public purpose. As I write at the beginning of chapter 1, the public realm is in eclipse. It is almost as though citizenship has gone into abeyance.

And yet there remain great issues. The terms of society's social contract remain as vexed and contentious as ever. The rich grow richer while disadvantage remains acute. Equality of opportunity, let alone of income and wealth, remains elusive. Public services are inadequate. And since I began the book, the terrorist attacks of 11 September 2001 are a horrifying reminder of the scale of atrocity that intercultural hatred can spawn – and of the urgent need to find some form of international settlement, along with the necessary policing, that reduces and hopefully eliminates the risk of any repeat.

This book is a response to these concerns. It is profoundly critical of American conservatism, now the dominant political current in the US, and of its impact on the US and the world. It sets out to correct the torrent of criticism levelled at Europe as though the US were a paragon of all the virtues – rather than a country with some severe economic and social problems, whose democracy, where votes and office are increasingly bought, is an offence to democratic ideals. European capitalism and its accompanying social model – and its democracy – by contrast have much to offer. The old world, contrary to the internationally accepted wisdom, has much to teach the new.

So this is a book for the idea of Europe. In my view, the quest for European union is one of the great rousing and crucial political projects of our time. It is vital in providing a counterweight to the US and thus offering genuine multilateral leadership in the search for securing global public goods. It is a means of advancing core European values. It is also the way to reanimate our politics and the public realm – and, indirectly, to put our economy on an upward trajectory of productivity and to build a less unequal society. We British are more European than we begin to realise, and our alliance with the US – bound by history and language though we are – needs to be recast in the light of our European vocation. We should, of course, join the euro.

These are not the current accepted wisdoms, and if the book has done its work I expect a vigorous reply. The argument is much needed, and the Eurosceptics have had too clear a run for too long. But one charge that will be made I must refute from the outset. That I am critical of American conservatism and its impact on the US and the globe does not mean that I am anti-American. I have been careful to distinguish the American liberal and conservative traditions throughout. The world has been lucky over the twentieth century that at key junctures the politicians running the US, and the dominant discourse, have been liberal. We need them back. It is through a coalition between liberal America and a European Union confident about its values that a benign world order can be constructed. For non-American and non-European readers, this does not mean I neglect your proper claims and interests; I am merely being hard-headed about where power lies and to whom global responsibilities fall.

The US remains a remarkable country. Its noble traditions of democracy, its vitality and its commitment to the acquisition of education – one of the first institutions each of the new states of the union began was a university – continue to inspire. But all this is now obscured by rampant inequality and an increasingly feral capitalism, together with an overblown conservative rhetoric that prevents self-knowledge and intelligent self-criticism. Indeed, it is my affection for the best of America that makes me so angry that it has fallen so far from the standards it expects of itself. Nor do I share the condescension that some Europeans express for American culture. I enjoy Sheryl Crow and Clint Eastwood alike; delight in Woody Allen, *Frasier* and *Seinfeld*; love American football; am in awe of the intellectual firepower marshalled at the US's great universities; and am grateful for Windows 98 (and 2000) and the internet – only the latest in a long line of inventions the US has bequeathed to the world.

I have never doubted that the US had to respond to the terrorist attacks of 11 September by military intervention in Afghanistan; terrorism needs a place to operate from, and the elimination of its physical sites is a crucial precondition for eliminating terrorism. But I have always coupled this support with a demand for genuine economic and social reconstruction and the building of a juster international order less likely to incubate terrorism. What has been dismaying has been the readiness of the US to set about the first element of response while almost completely neglecting the second. The victors of World War Two would not have made the same mistake, spending many billions of dollars on strengthening an already impregnable military position while refusing to increase aid flows to the underdeveloped world to remotely adequate levels or develop multilateral institutions – but that was before the calamitous rise of conservatism.

Moreover, as should be clear from the notes and references, I have said nothing about the US that Americans have not said themselves. Without the existing body of critical American literature the book could not have been written. Those who try to win this argument by name-calling critics of the current order 'anti-American' serve themselves badly. There are plenty of Americans who will find themselves in some agreement with what follows, and as anxious as any European to develop a less one-sided world order. We simply freeze argument and exchange if all criticism gets dismissed as anti-American and thus invalid.

One last point. 'Liberalism' means different things in the US, Britain and Europe. I have adopted the American usage. Liberalism in the US is the creed that advocates a rational, universal infrastructure of justice built on complex trade-offs between liberty, solidarity and equality – and this is sufficiently near European conceptions of liberalism for the term to work in both contexts. 'Liberal' or 'neo-liberal' economics, however, is free market economics asserting the primacy of individualism, which I have chosen to call 'conservative' throughout to avoid ambiguities over the use of 'liberal'. American readers will know that there are a number of shades of conservatism; again for ease of exposition I have simply called all them all conservative.

That's it. For too long the European case in Britain has gone wanting. This is my attempt at correcting the imbalance.

1
The rescue

The idea of the public realm is in eclipse, and with it a conception of civilisation. We British are no longer citizens who make common cause and share common destinies. The scope for public initiative and endeavour through which our common values are expressed is contracting with giddy speed. Inequality of income and opportunity is increasing, with no ready check to hand. Wealth and stratospheric incomes are portrayed as the just reward for individual enterprise, badges of individual worth. The poor and disadvantaged, unless they declare their readiness to work, are increasingly felt to deserve their status. Government and its associated tools of regulation, legislation and taxation are a currency whose very legitimacy is in question.

Britain has not developed these ideas on its own; they would have neither their strength nor their respectability without the rise of American conservatism and the preponderance of American power. Britain's core beliefs are more European. The fruits of a successful economy should be spread around to produce a successful society. Inequality of income and opportunity cannot be indulged and as far as possible needs to be countered. Government is the means for expressing our social concerns and preferences. Through it we express our citizenship. To argue for its illegitimacy is to argue for barbarism.

Yet the discordant, even alien, ideas summarised in my first paragraph have become a central part of Britain's cultural and political landscape. In this respect the most salient political event of our times has been the rise of the American right over the last twenty-five years and the collapse of American liberalism. It has been in the US that this conservative philosophy has been most aggressively and successfully championed, and it is there that it continues to dominate. The apparent success of its economy at home and its victory in the Cold War abroad have been an ostensible validation of all that conservative America stands for.

Political ideas matter. They define what is possible and impossible; they win hearts and minds. As the new conservatism has honed its rhetoric and political programmes in the US to celebrate individualism and denigrate the state, so that same philosophy has become seamlessly part of the new international 'common sense'. The American example, the scale of American power and its control of the means by which ideas are disseminated – from the financial markets to the great international institutions – have all combined to transform the political geography of the West. We are all becoming American conservatives now.

The barren triumph of conservatism

So it is that we subscribe to the curious syllogism that the rights of the propertied and the freedom of business come before any assertion of the public interest or social concerns, because these are the only circumstances in which wealth generation and employment can be assured, and thus the citizen stands to lose more by putting these at risk than he or she might gain from public action asserting common interests. The law of private property rules supreme. In this climate taxation is depicted as the confiscation of what is properly our own – an intolerable burden that should be reduced. The social, the collective and the public realm are portrayed as the enemies of prosperity and individual autonomy and, worse, are opposed to the moral basis of society, grounded as it should be in the absolute responsibility of individuals to shoulder their burdens and exercise their rights alone.

To maintain our schools and universities, our hospitals, our pensions, our welfare system and even our public transport has become an uphill struggle, prosecuted in the teeth of a consensus that the taxation that sustains them is a moral and economic evil. It is impossible to argue that wealth generation is as much a social as an individual act, and that successful companies are more than money-making, profit-maximising machines. It is not capitalism's job to serve us; it is our job to serve capitalism.

This is not a sustainable or a workable philosophy. It is not just that our public structures and social contract are of profound importance, and that patterning a society so that the rich are in a position of self-perpetuating dominance and the poor trapped at the bottom offends the canons of justice. It is that the resulting economic model does not itself work. For wealth creation *is* a social act. Companies that last and prosper are motivated by a vision of their purpose that transcends maximising their shareholders' immediate profits. The workforce that is productive and creative is the workforce that is not treated as so many economic chattels but as a group of respected human beings. Business organisations profit from the social and public infrastructure in which they are embedded and where they trade. The stronger a country's society, the stronger its business community.

The weaknesses of our civilisation consecrated to the contrary, conservative propositions are becoming ever more evident. The supremacy of market contract mean that careers, living standards and relationships are in a permanent state of contingency, dependent upon the next twist in the markets' volatile judgements and increasingly unprotected by commonly held institutions or systems for sharing risk. Civility is under siege as a market society makes strangers of us all. While our public horizons shrink, we search for satisfaction and contentment in our inner, private lives – but we turn in on ourselves thus not of choice; rather, we recognise that engagement with the world on any other terms than those that enthrone the primacy of market values and diminish those of public citizenship is increasingly without purpose.

The international system, run as the new conservatism dictates, is demonstrating its frailties. The financial crises and bankruptcies grow larger; in the autumn and winter of 2001–2 the world witnessed its biggest ever corporate bankruptcy (Enron) and largest ever sovereign debt default (Argentina). These followed the largest ever global stock market boom and bust in history, which left in its wake a trail of bankrupt and overly indebted companies, especially in the over-hyped telecommunications and high-technology industries. The shock waves ripple over the world with only weak instruments through which to attempt an internationally co-ordinated response. When and if recovery comes, too many businesses and workers will have been unnecessarily scarred from a boom that was unnecessarily frothy and speculative and an economic slowdown that was protracted by the way it simultaneously assaulted so many countries. The legacy of debt and bankruptcy threatens to dog our economies for years.

The moral asymmetry on which the relationship between business and society has been based lies ruthlessly exposed. Formerly triumphalist business looks for bail-outs from governments whose public purpose values it so recently mocked. The fantastic inequalities between the less developed and developed parts of the world, disregarded for decades, suddenly snap into focus as Western societies ponder the relationship between poverty and disappointed expectations and the incubation of international terrorism. It becomes clear that simple initiatives on debt relief, aid, the promotion of health and access to Western markets that would have improved the condition of poorer countries have not been undertaken. Our open, interdependent societies have made themselves vulnerable by their own selfishness and self-interestedness. There needs to be change.

Within the US itself, the spread and entrenchment of the belief that an effective capitalism must necessarily be ungoverned and that society has no choice but to submit to the dictates of business has had baleful consequences. As the last remnants of the postwar liberal ascendancy inherited from Roosevelt's New Deal have been shattered, American capitalism and society have become harsher, more unequal and less generous. The US that could launch the Great Society programme in the 1960s has disappeared as completely as the US that initiated the Marshall Plan after World War II. American liberalism certainly made mistakes; the system of support for the poor it developed had unwanted and undesirable side-effects, and in championing the interests of minorities it lost sight of the universal values that might have united all Americans.

Equally, there have been some important benefits from the conservative pressure to deregulate – such as mass cheap air travel and the rapid development of the information society – although the hidden and less apparent costs of much deregulation are beginning to show through. The regulatory and auditing failures that allowed the Enron debacle to happen are a salutary warning. Any rational calculation of the over-all costs and benefits of the whole conservative experiment must give a negative result.

The costs mount if the calculation is extended to include what has happened through the extension of conservative principles abroad. The principal reason why so many simple initiatives that might have improved the global infrastructure necessary for a properly functioning globalised market economy have not been taken is because conservative America has been opposed to them. It has sought to maximise its own freedom for manoeuvre rather than setting up rules that might con-strain it. American national sovereignty – America First – is seen not just as a principle which bolsters corporate economic freedom but as a philo-sophical and moral imperative.

This has meant that the entire international order should privilege American autonomy of action and its capacity to act unilaterally, both as a matter of self-interest and as a matter of conservative ideology. Even in the 1970s and 1980s the US was looking outside the international framework of treaties and institutions to secure what it wanted by uni-lateral action – whether pressurising Japan to invest in American government securities in the 1980s or, for example, lobbying Germany to open its telecommunications markets in the early 1990s. But over the last decade the US has increasingly subscribed to a highly and exclusively conservative definition of its interests – a process accelerated in 2001 by the Bush presidency – so that on climate change, on the regulation of international criminality and even financial markets, and over the system of international nuclear missile treaties its stance has been wholly defined by a unilateral assertion of the US position.

Hopes that after 11 September 2001 this would change have been dashed. The US, it was said, would re-engage with the world as it sought to build and sustain a coalition against terrorism. But it has become ever clearer over the months since the attacks that, whatever the initial impulse to organise a multilateralist response, the US's unilateralist, go-it-alone instincts have subsequently been entrenched. Its victory in Afghanistan after three months, with the loss of a handful of American lives, proved its vast military technological superiority and was gained with only token support from its allies. In the defence of the 'homeland', as it is now known, the old conservative urges to secure America behind a unilateralist military shield are rampant. Witness the Bush administration's request in early 2002 for an addition in defence expenditure of $48 billion – equivalent to Italy's entire defence budget – despite the disparity between US defence spending and the rest of the world's having reached unprecedented levels.[1] Whatever coalitions the US builds are tactical and self-interested. NATO may have offered its collective help in the action against terrorism; but it might have compromised the US's capacity to act as it chose, so it was not called upon. Its allies may be allowed to help the US, but only by invitation and on American terms. The mindset that has fuelled unilateralism and the building of a global capitalism on conservative terms remains no less entrenched, and may now imperil even NATO itself.[2] It is just having to be more apparently accommodating in how it reaches its ends.

Yet the big question of how internationally to construct a just society and just capitalism has been given extra urgency by the emergence of international terrorism. Military action by the US and the West to eliminate the safe havens from which terrorists operate was – and is – an imperative, but punitive action alone is not enough. The West needs to prove its legitimacy and build a system in which the ideologies that succour terrorism are less likely to flourish. But while some countries in the industrialised West, notably Britain, France and Germany, are interested in reproducing the US's own generosity after World War II with a new 'Marshall Plan' for the less developed world, conservative Washington shows little interest. Its preoccupations are increasingly militaristic: to repress the symptoms of the problem rather than address its cause. America's intervention in Kosovo in 1999 to prevent ethnic slaughter looks increasingly like the last act of the best of the twentieth century US. The twenty-first century US is a darker and less altruistic country.

The issue of justice, and how it is expressed economically and socially, has become the over-riding issue of our times. The refusal of

American conservatives to brook any interpretation other than their own – and the adoption of their analysis as the world standard, enforced by the transmission mechanisms of American finance, multinationals, military superiority and culture, along with the poverty of international governance – is not just a democratic offence both within the US and beyond. It menaces the future.

The lesson of the last decade, a warning for the twenty-first century, is that the world needs an order that is more subtle and more sophisticated. Security, prosperity and justice are global public goods. They cannot and should not be provided as any one country dictates, or as a by-product of what it considers its interests; rather, their provision needs to be international and predicated upon an acknowledgement of interdependence. Moreover, there must be scope within globalisation for different cultures and approaches to capitalism to flourish; we cannot all be homogenised around the principles of American conservatism. In other words, the world needs a different set of principles around which to organise, and leadership that is more generous and more respectful of diversity than that provided by the American right. The only bloc with sufficient economic and political clout to offer these vital qualities is Europe, to which a new challenge falls. There is reason enough to build Europe to secure and protect its own vision of capitalism and accompanying social contract. Now it has a global responsibility to become the countervailing force to the US around which a more enlightened and liberal global order can be formed.

The creed and the challenge

The conservative creed we have been asked to accept barely needs rehearsing. The Americans live with increasingly unequal distribution of income and wealth – indeed, many argue it is the necessary stick and carrot upon which a successful capitalism depends – so others should follow. The message is merciless. The object of companies is to maximise profits for their shareholders, so that all obstacles to that end – from trade unions to planning laws – should be as minimal as possible. Taxation is seen as a distortion of business decision-making and a confiscation of what belongs to individuals by right. Welfare is portrayed as disabling the poor from taking proper responsibility for themselves. The rich and business have only the obligation to the poor or to society as a whole that their own conscience and philanthropic instincts dictate. The poor and disadvantaged should expect no more than minimal, time-limited and means-tested assistance; they should essentially take their chance in a culture in which, if they work hard, there is no barrier to their upward mobility, as successive waves of immigrants have proved.

The conservative American presumption is that the federal government, conforming to the spirit of the founding fathers of the American constitution, should exercise its authority as minimally as possible – and that any departures from that rule should be temporary. Individual states in the union should be given the responsibility for doing as little as they can, and the federal government should confine itself to the provision of national security. Governance in the rest of the world should follow suit. But the so-called 'Washington consensus', enshrining balanced budgets and the urgency of implementing pro-market solutions, is not just an economic doctrine to be applied universally; it has profound social and political repercussions. The prescribed response to these is equally blunt. If there are malevolent social consequences, then react with a tough welfare system and repress crime. Do not wring your hands over the causes of crime; stamp it out with a repressive criminal justice system, extending even to endorsing the death penalty.

This is a very particular set of propositions supported by a very particular American value system which US conservatives have cleverly exploited. The experience of settling a continent, of pushing a frontier ever further and of representing an escape from a tired European civilisation dominates the American imagination – and gives American conservative ideologists the opportunity to align their own support of rugged individualism with the wider culture. Equally, the American constitution confers a notion of opportunity for all – supported by the social myth of the rise from log cabin to White House – that permits the legitimacy of an otherwise vicious pattern of income inequality that is insupportable in the smaller environment of Europe, where notions of equality are more deeply embedded and socially necessary.

No account of the rise of conservatism is complete without reference to the extraordinary grip of Christian fundamentalism in mainstream American life. The view that the injunctions of the Bible have unbending authority is uniquely shared across the majority of America's religious spectrum – in sharp tension with the secular liberalism of America's non-believers – and since the majority of Americans are religious, public life draws its moral authority from this discourse. This was a country, after all, settled by Protestants to protect their faith, and the culture lives on. Conservatives have exploited this public religiosity to support their arguments for low taxes, welfare minimalism and capital punishment (which exists in thirty-eight of the fifty-one states). It is this very particular cocktail of values that allows American conservatives to yoke together propositions that in Europe would be seen as frankly incompatible; that low taxation, for example, is the badge of a moral society whatever the consequences for society or the wider public realm.

Yet most countries have been so dazzled by America's economic success – its recent record in job generation and creating the information revolution seem to speak for themselves – that the question has been not how to arrest Americanisation on conservative principles but how to promote it. Over the last decade the US recovered its twentieth-century reputation as the embodiment of modernity. That American civilisation was exceptional, with a special vocation to show the world the merits of enshrining liberty at the heart of economic and social organisation – the arrogant assumption at the core of conservative American values – has seemed amply validated. It is only now, as the stock market bubble deflates and prosperity seems more qualified, that the American success story seems shakier. But the basic message stands: in the essentials, the US has got it right.

In Britain and Europe this conviction has induced a collapse of self-confidence in liberal social democracy and a belief that they too must join in the criticism of the public realm and the institutions of the commonweal. In Britain it has been an important, even crucial, element in the evisceration of political exchange. Western democracies have been characterised by one broad family of ideas that might be called left – a belief in the social, reduction in inequality, the provision of public services, regulation of enterprise, rehabilitation of criminals, tolerance and respect for minorities – and another broad family of ideas that might be called right: an honouring of our inherited institutional fabric, a respect for order, a belief that private property rights and profit are essential to the operation of the market economy, a suspicion of worker rights, faith in the remedial value of punitive justice and distrust of the new.

In Britain these distinctions no longer operate. The senior party of the left does not champion the family of liberal left values; rather, New Labour cherry-picks from both traditions to construct a new family of values under the rubric of the 'third way' and tries to make it consistent. Thus it is the party of both enterprise and regulation, of flexible labour markets and trade unions, of repression and rehabilitation, of change and no-change. Since its second general election victory in 2001 it has grown marginally more confident, opening up a debate about the case for taxation to fund an improved National Health Service and insisting that the priority for the use of public resources at the margin is not tax cuts but increased public spending. Yet there remains ample evidence of its leadership's judgement about the overweening ascendancy of conservatism in the extreme caution with which it moves, still respecting the essence of the conservative economic and social model. This leaves little ideological or philosophical headroom for the British right. The result has been an extraordinary narrowing of the British national conversation, the near-fatal implosion of the Conservative party and a House of Commons that offers no sustained opposition or coherent critique of the government – no voice of the government-in-waiting that is a critical part of British democracy.

This is no accident. New Labour has read the runes of our times correctly; to challenge an orthodoxy that is transmitted through every paragraph of the dominant conservative press and every axiom of the accepted economic consensus is to invite intellectual ridicule – and, worse, to hand the business community and international financial markets a stick with which to beat the party and deny it legitimacy. The social democratic parties in Germany, the Netherlands and Scandinavia have made similar choices (though they have given up less ground than New Labour), and even French socialists have followed the trend. Conservative parties in Italy and Spain have been quick to remodel themselves so that they can claim to be part of the new consensus and win power. European summits in Lisbon and Stockholm have endorsed Europe's embrace of a cluster of propositions whose aim, though hotly denied, is in effect to Americanise Europe.

Within Britain these concessions have not been sufficient to placate an angry and disenfranchised right. Casting about for some ideological purchase on the new consensus which has stolen their clothes, they have become fervent opponents of the process of European integration. They will associate with the European Union only to the extent it allows Britain the scope to pursue its proper vocation of adopting whole-heartedly the axioms of the American right and building a mini-America within Britain. One element wants to entrench this commitment by renegotiating the terms of our membership of the EU and joining the North American Free Trade Association (NAFTA) along with Mexico and Canada. Britain, it believes, should associate itself with a cultural 'Anglosphere' of English-speaking nations. This is now, for example, the public position of former British Prime Minister Lady Thatcher, who in her book *Statecraft* urges 'fundamental renegotiation of Britain's terms of EU membership', withdrawal from the Common Agricultural Policy, fisheries policy, all 'the entanglements of common foreign and security policy' and a reassertion of British trade policy. In other words, Britain's membership of the EU would be eviscerated of any substantive content – a process she would complete by applying to join NAFTA, insisting that British values and essential interests do not lie with Europe.[3]

In the absence of a proper argument between left and right, a new and vicious political exchange is emerging that has the character of civil war: Britain must choose to which civilisation it belongs. For British conservatives, the only choice is to side with the Americans completely in any position they adopt and to support the Europeans only to the extent that they wholly back the US. US and British interests are exactly the same, and anything the US does must necessarily be defensible against any European criticism. It is an argument that will surface with full fury when the referendum to join the euro is finally held.

But America is a very different civilisation; its values, interests and politics are not a mirror-image of Britain's. Its dominant conservatism is very ideological, almost Leninist in its tendency to insist that its principles be adopted completely and that its adversaries are so wrong their views have to be resisted to the last. Newt Gingrich, the former Republican leader of the House of Representatives and author of the right-wing 'Contract with America' in 1994, characterised his mission as war – and he spoke for the conservative political tradition. Tom DeLay, Republican leader of the House in November 2001, told airline lobbyists that they had to back the Republican opposition to the proposal in the wake of 11 September that airport security become a federal responsibility, with government employees, in these terms: 'You've got to back us on this, it's ideological.'[4] His resistance succeeded and the bill failed by 218 votes to 214. The American right takes no prisoners – even, or especially, in the wake of a terrible atrocity.

If this war against liberalism had produced more economic and social success it might be validated; but it has not. The US economy constructed around conservative principles is beginning to reveal its weaknesses. It is volatile. Its underlying performance, despite the brouhaha, is nothing like so strong as conservatives pretend. (US companies are much more brittle than their European counterparts. A huge responsibility for successful economic management falls to one institution – the US Federal Reserve, the country's central bank.) There has been an enormous build-up of personal and business debt. The trade deficit cannot continue to expand indefinitely. The social consequences of inequality are impacting on social mobility and the integrity of the political system alike. The bottom half of Americans are treated wretchedly. American conservatism has no reason to make the bold claims it does; it is time for more scepticism about its alleged achievements.

Some values are shared across the West – the rule of law, the commitment to democracy, religious toleration, and the view that markets and profits are the best precondition for an effective economy. But, as we will explore in chapter 2 over three core clusters of values – around the obligations of the propertied to society, the need for a social contract and the centrality of a public realm and government to a happy community – there are sharp differences between mainstream European views and those of American conservatives. This is not a continuum on which Britain lies somewhere about halfway between Europe and the US; Britain lies decisively with Europe.

Capitalism is an immensely adaptable system. Of course it rests upon the principles of private property, enforceable contract, the legitimacy of profit and flexible prices – but this is only the beginning. The legitimacy of each particular capitalism is built upon the acceptance of the mores and values of the community in which it trades, and those are in turn built into the body of its law, its financial system, its contracts and its culture. Those values are not trifles to be cast aside because of the transient success of another variant of capitalism. They are inherent to the vitality of the civilisations in which capitalism is embedded, and which capitalism can and must respect.

In this fundamental sense the current British disillusion with the European Union and European values is self-defeating; for it represents a disillusion and disaffection with ourselves. Britain and British culture have been constructed over centuries from the same crucible and influences that have created European culture; we cannot suddenly adopt conservative American values, because we have not lived the American experience. So much is obvious; but in the face of the anti-European offensive it needs to be restated. The argument between left and right should not mean a choice between Europe and America; it should represent choices here within Britain that respect who we are and why we have become who we are. Once this recognition is made, the avenue is open to acknowledging our shared European heritage and making common cause with countries whose attitudes to twenty-first-century problems correspond so nearly to our own. This is important not just for Britain, but for strengthening Europe's capacity to refashion the world's economic and political dynamics.

The construction of a new international settlement calls for change in the US as well. Unless American conservatism modifies its profound attachment to the notion that the US is an exceptional civilisation, that individual freedom is a transcendent value, that the US has a right to act unilaterally to pursue its interests and that no infringement to its sovereignty can be countenanced, there is no chance of getting even to first base. There can be no durable settlement without America; but without a more liberal America, there can be no such settlement. The strengthening of the American liberal tradition is thus central to any such project. It has become a global concern that it reclaim its position as a force in American life. To succeed in its battle with American conservatism it needs to reconnect to the Enlightenment principles that still dominate Europe and rediscover a language that works in an American context which can again popularise its appeal among the American majority.

American liberalism is not dead. It has fiercely resisted conservatives' attempts to extend their propositions into family and sexual life. America is the home of modern feminism, and there is among Americans a strain of powerful social liberalism which is as suspicious as mainstream European opinion of conservative moral absolutism over abortion, sexual preferences, the role of women and indifference to poverty. There are signs, too, that less vengeful attitudes towards criminal justice may be gaining salience. The US has a proud record of social movements campaigning for justice, and the civil rights movement achieved important gains for blacks. There is a strong, if currently cowed, tradition of genuine liberal egalitarianism in the US that has always reflected itself in its commitment to education for all, its genuine belief in equality of opportunity, its neighbourliness and the individual generosity of many Americans. In a country that is a continent, individual states and cities still guard and protect these values and accompanying institutions. The US liberal tradition could reassert itself again.

The battle for this renaissance must be fought and won on American terrain. However, Europe can help in two vital ways. It can be explicit about the importance of those liberal values itself; and it can demonstrate that they work effectively as a platform upon which to construct a just economic and social order. The old world, in short, needs to become an exemplar of what is possible for the new world – and, around the rebirth of a hard but tolerant liberalism, it needs to offer the rest of the world in general, and the Islamic world in particular, a settlement based on interdependence, reciprocity of obligation and the recognition that there is a global interest. It is the moment when Europe must come of age.

Britain faces a decision. It has the opportunity to join in the process of laying the foundations for a European political architecture that allows Europe better to shape its own destiny and that of the globe. It is this Europe that alone can temper conservative America's urge for autonomy, revenge and repression, and build a more liberal international settlement. Those in America who want to challenge the conservative take-over, to re-establish new terms for American democratic discourse and play a part in building such a settlement will have their position reinforced by a stronger Europe. Britain can stand to one side in this political project – or it can engage with it. There is no doubt about the decision it should take.

The critique

The United States is a continent of 280 million people who share the same language, government, market and legal system. Its companies throughout the twentieth century have been able to organise production on a scale unknown in other countries, taking advantage of the simple rule of production that the more that is cumulatively produced the lower unit costs tend to be. Moreover, corporate America is the beneficiary of a workforce that has had to accept that it may be fired at will with minimal compensation as market conditions change, and that it may have to move to find work – in short, that it has to accommodate to the requirements of the market. Successive waves of immigrants – culminating in a new high with the ten million Hispanic immigrants over the 1990s from Central and South America – have provided a pool of cheap and willing labour, buying into the great American work ethic and the dream that nothing is impossible provided you work hard enough. Abundant and cheap land has made Americans unfussy over planning and the environment. Towns and factory sites rise and fall depending on the vitality of their economic base. And Americans are risk-takers, culturally dismissing failure and moving on in their large country to new prospects, with a flow of rich investors and markets prepared to support innovation and new ideas.

With these advantages of scale, cheap land and cheap labour, the US should be an extremely productive economy. But while it is true that the US enjoys higher average incomes per head than western Europe, this is not because it is extraordinarily productive. In fact, though this is little

19

reported, over the last 20 years output per hour worked in France, the Netherlands, Belgium and the former West Germany has risen so that it is now higher than that in the US, because the Europeans have invested more. It is only fractionally lower in Ireland, Austria and Denmark. The only European country not to have significantly closed the productivity gap with the US is Britain. What still gives the Americans the advantage is that more of their women work and that on average men and women work longer hours – a trend explored in more detail in chapter 5. Put another way, the Europeans have chosen to invest heavily so that they can work shorter weeks and have longer holidays – a perfectly reasonable choice.

After all, as recently as the late 1980s Americans were concerned that they were losing ground to the European and Asian economies; the education and training of their labour force were poor, their investment record was indifferent and their weakening capacity to compete internationally across a range of industries was exposed by the growing trade deficit. American companies were more concerned with financial engineering, merger and takeover than with building value through the patient business of investment and husbanding human resources. In 1992, for example, the future US Treasury Secretary Larry Summers contributed a paper to the famous Harvard Business School Time Horizons Project confirming that US companies wanted investment to pay back in incredibly short periods, and set very high rates of return compared to other major economies; as a result they invested less across the board. But, as the 1990s slid into the stock market boom, with the infamous bubble in high-tech shares, short-term time horizons and a fixation with the stock market's priorities seemed positive benefits – and the economy's weaknesses were temporarily masked. For five years between 1995 and 2000 the economy grew at 4 per cent a year, with unemployment falling in its wake.

But this had much less to do with native entrepreneurial zeal, go-getting capitalism, hire-and-fire labour markets and an embrace of technology at which other countries balk than the barrage of propaganda from American cheerleaders and British Eurosceptics would have us believe. On the contrary, this was more of an old-fashioned consumer boom built on record credit and a monumental inflow of foreign capital to finance the consequent trade deficit – all justified by the mas-sive rise in share values that made consumers feel wealthy and foreigners anxious for a share of the action. Nor could this model have been copied by others, even if it were desirable; the US's relation with the rest of the world and its capacity, with the world's most liquid capital markets and ownership of the world's currency, to attract inward capital flows is unique. Globalisation over the 1990s worked very much to the advan-tage of the US; cheap oil and a worldwide glut of manufactured goods kept inflation low, allowing the Federal Reserve to avoid raising interest rates even as credit and consumption boomed. Indeed, some econo-mists view cheap oil as being the single most important source of rising investment, growth and profits.[5] Moreover, the profits of US multina-tionals abroad have grown at twice the rate of profits at home,[6] and the increasingly credible threat to relocate overseas, as I argue in Chapter 4, has been an important factor in checking the growth of real wages and ensuring that profits have risen as a proportion of US GDP. Globalisation-cum-Americanisation has been very good to corporate America, and thus to Wall Street.

Yet even for the US these trends proved unsustainable. Already the collapse in high-tech shares has brought the allegedly dynamic infor-mation technology sector to a shuddering halt, exposing the massive financial malpractice and technological mistakes committed as the hunger for instant riches tempted companies to float on the stock market with innovations long before they were ready. Even the produc-tivity 'miracle' (explored in more detail in chapter 3) is more a by-product of the boom rather than an entrenched new trend, and recent downward revisions make it less than miraculous. Britain's Professor John Kay, for example, goes further and argues that the US so inflates the growth of US GDP by over-estimating the impact of infor-mation technology investment compared to European statistical practice that this accounting difference alone is equivalent to the main part of the so-called US productivity miracle in the late 1990s.[7] If the adjustments are made there was little or no relative improvement. Even before making these accounting adjustments Julian Callow of Credit Suisse First Boston shows that between 1991 and 1998 productivity growth in Europe on average exceeded the US.[8] American success is a shaky edifice; and the problems that haunted the US only a decade ago remain largely unresolved.

The long run impact of the revolution in information and communication technologies (ICT) is likely to be considerable, but it will not necessarily be the American economy that leads either its development or its exploitation. The technology is ubiquitous, and exploiting its application requires a highly skilled labour force and patient investment – neither of which the US possesses in any abundance. The riddle of the American economy is less its success than why, with so many incomparable assets, it has wound up in such a precarious position. The answer is the opposite to that supplied by the conservatives. It is not the free market and tolerance of vast inequality that drive America, with government the obstacle; rather, it is the same subtle interplay of the market, society, patient finance and government that breeds successful capitalism everywhere – and these relationships have been under siege and deliberately weakened by the conservative revolution.

For where America has enjoyed success, it has been due to much more subtle factors than those conservatives believe responsible. The recent improvement in productivity in ICT – much more modest, in any case, than the hype suggested – was no more than the typical phenomenon of productivity gains working themselves through the economy after a paradigm-changing technological innovation – just as they have done in the past, as Barry Bluestone and Bennett Harrison describe in their important book *Growing Prosperity*. Moreover, the ICT revolution was itself spearheaded by government investment, notably led by the Pentagon; the internet, for example, grew out of the decentralised networked system developed to co-ordinate the responses of a multiplicity of military decision-making and operational sites. US leadership in satellite and aerospace technology has been the direct consequence of defence spending, although even that has been challenged by Europe's Airbus, as described in chapter 4. Even the emergence all over the US of the high-tech 'ideapolises' – the clusters of high-tech companies and new start-ups around leading universities – is not a free market phenomenon. It is federal- and state-funded research that generates the intellectual capital that lies at the core of the ideapolis and then becomes the heart of the new economy base. And although the venture capital industry, at least until the bubble burst, played a key role in funding the start-ups, it operated in a social milieu and within a set of networks that celebrated technology and risk; it was always phenomenally short-term and greedy. Now that the markets are in reverse and government spending on research is falling, the whole delicate mechanism is at risk; but there is little appreciation in the US of either why the high-tech boom got under way or why it is now failing. So prevalent is conservative ideology that many Americans are incapable of understanding what it is they are doing right for fear it might contradict conservative canons.

In fact, the quest for high short-term profitability has set spinning a pitiless and self-defeating vortex, a generator of corporate strategies that enthrone aggressive cost reduction together with investment minimalism and a peripatetic approach to hiring and growth – an approach that unites all the members of the Fortune 500.[9] Indeed, the lionisation of Jack Welch, chief executive of GE for twenty years until his retirement in 2001 and the man who earned legendary status by presiding over eighty consecutive quarters of profits growth, is profoundly symbolic of the US's corporate problem. GE, as James Collins and Jerry Porras explain in *Built to Last*, had been a quality company at the frontier of innovation and progressive management since its foundation in the early 1900s. Even before Welch took it over it had enjoyed years of sustained profits growth, and it had a well-established system for grooming cohorts of able executives. But what Welch saw more clearly and earlier than any other executive of his generation was that if GE redefined its priorities to mirror those of Wall Street it would win a star rating. GE's business aim would move from excellence in engineering to excellence in financial engineering.

Welch declared his objective as being to maximise shareholder value, and he shaped GE to do just that. As Alan Kennedy brilliantly describes,[10] his priority was cost reduction, which he achieved by massive redundancies and allowing the R&D spend to dwindle as a proportion of revenue to below the US corporate average, while transforming GE via a string of deals into a half manufacturing, half financial services company. Everything was subordinated to ensuring that profits grew smoothly quarter by quarter. Contributions to the pension fund were reduced as the stock market boomed; accounting conventions were stretched to smooth out profits and losses, producing the quarterly upward trend that Wall Street liked.[11] Beyond that, the company stood ready to buy back its own shares to ensure they sustained a high rating, putting a total of $30 billion into stock buybacks rather than investment in the core business – an exercise from which Welch, with his extravagant share options that aligned his interests with those of shareholders, benefited directly, ending up with share options worth between $750 million and $1 billion.

When asked how GE had managed to increase its earnings by 14 per cent a year over nearly twenty years, vice-president Frank Doyle replied, 'We did a lot of violence to the expectations of the American workforce.'[12] Indeed: GE sacked over 100,000 of them.[13] The assumption behind the current share valuation is that the earnings growth of the last twenty years can be repeated over the next twenty. But what will be the products and skills that will propel the company's growth? Another round of sweating assets and sackings on the same scale is impossible; the company would cease to be sustainable. Already there are doubts over its future – notably, in the wake of the Enron scandal, its aggressive approach to accounting: paradoxically, the markets are now punishing it for its slavish adherence to their values rather than to those of its business. Setting corporate objectives in line with those of footloose shareholders and not fundamental business needs turns out to be truly a Faustian bargain.

Throughout the 1990s Wall Street and company boards made increasingly common cause in overtly copying the trail blazed by Welch, with company directors being given options to buy their own shares cheaply so that they would benefit directly from a higher share price. The cumulative value of share options in the US in 2000 was some $600 billion, up more than tenfold in a decade – one of the greatest wealth transfers recorded in world history. In this environment the $200 million a year package achieved at the peak of the boom by Michael Eisner, chief executive of Disney, was no longer remarkable but merely another temporary benchmark that others aimed to match. The message is explicit: Don't mind the gap between rich and poor; just enjoy the consequences in terms of 'wealth generation' from which everyone will ultimately benefit.

Income inequality in the US is endemic. The gap between the top 10 per cent and bottom 10 per cent of earners is so large that those 10 per cent at the bottom are considerably poorer than the bottom 10 per cent in most other industrialised countries – the US ranking nineteenth – even while the US has the highest average per capita incomes.[14] This is not a source of economic or social strength. It reduces social mobility, ossifying the US into a class society as the rich gain a stranglehold on the elite educational qualifications that pave the way to the top while those at the bottom are trapped on low skills and low incomes. US social and income mobility is no higher than in Europe, and on some measures, as I explore in chapter 5, it is actually worse.

Moreover, inequality has, as Professor Robert Frank details in his subtle and important book *Luxury Fever*, been an important driver of almost baroque levels of personal spending – on which the growth of the economy so heavily relies and which has reached the limits of sustainability. The first-round effect of this concentration of spending power at the top – the US now has over three million millionaires – is that the rich spend increasingly on luxury items, splashing out extravagantly on everything from their ever larger houses to their over-sized, over-powered cars. These then become the target for the middle class below them; for example, the average new American house is now 2200 square feet, having expanded from 1500 square feet in 1970 as the middle class trades up to meet the new standards of opulence.[15] American consumption is driven by an obsessive desire not to be left behind in the race to show your peers that you are at least as affluent as they are.

However, because hawkish companies bent on maximising value for shareholders are constraining the growth of real wages, spending on this scale has been sustained only by debt. By mid-2001 the total stock of personal debt in the US had climbed to a record 120 per cent of personal income; and the net annual flow of credit to consumers has been running at some $800 billion a year at an annualised rate.[16] Astonishingly, in the first three months of 2001 American consumers not only did not save, they spent 7 per cent more than they earned by using their credit cards and borrowing capacity to the limit. The excuse was that if personal borrowing was high, so were the assets against which the borrowing was made; but this was hardly a sustainable position, dependent as it was on the feelgood factor or wealth effects generated by rising share and property prices.

As recently as the mid-1980s Americans held about a quarter of their savings in Wall Street; now the proportion stands at nearly three-quarters, making the relationships between share price movements, wealth effects and spending even closer. At the time of writing in March 2002, Wall Street is holding its value and there are signs of economic recovery, supported by sharp interest rate reductions, but the entire fabric is on a knife-edge. If share prices were to fall, as a result of mounting doubts about the real profitability and productivity of corporate America in the wake of the Enron scandal, and as indebtedness threatens companies with collapse, or if American consumers were to start to build up their savings again because of loss of confidence, then the consequent fall-away in consumer spending would be very considerable. Whatever happens in the immediate future, it is unlikely that with indebtedness at current levels spending can continue to grow at the same rate over the next decade as it has over the last.

It is also becoming obvious that today's US economy is structured to emphasise both upturns and downturns – in economic jargon, it is pro-cyclical. American companies, anxious about share price and profitability, are quick to lay off workers and cut production to lower their cost base. In October 2001 the US suffered 415,000 lost jobs outside agriculture – the biggest one-month loss for twenty years and a tribute to the new pro-cyclical volatility. This implies another round of falling demand, because companies further down the supply chain respond no less quickly in reducing their production and employment. The weakening of the social safety net, with no more than 39 per cent of unemployed Americans having access to unemployment benefit compared to as many as 70 per cent fifteen years ago, removes a further floor to consumer spending; Richard Freeman, leading labour economist at Harvard University, predicts that the poverty rate could climb well above the 12 per cent level of the last two recessions.[17] The consequent fearfulness makes every worker try to build up a savings cushion as times turn hard in case he or she is hit by redundancy. And, as demand falls and recessionary impulses take over, state tax revenues get hit, especially for states like Florida and Texas reliant on sales taxes whose yield tracks overall consumer spending very closely. State governments are in turn obliged to make a round of public spending reductions – most are constrained by law to balance their budgets – further reinforcing the downward economic momentum.

So it is that the US economy, pressing at the limits of productive capacity in the spring of 2000, then moved into a self-feeding downward lurch in the wake of the collapse of the high-tech share bubble in the early spring of 2001, with multiplier effects kicking in as rapidly in the downturn as they had in the upturn. In the winter of 2001 the economy was in a full recession. By the autumn of that year industrial production had fallen for more than fourteen consecutive months to register the longest decline in output since the 1930s. An economy based on market contracts – from the stock market to the labour market – that can be unravelled at will, and which is susceptible to either real or perceived changes in wealth through share price movements and their impact on consumer spending and business investment, is inherently volatile. The number of recorded bankruptcies in the current slowdown is twice that of the 1991/2 recession. The conservatives have constructed a world that moves rapidly from boom to bust. Small wonder that the Federal Reserve, the US central bank, is increasingly obliged to set interest rates to maintain share prices at high levels. Wall Street is some 50 per cent higher in real terms than any other peak over the last hundred years;[18] if it were to fall towards more normal levels the consequence would be a recession of awesome proportions.

Nor is this the only threat to the precarious US economy. As American consumers spend and uncompetitive US industry fails to meet demand, so the US has sucked in imports on an epic scale. The US trade deficit reached $477 billion in 2000 and scarcely fell in 2001. These are incredible numbers – more than 4 per cent of GDP. The Americans can square the financial circle without the dollar collapsing only because foreigners are prepared to invest in the US on an equally epic scale, spending more than $100 billion a year directly buying American companies and more than $150 billion a year buying American shares and bonds. Foreign ownership of American assets doubled to $6.7 trillion between 1995 and 2000, equivalent to some two-thirds of American GDP. Without such inflows the US economy could not continue to grow; yet they are unlikely to double again over the next five years.[19] Put another way, the net international investment position in 2000 was minus $2.187 billion, a fifth of GDP: if there is only modest growth and no fall in the dollar then the stock of the US's international debts will explode to anywhere between half and two-thirds of US GDP over the next five to seven years – a completely unsustainable position.[20] For the inflow of foreign capital is entirely dependent on the expectation that the good times will continue to roll, and in any case is dwarfed by the size of the trade deficit and deteriorating international balance sheet. If foreigners ever began to believe that share prices might fall, there could be only one consequence: the dollar would fall sharply. It is a commonplace among economists that the dollar needs to fall at least 30 per cent to correct the trade deficit; and a fall of that magnitude would trigger potential inflation, a rise in interest rates and a crash in Wall Street that would in turn provoke the dramatic and self-feeding cutbacks in spending that could drive the economy into a recession. So bleak is this prospect that conservative America will resist it. Trade protection, as the levying of 25 per cent tariffs on steel has forewarned, will be a more tempting option.

Thus the American economy rests on an enormous confidence trick; and if either of its twin supporters – foreign investors or domestic consumers – were to withdraw their support, it would be set back for years while the imbalances worked themselves out. Thus everything is consecrated to maintaining growth, and to maintaining confidence that this is understood by policy-makers. Hence the 4.5 per cent cut in short-term interest rates between autumn 2000 and autumn 2001. Hence the way in which the incoming Bush administration presented its ten-year tax-cutting package as a growth package. And hence, after 11 September, the further package put forward, allegedly to stimulate growth.

Here again conservative ideology was in full view. If the tax reform package was skewed to help the rich and corporations, it was small beer beside the structure of the proposed stimulus post-11 September. This concentrated on cynical tax breaks for large corporations, notably the abolition of the alternative minimum tax – a measure favouring mining and oil companies, large contributors to the Republican party – while setting aside a derisory fraction of the package's value for tax cuts for middle- and low-income families, who in any case save four dollars of every five they are offered as tax rebates.[21] In the event the administration was unable to get congressional assent for its wild ambitions, in part because the economic danger seemed to recede and in part because a Democrat-controlled Senate insisted upon some essential equity, directing help towards the newly unemployed. Nonetheless the US's apparently impregnable budgetary strength has evaporated within fifteen months of Bush's election. The combination of tax cuts, increased defence spending and more modest forecasts of economic growth has shrunk the projected cumulative government budget surpluses up to 2011 by a stunning $5 trillion – with precious little to show for it.

Nor is this the only casualty of harder economic times. The ICT revolution is imperilled. For as Michael Mandel, the economics editor of *Business Week*, warns in *The Coming Internet Depression*, 'the close relationship between the pace of the technological innovation and a buoyant stock market means that once the process goes into reverse, the much famed pace of technological development stops too. Never has technological progress been so closely related to the vagaries of the stock market.'[22] Yet it is upon this rickety economic and financial structure that the US has built its record of jobs growth.

This too is a lot less impressive when examined closely (see the account in chapter 5). According to conservatives, employment growth in the US is entirely attributable to its 'flexible' labour market – code for the ease with which labour can be hired and fired. But look more closely and it becomes apparent that the employment growth is demand-led, pulled along by the long American consumer boom whose sustainability is now in question. The US has not been generating employment for men; the phenomenon affecting all Western industrialised countries – declining participation of older men (over age fifty-five) – has hit the US as well, even if less severely than many European countries. Male participation in the labour force has *shrunk* by more than 2 per cent since 1973. Where the US has excelled is in pulling women into work in the growing service sectors – education, health, hotels and restaurants; their participation rate has jumped nearly 20 per cent over the last twenty-five years.[23] But this has less to do with the structure of the labour market and more with the sexual revolution and the pressure on male, and thus family incomes. Many women have joined the labour market because their family budgets require two incomes. If the spending slows or even stops, the sectors which favour female work will come under unusually severe pressure, with potentially calamitous social repercussions. Without either the income or the now pared-back access to social security, many households will be in severe financial difficulties.

These economic deformations have begun to have consequences right across US life. American politics, always wide open to the influence of hard cash, has descended over the last twenty years into a bidding war of fund-raising from the corporations and individuals growing fat in the US's booming but unequal society. Four billion dollars was spent on the presidential and congressional campaigns in 2000, with Republican presidential candidate George Bush outspending his rival Democrat Al Gore by close to two to one in the last six weeks. Bush's backers – the oil, drugs, film and banking companies – knew what they wanted: more deregulation, more 'freedom' and more tax breaks; and with his election came payback time. Tough regulations policing stress at work were rescinded within weeks of Bush's taking office after lobbying from campaign contributors; commitments to restrain carbon dioxide emissions were abandoned to placate the oil and coal lobbies. The proposed abolition of the corporate alternative minimum tax will be particularly kind to Texan oil producers – all Bush backers. The Enron scandal racking Washington in early 2002, swirling around the bankrupt and disgraced company which obviously bought favours and access with its political donations – favours culminating in the selection of regulators for the energy industry in the wake of Bush's election victory, for which it had contributed more than $1 million – has become a symbol of the corporatisation and corruption of American politics.

To campaign effectively in the US you have to have cash – to pay for TV advertising, telephone call banks and direct mail shots – and the candidate with the most cash wins with depressing regularity, as in the presidential primaries. In House and Senate elections the incumbent is almost impossible to beat as he or she is always best placed to raise money: in 1998, 98 per cent of House incumbents and 90 per cent of Senate incumbents were re-elected.[24] And because of the rules on 'soft money' – allowing organisations to advertise in support of a party's campaign issues as long as they do not urge a vote – Republicans, with their richer corporate backers, tend to outspend Democrats, so driving the whole political discourse to the right. Membership of the National Rifle Association, campaigning to resist measures to control the distribution and ownership of guns, may be falling, alongside that of the Christian Coalition; but because they are rich and deliver blocks of votes, the impact of these bodies on US political life through their influence on the Republican party remains immense. American disillusion with US politics is growing; membership of political parties is declining and their direction is falling into the hands of professional activists, fund-raisers and full-time party officials.

This shrinking of the public domain is accentuating the individualism that has always permeated the US. Locked into jobs that demand longer hours and which require extensive commuting – Americans spend an average of seventy-two minutes a day alone in their cars[25] – the average American is necessarily finding the boundaries of his or her social life narrowing. The redeeming feature of American life has always been the vibrancy of its community life, the wealth of what de Tocqueville called its 'associations' and the generosity of its spirit. Americans were a nation of joiners and club-builders, constructing in the process an immense reservoir of social capital and civic trust. In their bowling clubs and rotarian associations Americans participated in the life of their communities, learning the rewards of social reciprocity and negotiation and the sheer pleasure of giving. Americans were individualist, certainly; but theirs was an individualism tempered by membership of many networks of clubs and associations. There was a willingness to vote, to attend a political meeting or join a parent–teacher association. A concern for what the community held in common ranked alongside a concern for one's own individual well-being.

Yet over the past thirty years there has been a marked growth in American selfishness and introversion. Americans have turned away from the great marches and civic disturbances of the 1960s; instead, they look for happiness through the development of their internal selves, by means ranging from the psychiatrist's chair to the range of new age fads and therapies. Collective acts, from participation in team sports to attendance at the theatre, are in decline. Obesity has reached unprecedented levels, with the US Surgeon-General reporting that 61 per cent of Americans are now fat or obese; mental and psychological disorders are climbing to new peaks. Even though the crime rate has fallen, this society of strangers is ever more willing to use the guns whose control conservatives stubbornly resist. Every two years some 50,000 Americans die from guns; between 1993 and 1998 alone there were 200,000 such deaths.[26] Above all, Americans watch television – on average, some four hours of it every day.

Television is provided by great TV companies, part of larger conglomerates that are seeking to maximise shareholder value. So the plot lines of their dramas grow more surreal; the object of talk shows is to shock and titillate; news is compressed into ever shorter slots with ever shorter soundbites; current affairs becomes obsessed with celebrity and discussions that generate controversy and heat – all in the search for audience and market share. American TV journalism has reduced political debate to a kind of sport in which the task is to score politicians for their performance and second-guess the impact on public opinion; little attempt is made at exposition or explanation for fear of losing the audience's attention. And the networks are right; more than half of Americans reported that they watched television news with a remote control in their hand.[27]

This is the culture and society through which the conservatives have mounted their assault on liberal values and policy programmes. As the public realm has shrunk, so the cultural case for sustaining federal and state spending and its necessary taxation – already faltering under sustained intellectual assault – has steadily weakened. The scope of and access to welfare has been steadily pared away with the scarcely subliminal message that the recipients are largely black and the taxpayers who fund it largely white; the charge that welfare creates a dependency culture is only the old Confederacy assumption that blacks are inherently lazy dressed up in modern guise. If the US possesses the best doctors, hospitals and medical technology in the world, forty-three million of its people remain without any form of health insurance.[28] If the US has a top tier of world-class universities, they exist alongside a public education system creaking at the seams, with US students achieving among the lowest scores in international rankings for performance in maths.[29] The country's physical infrastructure, as described in chapter 4, is run down and crumbling.

One of the few areas in which conservatives consider public spending legitimate is countering crime. The US has 5 per cent of the world's population but 25 per cent of its prison population – overtly approved as a means of neutralising the troublesome adults (most of them black) for whom there is little chance of rehabilitation and no likely work. The dehumanisation of prisoners has been accompanied by increasing violence in the way they are treated, with guards resorting to chemical and electric shock treatments to achieve restraint. With a shrivelled public realm, no challenge is mounted to the proposition that prison works and that rehabilitation is 'soft'; and the prison population heads inexorably towards two million. Because most southern states disenfranchise convicted felons, there are now 4.2 million disenfranchised voters – 2 per cent of the electorate – most of whom, given the chance, would vote Democrat; this is the key reason why in 2000 George Bush won Florida and thus the presidency. Disenfranchisement was a potent political weapon in sustaining white supremacy in the post-Reconstruction south; now it is an important instrument in sustaining Republican rule at both state and national level.

This, then is contemporary America. If it is rich and entrepreneurial, it is also economically volatile, profoundly unequal and nothing like as productive as it could be, given its enormous assets. Its democracy, one of the great Enlightenment triumphs and a beacon of hope to many societies around the world in both the past and present, now resembles pre-Enlightenment Europe in its dependence on money and private power. This is the orderly country whose citizens routinely shoot each other. This is where worship at church is rivalled only by worship of the shopping mall. It is becoming a land of individual strangers questing for their inner happiness because the public realm is so corrupted and depleted. It is a country that has burst its limits; an economy that is on the edge. And the whole is overshadowed by a tenacious endemic racism that is the still unresolved legacy of slavery and civil war.

The American dream is of the pursuit of life, liberty and happiness; but the gap between dream and reality is lived out daily with increasing bitterness. America fails almost half its citizens. Cynicism about public and cultural rhetoric compared with actual experience is profound. This is hardly a desirable economic and social model within its own terms; to try to export it to the rest of the world is risible.

The island that lost its way

Ever since the early years of World War II, when Britain realised for the second time that it could not win a global war without American help, the British have taken the view that American and British interests are so intertwined and coterminous that British interests are best served by defining ourselves as partners, if in a very junior role, in a relationship with the US. Britain has actively sought to enmesh its military and defence decision-making with that of the US, accepting that while this involved important losses in sovereignty they were more than offset by the gains – and that in any case there was little choice before the threat of first Nazi Germany and latterly the communist Soviet Union. Thus, whether turning over British atom bomb research to the US in 1940 or allowing a remnant of the British empire, the island of Diego Garcia, to be a key American base, the deal is the same. Britain is the loyal ally and junior partner of the US; in return, Britain gets access, albeit on American terms, to state-of-the-art military technology and nuclear weaponry – and maybe some marginal influence on American decision-making. Better this than no influence at all.

In his support for the coalition against terrorism and the war against the Taliban, Tony Blair has been only the latest in a long line of British prime ministers who have closely aligned themselves with the US – among whom Margaret Thatcher almost stepped beyond the role, famously telling George Bush senior during the Gulf War not to go 'wobbly' on her. Britain's position over Afghanistan in autumn 2001 was no less bellicose than that of the US; the twin towers of the World Trade Center could almost have been in London, with British public opinion strongly if not unanimously behind British involvement.

But, as argued earlier, since the fall of the Soviet Union the American defence and foreign policy stance has become openly more unilateralist, disregarding the formal mechanisms for consultation and formulation of strategy within NATO. The British military, for example, learned only after the event of the targeting of the Chinese embassy in Belgrade for missile attack during the Kosovo war, or of the decision not to proceed with the invasion of Iraq during operation Desert Storm (to eject the invading Saddam Hussein from Kuwait). During the Afghan war the US was happy to have the extra legitimacy conferred by British involvement, but it kept its options and decision-making closely to itself. No less unilaterally, the US has decided that it must rewrite the network of nuclear proliferation and missile treaties itself in order to create the National Missile Defense System which allegedly will shoot down incoming missile attacks on America from rogue states. The rawness of American power aspirations and their conservative inspiration are becoming more fully exposed. The question for Britain is whether the defence and security deal that has served the country since 1945 still serves British interests.

The US has become a genuine hegemonic power; what the French foreign minister Hubert Védrine, after the collapse of the Soviet Union, now calls a 'hyperpower'.[30] Even if the US government were purely passive, the sheer scale of the US economy means that American priorities, interests and values would predominate in global affairs to the extent that other countries would find their options to develop alternative economic and social models severely limited. As Michael Crozier puts it, in the current world power structure it is the dominant who have freedom of manoeuvre while the dominated operate under the strictest possible constraints;[31] the US can ensure compliant behaviour without having to enlist any instruments of formal enforcement. In reality, the US government is not passive. Moreover, standing behind it is the awesome military might that exceeds the rest of the world's military capacity combined; and alongside it there is the appeal of American popular culture, transmitted by the powerful American media. Together these are the instruments of a new form of dominance, for which there are no ready historical analogies or categories.

This power system is complex. The US does have freedom of manoeuvre, and its priorities have been increasingly driven by conservative principles; but that does not mean that there is no countervailing power, or that the power system in Washington is monolithic. While conservatives champion the cause of America First, there is a rival, liberal view of America's responsibilities that accepts that the country must engage with and lead the world in pursuing genuine global interests – and that this implies compromise and recognition that the US, despite its power, must accept common rules of the game. One of the assets Blair won through his support of Bush over Afghanistan was moral authority and political capital, the withdrawal of which would have damaged the US – so that the conservative administration has had to limit some of its wilder unilateral ambitions to sustain his support. The twin propositions at the heart of this book are that such countervailing power would be stronger if the Europeans acted systematically and in concert – and that Britain can no longer take it as axiomatic that British and US interests will always be identical. Moreover, there would be more purchase on American defence policy if the EU had a joint military capacity and a commitment to technological parity with the US defence industry; so the old British reliance on the special relationship should be superseded. Britain needs to remake its relationship with the US, supported by a power bloc with an independent military capacity in the form of the emerging European Rapid Reaction Force.

The second area where Britain has been the willing object of the American embrace is finance. Here too there are grounds for a reappraisal of whether reproducing Wall Street and its value system is completely in Britain's interests. From Britain's failed attempt to return the gold standard in 1925 to the systemic trade deficits of the immediate postwar era, it looked as though the City of London would have to cede its role as an international financial centre to New York because of the weakness of sterling and the strength of the dollar. But from the mid-1960s the City took advantage of an offshore status manufactured by British taxation policy to create a market in dollars owned by non-Americans (eurodollars), the supply of which was assured by the ambitions of American multinationals and America's trade deficits. London, in short, became an offshore extension of New York, creating a major market in eurodollars which now makes it the world's biggest international financial centre.

It has proved a lop-sided bargain. The leading British investment banks and stockbrokers are now wholly foreign-owned. In 1983 the three leading investment banks in London were British-owned – Morgan Grenfell, Warburg and Hill Samuel; by 2001 the leading City investment banks were the American firms Goldman Sachs, Morgan Stanley and Merrill Lynch. This shift has turned London into a financial centre that faithfully apes New York.[32] The attempted sale of the London Stock Exchange to Frankfurt in 2000 was spearheaded by US investment banks anxious to create a pan-European market in company shares which they would dominate. If Britain wants the City to remain the pre-eminent financial market outside New York, then it has to respect US sensibilities over taxation, accountancy, disclosure and regulation. American investment banks are agile and internationally mobile; they are not shy about stating their preferences for government policy or what the consequences will be if their views are not heeded. Britain's system of regulation of its international money markets is constructed and maintained with a close eye on what they want.

The bridgehead established by American investment banks has also been the means to an extraordinary takeover of corporate Britain by corporate America (see chapter 7) and an infusion of US corporate values and practices into British boardrooms. Merger and acquisition activity has always been a feature of the London stock exchange, but since the end of the Cold War, with the increasing influence of American investment banks and business practices, the pace of takeover has accelerated. The key indicator of business success has become the share price, and the American doctrine that the sole purpose of enterprise is the maximisation of shareholder value has taken an iron grip.

The pattern of British chief executives' pay is now openly modelled on the American lead. As the boom reached its climax in the late 1990s it was CEOs like Jan Leschley, assuming the chief executive role in SmithKlineBeecham with a cash salary of £4.6 million and share options worth up to another £90 million, or Paul Chisholm of Colt Telecom (who had actively campaigned for telecoms deregulation earlier in his career), with a salary of £15.2 million and unexercised share options worth some £146 million at their highest price, who openly insisted that their companies should offer American-level remuneration packages – so paving the way to more extravagance by their example.[33] Both men retired after brief periods in office handsomely enriched. Over the last five years the average salary of a chief executive in Britain's leading companies, including bonuses, has more than doubled to £717,000 (excluding share options),[34] following the trajectory of the growth of American remuneration and bearing increasingly little relationship to company performance. Britain is importing American conceptions of inequality wholesale – but in a wholly different cultural, political, economic and social context. British employees and the wider society alike are much less tolerant of pay on this scale than Americans – not least because it has real consequences that are socially divisive. The upsurge in house prices, for example, in the smart parts of British cities and especially in London, effectively pricing them out of the reach of most income groups, is closely related to the new patterns of American-style executive pay transmitted by winner-takes-all effects throughout the senior managerial job market. The impact of income inequality on the American model in a country whose land area is very much smaller creates extraordinary pressure in the land and housing markets, with disastrous social results. Britain remains a European country with European instincts, and it has to take an intolerant European attitude towards inequality – as much from sheer practicality as from adherence to different values.

Finance is not the only strategic area in Britain dominated by US players importing their own distinctive commercial attitudes. Electricity distribution and ICT are largely dominated by US firms. Wal-mart, the US owners of the supermarket chain Asda, has begun to remake British shopping in its own image by putting up giant 100,000 square foot shopping sheds, and wants changes in British planning laws to accommodate its ambitions for more. It is disputable whether the aggressive challenge to high street shopping can be justified, given the social costs of the associated traffic congestion and allocation of scarce land to this kind of retailing. The Wackhenhut Correction Corporation is one of the two principal companies running Britain's growing number of private prisons, and is a powerful lobby for the further extension of the private sector into the prison service. The collapse of Enron in December 2001 had an immediate impact on the British energy market, most directly on Wessex Water, which it owns. Without fast action by Ofgem (the merged regulator of the electricity and gas distribution systems) the British electricity market would have been disrupted and the lights would have gone out. Worse, Enron had exported its enthusiasm for buying access and favours to Britain, embarrassing both Labour and the Conservatives with the scale of its political gifts. The cavalier attitude to the public good prevalent in US business is having its effect on more and more areas of British commercial life.

Brand names like Heinz, Kelloggs, Starbucks, McDonalds, Nike, Marlboro, Woolworth, Hoover, Ford are as pervasive in Britain as they are in the US. All these companies aim to maximise shareholder value as their over-riding priority, and they bring with them the same approach to capitalism that they follow in the US. They want 'flexible' labour forces and as little regulation and business taxation as they experience at home. Advertising is as American-dominated as investment banking, and a new political lobbying industry has grown up trying to reproduce in Britain the access to political decision-making that is common in the US. When the British government proposed in 1997 to limit the extension of gas-fired power stations to help preserve demand for coal, a powerful lobby was mounted by American firms (including Enron and GE, which had contributed to New Labour funds on American lines), backed by the American government; the decision was reversed.[35]

Nor is American power over Britain simply corporate, military, financial and political. It is intellectual and cultural too. British academics seeking to advance their careers have always needed to publish in American academic journals, refereed by American academics; but the sheer wealth and size of the US academic sector has made this an increasing imperative. In British university research rankings for economics, only one British academic journal now counts; the market leaders are American. At the same time as American dominance of academic fora has become uncontestable, the conservative advance has pushed the norms and underlying value judgements in areas like social science, management and finance steadily to the right.[36] It is this intellectual climate that made it possible, for example, for an *American* academic to devise the notion of developing an internal market in the *British* NHS – with disastrous results (discussed in more detail in chapter 5) – while British management theory has been heavily influenced by passing American fads ranging from conglomeration to gain 'synergies' to the now derided 1990s fashion for 're-engineering' the corporation which was used to justify many ill-judged takeovers.

Meanwhile, the US's long-standing dominance of intellectual property rights, notably in science, continues. US needs and standards are paramount. Registration at the US Patent Office is the ultimate arbiter of intellectual property rights. Approval by the Food and Drug Administration is central to the success of any drug because it provides access to the world's richest market – a prime factor driving the relocation of SmithKlineBeecham and Glaxo Wellcome's research headquarters from Britain to America after they had merged to form GlaxoSmithKline. Company accounts must be passed by the Securities and Exchange Commission if a company wants to raise cash in the US.

By all these transmission mechanisms American values and policy approaches are inserted into the British debate – cemented by the cultural impact of film, music and television. American control of film distribution in Britain is near total, the ambitions of the Hollywood studios aided and abetted by the lobby of the Motion Picture Association; thus the British film sector has long been trapped in a cottage industry of one-off productions. Consequently the cultural impact of film is founded almost entirely on the priorities of another civilisation. World War II, for example, is seen through the eyes of the US, so that the British watch *Pearl Harbor*, *Saving Private Ryan* and *Band of Brothers* – with no comparable offering of their own. There are no films with Dunkirk or the Battle of Britain as their central theme. It is American rather than British bravery that is celebrated. The increasing nationalism in the US is reflected by Hollywood's careless disregard for historical truth. British acts of wartime heroism – the British navy's capture of the German decoding device for the famous Enigma code (U571) or British escape exploits from the Colditz prisoner of war camp – are casually recast as American; US audiences do not want to watch British success. British characters are inevitably cast as odd, if not actively malevolent; in *The Patriot*, British soldiers during the American War of Independence were portrayed as cruel and evil. The British collude in their own character assassination to serve the cultural and political agenda of another country.

This agenda is also being imported via more direct routes. Labour and the Conservatives are quick to take their respective cues from Democrats and Republicans, even though the American political debate takes place in a wholly different context. The rise in American conservatism has been faithfully copied in Britain, and with disastrous consequences for the British Tory party. Whatever the early successes under Thatcher, the mix of anti-government, anti-tax, pro-market individualism laced with passionate religious belief and intense nationalism has not travelled well across the Atlantic and has certainly not taken root in Britain. There is a much stronger commitment here to fairness and tolerance, and a greater willingness to accept the legitimacy of the state which the Tories have fatally neglected in their open admiration for Republican extremists. In a political landscape where delivery of high-quality public services has become an imperative, British Conservatives have become fatally disabled by their unthinking fealty to public minimalism and championship of private-only solutions.

New Labour is no less an enthusiastic borrower of American social policies, notwithstanding the vastly different terrain on which they operate in Britain. President Clinton, retreating before the conservative ascendancy, felt that his only chance of advancing liberal social goals was through targeted tax credits which a Republican Congress would accept – rather than through public spending increases. He also conceded the massive rewriting of the US welfare state, making social security much meaner, more conditional and harsher – a process which needs to be understood in the US electoral context where, as noted above, welfare is understood to be largely an income transfer from whites to blacks. Nor did he make any attempt to challenge the increasing severity of America's penal codes, even consolidating them with the famous 'three strikes and you're out' legislation (see chapter 3). In all these areas New Labour has imported Clinton's ideas, introducing in Britain tax credits for the working poor, more conditional social security and tougher mandatory sentencing policies. The social contract component of Britain's welfare state has been reshaped, making it yet more means-tested and ungenerous. What worked in the US, reasoned Labour strategists, would work in Britain.

The march of the American conservative right and the eclipse of

American liberalism have helped to undermine our own conceptions of the proper relationship between the market and society. And yet, as I will argue in chapter 2, British values – and British expectations – are much closer to those prevalent in Europe than to those of American conservatism. New Labour is under intense pressure to deliver improved public services and a more robust social safety net; widespread distrust among its own supporters of the borrowed American conservatism that informs many of its criminal justice and social policies has given rise to extraordinary internal political rancour. In response, the Blair government plans a second three-year period of rising public spending and real efforts to alleviate the position of the poor, especially poor children, and has begun overtly to stress European ideas of rehabilitation in its approach to penal and prison policy. If Britain is to address its long-standing productivity problem or the weaknesses of its public services, it will need to be more open to European examples and models rather than having its options closed down by a blinkered focus on America. In the same way that Britain should reappraise its relationship with American defence and security policy, so it must reappraise its approach to the American ideas of economic and social organisation that have been so readily imported. It is time the British recognised who they really are.

Europeans are different

It is not just geography that defines Britain as a European country; it is a value system born of sharing the same essential history. Whether it was being conquered by the Romans or wrestling with socialism, the British experience over the last two millennia mirrors that of the rest of Europe. This history matters. We cannot, for example, share the indifference of American conservatives to inequalities of income, property and wealth. Catholic feudal Europe, of which Britain was part, insisted that wealth and property were associated with profound reciprocal social obligations; and it was this ethical view which partly inspired socialism when it advocated common ownership of the means of production and proper respect for the rights of workers. Although both

Christianity – or certainly the organised church – and socialism are in eclipse as vital, dominant philosophies, the ethic that underpins them both survives. No population in any single European country shares the American majority view that the government should not redistribute income; 63 per cent of British are in favour of income redistribution, for example, compared to just 28 per cent of Americans.[37] This is a formidable statistic, and part of a complex of values that are deeply entrenched.

The starting point for understanding what the American sociologist Seymour Martin Lipset calls 'American exceptionalism' is the American constitution. It is a remarkable document, providing an admirable protection of individual liberties, so that from freedom of information to freedom of speech Americans enjoy a degree of entrenched rights that is a global exemplar. However, it embodies a conception of citizenship in which rights are essentially political: the right to vote, enjoy a fair trial or, famously, to bear arms. But this same constitution is paradoxically a source of weakness for the liberal wing of American politics. For its definition of rights does not extend beyond the political to the economic and social, and the political rights it protects can be easily portrayed as for the individual and against government – a gift to the conservatives. The judicial component of the constitution, notably the nine-member Supreme Court, defines itself as the protector of this essentially conservative order. There have been moments in American life when the Supreme Court has sided with progressive elements in American society, notably in advancing the cause of civil rights in the south during the 1950s and 1960s. But in the main it has been a bastion of conservatism, defending governmental minimalism and the primacy of individual property rights. Its most complete conservative moment came in the famous judgement on the disputed hand recounts in Florida in the presidential election of 2000. By accepting that hand recounts were reasonable in principle but not as they were practised in Florida because of the danger of subjectivity in interpretation of the recounts – a vote that went five to four, reflecting the conservative/liberal split among the judges – without demanding either a fresh election or a recount of all the votes cast in Florida, the court in effect gifted the election to George W. Bush. In the event Bush would have won on the basis of the votes

43

cast in the disputed four counties (though he would have lost in Florida overall if so-called over-votes – where a voter writes in the preferred candidate more than once – had been included[38]); but it remained – as Vincent Bugliosi has so passionately written – the most partisan legal judgement in recent political history.[39]

The European conception of rights is much broader, and judicial obstruction to economic and social advance is much less. The right to free health; the right to free education; the right to unemployment insurance; the right to fair treatment at work, and so on – all are regarded as key parts of the social contract and as elements of citizenship just as important as political rights. In the New Deal and afterwards US liberals succeeded in winning parallel rights for Americans on education and the right to join trade unions – but these are derogations from the basic minimalist, individualistic model, and as such their legitimacy has always been disputed by the political right. The Democrats have never been able, for example, to develop Medicaid and Medicare into a national health scheme for all Americans, frustrated by conservative opposition; the view that such a scheme would imply too much federal and government power trumps the social argument.

It is not that European ideas of economic and social citizenship, together with the social contract, do not have powerful echoes in the US; it is that the liberals who champion these ideas do so against a hostile political and cultural backdrop. This is one of the reasons why there has never been a strong socialist or labour movement in the US. There have been gains – the US has had a strongly progressive tax system, for example – and there are periods in US history defined by social advance and concern for social justice. It may even be, as commentators John Judis and Ruy Teixeira argue in *The Emerging Democratic Majority*, that the combination of the liberal values of the New Economy of the information revolution, the dynamic growth in the Democrat-voting Hispanic and black population, and growing concerns about the character of American society presage another period of liberal strength. Certainly there are signs that a new liberalism is struggling to make itself heard in, for example, attitudes towards criminal justice, with a growing proportion of Americans in favour of rehabilitation rather than unadulterated punishment for criminal offenders. In 1994 16 per cent of Americans thought the purpose of prison was rehabilitation; in 2001 the proportion had jumped to 40 per cent.[40]

Even so, the framework in which this liberalism is stirring is profoundly different from that which exists in Europe. In the US the most basic call is to be given a chance, to be offered an opportunity. The reciprocal obligation is that the individual taking the opportunity accepts the risks and expects no social intervention to cushion the blow of failure. The fair society is thus one which promotes opportunity for all, but which is indifferent to the prior or consequential distribution of risk and rewards. Private education and private health care play a much larger role, and there is less willingness to use the power of the state to equalise the chances of those at the starting line, or to underwrite their circumstances if they are unlucky or simply fail. Trades unions and notions of social partnership are regarded with profound suspicion. Business must pursue its interests as free from constraint as possible.

The European conception of the fair society comprehends a larger, integrative role for the state as actively conciliating social partners, providing public services, and regulating business and society. It is not conceived as a mere night watchman or umpire; it is an actor, ensuring that risk and reward are fairly distributed in what the liberal political philosopher John Rawls calls an infrastructure of justice. A powerful system of collective insurance underwrites the risks of poor health, disablement or unemployment. Worker rights are supported and entrenched. Risks and rewards are not allocated by chance and market forces; rather, their final balance is settled by an activist state, expressing and enforcing the choices made by the community. Europe has been richly endowed with social and political theorists who accent the primacy of the public realm (as Habermas does in Germany), who insist that capitalism must be enmeshed in society (the great Durkheimian sociological tradition) and who argue that the precondition for a just society is a narrowing of inequality (the British tradition embodied by Richard Tawney).

Beneath these political values, moreover, lies a wholly different conception of religion and morality. Europe has for long accepted that reason and science are the twin underpinnings and driving forces of Western society; that religious faith cannot trump or obstruct science but must seek reconciliation with it. No European country would accept that the teachings of Darwin, for example, could not be taught because they challenged the precepts of the Bible; the Bible may be taught, but so must science. The same is not true of the US, notably in the south. The early settlers believed that America was a holy country with a special divine providence, and the same belief is still alive today, giving American Protestantism its particularly evangelical and highly personalised character – reinforced by the country's cultural egalitarianism. Ordinary worshippers come to believe that they can be individually blessed and saved – indeed, their standing as self-governing, God-fearing Americans demands no less. They can be and are 'born again'. As a result, America's religious culture, or at least the dynamic element over the last twenty years, has stressed the morality of individual self-interest and self-help, characterising social and public initiatives of the type widely supported in Europe and by liberals in the US as somehow inimical to morality because they minimise individual responsibility.

These are not differences of emphasis; they go to the heart of what lies between American and European culture and of how American conservatism has arrived at a position so very far away from the European mainstream. For these approaches to citizenship, fairness and justice cascade into how Europeans conceive of property, of the role of business, of welfare and of inequality, and where they draw the boundaries between the public and private sectors. Nor is the resulting European economic and social model inefficient. It produces, as discussed in chapters 8 and 9, high-performance companies and fair societies.

If these values and outcomes are to be sustained, Britain must act with other European countries to advance and protect them – not least from the conservative American advance. If we want to keep a progressive tax system that distributes income more fairly, it must not be undercut by other European countries. If we want to reduce carbon dioxide emissions and not lose our international competitiveness, then we had better persuade other European countries to follow suit. If we wish to regain some control over our exchange rate and interest rates in an environment where the scale of capital movements can unsettle even continents, we had better make common cause and pool sovereignty with other Europeans in creating a single currency. Similarly with defence, or the fight against the mafia and international criminal cartels.

In an era of globalisation all nation-states need to co-operate and collaborate if they want to represent their citizens' interests. Such co-operation works best among those who share values and goals; and it works most efficiently if it is entrenched in permanent institutions so that each act of collaboration does not have to start on a greenfield site. Moreover, those institutions need to be accountable if they are to be legitimate – which is why the EU is moving to turn its processes from those of a diplomatic quadrille into more transparent and politically accountable forms. This is the proper sphere for arguments between the European left and right; we should be debating the shape of our common institutions rather than pitching the political debate as a dispute over which side of the Atlantic boasts the superior civilisation. Even if we wanted to make Europe into a form of America it would be simply beyond us.

This is a leap into a new discourse, and Eurosceptics are right to say that as matters stand such political institutions have little legitimacy because there is no functioning European political community or Europe-wide political argument to hold them to account. The explicit invitation is not to rock the status quo, to freeze the European experiment, making no effort to construct such a community, debate or accompanying institutions. But the status quo is not stable. The paradox is that in order to regain sovereignty and relegitimise their national political processes, European states need to act together. The power with most to lose from that overt assertion of European interests and accompanying commitment to internationalism is the US. Every international agreement or treaty supported by the EU – whether the International Criminal Court or a renegotiated climate control agreement – consigns the US, if it holds itself aloof, to increasing isolation and challenges its leadership of the West.

Thus we need to address the deficiencies of the current EU institutions and processes and build a stronger, more accountable European Union around powerful, restated European values, both for ourselves in Europe and as a counterweight to a conservative hyperpower. Those in the US who adhere to liberal European values will derive strength from the emergence of such a political grouping. If America championed a liberal world order in the twentieth century, Europe will have to sustain that vision in the twenty-first, either alone or in partnership with a newly enlightened US. It may be that the terrorist atrocities of 11 September 2001 will trigger change in the US; but until its national conversation is transformed and the conservative grip loosens, the chances of this happening are not great. In any case, this is beyond European control. What we can do in the quest for a better world is to build a more self-confident, integrated Europe clearer about what it has to offer. To do that, we need to understand what it is Britain and the European countries hold in common, why US conservatism is in truth an eccentric, idiosyncratic creed, with only a tenuous relationship to the core values of European civilisation of which it purports to be such an ardent defender. Just how eccentric, and ultimately how dangerous, is where our study goes next.

2
Custodians of the light

Europe and the US would not be easy partners even in the best of circumstances. The rise in American conservatism has made the relationship even more difficult as the barrage of strident criticism directed at mainland Europe has grown more intense. The charge sheet is extensive. As European growth rates in the 1960s and 1970s pulled ahead of those in the US while Europe simultaneously ran a trade surplus, the criticism was that Europeans were not genuine free traders, exploited the US's open markets unfairly and did not do enough to support world growth. They did not even do enough to pay for their own defence. They were decadently free-riding off America's generosity in defending the free world while keeping its markets open to all imports.

Europe: the past or the future?

During the 1980s a second front was opened up as the American right consolidated its grip on Washington and the Cold War bubbled to its climax. Europeans were worse than free-riders; they actively sapped their economic and social vitality under a dead weight of taxes, welfare costs and regulation. And as the 1990s wore on, America's boom and accompanying record in job generation were constantly held up as evidence of

US dynamism and proof positive that American-style flexible labour markets and an enterprise culture were the key foundations of economic success, in contrast to which the Europeans were sclerotic and soft. For American conservatives, Europe's economic and social model is incapable of delivering the robust individual morality that drives entrepreneurship and self-help for rich and poor alike, and which lies at the heart of successful capitalism. American capitalism and its accompanying civilisation are the future – Europe, the past.

It is true that two different models of capitalism have emerged, although in all the commentary on the distinctions – which this book continues – it is worth noting what the two systems share. They are, after all, both capitalist in their roots, committed to profits, private property and the use of price signals in markets to allocate resources. But for all that, the two civilisations in which they are rooted have different sets of values and priorities – the difference more marked than ever now, given the new dominance of conservatism in American life – that confer on their respective capitalisms distinct dynamics. The conservative contention is that Europe's choices are wrong; but the following chapters will demonstrate that US conservative values have led the US into an economic and social blind alley while Europe, although it has grave problems, is nearer than America to finding out how to build a functioning, efficient, socially fair economy and society. For while there are important differences of emphasis between parts of Europe, its civilisation is united by a common set of values in respect of four critical and inter-related areas of human life that are distinct from the canons of American conservatism. European attitudes towards property, equality, social solidarity and the public realm are different from those that currently dominate discourse on these subjects in the US. They express themselves in cultural mores, law and social choices which in turn shape the way European economies and societies function.

In the first place, property is not seen in Europe as an absolute right, as it is by US conservatives. Rather, it is a privilege that confers reciprocal obligations – a notion captured by article 13 of the postwar German constitution, which specifies that 'property imposes duties. Its use should also serve the public weal.' Those who hold and own property are members of society, and society has a public dimension to which necessarily they must contribute as the *quid pro quo* for the privilege of exercising property rights. Nor is this attitude towards social obligation just directed at property-holders. Across Europe there is a profound commitment to the notion that all citizens should have an equal right to participate in economic and social life, and that the state is more than a safety net of last resort: it is the fundamental vehicle for the delivery of this equality. It is not just the institutions of social order and defence – for example, courts, prisons and the military – that it is acceptable to hold in common, as American conservatives contend; Europeans extend the remit to include hospitals, schools, universities, utility networks and even scientific knowledge. A publicly founded infrastructure supports equality of membership and participation. This principle of participation extends to notions of social solidarity – or 'fraternity' as the French constitution would have it, one of the three values on which the French Republic is declared to rest, along with liberty and equality; a constitutional commitment that in some ways speaks for the continent. Fraternity means that Europeans believe in looking out for one another to insure against life's hazards – the principal reason why social spending in Europe runs some 50 per cent above that in the US.

All this implies a much greater role for the public sphere and the state than conservative Americans could countenance. For Europeans, the state and government cannot be so easily portrayed as enemies of the people as they can in the US (although there are growing concerns about their efficacy and the shortcomings in their accountability); they are seen rather as upholders of, and means of expressing, public values. Europeans expect the state to finance scientific research or, by owning television and radio companies, to serve a notion of public service broadcasting, just as much as they expect the state to tax and spend to provide public goods like defence and education. The public realm is larger than the state, but the state is easily its most important component. It protects what society holds in common.

The contention of American conservatives is that this complex of values is economically inefficient, socially counterproductive – and immoral, in that it undermines sturdy individualism and obstructs the natural impulses of competitive capitalism. I argue the opposite. Of course some particular manifestations of these principles may be imperfect and susceptible to reform, but the value system that underpins them is perfectly consistent with a high-performance market economy. In one respect the argument is beside the point; for these values, as this chapter will show, are so deeply embedded that they could hardly be changed even if Europeans wanted to relinquish them. They help to define Europeanness. But there is no need to change them. The conservative American charge sheet, on closer examination, proves to be empty – indeed, the kind of capitalism European values generate is in the long run no less productive than the American kind, while respecting instincts that are fundamental to living in a just and civil social order. In detailing just what those values are, it becomes ever more apparent to which civilisation Britain belongs. We are Europeans.

Property – the American conception

North America was discovered as a wilderness pregnant with riches by settlers who had risked all crossing the Atlantic and who, as fervent Protestants, believed they had a direct relationship with God. They carved plantations and farms out of natural forest under attack by – as they saw them – cruel and barbarous savages. But there was no restraint on their capacity to own land, even if the British, through the 'headright' system of assigning ownership, tried to maintain the essentially feudal assumption that property was held in trust for all by the Crown and that it was only the Crown that could assign true legal ownership or freehold. On this view – a view of the legitimacy of ownership that would be of fundamental importance in the American War of Independence – it was not the settlers' land to discover and claim, but the Crown's. But whatever the legal stipulations, the headright system for granting land by the distant British Crown was no more than a titular formality – in practice, land was available to all. And, as they fanned out across the thirteen colonies, the mainly English opinion-formers deployed John Locke's famous philosophical dicta to justify the claim that what the settlers found and created was theirs – and nothing to do with the constitutional and political framework which formally assigned ownership. The seeds of dispute, and of a very different conception of property, were being sown.

'In the beginning all the world was America,' Locke had proclaimed.[1] If God had given the world to all men in common, then he had certainly given America to the settlers. They were serving God's purpose by taking possession of it and using it for their own individual good. But this was only the beginning. 'Men being, as has been said, by Nature, all free, equal and independent, no one can be put out of this Estate, and subjected to the Political Power of another, without his own *Consent,*' Locke had written. 'The only way whereby any one divests himself of his Natural Liberty, and puts on the bonds of Civil Society is by agreeing with other Men to join and unite and into a Community, for their comfortable, safe, and peaceable living one amongst another, in a secure Enjoyment of their Properties, and a greater Security against any that are not of it.'[2] It was a message picked up by preachers and politicians alike. The purpose of society was to further the enjoyment of property, and political power was only legitimate if it served this end.

Moreover, as he laboured, man created his property with God's blessing. 'Every man has a property in his own person. There is no body has any right to it but himself. The labour of his body, and the work of his hands we may say are properly his. Whatsoever then he removes out of the state that nature has provided, and left it in, he hath mixed his labour with and joined to it something that is his own, and thereby makes his property.'[3] For an early American settler, the proof was conclusive. God had created America; the settler had laboured to create a farm against all the odds. The farm was exclusively and completely his, and he owed nothing to anybody – the Crown, government or any other settler. The good man was the 'rational and industrial man' who followed this injunction.

Locke aimed to provide the rationale for both parliamentary government and the emergent capitalism of late seventeenth-century England, along the way inveighing against the divine right of kings, the doctrine that had prompted the English Civil War. Protestantism, representative government and private property went hand in hand. But if this was a useful ex-post justification of what was happening in England, it became the governing ideology of the American settlers, to which today's conservative ideas are linked by a golden thread. Government earned its place to the extent it protected liberty and property.

This early settler culture of the new world escaped all the anguished heart-searching of the old world about what the wealthy and propertied owed to the commonweal – a debate which went back to the early days of Christianity. Clement of Alexandria at the end of the second century had foreshadowed American conservative arguments when he argued that to own property was part of God's design; it was only excessive pre-occupation with wealth that was damnable, and as long as the wealthy acknowledged their obligations through charity, inequality of wealth was acceptable.[4] He was on his own. This was not a solid enough doctrine for the early Christian saints and leaders of the church, all of whom challenged the idea that property rights were absolute. St Augustine declared that 'he who uses his wealth badly possesses it wrongfully, and wrongful possession means it is another's property,' while St Ambrose – drawing on Cicero, who took the view that nothing natural justified private property rights – insisted that God's aim was that everything was commonly possessed. Those who held property had an absolute duty to support the poor. John Chrysostom, bishop of Constantinople, was no less radical, calling for the abolition of ideas of 'mine' and 'thine' and urging – as a forerunner of the best instincts of socialism – that all the Christians in the city put what they had into a common fund so they could achieve the great things otherwise beyond them as individuals.[5] St Thomas Aquinas argued that part of the obligation of government was to regulate private property for the common good and that 'a Christian is obliged to make his wealth available for common needs.'

The European feudalism that grew up on a foundation of Christian beliefs thus had at its core the value system that would later give rise to notions of equality before the law and that the exercise of social privilege by the wealthy came with wider social obligations that went beyond charity. Feudal barons might be delegated political authority by their sovereign king, but they held their lands subject to their obligation to offer its wealth to serve the common weal as the king decided. This might take the form of contributing men and munitions to defend the realm, or making regular payments to sustain the cost of administering justice and order. When barons died they could not expect their lands to pass to their sons without the payment of a levy, which today Europeans would call inheritance tax and American conservatives would describe as a death tax. The designers of feudal Europe understood it instead as a life tax – a tribute to the common weal as an acknowledgement that the holding of land was a privilege and that this payment on death was a key means of sustaining the life of the community. It is an important and vital distinction that has relevance today.

And if anyone was in any doubt that the wealthy and propertied were not necessarily the possessors of virtue also, there was evident in almost every town and village the infrastructure of monastic life, where monks attempted to approach the divine by living in a community that produced and consumed no more than it needed. Some, like the Franciscans, went further, insisting that it was only through living in a community of poverty that man could hope to earn God's redemption. Add this to the powerful millenarianism that grew out of St John's promise in the Book of Revelation that Christ would come again to overthrow his enemies – a claim that was periodically used by dissident clerics to threaten the wealthy with actual or possible revolt by the lower classes if they did not meet their side of the social bargain – and it was well understood throughout the middle ages that property rights were not absolute.[6]

Feudal Europe was not a terrain in which individualism flourished, in particular over religion. The authority of church and state, backed by the nostrums of Catholicism (and eventually in England its compromise version in the Church of England), was suffocating. The English puritans who first settled America passionately believed that they could individually establish a direct relationship with God – and that God-fearing industriousness was the best possible route to God's favour. They had crossed the Atlantic to win the opportunity to express their religious convictions freely. But their encounter with so much virgin land, together with the philosophy of Locke, would trigger the invention of an explosively new and radical ideology justifying an individualist rather than social view of property. God had not given the world to the lazy or even benevolent man, declared Locke: he gave it to the use of the 'rational and industrious'. Moreover, the property that such industry created was 'the best support of that Independency, so passionately desired by all men'. Property, ownership and the virtue of independence were thus indissolubly linked as part of God's plan – a world view that would find renewed legitimacy in the twentieth-century conservative idea that 'greed is good' and that the spirit of acquisitiveness benefits all.

Locke had been concerned that too much acquisitiveness might lead to hoarding and avarice, and that any right to appropriation was subject to there being 'enough and as good left in common – (of what God had given to the Earth to the Children of Men in common) for others'. But two hundred and fifty years later no such inhibition was felt by his conservative successors. Here is the important conservative philosopher Leo Strauss (of whom more in the next chapter): 'Far from being straitened by the emancipation of acquisitiveness,' declared Strauss, 'the poor are enriched by it . . . unlimited appropriation without concern for the needs of others is true charity.'[7] Strauss and the new conservatives built on the logic of Locke's position; if he justified the legitimacy of property as an individual's proper deserts for working on nature's endowment from God, they would justify it as the proper deserts for simply working. It was this tradition that helped form the 1980s conservative dependency theorists and their view that welfare actively increases poverty (see chapter 3), which, rather than springing from social and economic processes, should be seen instead as rooted in the motivational and psychological deficiencies of the poor themselves. They do not do enough to help themselves.

This is the first chasm between Europe and the US. The radical new world view of the early settlers was cemented into the centre of American culture by the writing of the American constitution. The settlers' rights to enjoy their property freely had been usurped by King George III's tyrannous government, went the popular cry, and so they fought the war of independence to assume responsibility for their own governance – but of a very limited and constrained kind. Their core view, as the citizens of Ashfield, Massachusetts, voted, was that their only true governor was the governor of the universe. This was the Lockean view in the extreme, with some communities insisting that it was not just George III whose governance they disputed, but anybody's: they reserved the right – as self-governing individuals, who had created their own property, owing allegiance only to God – to overturn any state legislation with which they disagreed.

As the war years passed on it became clear that this assertion of individual liberty, under which armed citizens felt justified in threatening state legislatures to do their bidding, could be wildly irresponsible. The principles of independence and individual reverence for God were in direct conflict with that of the proper protection and exercise of property rights. Some of the thirteen states issued paper money to clear their debts; others refused to honour their contracts, wrote off debt or raised taxes arbitrarily. Indeed, the whole approach was so haphazard that in the early 1780s the very success of the war was threatened, with some states refusing to levy taxes or hand over the receipts to Congress to conduct the war, while others paid up.

The federal state formed after the war was won and the constitution that was written for it were shaped by this tension and its resolution. The pro-central government 'federalists' knew that to establish any kind of central government which over-rode states' rights, they had to find a way of encompassing the revolutionary commitment to independence and liberty within an apparatus that, despite having the detested central authority, could be presented as promoting – in the words of the consti-tution – domestic tranquillity and the general welfare, i.e. the protection of property. It was James Madison who, in coining the famous phrase 'we the people' to begin the constitution, came up with the rhetorical flourish that solved the conundrum; federal government was the means to protect property-holders – 'we the people' – from the potentially capricious depredations of state government.[8] Madison even wanted a federal veto over state legislatures – which he did not get – but more importantly he insisted that the federal government had to represent the national interest, and as such had to possess some capacity to be disinterested and objective in its deliberations in order to 'filter' vested private interests. Hence the powerful office of the presidency to hold the ring between the interests of the haves in the Senate, as Madison saw them, and the have-nots in the House. He could not prevent the states continuing to exercise as much government power as possible, so that the US ended up with two sets of checks and balances: one within the federal government, and the other between the federal government and the states. In the wings was an inde-pendent judiciary that was to be another source of independent power.

Three years later, in the fifth amendment, the constitution extended constitutional protection to individual property rights, preventing gov-ernment from depriving an individual of 'life, liberty and property without due process; nor shall property be taken for public use without just compensation' – but nowhere is there any notion to parallel the German constitution's stipulation that property imposes reciprocal duties. The federalists counted themselves lucky that they had got their constitution ratified as quickly as they had in a climate in which to acquire and hold property was held to be a necessary and sufficient expression of republican virtue, which a broad strand of opinion felt should express itself in self-governing autonomous units in villages, towns and member states rather than any federal government. The federalist counter-argument was to acknowledge that while property underwrote independence and thus virtue, it was insufficient alone to produce a virtuous order. That required the disinterested arbitration that only federal government might bring – without which the community threatened to break down into warring factions and vested interests. The most practical expression of the principle was the constitution's commerce clause, drafted in recognition of the evident need to regulate the terms of commerce between states and insist on good transport links.

Government had to be argued for via the back door; not as an expression of a social contract or general will, but rather as a means of reconciling the clash of interests disinterestedly. And there was also the ugly question of slavery. To attack this property right in any way would imply that the southern states of Georgia, Virginia and South Carolina actively expanding their plantation economies through importing slaves could not economically afford to join the new United States.[9] Slavery was thus not forbidden. The new republic would deal with the issue eventually as a matter of federal political authority – but not yet as an embedded constitutional clause. It was a fateful decision that has traumatised American culture.

The American story unfolds

From the start, then, the autonomy of private property rights in the US has been seen as the legitimate consequence of man's interaction with nature; civil society naturally respects property and government is cast as its protector. Any notion that property rights were a concession granted by the state in the name of the common interest – the European tradition, represented in America by the colonial headright system – had been dispelled by the revolution. As for redistribution, that was an even greater offence against nature. The acquisition and holding of property was a private initiative, and what was required of the federal state was that it policed, upheld and arbitrated between the resulting private contracts between property-holders. The constitution's clause insisting that no state could do anything that might impair the obligations of contracts became the legal lodestar of the Supreme Court, which throughout the nineteenth and early twentieth centuries interpreted the provision as conservatively as possible. Once it had been established, under *Dartmouth College* v. *Woodward* in 1819, that after any state had given a corporation the right to enter contracts then it had no more right to interfere in its affairs under the contract clause, the stage was set. The Supreme Court would permit the federal government only to regulate commerce between states as it was constitutionally permitted, requiring it to refrain from any other intervention. In *Lawton* v. *Steele* in 1894, for example, the court ruled that 'the legislature may not, under the guise of protecting the public interest, arbitrarily interfere with private business, or impose unusual and unnecessary restrictions upon lawful occupations.'

The sanctity of ownership and the rights of property were being spread from the settler farmer to the company. The Supreme Court's extension of the fourteenth amendment, guaranteeing the property rights of 'persons' in an overt protection from slavery, to corporations, conferred on the latter the same uninfringeable property rights. The federal government should not interfere with how the owner of a company chose to organise his enterprise or how he related to his shareholders – except if he exercised excessive and abusive market power. A company's founding legal document thus became an absolutist expression of property rights in which Washington had no right to interfere.

In any case, even if the federal government wanted to interfere, the registration of individual corporations was not seen as a federal duty, so there was no direct capacity to make any intervention or construct a purposeful constitution for companies; that power rested with individual states, which guarded it jealously – Delaware, the state in which most companies incorporate with the most minimalist requirements, most jealously of all. When New Jersey, in 1896, decided to exercise its rights and drop all restrictions on what companies registering in the state might do, Delaware followed suit three years later – and added in some tax incentives to register with it for good measure. American corporations and the American financial markets developed as they chose.

For the next three decades, up to the Roosevelt years in the 1930s, the Supreme Court and Congress were locked in arguments about what the federal government could and could not do, with the court taking the defence of property interests to what even contemporaries regarded as absurd limits. The court ruled against measures to ban interstate trade in goods produced by children and against state laws limiting work to ten hours a day. The sixteenth amendment in 1916 was passed to permit the levying of income tax, which the Supreme Court had ruled as unconstitutional in the 1894 *Pollock* judgement – as it had later ruled against a heavy tax on phosphorus matches, imposed on health grounds. The Court carried on its conservative mandate against key New Deal legislation and it was only (as described in the next chapter) when Roosevelt threatened to pack it with liberals after his re-election in 1936, that it finally backed down and allowed a raft of regulatory measures to be deemed constitutional. As Leo Pfeffer wrote in his history of the Supreme Court, from its inception 'the Court deemed its mission to be the protection of property against depredations by the people and their legislature. After 1937 it gave up this mission.'[10] The first to make the attempt since the US's foundation, the New Dealers – as we will see in the next chapter – began to put in place a system of regulation and limits to property rights. But it rested on shaky foundations.

For the constitution remains explicit. Without powerful popular support and a clear sense of national crisis – as over slavery in the 1860s or unemployment in the 1930s – the American constitutional conception is that government at federal and state level is the custodian of private property rights; and the Supreme Court sees its task as policing that injunction. Thus, as the passion to unwind Rooseveltian regulation has mounted, so the Supreme Court has kept pace. Conservatism's success in promoting shareholder value, the minimalist approach to corporate governance, the objections to capital gains and inheritance tax, the indifference to growing inequality, the detestation of organised labour, the resistance to land-use planning and even to the reform of campaign finance have all been immensely assisted not just by the cultural belief that private property rights are unassailable but by the constitutional buttresses to this value system. America's rich still believe in charitable giving to an extent unrecognised in Europe – one positive by-product of the Lockean inheritance – but the basic stance is the same. What is mine is mine, and well-deserved because otherwise I would not have it.

Property – the European conception

European attitudes, by contrast, are more complex. Here the notion persists that property is held in trust for all and only delegated to individuals for as long as they accept reciprocal social obligations. This is the legacy not only of the early Christian church and feudalism, but of the fact that Europe was already settled. America's founding fathers operated in an environment where there was almost limitless virgin land; 80 per cent of the colonialists were property-owners and thus middle class, and there was every expectation that this would remain the norm. When John Adams argued in 1776 that the acquisition of land should be made easy for every member of society in order to achieve equality and liberty, he could disregard European concerns with how the state had to intervene to construct a just society; a continent lay before him waiting to be claimed. The same populism about property informs American conservatives today; their continent may now be settled, but by transferring the idea of property for all to the realm of share ownership, so that even small investors should speculate on Wall Street as their sacred right, they have given the notion of property for all without pain new life. The current Republican obsession with making private investment accounts a major part of the social security system comes from the same tradition.

In Europe, propositions about the possibility of individual ownership for all could not be made so easily. Thus when, after the English Civil War, the radicals in the New Model Army – notably the Levellers – wanted equality, liberty and universal suffrage, informed by almost exactly the same set of Protestant values as the American settlers, the only avenue open to them for the creation of fairness for all was to argue for redistribution and common ownership – and to anticipate, along with the millenarians, that Christ's second coming would bring this about one day even if it was not achieved politically in the here and now. If all property had been created by individual labour, then if the majority had none and the minority a lot the rest of the syllogism was easy to complete. Great private wealth could be accumulated only by exploitation, and the political solution had to be redistribution from the few to the many – a solution validated by a Christian tradition that ran back for centuries. But in the 1650s Cromwell and his son-in-law Henry Ireton, taking the same position as John Adams that individual property ownership should be the foundation of the country, were on the side of reaction rather than revolution. At the Putney debates they resisted the argument for universal suffrage because it might threaten property; England had no virgin land that it could offer the radicals to square the equation by making them property owners without redistribution. Eighteenth-century republican America, however, could be both egalitarian and for private property.

The constitutional compromises reached in England allowed parliament to assume the feudal authority of the monarch, keeping alive the notion that property was a concession that demanded reciprocal privileges in the common interest. The early English corporations, like the East India or Hudson Bay Companies, were exclusive licences to trade, made by the Crown-in-parliament, that involved reciprocal obligations upon the corporation to pay dividends to the government, conduct trade as directed and open up lands for English settlement. Indeed, the early American colonies were founded on the same principle of delegated sovereignty and reciprocal obligation – the very principle that the colonialists were to dispute.

It was the industrial revolution that was to dramatise the social weaknesses of unrestrained property ownership and capital accumulation – and the need dramatically to widen the obligations that went with property ownership if the very system was to survive. Adam Smith, the revered godfather of *laissez-faire* economics, could suppose that a market system would find a natural point of balance only by arguing – along with John Locke – that all value originated in individual labour and that market prices would converge with the natural prices reflecting the labour content. David Ricardo went one step further and argued that value lay purely in the conditions of production; he showed that the lower real wages were, the higher rents and profits would be. Marx's contribution was to argue that common ownership was politically inevitable as the consequence of Ricardo's predictions about falling wages, secularising the early Christian insistence that property was expropriation, along with its millenarian promise that there would be redistribution on Christ's second coming. Marx instead foresaw revolution.

The secularisation of the medieval millenarian predictions about the overturning of an unfair order, together with a highly plausible economics, made Marxism extraordinarily influential. Europe's cities, growing explosively in the wake of industrialisation, were social tinder boxes in which the old notions of socially obligated property seemed risible, creating a new class of industrial workers all too ready to listen to the moral content of Marx's message. The conditions of factory work were miserable, and factory owners paid money wages that might or might not offer subsistence. The contrast to life in feudal communities where payments were made in kind – or in towns, where powerful guilds had the power to regulate the labour market to ensure that workers received a just wage – could not have been more marked. The emergence of a mass labour market upon which the enormously new productive factories depended but which respected none of these ancient means of securing justice required an antidote; Europe's new urban working class found it by organising in trade unions and becoming wedded, if not to Marxism, at least to socialism.

The values that created the European labour movement thus had long roots, notably in feudalism and Catholicism. Social Catholicism, in this respect, anticipated socialism. It was no less fierce a critic of free market economics, and over the nineteenth century sought to recreate what it imagined to have been the organic bonds of pre-industrial society through a network of enlightened employers, workers' self-help groups (St Vincent de Paul societies in France and Kolpings Gesellen circles in Germany), the first mutual funds and early Catholic trade unions – all inspired by a commitment to Catholicism. In France Leon Harmel, industrialist and devoted Catholic, encouraged his workers to meet and organise themselves collectively, setting up an insurance fund to which he contributed half and creating savings and sick funds on top. In Germany the Catholic industrialist Franz Brandts followed suit, with Bishop von Kettler providing the religious leadership. Profit, declared Kettler, does not belong exclusively to the owner but should benefit everybody.[11] In France, Austria and Germany the first tentative regulation of the labour market was prompted not by socialist or liberal members of their national assemblies – but by social Catholics. Even Bismarck's programme of social insurance was partly inspired by a desire to spike the arguments of the growing Catholic movement.

Harmel and Brandts had a British echo in Robert Owen, the inspirer of the British co-operative movement, while the French and German worker circles had parallels in the Victorian friendly societies, created to help workers save and insure themselves but stopping short of being even a shadow trade union. But the social movements that pre-dated socialism were much weaker in Britain. Here the Catholic tradition was virtually extinct, and the marriage between Protestantism and *laissez-faire* economics that was flourishing in the US had as firm a foundation in British values. The economic orthodoxy insisted that intervention in the operation of markets would impair their functioning, and that the Samuel Smiles doctrine of the virtues of self-help was the route to individual salvation. There were 'laws' of labour and property that simply had to be observed. Yet such was the wealth being generated by the new forces, and such the scale of the poverty created in their wake, that it became increasingly difficult to stand by the maxim that the wealthy deserved to receive their profits in full without incurring any obligation to those who were impoverished other than what charity and Christian instincts might dictate. The nineteenth-century Factory Acts, in any case bitterly resisted, ameliorated conditions for women and children, but left male employment largely unregulated. For that the system had to be recast.

This was what socialism promised. The paradox was that, once the early socialist thinkers had cast aside the Marxist notion of revolution as a consequence of capitalist collapse and accepted that the socialist project was to reform capitalism – the explicit goal of the German Social Democratic Party's 1891 Erfurt programme, which became the benchmark for European socialism[12] – socialism was in its values as much backward- as forward-looking. Its attitudes towards property, work and wealth were strongly influenced by feudal and early Christian notions of the organic community, in which property-holders accepted obligations to the common weal – and that work in particular should not be exploitative. The tension was how far those aims could be achieved by legislation, regulation and taxation through parliamentary action, and how much they would require public ownership of the means of production – and if so, of what industries. Politically, socialism looked for the same democratisation and enfranchisement achieved by the American settlers in 1787, but wanted to extend those political rights to the social sphere – notably by securing free education and health care funded by progressive taxation on incomes and wealth. It was a tougher set of demands than the American labour movement, growing at around the same time, needed or wanted to make – but then, the US had already made more progress in extending suffrage, if only to white males (women of all races had to wait until 1920). Culturally, the American belief that property is natural and more likely to be conferred on individual Americans by the operation of the system is deeply seated. That socialism never happened in the US is attributable to the differing values of the two continents.

The parliamentary attempt to arrive at a new social settlement in Europe was shattered by World War I and the Russian Revolution. The emerging competition between European parliamentary socialist parties and the first Christian democratic parties growing out of social Catholicism might have delivered a durable social contract without political upheaval. Both traditions championed a curtailing of private property rights and advanced notions of a just wage and the outlines of a welfare state. But the process was never tested. A substantial part of the European labour movement was committed to communism as a more radical solution to the property question. As Europe descended into depression and mass unemployment in the interwar years, fascism emerged as a parallel phenomenon on the right as the democracies and their parliamentary parties of left and right seemed helpless to act before the dictatorial ambitions of communists aiming to confiscate private property. Fascists were content to permit the autonomy of private property, but only, in Hitler's formulation, to produce results 'in line with the ideas of the common good under state control'.[13] As a German civil servant put it, 'at bottom we do not seek a material but a mental nationalisation of the economy.'[14] The people, racially pure, would represent their collective will through a strong state. That would suffice to produce socially desirable behaviour from those who held property and ran the private enterprise system.

European communism and fascism were thus two extreme routes to the same end: solving the riddle of how property rights were to be exercised for the common good in the face of mass unemployment, poverty, depression and hyperinflation. The liberal parliamentary system had proved inadequate to the task, and, desperate for prosperity and stability, societies in which property ownership was not widespread readily turned to totalitarian solutions. To complicate matters, German fascism had territorial ambitions as much as Soviet communism had global ideological ambitions. This menacing, evil marriage of ideology and power was to trigger world war.

Beside these developments in Europe the American political settlement, although also challenged by depression and unemployment, was not only an effective defender of liberty and democracy; in the New Deal it proved a creative source of economic and social responses to the problems of the time. The founding fathers had provided a political constitution and value system that could hold a continent together, and in so doing created the country that was to save Europe from itself. Without the US it is difficult to imagine Hitler being beaten so quickly, if at all – or Stalin's advance into Europe after the war being halted along the Iron Curtain. The inability of Europe's nation-states to provide a durable social and political settlement had put European civilisation itself in jeopardy.

But that does not mean that Europe could, or can, solve the property and wealth questions as the Americans have – or that it can freely import the canons of American conservatism. Private property and wealth simply do not have the same legitimacy in Europe as they have in the US – witness again the qualification in the postwar German constitution that the common will over-rides private property rights. If the EU and its members were to copy an absolutist conservative view of government, and say that their only role was to protect private contracts and the right to sack workers at will (see chapter 4), while promoting only interstate commerce, they would be laughed out of court. It is a far too limited conception of property and its obligations for Europeans to accept.

Europe instead has had to continue to develop and protect a distinct model that is true to its values – not only so that it will never again fall prey to communist and fascist temptations, but because that is the only way for European capitalism to win long-run legitimacy. The idea that property must earn its rights through accepting responsibilities to the community of which it is part is deeply embedded in a tradition that extends from John Chrysostom through Robert Owen to the Erfurt programme – a tradition that includes Britain. As a result, the notion that companies must earn their licence to trade through operating in a socially legitimate fashion and accepting that responsibilities accompany ownership is very much alive in Europe. Property is not a right or a simple network of private contracts; rather, it is a concession made by the society of which it is part that has to be continually earned and deserved. Employees insist on just treatment, ranging from their wages to the acknowledgement that their attitudes and dignity matter in how the organisation for which they work develops. Progressive taxation – including tax on property – is an imperative to finance universal health care and education.

Europe's attitudes towards property *are* different from America's – not just because of the experience of war and totalitarianism and the legacy of Catholicism and socialism, but because they are linked ineradicably to distinct European attitudes towards equality, social solidarity and ideas about the legitimacy and extent of public discourse. The distinction is fundamental – and it is of correspondingly fundamental importance that Europe continues to answer the property question in its own way. Indeed, it may even be that over the next century America has to borrow from Europe.

Equality and social solidarity – Utopia in dispute

The early American settlers prized liberty. It was liberty that allowed them to worship as they chose; and it was liberty that protected them from any coercive constraint or direction on how they acquired, used and disposed of their property. Governmental minimalism and the free exercise of property rights are thus the bedrock of the good society, a tradition exemplified by the leading American conservative political philosopher Robert Nozick in his *Anarchy, State and Utopia*, where he takes the conservative argument to the extreme. He depicts taxation to finance any minimum income for the poor as a form of forced labour and all forms of redistributive justice as essentially coercive. The reduction of inequality presupposes an authority to discharge the initiative which must of necessity be coercive, and thus endangers the state of liberty which all individuals must prize as an absolute virtue. The quest for equality threatens the onset of totalitarianism, and as a result all citizens must wish for as small a state as possible. This is the utopian condition.

Nozick's propositions strike most Europeans – including mainstream European conservatives – as close to absurd. Of course, pushed to its logical conclusion, what defines state power is that it cannot be resisted, but Nozick sees only the dark side; in the real world the propertyless are coerced through their powerlessness and the state is the means by which many are enabled to do things that would otherwise be impossible for them. Indeed, we accept state authority precisely because we know that the acts of the whole enlarge the possibilities of the parts, just as we accept rules for membership of any club because we are both protected and our interests furthered by membership. The perverseness that denies such self-evident truths begins to make sense only in an American context in which liberty and individualism are so highly valued – and where property has never been associated with any conception of reciprocal social obligation.

Ever since the American constitution banned the conferring of European-style titles associated with aristocracy, feudalism and monarchy, Americans have believed that theirs is a fundamentally more egalitarian society; but that ostensibly egalitarian culture has only served to mask, as I will argue in chapter 5, massive inequality and disturbingly indifferent rates of social and income mobility, despite the massive propaganda to the contrary. Inherited property and the accompanying titles were properly an offence to the American revolutionaries, just as they were to European radicals, but they had one crucial source of legitimacy which most parties to the debate – with the exception of classic one nation Tories – missed. Aristocracy contained the notion of *noblesse oblige* – literally, 'nobility obliges' – that in turn is rooted in the conception that property is held in trust for all, and that those who enjoy sovereignty over it exercise their privilege subject to their recognition of their obligations to the social whole. Part of the moral force of the French Revolution in 1789 was the conviction that this explicit social contract had been profoundly abused, and that the overturning of monarchy and aristocracy would permit a new social contract along the lines set out by Rousseau to be established. No such thinking informed the American Revolution, and so it created a culture in which, two hundred years later, clever social nihilists like Nozick can exercise a strong influence in American life.

The European tradition is much more mindful that men and women are social animals and that individual liberty is only one of a spectrum of values that generate a good society; indeed, the pursuit of liberty cannot be considered as an absolute value because at some point one woman's liberty involves a constraint on the exercise of that of another man. As the leading English socialist of the interwar years, Richard Tawney, put it in his famous book on equality: 'Every man should have his liberty and no more, to do unto others as he would that they should do unto him.' But the instinct of being ready to empathise with others requires in turn some sense of altruism and co-operativeness that itself has to be sustained and nurtured – and which is unlikely to emerge spontaneously from a Darwinian struggle of all against all which necessarily creates a wide spectrum of inequality. To achieve a proper balance of liberties, in short, requires a recognition of the needs of others which comes from knowing you are a member of a social collectivity.

Now I make an explicit European value judgement – but I believe, notwithstanding Nozick, Strauss *et al.*, that it also applies to Americans. Human beings depend for their humanity on association, and this requires that they participate in a collective consciousness and shared belief system that allows them to empathise with the conditions of others. Membership of an associative conscience is essential to human well-being; but an associative conscience cannot be established if there is not a common culture, which in turn implies that everyone can belong to it on the same terms and has the same chance fully to participate in the civilisation that creates it. These are the preconditions for any individual to have the altruistic impulses that underpin human association – and which allow the boundaries of the exercise of liberty to be established.

If these interlinked propositions are to be sustained, they have to be underpinned by a social organisation that allows every citizen the equal possibility of participation. To attempt to create this social organisation can be described as coercion – as the American right do – only if one is to describe, say, observing common rules of grammar and syntax through which to communicate as coercive. The convention that requires this sentence finish with a full stop could be described as coercive, but I observe it because I want to communicate. On the same terms, the tax I pay to ensure that the socially needy can participate in society could be described as coercive, but I pay it willingly because I accept the justice of the transfer. The contrast with American conservatism is that every European country accepts that it needs public organisation to achieve the social goals which as an explicit social contract underwrite its civilisation, and understands that of necessity the state must be the social contract's trustee. The American conception, pushed to its limits by conservatives, is that no social contract exists or is achievable without an unreasonable extension of state power; the rationale of the state is to protect individual liberties.

This conception of membership of society on equal terms as an intrinsic component of an implicit social contract is fundamental to the European tradition on both political right and left. It is the reason why across Europe there is much greater popular support for state initiatives to guarantee income and much greater dislike of inequality than in the US. In *It Didn't Happen Here*, Seymour Martin Lipset and Gary Marks present a table showing that only 12 per cent of high-income Americans believe that the state should offer a basic income to all citizens; among low-income respondents the proportion is still only 33 per cent. Yet in Britain, the former West Germany (the data are for 1990 and thus pre-unification), the Netherlands and Italy the proportion of low-income respondents backing the idea is a massive 71 per cent, 66 per cent, 58 per cent and 80 per cent respectively, with 47 per cent, 45 per cent, 39 per cent and 53 per cent of high-income respondents also supporting the notion. Richer groups in both Europe and the US are more distrustful of a basic income than their poorer counterparts (they have less need for it), but in Europe three to four times more of even the rich are in favour than their American counterparts.[15]

A similar pattern is evident over attitudes to inequality. An intriguing paper by Alberto Alesina, Rafael di Tella and Robert MacCulloch shows that Europeans dislike inequality more than Americans, with the poor feeling particularly strongly.[16] In the US the only group worried by inequality is rich leftists; every other group is indifferent. The authors' view is that the reason the American poor are less concerned than their European counterparts is that they think they have greater chances of upward mobility, the reflex assumption being – as with so many inquiries of this type – that mobility is necessarily greater in the US. This is not in fact so, even if it were for the early settlers, but that does not matter; it is believed to be so by almost every American, including most social scientists, and so this perception governs attitudes despite its lack of correspondence with reality. Americans are cultural egalitarians to a degree that makes real income redistribution – and the demand for income redistribution – less necessary than in Europe despite objective conditions that are more or less the same. The American dream underpins egalitarian social attitudes and culture even if it is increasingly hogwash in practice.

The European dislike of inequality and accompanying willingness to support measures that underwrite a minimum income, and indeed a range of social benefits, should not be understood as surrogate communism – the critique levelled by American conservatives. The European acceptance of the need for a social contract is not the same as the communist campaign to redistribute resources exactly equally in a universe in which property is held in common; even some European socialists before the communist revolution (and all of them after it) understood that this approach is economically unworkable and morally undesirable. Tawney, for example, made no such demand, acknowledging not only that individuals would receive different levels of remuneration according to their skills and qualifications, but that such a pattern of differential rewards was necessary to ensure that such skills were acquired. Inequality of that type is ineradicable, and the attempt to abolish it should not be made.

Rather, the objection is to the conservative American justification of inequality as the natural outcome of a process of Darwinian selection, laced with Lockean justifications that obligation-free property rights are natural, leavened only by the need to provide subsistence income for the very poorest if they can prove that they cannot look after themselves. In this universe the losers in the race may be permitted to subsist, but they cannot achieve the broader level of social well-being which allows them to be participants in and members of the whole. Citizens, however, are defined not by mere subsistence, but by the cultural knowledge that they stand in a position of equality with others notwithstanding their low income; they are as much part of the civilisation as everybody else. For this they need their incomes to be higher than subsistence level, and to know that whatever their circumstances they have had an equal right to achieve happiness even if it has not been achieved, and that whatever their current economic and social position they are of equal worth to those more successful, luckier or better endowed with skills and talents. Tackling inequality is as much about symbolically 'stripping inequality of its esteem', as Tawney put it, as it is about providing every citizen with the material means to live above subsistence level.

If this is not even attempted, then the business of creating and sustaining the civilisation of which the losers need to be part – and of which the civilisation in turn needs to make them part if it is to make the claim to be a genuine civilisation – is left to the winners. But this is at best an incomplete civilisation, because it accepts that a significant class of its potential members is not eligible to have a stake in the common interest. Unless the working class feel they belong to their society as much as the middle and upper classes, and have a fair chance of raising their status because the odds are not stacked against them, then there is no chance of creating the equality of standing on which social solidarity depends. If that is to happen, then the state has to be vigilant about ensuring that the rich do not exclusively look after their own children and their own networks through inheritance, favoured education and nepotism. In other words, the rich have to accept the legitimacy of the state working to see that they discharge their obligations to the whole. A culture that accepts the principle of egalitarianism, in the sense of acknowledging the legitimacy of some form of social contract, has to be embraced by the better-off as much as the poor if a civilisation is to function.

Of course, the degree to which this analysis should be accepted is a matter of political dispute between the European right and left – Christian democrats and one nation conservatives arguing that the system has to accept a measure of 'natural' inequality while social democrats and liberals argue for more redistribution of income and wealth and high levels of basic income. Nor does the exact means by which the social contract is expressed take the same form throughout Europe. My point is rather that these sometimes significant differences should not be allowed to mask the truth that European cultures hold an idea of the social contract in common. If Tawney is among the most eloquent British thinkers to express the concept, the French, for example, can boast Emile Durkheim.[17] The great French sociologist's preoccupation is to identify the importance of social solidarity as not just material but psychic social cement, and in doing so he inverts the arguments made by the proponents of *laissez-faire* economics. Individual competition, market exchange and the exercise of liberty do not spontaneously create co-operation and a vigorous social life – on the contrary, they destroy it. It is only when there is strong social solidarity and a powerful collective conscience that individuals have the platform on which to express their individualism; otherwise they risk being isolated by the pressures of the modern market economy and getting lost, resulting in alienation and what Durkheim calls *anomie* or a sense of purposeless anonymity. The task is to make people feel part of the whole, and that requires Tawney's approach of trying to ensure an equal chance of social membership. Durkheim's idea of a collective conscience may now be regarded with some suspicion, but his view that a successful market economy is embedded in a strong society survives. When French prime minister Lionel Jospin uses the formulation of being for a market economy but against a market society, for example, his ideas descend directly from Durkheim – but then, Durkheim is articulating a common European preference.

The infrastructure of justice

Europeans do not have a monopoly of the idea that equality and the social contract are linked. After all it was John Rawls, professor of philosophy at Harvard University, who attempted to prove from the first principle underpinning American culture – that all citizens are free – that a social contract approach self-interestedly produces the best society, and goes on to outline what the most robust social contract would be. He is trying to reconcile the European notion of a social contract with American preferences for liberty and individualism, as he openly admits in citing his admiration for European social contract ideas. Yet for all its insight and remarkable reception in the world of philosophy and intellectual liberalism, *A Theory of Justice* (published in 1971) has not entrenched itself in the US with the same force as the new conservatism. It has not informed the policy programmes of the Democrats; it has not been deployed to justify any social programmes or criticism of America's money-dominated politics. It did not check the conservative advance – indeed, if anything it served only to sharpen conservative arguments in reply. Robert Nozick's *Anarchy, State and Utopia* was written in part as a refutation of Rawls. If a culture is not equipped to hear a philosophy, then it remains deaf.

The Rawlsian thesis is well-known and I will rehearse it only in brief. Rawls invites us to indulge in a thought experiment about what would be the nature of the social contract to which we would consent if we were in the 'original position'; that is, if we were situated behind a 'veil of ignorance', knowing nothing about ourselves and our future life-chances but wanting to live in a just order in which our own and others' liberties were respected. He does not put it this way, but you might imagine you were a new puritan settler imbued with the teachings of John Locke and a love of freedom; what would be the social order you would want to construct in your new land? Rawls sets out to prove that even as liberty-loving individualists, the rational strategy would be egalitarian subject to the freedom to exercise one's basic individual liberties. Rawls defines these essentially as civil liberties – the right to vote, freedom of thought and the like – consistent with offering a like liberty for others, which on close examination looks astonishingly like the first amendment.

But in elucidating his second principle – 'the difference principle' – Rawls tries to persuade his compatriots that the Europeans are right to be concerned about the conditions of the poorest, if only because anybody could have been one of them. Any individual making a choice about the ordering of society behind a veil of ignorance would want to make sure that the worst outcome that might befall him or her would be manageable and that he or she would still have access to key primary goods – some reasonable level of income and material well-being, access to opportunity, and the exercise of basic rights and civil liberties – which together allow the individual the self-respect on which membership of society depends. The chance of making a very high income should be constrained by the taxation and constraints on the use of property necessary to provide the infrastructure of justice that provides such key primary goods – an infrastructure which ensures that the greatest benefits go to the weakest so that they have no reasonable grievance against the rich. We can only enjoy very high incomes to the extent that we have ensured that the poor are in the best position we could conceive – the yardstick being that were we in their place we would consider the arrangements fair. Importantly, this infrastructure of justice is not only about a minimum level of material well-being; it must also ensure that the disadvantaged enjoy minimum basic civil liberties.

This two-paragraph account only hints at the sophistication of Rawls's model social contract, which he considered superior to other attempts because it guarantees that no section of the community can ever have their well-being neglected, even if that would benefit the general good: unless everybody has primary goods and self-respect (the echoes of Tawney and Durkheim are obvious) then one cannot be said to be living in a just society. What is intriguing is that this attempt to transplant European social contract theory to the US has not taken off in either theory or practice. When Rawls's broad conception of an infrastructure of justice goes head to head with Nozick's insistence that liberty is so important that it over-rides the legitimacy of any attempt to redistribute income, Rawls has emerged the loser. The conservatives have so resoundingly won the cultural argument that in America, and to an extent in Britain, we opt for liberty and inequality. Thus advocates of the Rawlsian position, if they are to make any ground, find themselves taking the softer position that the good society is simply a meritocracy with a reasonable social floor – rather than the social floor that we would consider fair if we were in that position and that is the very best we could conceive. We should not 'mind the gap' as long as there is a basic minimum safety net. This is the position of some New Labour theorists. Philip Collins, for example, director of the Social Market Foundation, advances the thesis that the good society is one with a high social floor and a meritocracy with no limits to incomes at the top, looking to Rawls for justification.[18] Rawls's egalitarian liberalism (as we will call it) goes much, much further – but it is the radicalism that currently dare not speak its name.

A Theory of Justice assumes that society is solidaristic enough for us to posit that individuals rank their desires similarly. Perhaps the most expressive sign that his ideas have gained little purchase in the US is the drumbeat of insistence that in contemporary America minority groups in society will not make the same choices about the level of primary goods they might need because their values are different. A Theory of Justice presupposed a universality of moral choices that cannot be possible, allege the apostles of cultural diversity, given the different world views of say, blacks, or religious groups. In short, in an immigrant society with many sub-groups and competing moralities, it is impossible to presuppose a universal morality and commonality of moral codes to guide individual choices behind the Rawlsian veil of ignorance on which the just society is founded.

Here Rawls's thesis is trapped by the character and conservatism of American society; a social contract cannot fly in such an environment, and conservative intellectuals will not let it pass. Even if they were to drop their guard, powerful minority groups in American society would continue to use the protections afforded by the constitution over their individual rights, backed by the courts, to insist on preferential treatment. These are the culture wars that have plagued the US for the last twenty or thirty years. Blacks, for example, campaign for reparation payments to compensate for slavery, and religious groups insist that their primary goods include a commitment to ban abortion: all can use the rights entrenched in the constitution and the conservative instincts of the Supreme Court to press their cases as minority groups whose grievances must be respected. Thus the US descends into a cacophony of competing group grievances, with no common view about what the social contract or infrastructure of justice might be that would reconcile them equitably. American blacks are right to argue that they have been systematically discriminated against; the response that would hold American society together would be to redress that grievance over time through an infrastructure of justice that is neutral to all minority groups and mindful only of equivalent disadvantage. If, instead, the claim for hundreds of billions of dollars of reparations ever makes progress, it will poison America's already disastrous race relations for yet more decades. It will be more important to be black than to be an American citizen. Rawls, properly applied, would avoid this social disaster – but destructive conservatism dominates.

Ironically, Rawls's model does capture what is happening in Europe, especially in the Nordic states and the countries that practise what Michel Albert in *Capitalism against Capitalism* describes as 'Rhineland capitalism', where there is the necessary egalitarian liberalism to build an infrastructure of justice; and there are shades of this all over Europe as the legacies of social democracy and social Catholicism that form the foundation of the European welfare state. The call to abandon this moral world view by Europeans openly admiring of the US, and to follow the doctrines of multiculturalism in the name of diversity to reproduce America's approach to recognising minority groups, is a calamitous mistake. Once group politics trumps the politics of social solidarity, the foundations of further injustice are laid for everyone. Massive inequality and falling social mobility result as it becomes impossible to articulate any sense of a social contract or common purpose once group rights overwhelm the belief in collective efforts and collective responsibilities.

There are plenty of multiculturalists in Britain insisting that Britain should conceive of itself as a community of communities, conceding religious schools to ethnic and racial minorities and all the other social instruments that balkanise and destroy a common civic culture. Indeed, this is declared New Labour policy. But, as Brian Barry argues in his powerful book *Culture and Equality* – probably the best egalitarian argument since Richard Tawney – you cannot create a fair society without a common civic culture committed to some notion of liberal egalitarianism. Lose that, and we are on the road to perdition – legitimising alike the noxious politics of the British National Front and the separatist Asian groups protesting that their own subcultures have equal worth whatever their values – and however they obstruct the creation of wider solidarities. As the clamour for compensation, reparations and minority group 'separate development' with their own religious schools grows, we have to be clear-headed. A society can hold together only if it stands by universal egalitarian values and a universal infrastructure of justice – and it is within those that we design our responses to racism and poverty alike. Tawney, Durkheim and Rawls are right in their conception of what produces a just society. Europeans must stand by their values which underpin the social contract, not give them up. The road to hell is paved with good intentions.

Last but not least – the public realm

If there is to be a social contract, then there has to be a collective agent that can organise it – and there has to a public space within which the social contract's character and structure can be debated. In short, there has to be a state, and the state has to be part of a wider public discourse in which its actions can be publicly discussed, evaluated and held to account by the citizenship at large. For any European – or indeed any Rawlsian American – this is a pretty tame lowest common denominator of agreement.

The European tradition of central public authority that can command individual allegiance in the name of the common good goes back to the justification of monarchy as the trustee on earth of God's interest in humankind. While it became obvious during the eighteenth-century Enlightenment that monarchical rule was not consistent with the creation of a free public realm where free argument could be had and debate settled on the objective merits of proposals – not just about politics but across the gamut of human endeavours – the idea of a common interest lived on. Thus the emergence of representative government in Europe had two features that its corollary in America did not. First, political democracy was a consequence of the joyous Enlightenment liberation from the suffocating imprisonment of thought within the tramlines set by church and monarch. There was a demand for a public realm in which individuals could be free to think as they wanted; the democratic *political* domain was a vital component of this public realm, but it was only a critical subset. Second, the notion of the state as somehow embodying a common interest and thus fundamentally legitimate was handed on to the new world of representative democracy. Thus, as democratic government spread around Europe, the combination of the legitimacy of collective agency as embodying a common interest, the need for public space and public deliberation beyond the state, and the necessity of a social contract together with the requirement of accountability and representativeness became integrated into a European world view about government that is distinct from the American.

This has been a hard journey, disfigured by the interwar flirtation with fascism and its more radical version, Nazism, and the resulting second world war. As the historian Mark Mazower observes in his powerful book *Dark Continent*, one of the more unpalatable truths for contemporary Europeans is how attractive many Europeans once found the prospect of fascism; had Hitler had been less of a barbarian and less exploitative of the countries he conquered, fascist doctrines might have taken root. The values celebrated in this chapter – centrally, that property rights cannot be unqualified – can in different circumstances be exploited for uglier ends. The emergence of European states with a clear and profound commitment to democracy within a European Union which makes democracy its cornerstone, along with a self-conscious desire to construct a powerful social contract and welfare state, has grown out of the desire never to repeat the experience of the 1930s and 1940s. Europe must never again make the same mistakes.

There were and are important variations in these developments across Europe. Britain, for example, in not writing a constitution that reflected Enlightenment values and merely bolting representativeness on to its old monarchical political system, has a much weaker conception of the public realm than is common on mainland Europe. Its state structures, though, retain immense legitimacy. France has the clearest and most explicit identification of the state as personification of the general will, while the modern German state draws its legitimacy from being the trustee of Germany's complex social contract – the social market economy. But for all their differences, these European states are there to act. Once a course of action has been settled, there is common agreement that each citizen will abide by the rule of consequent legislation or executive action – and has a duty to do so because that is part of the political and social settlement. Individual liberties might be constrained by majority decisions, given the uninhibited nature of state power; but better that than the lack of any capacity for collective action which represents a common interest. Because of its greater legitimacy, the political realm is where normative judgements are made, where political parties compete to tell different narratives about what might or might not produce the good society, drawing from the narratives developed in the wider public realm – and where the state will follow through with prescriptive action.

The American state tradition has significantly different roots which have allowed the conservative revolution to lead it towards a very different conception. As described earlier, this was never a state constructed to embody any notion of collective will or build a social contract; the contract was the narrower one of protecting the settlers' individual liberties and property rights. As de Tocqueville remarked over a hundred and fifty years ago, American patriotism is not a patriotism that celebrates a common interest; it is a patriotism that celebrates a state that protects individual interests – so that love of property and love of country are united.[19] The state does not and should not embody or represent a common interest, and its capacity to act is restrained not just culturally but by the complex system of constitutional checks and balances that prevent it from acting. This produces the advantage of much more open government and disclosure of information to citizens, because in an important sense they own the state, and its legitimacy resides only in its purpose of serving their individual interests. Its weakness is that, unlike in Europe, it is not supported by any substantial idea of the common interest; there is only a shrivelled conception of the public realm, which indeed hardly exists beyond the US's now chronically impoverished political arena.

For America's conservatives, this is the utopia imagined by their philosophers, like Robert Nozick and the anti-state minimalists in the Republican party. Their core conception is that of a virtuous individual unencumbered by obligations or constrained by public regulation: minding one's own business, staying in one's own space, and sticking to one's last. No coercive obligation is laid on others, and none is expected from the state. Indeed, state action that in Europe is seen as a natural outgrowth of any attempt to assert a common interest is quickly labelled coercive by American conservatives – and such is the resonance of this idea in American culture that it has paralysed the American liberal tradition.

The consequence of this conservative distrust of the state as coercive, anti-libertarian and inefficient, together with American liberalism's reluctance to risk conservative wrath by deploying state power to make morally based collective interventions, has been the collapse of what little capacity the US constitution confers for constructive state intervention, regulation and institution-building. Indeed, the constitution itself both creates and compounds the problem. It and the bill of rights are seen as the acme of democratic perfection, so that all problems should be solved within their carapace; politics, as Daniel Lazare perceptively writes, is conducted by constant deference to what the constitution says and how it should be interpreted.[20] It thus becomes difficult to use the state to exercise popular sovereignty, for the constitution was drawn up not so much as to check or balance such sovereignty as to deny it. Worse, contends Lazare, because the constitution is almost impossible to rewrite – it has been amended only fifteen times since 1791 – arguments over civil liberties and social progress are frozen, locked in what the unchangeable bill of rights asserts. 'By externalising civil liberties in the form of an untouchable Bill of Rights,' he writes, 'US constitutionalism has prevented their internalisation as part of the democratic political process.'[21] It is a deformation that bubbled to the fore in the aftermath of 11 September 2001 when Attorney-General John Ashcroft, a convinced Straussian, and President Bush adopted measures permitting the private military trial and execution of any non-American deemed to be a terrorist, along with extensive new powers to wiretap phone calls and e-mails. The scale of this withdrawal of civil liberties to combat terrorism is excessive and hard to justify in terms of potential results; it was a populist response which has become law without any political debate or opposition. The thinness of American political culture was exposed to full view. More limited measures in Britain were the subject of intense debate and parliamentary scrutiny, and were substantively amended by the House of Lords.

In the formulation famously coined by Professor Michael Sandel of Harvard University, the US has become little more than a 'procedural republic' which is ever poorer in expressing collective choices and moral preferences.[22] Instead, he argues, the political debate is constrained by a suffocating combination of constitutionalism and the canons of conservatism, leaving wider challenges to be fought out in the bearpit of individuals

asserting their individual rights in the courts or through corporate lobbying and allegiance to the latest new age fad. Essentially, economy and
society are now developing according to private choices, with little or no
intervention from the political process or wider state except to accelerate
the drift towards ever more extreme conservatism.

Those areas of American life that might constitute a public realm for the
criticism of government and deliberation about public action have shrunk
to almost nothing – not that the US public realm defined in these terms has
ever been very vigorous. De Tocqueville, writing of his experience in 1835,
found the American press shallow and uninterested in driving public
debate; in a country founded on liberty, he observed, the press defines
itself as serving liberty by prescribing little.[23] It is a tradition that has continued. The American media wants to portray itself as value-neutral and
non-prescriptive, as the state has become – and in any case, the physical
space and time devoted to public issues, as described in chapters 1 and 5, are
continually eroded by market and commercial pressures. As a result, writes
Sandel, American public life has no capacity to develop political stories
with any soul apart from those that celebrate individualism; it is vacuous –
much to the delight of American conservatives, who see every impover-
ishment of the scope for collective initiative as another liberal scalp.

Sandel is part of a growing movement that is fundamentally critical of
the way American democracy has developed. The democratic template
embedded in the American collective consciousness is of some New
England public square in the mid-1750s, in which the colonists are debating how to protect their liberty from George III – the liberalism of what
one American commentator has called the 'naked public square'.[24] It is
this image of protecting liberty at all costs that has been captured and permanently bottled in the US constitution and bill of rights, and which
explains the attitude of the American media. Newspapers, television and
radio regard themselves as electronic public squares – facilitating debate
rather than being active political players.[25] But while the civic republicanism of the eighteenth century was properly concerned with asserting the
liberty of the colonists, it is a travesty of its spirit that traps American political debate within incredibly narrow tramlines, laid down according to a
diminished conception of the public interest that in turn shrivels what is
politically possible. For Sandel as much as Rawls, a precondition of launch-

ing a more determinedly liberal America is to break out of these constraints and recover the ambition of a genuine civic republicanism.

So Europe points the way

In a sense, the US needs to follow the path postwar Europe has blazed, however uncertainly. From Immanuel Kant's rejoicing in the new freedom for public argument that the Enlightenment offered,[26] to the way Jürgen Habermas defines the public realm today – as any forum where debate and argument can take place – Europe has had, and retains, both an idea of the public realm that transcends the formal institutions of democracy, justice and government and a recognition that it is legitimate for the state to act purposively to shape economy and society. From the scientific journals where information should be available to as wide a public as possible rather than preserved in secrecy for private clients, to the political stances of its great newspapers, Europeans see a wide range of areas where it is legitimate to insist that public values are expressed and debated. Hence the commitment to publicly owned TV stations with a mandate to provide a universal public service as guarantors that ordinary citizens will have access to core news and comment delivered as objectively as possible – without which participation in the social and public life of the nation is much harder.

The American champion of such an approach is PBS (the Public Broadcasting Service), but it is not offered public revenues or privileges that might allow it to rival the commercial networks in its programming ambitions. Even before the conservative revolution Americans would have hesitated about making such a commitment; now it is impossible. Instead, PBS is a membership organisation relying on subscription and public donations from those members of the public willing to join it; it is not a station that has a statutory obligation to broadcast to the universe of American citizens and as a *quid quo pro* enjoys special state support. This contrast with European public broadcasters encapsulates the different approaches to ideas of the public.

This cuts to the quick of both civilisations. According to a Western tradition which began with Aristotle, the complete individual is one who is capable of expressing in his or her life both the public and the private; but this is a tradition from which the US is increasingly declaring independence. It is not just a matter of accepting that the state can and should act to build an infrastructure of justice that diminishes inequality, equalises opportunity and tries to enlarge individuals' capacity for self-respect. It is, as the German philosopher Hannah Arendt argues, about our needing a public realm to allow the full flowering of our human sensibilities.[27] For, taken to its limits, a society peopled only by conservative 'unencumbered selves' jealously guarding their individual liberties and privacy is a denial of the human urge for association and meaning. The musician at the peak of her powers gives a public performance as a celebration of her prowess at which we are delighted to be present. The gardener delighting in his private garden understands its value because it expresses a value a public park cannot; but equally, a public park offers a grandeur and collective space that is a pleasure in itself, complements what is offered by a private garden and in so doing underlines the character of privacy whose meaning is better comprehended because there is a public park with which to compare it. Similarly, a city needs to have public spaces for us to make sense of and value the private; but if every corner is privatised, those who are offered no access to anywhere are reduced to aliens. Contemporary American cities have this feel more and more; their public space diminishes as they become consecrated to the primacy of the private.

In a world that is wholly private we lose our bearings; deprived of any public anchor, all we have are our individual subjective values to guide us. Public parks, public squares, publicly owned television, public museums, public art, public science and public transport – to name but a few – should be seen not just as essential expressions of the collective but as vital means for framing and understanding our private choices.

Europeans of both left and right understand this, as do American liberals – but they are under assault from the values of American conservatism driven by the process of globalisation. Arendt, writing in the 1950s, was alarmed that the onrush of a market economy and society was gnawing away at conceptions of the public realm. She warned presciently that the public sphere was becoming reduced, and that as this happened government was becoming little more than administration and individuals would seek refuge by looking for meaning in their intimate relationships – but that even these would become harder to negotiate successfully as we loaded so much emotional weight on them while simultaneously reducing the anchorage offered by a vigorous public domain. In the first decade of the twenty-first century these processes are much further advanced – and will accelerate if American conservatives have their way. Protecting European conceptions of the public realm, the social contract and the obligations owed by the wealthy and propertied is becoming ever more urgent, not just for wider justice but also for our individual well-being. The most striking evidence for that is what contemporary America has become – and to explain that, we first need to explore the rise of American conservatism.

3

Waging war without blood: the collapse of American liberalism

American conservatives can be pleased. At the beginning of a new century they have succeeded in binding America's long-standing scepticism about the merits of government, its Protestant religiosity, its belief in its special destiny, and its faith in capitalism and individualism into the country's dominant conservative ideology. To be conservative is to be patriotic – and, even more extraordinarily, to be populist and the champion of ordinary people. Yet only twenty-five years ago this brand of conservatism seemed at the political margins, its fate uncertain before the moral ascendancy of liberalism – which had established a consensual acknowledgement that government was central to the creation of a fair and prosperous society, in particular to dealing with race – and a spreading secularism that seemed set to undermine conservatism's religious strongholds. Today that same liberalism is charged with intellectual incoherence and is placed permanently on the political defensive. To be a liberal is no longer just a dirty word; it is associated with the venal crime of being un-American.

It was not ever thus. In 1960 John F. Kennedy won a closely fought election that was to open up another wave of liberal reform, building on the work begun in the progressive era of American politics in the early years of the century and resumed by Roosevelt in his New Deal. It was the progressives around Theodore Roosevelt who had fought for and won acceptance of the principle of income tax and the trust-busting of monopolies. And it was the New Dealers who later made the banking system more robust, organised long-term credit for farmers and home-buyers, established collective bargaining rights for trade unions, instituted a proper system of unemployment benefit and were ready directly to employ the unemployed or create work for them in huge public works programmes. The liberal project in the 1960s was to carry this vision for-wards; to civilise American capitalism by protecting workers and consumers alike while providing genuine equality of opportunity for all. New Dealers might have relied on votes from blacks, but they had done little or nothing to promote their rights or opportunities. The priority now was to make sure that black Americans could become equal citizens and share in the wealth and opportunity of a dynamic economy and society.

Kennedy's inaugural speech, famously inviting his fellow countrymen and women to ask not what their country could do for them but what they could do for their country, was not just a classic statement of the best in the American liberal tradition but brilliantly identified liberalism with the American way. After Kennedy's tragic assassination Lyndon Johnson was to carry the programme forward in his vision of a Great Society, setting out to achieve the elimination of poverty, the genuine enfranchisement of all American citizens regardless of their race, the extension of medical protection to every American, the championing of the environment, massive training of the unskilled and the establish-ment of model cities. Nor did this vision represent just the idealised hopes of liberal America; the American business establishment backed the programme enthusiastically, and when Johnson lost office even the Nixon administration was to establish the Environmental Protection Agency and act to ensure minimum standards of health and safety at work.

Thirty years later, the whole apparatus, together with the thinking behind it, is decried and vilified; it is impossible to imagine a similar impetus being established today, let alone supported so extensively by the business community. George W. Bush is pledged further to emasculate what remains of the New Deal settlement, whether in worker rights, business regulation or progressive taxation; his brand of conservatism, masquerading as 'compassionate', is the apotheosis of the thirty-year struggle to vanquish liberalism. It is a story so important both to America and the globe that it is worth analysing in detail.

Sowing the seeds of decline: triumphant liberalism and its weaknesses

When Lyndon Johnson signed the Civil Rights Act in 1964 he made the famous aside that he had just lost the Democrat party the south. This was no casual quip; in private White House discussions over civil rights he had openly conceded that it might destroy the Democrats – but never-theless maintained that the principle of establishing civil rights for blacks had to be 'pressed for as a matter of right'. The hope, of course, was that the Democrats could more than compensate for such losses by gaining ground in the north; the fear was that if the huge expanses of the south and west of the US ever became more fully populated and industrialised, the Democrats might become a permanent minority party.

Johnson's words were prescient: subsequent history has more than born out his prediction. The states of the old Confederacy are the heartland of American conservatism. Until the last thirty years these had been predominantly agricultural economies – even now, large plantation-style farm units remain at the core of agricultural production – and natural homes for the unique combination of macho individual self-reliance, religious fundamentalism, nationalism, hatred of blacks, belief in private property and free enterprise together with sexual and social reaction that defines American conservatism. These are the apostles of the states' rights against the reach of the federal government in Washington – the inevitable consequence of the Civil War – and the rights now advocated by the new conservatives as an entrenchment of freedom.

Above all, these are the old slave states, where 250 years of slavery casts its long and ominous shadow into the twenty-first century. The Confederate cause might have been lost militarily in 1865, but thirty years later the condition of southern blacks had scarcely improved, eco-nomically, socially or in terms of citizens' rights. So-called 'Jim Crow laws' enforced a form of apartheid, so that blacks travelled, lived and were educated separately from whites, and could not exercise basic rights such as voting or testifying in court without the threat of beatings, burning and even murder executed by the Ku Klux Klan. Even as late as the early 1960s the Klan bombed black churches and killed blacks without any fear of being brought to justice. The racism was endemic; but slavery and its shadow also cemented the cultural view that labour should be cheap, disposable and without rights. Over the twentieth century the south became the centre of anti-unionism as part of the southern ideological cocktail of anti-federalism and suspicion of government and its intentions.

The violence lives on, now in the form of scattered, lunatic but dangerous militias that exercise their constitutional right to bear arms in the woods and hills, rehearsing armed resistance to what they believe are the dark ambitions of the federal government, or invasion by the UN or communist forces. Nor is this paranoiac element confined to the south. One of the largest of such groups, the militia of Montana, hides out in the hills, grimly warning in its feverish newsletter about how America's white population is about to be overwhelmed and issuing warnings about the anti-American ambitions of the state and the loss of individual freedom. It was this same pathology which drove the mad group led by Timothy McVeigh to bomb federal offices in Oklahoma City in 1995, causing over 160 innocent deaths. Others of this ilk are linked to the sending of letters with anthrax to pro-abortion groups. They may be light years away from the right-wing think tanks, but they are linked by the same thread.

The picture is not one of wholly unrelieved reaction. Politically the south has necessarily been sympathetic to state-led initiatives for economic development as the only means of alleviating desperate poverty; Louisiana provided the political base for Huey Long's populist economic Keynesianism in the 1930s and, for all his segregationism, Alabama's George Wallace was enthusiastically committed to building up the state's public infrastructure. Here social conservatism and racism have sat side by side with deployment of the state to serve the free enterprise system, but only if the essential pillars of the southern order are left in place – in particular a subordinate role for the black man and woman. It has always been clear that if this culture ever became predominant nationally, the prospects for American liberalism would be poor.

In a sense, what has happened to liberalism is the north receiving its dues for never properly engaging with the different civilisation that constitutes the south. The founding fathers of the US constitution – Washington, Hamilton and Madison – all knew that a constitution that proclaimed the equality of all men and women could never be squared with slavery. But they also knew that the political necessity of combining all the former British colonies – even those whose economy was dependent upon slave-ownership – into a United States of America trumped the need to offer any constitutional injunction enfranchising the black population. And as slave-owners themselves they were in any case compromised. So – better leave the issue to the individual discretion of member states. It was a hypocrisy and a betrayal that has bedevilled the US to this day.

Even after the north under Lincoln's Republicans won the Civil War, the same ambiguities remained. The north turned a blind eye to the devices deployed by white plantation owners and the southern white political establishment to sustain white supremacy after the Civil War – ranging from setting literacy tests for voters to disenfranchising felons. Moreover, the Democrats, then, as the anti-Republican party, holding the advantage in the south, needed to secure their southern base if they were to mount any effective national challenge to the Republicans, on whom victory in the war had conferred a new and immense legitimacy. Add this political calculation to the pork-barrel nature of American politics and the constitution with its checks and balances and it is not surprising that it proved impossible to assemble any national majority in favour of asserting proper civil rights.

The progressive movement avoided the issue, as did Roosevelt's New Dealers. Their initiatives were aimed at improving the condition of American working people as a class against the rich and powerful rather than championing individual rights – an approach that poor southern whites and the Democratic southern establishment were happy to support, given their own willingness to use the state to promote economic development, just so long as the racial question was not raised. Louisiana's Huey Long, for example, was in economic terms more radical than Roosevelt. In an American context the creation of the progressive coalition was something of a political triumph, implying as it did and does that the minorities who together formed the coalition put aside the advocacy of their individual rights and instead made common cause. All politics in democracies is about the art of coalition-building; it inevitably involves compromises, but as long as there is a sufficiently large core group and a robust enough sense of overall mission, the coalition will hold. In the US the task is made more difficult because necessarily in a polity that encompasses a continent the core group in any coalition is smaller; coalitions are more a plurality of minorities than an anchored political grouping. In addition, all interest groups in the US are versed in the language and culture of rights, which makes them intrinsically less willing to make common cause around a common agenda.

The progressive and liberal approach was to borrow the European centre-left language of a working-class interest that needed to be asserted against the rich and business, but rather than use the language of socialist transformation, instead campaign for practical ways for improving working people's lot in a capitalist society which would remain capitalist. With a tacit silence on the civil rights question (for example, the New Deal Social Security Act conveniently excluded agricultural and domestic workers, who were predominantly black), southern Democrats could sit as easily as northern trade unionists in the liberal coalition – which thus encompassed a range of religious beliefs that stretched from Catholicism through to southern fundamentalism.

Eisenhower's election in 1952 did nothing to threaten the new consensus. The new Republican administration respected the essentials of the New Deal framework, at least in part solidly to bind in the American working class to the Cold War confrontation against communism and head off the potential appeal of left-wing ideas to organised labour. In any case the experience of World War II, together with the New Deal, had immensely enhanced the authority of the federal government. It had been government contracts that had underwritten the immense increase in US production and scientific leadership during the war; and it was the government's GI bill of rights that guaranteed every American serviceman the chance to acquire the skills and education necessary to succeed in civilian life. *Laissez-faire* and free markets meant depression, unemployment and lack of opportunity of all; government meant growth, work, new life-chances.

With business accepting the enlargement of the government's role, the liberals felt that the coalition they had built to support activist government was solid. The next phase in the progressive journey was to back the growing civil rights movement in the south, agitating to end segregation and discrimination, and to complete the task that should have been finished in 1865. The US was the richest and most productive economy in the world. It was an age of extraordinary optimism and self-confidence; there was nothing that the US could not attempt and succeed. It was politically impossible not to include southern blacks in the fruits of the postwar boom – and the country, it seemed, could comfortably afford the necessary social expenditures.

The resulting Civil Rights Act of 1964 in many respects marked the beginning of the high tide of American liberalism that would end a decade later with the Supreme Court's judgement legalising abortion in 1973. Federal spending on the poor during these years more than quadrupled and there was liberal progress across the board, with the distribution of guns by mail order being limited in 1968 and states like Arkansas and Mississippi finally losing the right to ban the teaching of Darwinian theories of evolution. By the time Congress passed the Equal Rights Amendment (ERA) outlawing sexual discrimination in 1972 the liberal advance seem assured; but the liberals were beginning to be overconfident and the conservative anti-ERA forces were determined to kill the measure. Too few states ratified it and it failed to become law.

The most important and politically potent initiative of this period was the launch of affirmative action, the concept that was to prove the fateful trigger to a massive conservative reaction. The Civil Rights Act itself, together with the Voting Rights Act that followed, carefully and explicitly avoided positive discrimination in favour of blacks as a group. Rather, the acts sought to outlaw any intervention that obstructed individual blacks from exercising their individual constitutional rights as citizens in elections. In 1964, for example, only 7 per cent of blacks in Mississippi had succeeded in registering to vote; by 1969, after the passage of the two acts, the proportion had grown to 61 per cent. There were parallel improvements across the south whose fairness and legitimacy it was impossible to contest.

But black disadvantage extended well beyond their lack of citizen rights; poor farm workers in the south, they were the ghetto-dwellers of the north. Redress demanded that the economic and social stigma of having a black skin be taken on directly, which meant giving blacks privileges as a group in order to give them the same proportional opportunities as whites. Thus employment quotas were established in the public sector and for public contractors; there were quotas for a fair share of good housing and special preferences for educational places. At the time, the movement to redress blacks' position was supported by the Republicans (the party, after all, of Lincoln), with Richard Nixon in 1969 fighting for affirmative action quotas against opposition from Democrats influenced by a trade union leadership that was fearful that white jobs would be stolen by blacks. However, affirmative action was ultimately to prove fatally divisive.

Doubts about affirmative action were not just rooted in racism; they went – and go – to the heart of the twin incompatibilities that form the basis of the American credo. Egalitarianism and citizenship demand affirmative action for blacks (or women) as a group; individualism and equality of opportunity mean that any help should be given only to individual Americans who earn their advance by merit, and those who try to achieve the American dream should not have their progress blocked by administrative fiat favouring a minority. If American liberalism had used the social contract framework to address the black issue, as argued in chapter 2, it could have avoided the political skewer on which it impaled itself and kept the white working class in the liberal coalition. As it was, it never sorted out its own ambiguities over the question – leaving an opening which conservatism was to exploit murderously to help end the liberal ascendancy.

Conservatism's revenge

For the first half of the 1960s conservatism seemed trapped. The US economy was strong; productivity and growth rose on average by more than 3 per cent a year. There seemed no problem in simultaneously financing the massive Great Society programme and the military competition with the Soviet Union. Indeed, this competition made the great civil rights and social programmes even more imperative. America's racial tensions and poverty were a gift to Soviet propagandists, so that even Republicans could share liberal concerns – if only as a tool in super-power rivalry.

But by the late 1960s severe strains were beginning to show. The US had decided after 1945 that its own security interests would be best served by throwing a military and diplomatic *cordon sanitaire* around the entire Euro-Asian littoral, so constraining the possible geographical advance of communism to the Pacific and Atlantic seaboards. Hence NATO, the Berlin airlift and the Korean War. When communism gained ground in Indo-China the doctrine demanded that the same stance be taken in South Vietnam in the 1960s to stop its conquest by the North and assim-ilation into a communist Vietnam, not least as a demonstration to America's Asian and European allies – and to Moscow and Beijing – that the US was not in the business of appeasement.

As defence expenditure jumped to nearly 10 per cent of GDP at the height of the Vietnam War, inflation moved towards 5 per cent and the trade deficit reached hitherto unprecedented levels. The dollar began to come under strain as the linchpin of the international financial system. In 1971 Nixon was forced to break the US currency's fixed linkage with gold and preside over the dismemberment of the Bretton Woods system of semi-fixed exchange rates, pegged to the dollar and thus to gold, that had held since the late 1940s. The US could not, it found, support the dollar, the Vietnam War and its Great Society programme simultaneously.

It was this failure that created the intellectual opportunity for which conservatives had been preparing. Kennedy had chosen to pump-prime the American economy with Keynesian-style tax cuts in the early 1960s, and the economic consensus was that the federal government should manipulate demand in the economy by changes in taxes and public spending in order to sustain the growth of employment or lower infla-tion, as the case might be. In essence the proposition was that the state could and must direct the economy to achieve public goals – anathema to the American right. In the mid-1950s William Buckley's periodical *The National Review* had begun to marshal a coherent anti-Keynesian, pro-free-market position articulating the philosophy of Friedrich Hayek, in which any extension of state activity was the thin end of a wedge destroying the functioning of capitalism and was literally *The Road to Serfdom*, as Hayek entitled his book of 1944. For Hayek, wealth creation was the product of economic freedom, which had to be protected from any kind of state intervention. But in the 1950s he had few listeners in the US. Arch-conservative Barry Goldwater suffered a landslide defeat in the 1964 presidential election, with Johnson dismissing him as nutty as a fruitcake – but his winning of the five states of the deep south was a harbinger of what was to follow.

As the 1960s wore on, the economic background became more favourable to conservative preoccupations, and conservative intellectuals intensified their case for free market economics, linking its precepts to libertarianism and the case for minimal government which conservatives believed underwrote the responsible, and thus virtuous citizen. These two streams of thought – economic and philosophical – were interwoven through the 1960s in the University of Chicago under the tutelage of philosophy professor Leo Strauss, a refugee from Nazism who blamed the liberal Weimar Republic for the Holocaust, and economics professor Milton Friedman. Strauss was to win the largest and most devoted following – or collection of disciples, as one of his students called them[1] – in American academic life. The good society, he insisted, was constructed upon virtuous, morally centred citizens of good character, and the case against state-led attempts socially to engineer more freedom or equality was that they undermined such virtue by relieving individuals of the necessity of facing the consequences of their individual actions. He thought that religion and nationalism helped to entrench such virtue, and that liberalism and secularism undermined it – and that unless the US was watchful it faced the same fate as the Weimar Republic. Even if religion was bunk and its moral codes impossible to maintain, said Strauss, the task of the educated elite was to keep quiet and maintain the fiction in the name of order. Although Strauss died in 1973, twenty years later Republican Newt Gingrich was to claim his 'Contract with America' of 1994 was inspired by Strauss – and almost every strand in current American conservative thought, from dependency theory to incorporating the evangelical movement into the Republican party, can trace its lineage back to him. Today the most militantly conservative members of the Bush administration – Deputy

Defense Secretary Paul Wolfowitz and Attorney-General John Ashcroft – are committed Straussians. When Wolfowitz insists on the US's right to strike militarily, unilaterally and pre-emptively against any state that might offend the US's will, or Ashcroft insists on summary justice for any suspect non-American, their philosophical and intellectual patron is Strauss. It is a lethal legacy.

However, it took Friedman and the University of Chicago's conservative ultra-free-market economics faculty to put some practical policy bite into the philosophy. Friedman's intellectual bridgehead was his explanation of inflation, which rose steadily over the 1960s and emerged in the 1970s as the leading economic problem. Friedman's proposition, which came to be known as monetarism, was that the rate of inflation was set automatically by the growth in the supply of money, which in turn could be generated only by the state, which has a monopoly of money creation. If inflation was rising, then either the government had mistakenly set interest rates too low, or it was spending too much and financing that expenditure by printing money – all in the attempt artificially to prevent the economy from doing what it 'naturally' wanted to do. The cure was to curb the role of the state and its associated spending, and thus the growth of money – and in the process inflation would settle at low levels and economic growth would be rekindled. Behind this view lay the judgement that a free market economy was essentially self-regulating and generated wealth spontaneously, and that government got in the way of these natural processes and damaged the vitality of capitalism.

A few lecture rooms away, Strauss was insisting that such a government-free environment created the virtuous citizen, especially if it was reinforced by powerful religious sentiment. The very particular brand of American conservatism began to take off in earnest.

Friedman and the so-called Chicago school purported to be 'scientific' economic theoreticians, but behind the panoply of monetarism and the associated theoretical toolbox that made it work, notably the theory of rational expectations and of the rational economic man, lay a Straussian and highly ideological conception of the world. In order to prove that markets tended to work perfectly, the Chicago school had to guarantee that individuals could be relied upon to respond to price signals and, if they made mistakes, immediately to change their behaviour – that is, they were rational, formed rational expectations and adjusted those expectations rationally – despite the overwhelming evidence, furnished by liberal economists, to the contrary. For example, it is simply unrealistic to assume that every market actor has perfect information and that the cost of acquiring information is equal for all, as the Chicago economists claimed. It is perfectly possible for, say, unemployed workers not to find available work because they do not know it exists – so that as a result wages get pitched above what they otherwise should be. Equally, bankers may ration credit to perfectly creditworthy borrowers because they are ignorant or have imperfect information about them – or, equally, lend to uncreditworthy borrowers for the same reason. In short, there is market failure.[2]

But the Chicago school could not admit this. At the centre of its universe was the conception of the self-interested, profit-maximising individual who definitionally cannot make systematic mistakes – first cousin to Strauss's virtuous citizen, and thus the coping stone of a healthy, free market American republic. It was this ultimately ideological conception that made the narrow economic critiques of the Chicago/Friedman position so ineffective, even though the Chicago school was largely wrong and the implementation of its ideas has gravely weakened the US economy. Ideology protected Friedman from the mounting concerns that his methodology, automatically and mechanically linking money supply growth and subsequent inflation over America's economic history, was wanting.[3] The monetarist theory had to be right, because it had to be right to minimise the role of government. The criticism that markets are not self-regulating, nor ever have been, was simply dismissed. It might be true that stock markets, for example, are well known for their bubbles and irrational depressions, or that capitalist firms rig markets to their advantage if they can. But the conservatives, instead of acknowledging these phenomena as inherent to the operation of markets, insisted they arose because some obstacle had been erected – usually by government or unions – which hindered their free operation.

As for the conservative claim that individuals are all-knowing, the human condition is that we face an unpredictable future which can engender irrational fears or hopes which then dictate our actions; the ridiculous expectations which generate irrational outcomes like a stock market bubble can make it rational to buy even in the middle of the bubble. For conservative economists such a suggestion is a logical impossibility; the theoretical framework cannot permit such heresies, for if admitted they would bring down the whole ideological house of cards. No less seriously, the conservative perspective that market economies are solely and completely about the capacity to exchange goods and services in a series of contingent, potentially reversible market contracts is a very limited conception of wealth generation and innovation. The market may be a necessary precondition for wealth generation, but by itself it is insufficient. It does not, as argued in later chapters, take any account of the necessary role of organisations in integrating and marshalling physical and human capital – people whose strategies and capabilities are determined by their histories. Innovation is not switched on like a light bulb inside an entrepreneur's head at the prospect of profits, as conservative economists hypothesised. Its roots are much more complex, as this book will explore.

The Chicago school view that markets are held together and wealth generated by no other means than mere economic self-interest is bunk. But conservatives are obliged to play down or ignore the complicated truth that markets depend upon webs of reciprocal obligations, trust and social capital that are created by conceptions of fairness and natural justice to which self-interest stands in tension rather than harmony. They cannot accept any criticism on these lines, or even allow it to dent the monetarist, free market thesis, because to do so would fatally weaken their objective – to delegitimise government, the social and the collective.

Because of the enormous care and effort expended by conservatives to make sure that their propositions were intellectually coherent, once the foundations were accepted conservative economics could be contested only if the philosophy and politics upon which it rested was challenged root and branch – but this American liberals failed to do. This is why Hayekian and Straussian ideas were so important. Hayek made the linkage between economic and political freedom; Strauss made the fundamental moral proposition that the good society depended on moral individuals – and that individual morality was a higher good than either equality or opportunity. Thus any economics that relied, as Keynesianism does, on the notion that government expresses the common will and public interest is automatically devalued – even if it produces results – first because it enlarges the role of the state and second because it represents a value system that attacks and undermines a superior universe of moral individuals. Conservatives do not even admit that any collective initiative should be taken to minimise inequality, for example, because in the last resort poverty is evidence of 'poor' character – that is further morally degraded by accepting welfare.

It was Robert Nozick, as we saw in the previous chapter, who took the conservative argument even further. All state action was characterised as coercive. If, in the name of fairness, the state tries to alleviate poverty, it must perforce confiscate part of some individuals' income as tax to support the incomes of others. The notion that tax is the payment citizens make for the public goods, ranging from pensions to health, that the market is incapable of providing, cannot be accepted.

This combined conservative philosophical stance that the state is amoral, inefficient and coercive was the platform for a savagely effective attack on American liberalism. It has been, in short, the ally of a new barbarism even while it purports to keep barbarism at bay; the sponsor of economic degeneration even as it advertises its commitment to wealth creation. But liberalism never understood the totality of the ideology it confronted, the persecution complex of those who developed it, their fanatical determination to press home their advantage or the degree to which America's cultural tinder would aid conservatism's advance.

Laying the conservative foundation

The south did not need to be told that religion was vital social cement; it knew that already. It did not need to learn that individual states' rights were part of America's natural constitution of freedom; that was the basis of the Confederate case. It understood what politicians meant when they spoke of welfare queens, family breakdown and the dependency culture; they were talking about feckless black sexuality and sponging off whites. The south was the natural political base of the National Rifle Association, Christian Coalition and Business Roundtable alike; and its willingness to mobilise behind the ideological openings offered by the great right-wing intellectuals – Ayn Rand, Milton Friedman, Leo Strauss, Irving Kristol *et al.* – has been at the heart of the conservative revival.

Even so, this ultra-conservative critique that aimed to destroy the postwar consensus and the foundations of American liberalism, might have remained at the margins of debate if the US had continued to prosper in the 1970s while healing its social and racial wounds. It did not. The Democrat coalition, incorporating northern blue-collar workers of all religions and ethnic backgrounds, southern blacks and the liberal professional classes, was already fraying before the advance of the right and its attacks on the implications of the civil rights revolution. Race was working its poison in American politics. For northern Catholics the issue might be abortion; for blue-collar workers in the south the flashpoint was affirmative action; suburban whites everywhere recoiled from bussing to limit educational segregation. As political analysts Ruy Teixeira and Joel Rogers observe, 55 per cent of American voters are white working class, and over the 1970s they deserted the Democrats in droves; to them, the party seemed more interested in helping blacks and gays than its traditional base.[4] At just this moment liberal America faced a gathering economic crisis. Inflation mounted; growth and productivity slowed. Imports soared; the dollar weakened. Unemployment grew – and blue-collar America was hurting, with its traditional champion apparently no longer focused on its core voters' interests. And if that were not enough, there was the ignominy of losing the Vietnam War. Liberalism at home and abroad seemed to have reached a dead end.

And, as the assumptions of the postwar era were progressively challenged, Nixon resigned over Watergate – his attempted impeachment by the Democrats an event which the Republicans would never forgive or forget, and which they determined they would one day repay in spades. For that they would need a dominance of Congress that had so far eluded them, and for which the necessary precondition was the building of a conservative coalition as strong as the liberal one they sought to demolish. The 1970s were to offer them four simultaneous advantages. The apparent failings of the economy gave Friedman and the Chicago school their chance to open up the entire economic argument, and with it create the space for conservative ideas deploring welfare and the state to enter the arena. The growing sense that the 1960s movement for civil and equal rights had gone too far allowed the right to play the subliminal race card – not always, indeed, very subliminally – so detaching the white working class from the Democrats. The shift of the US's centre of economic gravity to the south and west offered a natural strong hinterland and secure political base. And finally, the increasing role of the media made money ever more important in US politics, giving conservatism, richer than liberalism, an advantage upon which it has ruthlessly capitalised for more than a generation. The foundations had been laid of the conservatives' march to power.

By the middle of the 1970s the US was mired in stagflation, the rate of productivity growth was falling sharply and the dollar was consistently weak, reflecting in part the growing and persistent strength of Asian exports to the US, particularly from Japan. Nixon's wage and price controls had failed to curb inflation, and the Keynesian mainstream seemed to have no solution which would address the gathering sense of economic pessimism and evidence of failure.

In reality, America's economic problems were rooted as much in the way the international economic system it had created was now developing as in any domestic shortcomings – although this was never to be admitted by the right. Inevitably the rapidly growing Asian and European economies had gained a competitive advantage in some key manufacturing sectors – notably cars and consumer durables – through a heavy programme of investment in state-of-the-art technology that necessarily lifted them to the frontiers of productive possibility, and were taking advantage of the liberal world trade regime the US had devised to exploit the narrowing of their productivity gap with the US and raise their exports to the world's biggest market. They were responding to no more than the order the US had constructed for its own geopolitical purposes. Kennedy had pioneered a major round of tariff reduction in the 1960s – the so-called Kennedy round – largely to help consolidate the Asian and European economies into the American-led capitalist West. Khrushchev, the Soviet premier, had boasted that Soviet production and standards of living would overtake those of the West by 1970, saying that 'When we catch you up, as we pass by, we will wave to you.'[5] The Americans' angry response was to use free trade as a mechanism for spreading American living standards to Europe and the rapidly industrialising countries of Asia in order to limit any potential appeal from a successful communism. Thus part of US industry's difficulty in the 1970s was simply that of adjusting to the new international division of labour as production in Asia and Europe grew to the maturity that the US had wished into being. America's share of global manufacturing fell by 23 per cent between 1970 and 1980 – a decade in which the foreign share of the US car market rose from 8 to 22 per cent.

Similarly, the problem of inflation which began to loom large in the 1970s needs to be interpreted against the trends of the international financial system the US had created. Although the British (especially Keynes[6]) had lobbied hard during World War II for an international system less dependent upon the dollar, the Americans had insisted that their currency should be central – a position that in the immediate postwar years was almost unavoidable given that the US economy constituted nearly half the world economy. But the consequence of a generation of American trade deficits and the accompanying emergence of a vast offshore market in dollars (eurodollars) around which London rebuilt its pre-eminence as a world financial centre was to create a vast pool of dollar liquidity. The world had too many dollars chasing too few goods.

When the discipline of the Bretton Woods system collapsed between 1971 and 1973, Europe, Asia and the US all stimulated their economies apparently free of an exchange rate constraint, and it was against this background of surging demand and billions of footloose dollars that the OPEC countries were able to make the quadrupling of the oil price stick. Other commodity prices jumped in sympathy. As a result, American inflation rose sharply and the share of profits as a proportion of GDP nosedived because the oil-dependent structure of production could not be changed overnight; wealth was being transferred from the oil-dependent US to largely third world oil producers. Investment fell, and the lower trajectory of output growth implied slower productivity growth.

But the intellectual and political argument in the US was – as it is today – extraordinarily America-centred. Rather than describe the problems of the US economy as arising from a very particular international conjuncture, the conservatives saw their opportunity to press home their view of the world. In essence, as Jude Wanniski argued in *The Way the World Works*, one of the defining texts of the resurgent right, published in 1978, the natural productivity of the so-called supply side of the US economy had been fatally undermined by a burden of regulation and taxation that obstructed the pattern of incentives that go-getting Americans needed to deliver wealth generation. In the free enterprise system, enterprise had to be free – it needed to declare independence from the postwar bargain with government and return to the truths of the American way.

Together with the monetarist propositions of Milton Friedman, this protest amounted to a full-scale conservative assault on the liberal economic world view; it was liberalism, rather than the trends in the global economy, that was causing America's travails. If the US wanted lower inflation, it should generate less money supply growth, which meant reducing budget deficits – not by raising taxes, which would damage the supply side, but by cutting back federal spending, which had jumped by 5 per cent of GDP over the 1970s. Indeed, Wanniski and a little-known economist, Arthur Laffer – championed by a Republican congressman, Jack Kemp – argued that cutting taxes would so stimulate vital economic growth and boost accompanying tax revenues that the budget deficit could be cut – one of economic history's more famous delusions about having your cake and eating it. Laffer posited his famous 'Laffer curve' on a napkin in a Wall Street restaurant, and a theory that had no empirical or theoretical support took off. Conservatism had become the new orthodoxy so quickly that even its more absurd propositions could suddenly be inserted in the policy mainstream. For the first time since the gold standard and *laissez-faire*, the right had a complete economic theory with which to contest the liberal consensus. Moreover, as the Californians had proved in 1978 with Proposition 13 – a measure halving the state's property taxes which became the forerunner of similar anti-tax laws in more than half the states – it was connecting with a popular mood.

The great right-wing think-tanks – the reconstituted American Enterprise Institute, the Hoover Institution and the Heritage Foundation, set up in 1973 – promulgated this world view with the fervour of ideological zealots. Their most reliable outlet was the op-ed pages of the conservative *Wall Street Journal* run by the obsessive crank Robert Bartley, sponsor of the Wanniski–Laffer supply-side coalition; the number of anti-big-government leaders in the *Wall Street Journal* exploded in the first half of the 1970s.[7] Business began to shift its position. It had given the Goldwater campaign in 1964 a wide berth, but by the early 1970s there was a readiness to find cash to support the new think-tanks, and even begin to lobby for a more 'free market' approach to economic management. The Business Roundtable, founded in 1975 as inflation topped 10 per cent, brought chief executives together for the first time to make the business case directly rather than through the medium of trade associations; already some CEOs felt the postwar readiness of business to accept regulation, taxation and trade unionisation was now outmoded. Their initial particular obsessions were the need to challenge the power of organised labour and the growing consumer movement, whose most conspicuous and outspoken advocate was Ralph Nader. But as the 1970s progressed they began to think there might be something in the wider ideology of the right-wing think-tanks.

Nowhere was the need to assert conservatism felt more keenly than in the south, paradoxically the beneficiary of the adjustments being forced upon the US by the world economy. While the high-wage factories of New England, the Great Lakes and industrial midwest suffered from foreign competition, the low-wage, cheap-land economies of the south found themselves the object of new interest. The centre of economic gravity in the US moved south and west, aided and abetted by massive federal defence spending: during World War II 60 of the country's 100 new army camps were located in the capacious south, and by the 1970s it boasted more than half the US's defence installations. California, already the home of hi-tech industries related to defence, began to develop Silicon Valley, while high oil prices made Texas an *el dorado*. Over the 1970s more than one and a half million Americans migrated south. The men and women behind a new class of growing young businesses – the sunbelt entrepreneurs – made overnight fortunes apparently independently of the efforts of Washington, tripartism and the culture of the New Deal. They keenly appreciated the arguments of the new conservative think-tanks and the Straussian, Hayekian and Friedmanite intellectuals, and were ready to back them with time and cash.[8] In the conservative heartlands of the south and west, the American way was alive and kicking.

For the first time in the twentieth century the south was making sustained economic advances in relation to the north, and as a result was gaining in self-confidence. Newly and increasingly prosperous, the south felt able to associate its own long-standing prejudices with the intellectual nostrums of the new conservatism. Southerners delighted in the pro-quota, anti-war Democratic presidential candidate George McGovern losing every state except Massachussets in 1972; the cluster of ultra-liberal views associated with McGovern and his electoral failure has cast a shadow over the Democrats that lasts to this day. In 1977 the National Rifle Association moved its headquarters out of New York, dropped its image as primarily a lobby for field sports and instead, after an internal coup, decided overtly to copy the civil rights movement, campaigning for gun ownership as an individual's constitutional right.[9] After the famous 1973 *Roe* v. *Wade* ruling in the Supreme Court, abortion became one of the most divisive issues in the country, with southern Protestants establishing themselves as the leaders of a 'pro-life' movement that included northern Catholics. The poisonous divide on abortion marked the politicisation of American religion – again overtly borrowing from the civil rights movement – and in 1978 Jerry Falwell established the Moral Majority, whose prime aim was to persuade evangelicals to register and vote. The term he chose was a further extension of Nixon's 'silent majority' – the forgotten Americans, in his characterisation, who worked, saved and cared. Neither Nixon nor Falwell needed to say it overtly, but the moral and silent majority were white – it was blacks who did not work, did not save and relied on welfare. Here again race was being deployed for conservative ends. Formidable new forces were abroad in American politics, before which the Democratic coalition consolidated by Roosevelt and Kennedy began to wilt and fragment.

The last piece of the jigsaw was money. American politics have always been unapologetically about money chasing influence, but one of the paradoxes of the reform of campaign finance that followed Watergate, including the prohibition on direct funding of candidates and campaigns by corporations and unions, was the legitimisation of the political action committee (PAC) – a dodge that allowed corporations and unions alike to give money indirectly to support their candidates and causes. The result was a quadrupling in the number of PACs by the 1980 presidential election, the vast majority of them vehicles for the newly politicised business class to give cash to the Republicans.[10] In 1979/80 the Democrats received 21.7 per cent of the level of Republican donations; four years earlier both parties had received the same.

By 1979, when the Business Roundtable published its manifesto, essentially arguing for what was later to be dubbed the 'Washington consensus' (balanced budgets, tax cuts, tight money, deregulation, anti-union laws), with the Moral Majority and NRA campaigning hard on conservative social issues, the conservatives – spearheaded by the intellectual shock troops of the right – were on the move. They had cash, ideas and a background of economic stagflation. The centre of political and economic gravity was moving to the south and west. The liberal coalition was fragmenting before the charges that it was pro-black and anti-white, and that its economic and social policies did not work – and, worse, promoted the poverty and amorality that they intended to alleviate. What the conservatives needed was a leader, a man who could do for Republicanism what Kennedy and Roosevelt had done for liberalism; somebody who could translate their disparate ideas into an attractive political rhetoric, and then identify them with the American way. Enter Ronald Reagan.

The long conservative ascendancy

Reagan is one of the most underestimated political figures in modern times. Mocked by his opponents as a forgetful B-movie actor with a few folksy lines, a mouthpiece for policy ideas scripted by somebody else, through the 1980s he provided the platform for the consolidation of conservative ideas and policies and created a political coalition in support of them that survives to this day. Even if he vastly over-estimated the size of the Soviet Union's military arsenal, he saw more clearly than any of his circle the strategic possibility of bringing communism to its knees through ratcheting up defence spending to a rate the Soviet Union could not match – and if that, combined with the result of the other strategic necessity, tax cuts, was to produce an impossibly high budget deficit and an early recession, then so be it. Reagan was playing for high stakes, and with victory in the Cold War in 1989 and conservatism ascendant in the early 2000s he can claim to have won. In that sense he must rank as one of the most significant political figures of the second half of the twentieth century.

Yet despite all his advantages his winning margin over Carter in 1980 was comparatively tight, dependent on the 70 per cent of the southern white vote that went his way. Johnson's eerie warning back in 1964 about destroying the Democrats resonated ominously. From the outset Reagan conceived his mission as re-establishing what he saw as solid American values at home and contesting communism abroad, heavily laced by his romantic attachment to religion and the American way. The Soviet Union was a godless evil empire, while in the American heartland – weighed down by too much government and needy of spiritual revival – 'lives the hope of the world'.[11] He rarely talked about capitalism or markets, preferring instead to make a moral, spiritual and religious pitch in which the state was bad and individual freedom good. Reagan may never have read Strauss, Hayek and Nozick, but many who worked in his administration had; the president was their populariser.

After the initial depression in the early 1980s, brought about by sky-high interest rates trying to undo the twin inflationary effects of tax cuts and sharply rising defence expenditure, Reagan's government began to get into its ideological stride. By the mid- to late 1980s a consumer boom was under way, driven largely by an explosion of consumer credit after a massive round of financial deregulation. Americans saved less because they could borrow more easily, especially from the savings and loan associations (SLAs) that had been given more freedom to lend even while their deposits remained guaranteed – a right they abused, ending up confronting the American taxpayer with a bill recognised to be in excess of $200 billion for the subsequent bail-out (see chapter 4). But tax cuts and spending increases left the US with a persistently high budget deficit, while imports poured in to produce an equally large trade deficit – the famous twin deficits. Still, Reagan's sunny optimism remained undented; it was morning again in America.

His vice-president, George Bush senior, comfortably saw off the

Democrat challenger Michael Dukakis in 1988 by portraying him as an unreconstructed liberal who in particular was wobbly on capital punishment. An effective TV advertising campaign reminded voters that Governor Dukakis had released from jail on parole a convicted killer, Willie Horton, who had murdered again; Horton, inevitably, was black. With some 30 per cent of all violent crimes and 60 per cent of robberies committed by blacks,[12] the message was explicit: liberals and Democrats, wedded to affirmative action, could not face up to what was really happening in the US. It was this command of the cultural, racist and religious arguments that allowed the right to control the agenda irrespective of economic mishaps and disasters. This, after all, was the year Operation Rescue was founded, aimed at blockading abortion clinics throughout the country; it was to prompt 1500 arrests. Reagan had throughout his presidency maintained a drumbeat of pro-family, pro-life rhetoric, passing a largely tokenistic act gagging abortion counselling. He stroked the prejudices of Moral Majority and the gun lobby alike, and in 1986 famously legalised inter-state gun sales. In these years, too, the impact of money and lobbying in American politics exploded; it was in the 1980s that the lobbying industry based in Washington's K Street bedded down. Officials and ministers moved from government to lobbying company and sometimes back again with amoral ease, so that policy increasingly became determined by the relative financial power of the various lobbyists – a situation that benefited the right. The conservative ascendancy was complete.

In hard economic terms Reagan and then Bush presided over twelve years of indifferent economic performance in which the imbalances of the US economy grew more acute. The wages of blue-collar workers stagnated under the pressure of international competition and growing pressure on US corporations to maximise their returns to shareholders. This was the era of corporate raiding, merger mania and Wall Street excess. Financial deregulation was to leave most Americans with colossal debts. Income inequality began to take off, so that over the 1980s the top 1 per cent of families saw their incomes double while the bottom 20 per cent suffered a 10 per cent decline.[13] Meanwhile the country's infrastructure rotted. The competitiveness of the old industrial heartlands declined as investment stagnated and R&D expenditure was sacrificed for short-term profit maximisation. Steel, cars, shipbuilding and chemicals gave ground to foreign competition, while the Japanese threatened to dominate the emerging new technologies based on the microchip.

As Paul Krugman writes in *Peddling Prosperity*, the verdict on the supply-siders, monetarists and economic conservatives has to be a resounding indictment. Most Americans suffered declines or negligible increases in their living standards while little growth in productivity was achieved. Investment languished. Even the monetarist propositions of Milton Friedman proved to be wrong. There was no supply-side revolution at all; just a scale of enrichment at the top that beggared belief. By the end of the 1980s the national debate was beginning to change. In the universities conservative economic propositions were being comprehensively demolished, while discussion in the media was dominated by heart-searching about whether US economic power was sustainable – and whether the US, like Britain in the nineteenth century, was to suffer relative economic decline as a result of imperial overstretch.[14] A new consensus grew up around the need to develop a smart industrial policy, focusing on strategic trade initiatives, and to lower the budget deficit, if necessary by tax increases – a direct challenge to the conservative orthodoxy. After all, in 1987 the US became a foreign debtor for the first time in the twentieth century, and the national debt – propelled by an apparently unclosable budget deficit – climbed back to levels that hitherto had been produced only by war. Something had to be done.

During the Bush (senior) presidency, under pressure from economic and social reality – especially the ballooning trade and budget deficits – the conservative coalition began to fragment. The fundamentalists wanted to press home the cause; the religious wing of the coalition despaired at the lack of any real initiative over abortion, restoring family values and 'reforming' (i.e. phasing out) welfare, while the supply-siders wanted yet more tax cuts and resisted tax increases as an offence against nature. But the pragmatic wing of the coalition, especially those associated with business and Wall Street, began to argue that the primary task was to close the budget deficit as a precondition for anything, and in 1990 Bush – who a decade earlier had described supply-side economics as 'voodoo economics' – gave way to the pragmatists. Having declared at the 1988 Republican convention: 'Read my lips: no new taxes,' in 1990 he initiated tax increases.

The supply-siders and libertarians were appalled. A Republican president had turned his back on the conservative holy grail. Bush might be the president under whose watch the Soviet Union collapsed and who was to win the Gulf War, but his foreign successes counted for nothing beside the scale of this betrayal. Although his formal poll ratings were high, the underlying coalition he had inherited from Reagan was in disarray. Was the future pragmatic or ideological conservatism? Trade policy produced another split, with Pat Buchanan, Reagan's former speech-writer, championing trade protection and fewer overseas adventures as the response both to the trade deficit and to the stagnation of blue-collar wages. By the 1992 presidential elections the independent candidate Ross Perot could exploit the divide, marrying a conservative economic programme focused on reducing the budget deficit with a libertarian approach to social issues, suspicion of the religious right and a readiness to protect American jobs. Reagan's coalition had lost its glue. Perot picked up 19 per cent of the popular vote, largely from disaffected Republicans, so opening up the presidency for the Democrat Bill Clinton. The conservative revolution had lost its way, it seemed; surely now the liberals could mount their long-awaited fightback?

Clinton – the Eisenhower Republican

The conservatives might have been at odds, but conservative beliefs and values, along with the US's new electoral geography, continued to determine the political agenda. Christian conservatives extended their grip at local level across the south in the 1992 elections; in South Carolina alone they distributed 840,000 voter guides before the presidential election alone.[15] The defining economic arguments during the election were for deficit reduction and tax cuts. If Clinton talked about establishing a national health insurance programme, he was careful to make sure he talked lower taxes and a shrinking federal payroll at the same time. Although he was to win an overwhelming majority of the black vote, he was careful to position himself as pro-white; welfare reform and toughness on crime were clearly directed at blacks, although never stated in those terms. He did not challenge the conservative agenda, but rather worked within it, pursuing long-standing Democrat aims only on the three consensus 'e's' – education, environment and the elderly. But even so he won only 98 of the country's 435 congressional districts. Without disaffected Republicans voting for Perot, Bush would have won, notwithstanding the 1991–2 recession.

Eight years later, the valedictory comments on Clinton's presidency all agreed that, whatever his misadventures with the Starr inquiry and the Lewinsky case, one of his enduring legacies is that he firmly repositioned the Democrats in the political centre. The truth is that he had no alternative. From the outset of his presidency he never had a political coalition strong enough to do anything other than tack within an overarching conservative consensus; indeed, he famously remarked that he was little more than an Eisenhower Republican, and that the choice confronting America was between that and Reagan Republicans.[16] The Christian Coalition, the National Rifle Association and the right-wing think-tanks continued to press their fierce ideological offensive – aided and abetted by a new generation of right-wing talk-show hosts (notably Rush Limbaugh) who taught their audience to hate liberals as un-American. If there was a consensus that closing the US budget deficit – close to 5 per cent of GDP when Clinton took office – was an economic priority, there was none about how it should be done. For conservatives the deficit was just proof positive that central government was too big and too little had been done to reduce welfare and the dependency culture. That Reagan's tax cuts and recession might be to blame was beyond their recognition.

For the incoming Clinton administration, the issue was thus how to reduce the deficit while still retaining the core of a progressive economic and social programme, notably increasing investment in social, human and physical capital – but within an overwhelming conservative consensus. Clinton's response was to raise taxes, partially rescinding the tax cuts Reagan had given to the rich, lower expenditure on defence and launch new tax incentives for the working poor to find work – but he never dared take on the violent conservative reaction head to head. There was no increase in public investment, even in education and training, despite his ambitious talk. Indeed, over his two terms spending on education, transport and science – all initially earmarked for substantial additional investment – was in each case to fall dramatically as a proportion of GDP.[17] Without cash he could not lubricate his plan to establish a national health insurance system; so he tried to co-opt business. Business responded by using the new lobbying structures to oppose his proposals to devastating effect, portraying them as communist. The plan collapsed.

Clinton was, in short, unable to develop even the qualified, so-called 'modern' progressivism he had played a part in formulating before taking office. The Democratic Leadership Council, of which Clinton had been a founding member, had been attempting since 1988 to redefine the liberal agenda in the face of three lost presidential elections and the emerging changes in the US economic structure – eventually coming up with a position which Clintonites were later to characterise as the 'third way'. The conception was three-pronged: to re-invent and so relegitimise government; to recast support for the unemployed and poor, through massive investment in their education and training, so that they could help themselves to be less dependent on the welfare state; and to re-energise civil society through, for example, the launch of a new national service programme. At the same time the Democrats tried to inoculate themselves from conservative attacks by tactically moving to the centre on contentious issues like capital punishment or affirmative action.[18] The ambitions of the Roosevelt–Kennedy–Johnson tradition to reshape American capitalism and society around nobler ideals were jettisoned wholesale. As a strategy it may have helped win Clinton power, but it collapsed under the pressure of governing within a conservative consensus that the Democrats had not challenged and, in the absence of a sufficiently robust coalition to rely on as a counterweight, could not face down. Health reform, as we have seen, got nowhere, and even the token concession towards liberal opinion of recognising the rights of gays in the military had to be withdrawn.

But it was the tax increases that drew the hottest fire. The ideological right – the direct heirs of Strauss, Wanniski and Friedman, now in the hands of anti-tax activists like Grover Norquist – had been stung by the Bush tax increase to organise every incoming Republican member of Congress in 1993 to sign a pledge that they would not vote for any tax increase. Norquist, who had come to hate Clinton obsessively, assembled the 'Leave Us Alone Coalition' to bring all the elements of the right under one umbrella – and to co-ordinate opposition to Clinton and support for the Republicans in their bid to capture Congress in 1994. They worked closely with the Republican leader of the House of Representatives, Newt Gingrich, who brilliantly caught the mood with his 'Contract with America' – a wish-list of populist Republican measures that would allegedly strengthen the family and America's defences, and simultaneously weaken Washington insiders, cut taxes and balance the budget. In the 1994 congressional elections the Republicans won control of both the House of Representatives and Senate for the first time since 1952.

Prompted by two years of the most modest and compromised liberalism, the conservatives had healed their divisions; they had reunited the Reagan coalition and were back, even more nakedly fundamentalist than before. The conservative cocktail – against black welfare queens, for white gun-owners and anti-abortion, all laced with a generous dose of tax cuts, religion and the flag – was still triumphant. From then on the Clinton presidency became an exercise in holding off the resurgent right and securing the centre at all costs. His only prospect of legislative success lay in initiating those measures with which a Republican Congress could agree – hence the creation of the North American Free Trade Agreement, the deregulation of banking and telecommunications, and, famously, welfare 'reform' in which welfare benefits became time-limited to five years.

But, startlingly, the Republicans over-reached themselves. An over-confident Gingrich openly invited commercial concerns to write Republican pro-business legislation through the network of K Street political lobbyists, a surrender of political integrity that even Washington insiders found unacceptable. Most importantly, he and the Republican leadership were to find that America's appetite for tax cuts did not extend to finding the savings from cutting medical assistance to the elderly, Medicare. As Republican plans ran into public dissent, Clinton brilliantly turned the bombing in Oklahoma City to his advantage, associating Gingrichian fundamentalism with the lunatic anti-government fringe. Later in 1995 he was to manoeuvre the Republican Congress into shutting down the government for six days by vetoing the Republican plans for tax cuts paid for by Medicare cuts. In his memoir, Gingrich later acknowledged that 'we mistook the [right's] enthusiasm for the views of the American public.'[19]

As the economic recovery continued in 1996 it became obvious that, while Clinton was not strong enough to do anything of which the conservatives did not approve, he was powerful enough to block Republican fundamentalism. He comfortably won the 1996 presidential election, positioning himself carefully as both the pragmatic willing to steal Republican ideas when they worked and also a sound steward of the American economy who put the interests of ordinary working people first when he could. But his 1996 State of the Union address, declaring that the age of 'big government' was over, and his declaration later in the same year that his aim was to 'end welfare as we know it' only further underlined the strength of the conservative consensus.

'Triangulation' – the policy of taking the best of both parties' positions and adopting them as your own, as the pollster Dick Morris coined it – might have been a brilliant tactical ploy for re-election; but as a tool for serious coalition-building or constructing a coherent political narrative it was useless. As the 1990s wore on Clinton was the beneficiary of an extraordinary boom – whatever its ultimate lack of sustainability (see chapters 1 and 4) – which validated the fiscal conservatism that had been thrust upon him in his first term. In truth, US economic success in the 1990s had as much to do with the way the world system was now working in America's favour – as argued in chapter 1 – allowing low inflation and the financing of colossal trade deficits, as it had with any indigenous economic dynamism: the mirror image of the 1970s. The Democrats' position was strengthening despite their inability to find a political story to tell or to challenge the conservative hegemony – yet the Republicans were unable to turn the position to their advantage. Their most effective strategy was to intensify their efforts to destabilise Clinton personally, a front they had opened in 1993 with the Whitewater investigation into alleged irregularities when he was governor of Arkansas, and which they were to widen with the Starr inquiry leading to the Lewinsky affair and the attempted presidential impeachment in 1998 and early 1999. David Brock, one of the conservative journalists who led the assault on Clinton's reputation with fake allegations of sexual impropriety, abuse of power and even drug running, has recently openly admitted that there was a co-ordinated effort by conservative interests to denigrate the President.[20]

The Whitewater affair threw up no proof of any wrongdoing, and impeachment was always bound to fail (there was not the necessary majority in Congress); but for Republican strategists that was not the point. Conservative fundamentalists were genuinely outraged by the president's private peccadillos, notwithstanding the numerous parallels within their own ranks. He seemed to personify the moral decadence they were pledged to reverse. Moreover, the opportunity for paying back the impeachment of Nixon was too juicy to pass up. Politically, it would pose any Democratic presidential candidate in 2000 with a political conundrum. To claim credit for the Clinton boom by association would invite the accusation that the candidate condoned the president's behaviour; to dissociate himself from Clinton would legitimise the Republican accusation that the president lacked moral integrity while simultaneously neutralising the Democrats' greatest advantage, the performance of the economy. Gore fell into the elephant trap and ran a campaign distancing himself from Clinton. The Republican determination to stake everything on victory was starkly revealed by their astonishing capacity to outspend Gore on political advertising in the most costly ever presidential election; but even so Bush was to lose the national poll by 537,000 votes. Without their cash and the calculated destructive shock waves of impeachment, the Republicans would not have won back the White House.

Back on top – but for how long?

American conservatives had come to believe that liberalism in any guise was a mortal threat to the American way and that it was accelerating the drift to amorality of an already over-secular society. Sacred American rights – ranging from the right to bear arms to the right to do whatever a property owner wants on his or her land (e.g. drilling for oil in a conservation area) – required to be reasserted. Nor should the extension of individual civil rights be accorded to any group en masse – certainly not to gays or blacks. The American way was to live in a free market, to seize opportunity and to enjoy the fruits of one's work unoppressed by taxation or regulation, while offering due obeisance to God and country. This is George W. Bush's credo, and for all the talk of healing America, compassionate conservatism and bipartisanship, his administration is driven by the same conservative animus that propelled Gingrich and Reagan. And it is, as we have discussed, no less unilateralist after 11 September than before; indeed, it is arguably more so.

The condition of the US criminal justice system is perhaps the best indicator of the new ascendancy of conservatism and the retreat of liberalism. Although approaches necessarily vary from state to state, the trend towards repression is universal. Programmes for the rehabilitation of offenders have largely disappeared; parole is increasingly limited, and attempts at education and training have been largely given up. Over 1000 new prisons have been built over the last twenty years and yet overcrowding is endemic. The prison system now houses approaching two million prisoners, and official figures show that prisons were operating at 19 per cent above capacity in 1998. Sentencing is increasingly 'determinate', with state and federal laws insisting on mandatory minimum sentences for given offences. Bill Clinton himself, in the starkest repudiation of his party's liberal tradition, famously legislated in 1994 that after 'three strikes' 'you're out': that is, the offender must suffer a mandatory long-term sentence. In California, after a third offence as trivial as stealing a pizza the sentence is twenty-five years imprisonment.

The conservatives have pointed to a falling crime rate as justification for this harshness, but the degree to which its achievement can be directly linked solely to a penal and repressive sentencing and prison policy is unproven. The fall in unemployment, the ageing of the population so that there are fewer in the crime-prone younger age group, more effective gun control and more effective community policing – all elements in the liberal explanation for falling crime – are obvious contributory factors. However, they are neglected in the conservative rush to claim sole credit for the success of conservative measures. This 'success' may prove all too illusory all too soon. As leading criminologist Professor James Alan Fox of Northeastern University in Boston has noted, the rise in the prison population provides only 'temporary relief', 'because those people will come out of prison and many will still have inadequate skills and bad attitudes'. With over half a million prisoners now being released every year, of whom on current recidivism rates some two-thirds are likely to be re-arrested within three years, the 'gains' from conservative penal policy look fragile. Indeed, there are already signs that crime is beginning to rise again in some cities. And while violent crime may have fallen, homicide rates remain dramatically higher than in any comparable country; but still conservatives refuse to concede that this may have anything to do with that central article of their creed – the freedom of Americans to carry guns.

The conservative world view rules; yet there are cracks in its dominance. The US is dividing, even over crime. The long-standing division between two cultures – the culture of the orderly 1950s and that of the rebellious 1960s, in Gertrude Himmelfarb's formulation – is becoming more marked. Some half of the population – roughly the proportion that voted for Gore and Nader in 2000 – is increasingly secular, tolerant, accepting of the role of government, willing to make common cause and growing more suspicious about the death penalty and free use of guns. Despite the persistence of conservative penal policy at state and federal level, recent opinion polls, as we have seen, show a growing interest in the rehabilitative role of prison and an increasing awareness of the self-defeating nature of the conservative approach. Other surveys of American opinion show an almost European readiness to spend extra on education, health and social security.[21] The new ideapolises, as identified in chapter 1, are much more likely to be Democrat than Republican. Surveys of American values show a remarkable stability in adherence to the core principles of freedom, equality of opportunity, the importance of hard work and achievement, fairness, belief in religion and equality before the law that at a deep level underpin American culture.[22] These could be deployed to serve the liberal cause, as they have been in the past, if the American liberal tradition could marry its core intellectual propositions with American values and real interests as successfully as conservatives have done.

Conservatism may be in the ascendant now, but a powerful American liberalism lies beneath the surface of American life – and it is increasingly uneasy about the direction in which America's society and economy are developing. As we will see in the next two chapters it has good reason.

4
Greed isn't good for you

In the US private property is king, and the quintessential expression of this philosophy is the corporation. The American corporation, from the early business charters to the great monoliths of the early twenty-first century, has driven the rise of American capitalism; and it is in this corporate representation of individual property rights that the rise of American conservatism has had its most forceful impact. At the beginning of a new century the attempts to legitimise and constrain the exercise of those rights – from regulation in the public interest to the notion that companies should have a wider responsibility than profit maximisation to the communities in which they trade – have never commanded less support. The object of the US corporation is now naked and unashamed: it is to maximise financial gain for those who own it. Accordingly, it is to be freely traded, like any other commodity, on the stock exchange. Every business organisation in America is not merely seeking to make as much money as possible as fast as possible, it is permanently up for sale.

These are the basic principles of American capitalism; but they are also a source of economic weakness, and the vulnerability of the philosophy underlying them is now being exposed by harder economic times. Companies are more complex than financial poker chips, and the extension of this philosophy over the last twenty years has gradually undermined corporate America in ways we will explore in this chapter. But the conservative infrastructure of ideology that has driven this movement has had more pernicious effects still. It has obscured and deliberately neglected the real drivers of much US growth – for example, the importance of high-quality, government-funded scientific research; the impact of education, which at its best in the US is world-beating; the crucial role played by local and regional banks in supplying patient finance; and the importance of physical infrastructure – choosing instead to celebrate simplistic nostrums of entrepreneurship and to deify capitalism and markets. As a result there is widespread ignorance within the US about what has propelled its growth, a vast exaggeration of what has been achieved, an uncomprehending dismay at the consequences of the pricking of the epic 1990s financial bubble – and equal incomprehension of how something so irrational could ever have taken place.

In particular, the introversion of American conservatism has massively downplayed the importance of the US's hegemonic economic role in the globe, which allowed the build-up of unsustainable economic imbalances – notably the disappearance of saving and the emergence of a colossal trade deficit – that no other country could or should copy, and the redress of which threatens even the US with a period of prolonged economic underperformance, possibly even stagnation.

The unbinding of the corporate leviathan

Americans may have thought carefully about their political constitution, but they have never taken the constitution of their companies and the responsibilities of those who own and finance them as seriously. As noted earlier, companies were seen as no more than vehicles for the expression of individual property rights, and as such essentially unassailable. The view of the financial system is that it accommodates and facilitates the needs of property. Banks, for example, are not conceptualised as instruments for husbanding the growth of American companies; their historic role has been to supply trade credit and keep their distance – so that even when more fruitful relationships develop, these are felt to break the proper rules and are rarely admitted. Nor has the stock market's principal purpose been to raise money for business expansion, where the cumulative sums concerned are trivial; rather, it has been to allow founders of companies to capitalise on their success by selling their companies as a whole or in part to outsiders. This is before anything else a market in property rights and corporate control.

For nineteenth- and early twentieth-century America, unlike the countries of continental Europe, Japan or the Asian tiger economies, never had to use the financial system as an instrument of economic development. Growth was driven by the floods of innovative immigrants entrepreneurially combining cheap land and labour to exploit continental-scale market opportunities. Profits were high, and companies were largely self-financing. Wall Street in the first thirty years of the twentieth century resembled a gambling den more than a forum for mobilising risk capital for enterprise – a tradition to which it has recently returned with a vengeance.

This attitude bubbled to its climax in the stock market boom of the 1920s, when the entire nation was playing financial poker with its companies in a casino which seemed to guarantee profits as long as you speculated aggressively enough. This was a rule-free environment. Lack of creditworthiness was no bar to speculating in company stock by paying only a fraction of its worth and borrowing the rest – so-called margin trading – while companies themselves could report and account for their financial performance almost as they chose. Banks could use their capital to support lending or stock market speculation. It was a market free-for-all – and the natural culmination of the republic's attitude towards property and the sanctity of markets over its first century and a half.

Famously, the boom came to a shuddering halt in the Wall Street crash, whose financial losses spread first around the financial system and then through the rest of the economy as a cancerous, depressive contagion. The Great Depression was above all the result of a massive credit crunch; the financial system imploded. Roosevelt's New Deal was as much about the reconstruction and reorganisation of the hitherto self-governing and self-regulating American financial system as it was about the things for which it is more famous – establishing the foundations of the US welfare system, for example, or recognising trade unions and launching great public works programmes. There had been over 9000 bank failures that had inflicted incalculable harm on the economic life of the nation; firewalls had to be constructed to prevent the same thing happening again. For the first time the federal government took it upon itself to dictate how the self-governing autonomous corporation should be run – and above all, how the financial system was to operate.

The Glass–Steagall Act of 1933 forbade commercial and investment banking to be undertaken by the same company. Never again should losses in the stock market pollute the ability of the commercial bank to lend – the two functions should be kept separate. A year later the Securities and Exchange Commission was established to ensure that speculation would be curtailed by rigorous regulation of margin trading and ensuring that corporations disclosed systematic and honest accounts of their financial affairs to investors. And Roosevelt completed his reforms by creating a network of publicly owned financial institutions, ranging from the Home Owners Loan Corporation to the Reconstruction Finance Corporation. Their job was to do what the financial system had proved incapable of doing on its own; providing the 25-year mortgages to home-buyers and farmers that the privately owned savings and loan associations had not done of their own accord, and similarly offering long-term bank loans to industry. The financial relief and confidence these measures provided were the single most important contribution the New Deal made to economic recovery.

It was not until the tail-end of the New Deal period, in 1950, that the then ageing New Dealers turned their attention to creating a framework of company law, passing the Model Business Corporation Act as a template on which individual states were exhorted to model their own incorporation statutes. But even then, with federal government at the zenith of its prestige, having rescued the country from depression and won a world war, the approach was minimalist and cautious. The case for revisiting company law was made not in terms of a need to prescribe how the internal affairs of a company should be constitutionally arranged, but rather in terms of a recognition that increasingly owners of large corporations had to delegate management to professional managers, and there needed to be a legal framework within which this could take place. The company's founding document was moved to centre stage, and directors, managers and officers of a company were required explicitly to accept a fiduciary duty to the company. This had three components: managers were legally obliged to act in accordance with the principles of the founding document, to act loyally in the interests of the corporation and to accept a duty of care, which was defined as acting in a way that reasonably protects the interests of investors. If shareholders did not like the results of this delegation of duties they could sell their shares, and they could vote on their stock to replace the officers of the company.

The contrast with European and particularly German company law could hardly be more marked. The act made no stipulations about how a company should be governed, which was considered entirely the purview of the management and executives. Thus if a corporation decided that the roles of chairman and chief executive were to be merged and no independent directors required to be on the board, then that was (and is) entirely within its capabilities. Annual accounts were prepared for shareholders as an account of the management's stewardship of their assets rather than as an account to the world at large, including the government, of what the true performance of the company had been across a wide range of measures. This was and is a world of private property contracts; the central conception is that, whether decisions are taken by shareholders or directors, private contracts and rights are sacrosanct.

So if managers and directors had become the de facto exercisers of property rights over quoted companies, this was only because they were seen as the only practical place in which to vest those rights. Private ownership was a secret garden into which the state should never pry. It might regulate the outcomes of corporate behaviour – but never its internal processes. Indeed, there seemed little need to do so. Managers and directors exploited the latitude open to them and took their obligations to their companies' founding legal document seriously; the divorce between ownership and control meant their first obligation was to their company as an organisation. They expanded, husbanded and invested in their companies as never before. The legacy of the federal government's enormous build-up of defence spending was a vast array of new technologies, ranging from television to jet aeroplane manufacture, and corporate America fell on them hungrily. Boeing developed the first civilian jet by transferring the technology from the wartime B-47 and B-52 bomber programmes; IBM's leadership in computer manufacture hung on the pathbreaking computers it built for the new computerised air defence system, SAGE; the semiconductor industry was brought into being by defence orders, which accounted for 38 per cent of all production between 1955 and 1965.[1] The Buy America provisions, directing the US government to purchase strategic goods from US firms, meant that all the business went to US firms – giving birth to the military–industrial complex of which Eisenhower had warned. Between 1949 and 1973 annual productivity growth averaged over 3 per cent, and one key link in the virtuous circle of growth begetting investment begetting employment and spending that in turn generated more growth was the high-investment corporation feeding off government-generated state-of-the-art technologies. Indeed, all corporations shared the same dedication to growing their companies in the round. The delegation of control to directors committed to growing the organisation as a whole, rather than just serving the interests of the shareholders, was having remarkable results.

As the 1960s gave way to the 1970s the pattern of company ownership began to change, with consequences that are still unfolding. Share ownership began to migrate from individuals to large financial institutions, like mutual funds and pension funds, investing on their behalf. In 1945, 93 per cent of shares were held by individuals: by 1997 the proportion had fallen to 43 per cent.[2] A feeling began to grow among the powerful institutional shareholders that corporate America was interpreting its fiduciary duty with too little regard to their interests; the 1960s saw the first hostile takeover. CEOs might be effectively growing corporate America, but in the process they had become barons of all they surveyed, running companies as if they were the owners, even though they were only servants of the founding legal document and the shareholders beyond that. During the 1970s, as company profits reeled in the aftermath of the oil shock and growth and productivity fell, management theorists and the new powerful institutional investors began to agitate for a proper restoration of their property rights – and the running of companies to serve their owners. The shareholder value revolution was born.

This was disingenuously presented as an exercise in enfranchisement rather than self-interest, a campaign to restore property rights to those in whom they should properly be vested – the shareholders. By making management more responsive to shareholders, ran the argument, American capitalism would become more vibrant – neglecting the important fact that it had been managements' freedom from shareholder interests that had contributed so largely to making American capitalism so dynamic in the years after World War II. The United States Shareholders' Association, founded in 1986, quickly became a national movement of 'shareholder rights activists' (in a self-conscious reference to civil rights activists) and cast itself as the rescuer of American companies from greedy, lazy managements. Dividends should be put first. The mutual funds latched on to the mood, claiming to be the means through which small investors could exercise their property rights more effectively – and get richer quicker.

As the internet grew in importance over the 1990s, with 10 million shareholding accounts held in internet brokerages, websites like the Motley Fool kept up the dreambeat of hype that ancient American myths of the individual citizen–owner could be repeated in cyberspace. Suddenly the market had become cool and individual investment anti-elitist. The quest for shareholder value was nothing more than the legitimate desire by every owner – whether a small investor or a gigantic pension fund – to see his or her property managed to deliver the maximum gain that they naturally wanted. Chief executives should be given the incentive to act in the real interests of owners by hooking their own remuneration to the share price. So, as individual Americans trebled the proportion of their savings held in stock market assets within just fifteen years, CEOs enjoyed a parallel boom in share option schemes, which rose in value from $60 billion to $600 billion over the 1990s. Everybody wanted to be an owner, and to share in the spoils of a rising stock market. The powerful and moneyed might benefit most of all – 64 per cent of American households own less than $5000 worth of shares[3] – but a stock market that grew on average by 17 per cent a year over the decade seemed to offer sufficient gains for everyone. Wall Street had become the new embodiment of the American dream.

In this heady atmosphere the Rooseveltian restraints on American finance seemed like annoying Lilliputian bonds that must be broken as soon as possible to give the financial machine more room to move. Wall

Street had its own agenda, which aligned it with the shareholder rights lobby. It was having growing success in lobbying for the dismantling of international controls on the operation of US financial markets, as we will see in chapter 6, so increasing the volume of tradable financial assets; the promotion of shareholder value was a means of promoting the role of shares and share trading, and thus further swelled the business of Wall Street.

One of the great boons of the American financial system had been the plethora of its banks. For fifty years after the Great Depression the US enjoyed the services of 14,000 banks, which under the protections afforded by the Rooseveltian legislation had been able to become relationship banks, committed to offering medium- and long-term support to America's small and medium-sized business. The ideology of the American way, of course, continued to cast them in a different light as nothing more than market-driven facilitators of credit; but, ring-fenced from competition from banks in other states, their own competitive position entrenched by regulation, and their depositors given confidence by federal deposit insurance, they had created unique franchises – almost along north European and Asian lines – supporting local enterprise. America's great cities had become centres of regional banking, careful to nurture industry in its own backyard. If Germany had its great regional mutual banks and specialist industrial banks, and Japan its own industrial banking system, the Americans had their network of state and city banks which knew their business customer base well and wanted to support local business champions. This was grassroots business banking at its best.

For the shareholder value merchants, the American banking system was a ripe plum ready for the picking. There were too many banks protected by outmoded regulations. Some of the regulations, like the ban on interstate banking, were being made redundant by the explosion in mobility. Businesses were moving beyond their local bases, and businesspeople looked to banks that could offer them a national rather than a regional service. Other regulations, like the ceiling on interest rate payments, were being evaded by the capacity of individual Americans to invest on the New York money markets via mutual funds. As importantly, the banks and financial institutions themselves were agitating to be freed from controls over what they might do and to whom they might lend. Shouldn't they be able to do what they wanted with their property, like any other American or American business?

The experience of the deregulation of the savings and loan associations (S&Ls), mentioned in the previous chapter, should have been an awesome warning. In 1982 the controls were lifted on what the S&Ls could lend, but the guarantees enjoyed by their savers remained. The S&Ls saw the new structure – rightly – as a one-way bet; they could lend whatever they liked to whichever property developer they wanted – including themselves – confident that if things went well they would make millions, but if the return did not materialise then government deposit insurance would pick up the bill. What followed was one of the greatest orgies of unsound lending in history, including fraud on an epic scale, leading in 1989 to the creation of the Resolution Trust and a bail-out conservatively estimated at $200 billion.[4] Thus one industry in the private sector wasted more than the entire government had managed in the postwar period. But the conclusion drawn by conservatives was not that the Rooseveltian framework was sound and should be tampered with only cautiously; rather, it was that deregulation should have gone much further and much faster, removing the protections for savers as well. After all, in the land inhabited by conservatives all government is bad and everything in the private sector good. The clamour for deregulation and for shareholder value continued unabated – and against no very great opposition. This was a nation of wannabe owners, keen to extract value from their assets and ride the gathering stock market boom.

Meanwhile Wall Street and the banks combined to press for more financial deregulation for reasons of self-interest – and Washington, penetrated by financial interests and political lobbyists, and in any case seeing advantages from building up the size of US financial markets in order to finance the budget and trade deficits, was happy to oblige. Already the Federal Reserve had been allowing banks to offer a growing range of financial services; over the 1990s the pace of deregulation quickened. In 1994 the ban on interstate banking was lifted; in 1996 the rule (Regulation Y) limiting the pace and scale of bank mergers by stipulating that a bank could acquire another bank only if it was 35 per cent of its own size was abolished; and in 1998 the Glass–Steagall Act was finally rescinded after a lobbying campaign of more than a decade.[5]

Through the 1990s the pace of bank mergers accelerated at a bewildering rate; as Gary Dymski reports, by the end of the decade, the number of US banks had halved in twenty years.[6] The justification put forward is that larger banks are more 'efficient' – but, as Dymski argues, efficiency is identified in narrowly economic terms as closing bank branches and concentrating bank operations. The value of the banks' relationships and their capacity to support local business is ignored. Closures create a one-off boost in profits through a one-off reduction in fixed costs, and raise the merged banks' share price, usually enriching the bank CEOs and the investment houses that brokered the merger. But the price is the destruction of America's banking infrastructure that allowed the gathering of local knowledge essential to judging the true creditworthiness of borrowers, especially important if they are local businesses. Instead, loan applications are judged according to formal criteria by loan officers not rooted in local communities and who must necessarily ensure that business lending is backed by property collateral rather than the true strength of the business. The powerful results of local banks working with local businesses in local clusters exploiting informal networks and with strong incentives to develop the local economy are lost, and with them a major prop of local enterprise and American business dynamism. The beneficial wider social impacts are reduced and the public good of local banking diminished. But the value so extracted benefits profits and the share price, now more important than any other consideration to the US's business community – whose priorities seamlessly translate into Washington's political priorities.

Even the mounting evidence that bank mergers have tended to destroy shareholder value has been insufficient to halt the Gadarene rush.[7] With Wall Street reaching new highs as the new century began, the conservative position seemed amply justified. The paradox was that beneath the surface the underlying innovativeness and competitiveness of the US were being undermined. The infrastructure of supportive banking was being removed, and the new focus on boosting the share price at all costs would further hollow out American business. The triumph of the market had created a stock market bubble that would enfeeble the new economy it had helped to bring into being – an ominous echo of the 1920s. At its apparent zenith, conservatism has failed to meet its boastful promise.

The story of Boeing

The jumbo jet and the B-52 are two of the most visible expressions of American technological and military superiority – and Boeing, the company that made them, is a corporate name to rank alongside Microsoft, Coca-Cola and Ford as a global brand. But Boeing, like so many of the top American companies, is itself a victim of the collapse of American liberalism and the rise of the conservative right. Within a generation its capacity to take technological risks and to put building planes as its number one corporate purpose has been undermined by the extraordinary pressure of Wall Street for American companies to deliver immediate high financial returns as their over-riding objective. When the new superjumbo, carrying 555 passengers, enters service in 2006, it will have been built by Europe's Airbus consortium. Boeing is fading as a leading aircraft manufacturer. It will look less to innovative leaps to fuel its growth, as it did when building the jumbo: rather it will hope to grow its less risky aircraft service business, building avionic and air-traffic management systems.

The ascendancy of conservatism and its accompanying economic maxims has found expression in a new corporate doctrine in which investment, husbanding human capital and organic growth are seen as secondary to the real business of corporations: enriching their directors and owners in the name of shareholder value. The entire US economic structure and the society built upon it is now wedded as never before to the interests and needs of high finance and the financial markets. Four thousand executives on Wall Street earn more than a million dollars a year each,[8] and the chief executives of the 362 largest US companies in 1999 received an annual average remuneration of $12.4 million – six times up on 1990.[9] No economy and society anywhere have so interlinked their fate with the appetite of the stock market for short-term profits, or structured their financial system with such close attention to the interests of markets and short-term profit maximisation.

The story of Boeing offers a salutary lesson. In the mid-1960s this was a company dedicated to technological excellence and the development of its highly skilled, loyal workforce – and whose close relationship to government, rather than the hindrance painted by conservative ideologists, was a source of competitive advantage worldwide. Its managers were loyal to the company's founding document; this was an organisation dedicated to building the best planes in the world – and it did. It had developed the first generation of civilian jet airliners from the technical advances and strong financial position it had developed as a leading defence contractor during World War II and the early years of the Cold War; and it retained a healthily profitable military division. At this juncture, with the bulk of its shares held by patient individual investors and supported by a network of local state banks with a close interest in the company's growth, it embarked on the then vastly ambitious project to build the 747, the jumbo jet.

Part of the financial risk was underwritten by its own financial structure, with a multiplicity of small and loyal shareholders, and part by a large order from Pan Am, whose own ability to order aircraft was in turn underwritten by its own sheer scale and financial structure – and an airline environment regulated by the US government through the Civil Aeronautics Board (CAB), which kept airlines profitable by closely regulating ticket prices and boosted technological innovation. The project was plagued by technical difficulties and foreign cancellations of orders, but $2 billion ($6 billion in 2002 dollars) later in 1970 the first jumbo was delivered to Pan Am. Twelve and a half thousand engineers had worked exclusively on the project. The next five years were extraordinarily hazardous, with Boeing laying off 60 per cent of its 142,000 workers and actively considering abandoning the aviation business as sales of the jumbo remained stubbornly depressed; the company was found guilty of bribing foreign airlines to win orders. But by 1978 the colossal gamble had paid off. In that year a booming airline business placed orders for eighty-three 747s, and Boeing's financial returns climbed to the highest in the Fortune 500.

Over the next decade Boeing reaped the rewards for the risk it had taken, ultimately making $20 billion in profits from its $2 billion investment; with no competitors, it was able to insist on airlines paying full prices for the 747, and despite the launch of the airbus by its European challenger, Airbus, it consolidated its position as the dominant actor in the world aircraft industry.

But Wall Street was leery. This was a cyclical business that required high research and development costs together with sustained investment in people to stay ahead; it did not lend itself to quick dollars. Moreover, the new conservative economic thinking was undermining one of its chief supports – a domestic airline industry rich enough to pay good prices and provide forward order books for aircraft. Deregulation of tickets and routes, beginning with the abolition of the CAB in 1978, along with a wave of mergers and acquisitions aimed at boosting short-term profits, made US airlines more hawkish in their purchasing policy. The world in which a company like Boeing could in effect bet itself on a vast project embodying state-of-the-art technology was disappearing.

The pivotal year was 1987. Texan T. Boone Pickens, apostle of southern raw capitalism, supporter of Reagan and founder of the US Shareholders' Association, had already established a reputation for himself as one of the leaders of the new generation of 'corporate raiders'. Now he dared to try to buy a stake in Boeing as the first step to a full-blooded bid. The romanticism of their 'raiding' image belied the raiders' real aim; these were not swashbuckling adventurers so much as corporate vultures whose objective was to dismantle large organisations, stripping them of cash and assets in order to unlock 'value'; so long as the disposal proceeds were greater than the purchase price, they would make their profit. Pickens dismissed the charge that he was short-termist, saying it was no more than a 'theory that freed executives to scorn any shareholders they choose to identify as short-termers'.[10]

The raiders' operations had been made feasible by the new dominance of institutional investors – pension and mutual funds – that now owned the majority of any corporation's shares; instead of trying to persuade tens of thousands of individual investors of the merits of their case, as they would have had to do in the 1960s, raiders like Pickens had to convince only a dozen major institutional fund managers – who themselves were anxious for short-term performance to boost the sale of their units and pension plans – that they should be backed. Boeing's share price at this time – $7, compared with an estimated net worth of $75 a share – reflected the degree to which Wall Street shunned America's national champion in aircraft manufacture.

Pickens was seen off, but Boeing was never to be the same company again. Plans for new planes were frozen, R&D spending was slashed and close to 50,000 workers were laid off in an attempt to boost the bottom line. In taking this line Boeing was following the lead of the high prophet of shareholder value, Jack Welch, chief executive of GE. Welch had not needed the attentions of a corporate raider to persuade him that the interests of shareholders must come first; as described in chapter 1, he saw the quest for 'value' as focusing a management's objectives and ideologically the proper and only true purpose of a capitalist enterprise. This was the model that Boeing now set out to copy, fearing that if it did not it would suffer from the attentions of another corporate raider or the takeover ambitions of another large corporation seeking to sustain its profits growth by milking Boeing. Indeed, one of the companies eyeing Boeing was GE itself.

Throughout the 1990s Boeing's object has been building rapid earnings growth rather than developing new planes; in 1997 it bought its great rival McDonnell Douglas in order to boost the steadier income from military contracts. McDonnell Douglas's boss, Harry Stonecipher, had spent twenty-seven years with GE; this disciple of Welch's and apostle of shareholder value became Boeing's new president. When, that same year, Boeing declared that it had no intention of trying to build a superjumbo, the share price climbed to an all-time high of $60. Philip Condit, the then CEO, acknowledged the new order of priorities when he told *Business Week* that 'a very fundamental thing was going on'. In the old days the preoccupation had been meeting 'technological challenges of supreme magnitude' like building 'an airplane that went further than somebody else's'. 'Now,' he declared, 'we are going into a value based environment where unit cost, return on investment, shareholder return are the measures by which you'll be judged. That's a big shift.'[11]

But while a value-based environment may enrich executives and Wall Street, it is proving a pernicious context in which to develop and build aircraft. The nadir was reached in October 1997, when a combination of staff shortages incurred from too many redundancies and an overstrained

supply chain organised around minimalist 'just-in-time' delivery principles to boost operating margins forced a seizure in production; Boeing
literally stopped building aeroplanes for some weeks, for want of parts
and people, at a cost of $2.6 billion. Productivity per man had been
raised, but the production process had become so hollowed out that
continuous production was endangered. More seriously, it is simply
unable to compete with Airbus, now attracting half of all commercial aircraft orders even before the launch of its new superjumbo, the A380 – a
market that Airbus has to itself, for Boeing today has not the skills, the
engineering capacity, the financial stability or the access to long-term support. In short, it is surrendering technological leadership to the European
consortium, whose stabler ownership structure and long-term financing
environment leaves open possibilities for Airbus that no longer exist for
Boeing.

The development costs for the A380 will exceed $12 billion, a chal-
lenge Boeing might have considered in the mid-1960s but can no longer
entertain today. As Matthew Lynn has written, 'Where once Boeing had
led the industry, breaking new ground, inspiring new departures, it was
now content to leave the ground-breaking to others and give chase where
necessary.'[12] Each model it developed over the 1990s was a reaction to a
prior move by Airbus. Boeing concedes this, claiming it sees it as an
advantage in the short term. But in the long run Boeing's reputation as a
producer of quality innovative aircraft is suffering. In February 2002 it
had a smaller production backlog than Airbus. The US may protest that
Airbus enjoys government subsidy, forgetting that juicy defence contracts have been essential to US success (the arguments are examined in
more detail in chapter 9) – but that is not the point. Even if Airbus did not
exist, Boeing would be in trouble.

Conservative America has constructed a financial environment where
technology and manufacturing prowess take a back seat behind the financial criteria set by a Wall Street crazed by greed and rendered irrational
by the dictates of its own competitive dynamics. Senior executives in
investment banks can earn their $10 million remuneration packages only
by engineering mega-deals – and Boeing knows that if it bets $12 billion
on a new generation of planes, the result will be a plummeting share
price and a shotgun merger. To preserve its independence its strategy has

been to milk its existing range of planes for cash and profitability – for example, building a stretched version of the 747, the Sonic Cruiser, to rival the A380 rather than developing a new superjumbo – and to move into the aviation service business. Now even the Sonic Cruiser is in doubt. In a talismanic retreat of this once great company, it has moved its headquarters out of Seattle to Chicago. As the airline industry retrenches before the fall in demand prompted by the aftermath of the terrorist attacks of September 2001 and orders to aircraft manufacturers fall, Boeing's lack of financial solidity and new priorities are even more exposed. An industry that the US once dominated is being ceded to the Europeans.

The destruction of value

Corporate America now no longer principally seeks to innovate, build and marshal resources over time to create value; it tries to extract value by financial engineering. Wall Street, always an uneasy ally of US business, has become its master. In the 1960s 44 cents in every post-tax dollar of profit was distributed as dividends; by the 1990s the proportion had nearly doubled to 85 cents as companies sought to please the hawkish financial markets and support their share prices, to which CEOs' remuneration, via stock option packages, was so tightly linked.[13] Around half of CEOs' total earnings now comes from stock options.[14]

The institutional investors who own more than half the shares traded on the market are restless in their search for higher performance to please their own demanding customers; on average they turn over 40 per cent of their portfolio in a year looking for higher returns. By contrast, in 1960 Wall Street turned over only 12 per cent of its entire capitalisation. Every corporation does everything in its power to keep the fund managers happy, promising to deliver ever higher profits every quarter, topping up their efforts with stock buy-backs and financing investment by asking the markets for as little new cash as possible. Ninety per cent of business investment is self-financed; between 1985 and 1995 over $500 billion was spent by companies buying back their own shares to support the price.

The story, from the commanding heights of the Harvard Business School and the *Wall Street Journal* – aided and abetted by the all pervasive free market American economists – to every statement by a CEO, is that this new environment is the principal explanation for the recovery in American productivity and growth. The Business Roundtable in 1997 declared that 'the principal objective of a business enterprise is to generate economic returns to its owners . . . if the CEO and the directors are not focused on shareholder value, it may be less likely the corporation will yield that value.'[15] For George Baker of the Harvard Business School it was this change in attitudes and in the behaviour of owners and managers alike that had produced rising productivity and profits.[16] Michael Jensen used his presidential address to the American Finance Association in 1993 to insist that it was only because of pressure from the stock market that American corporations were likely to adjust quickly and efficiently to the realities of globalisation.[17] And all this is supported by a daily drumbeat from the American financial press and media.

The thesis is simple. Companies are driven wholly by price signals and the desire to maximise profits. They combine labour and capital as prices dictate in a network of contracts, for example labour or supply contracts, that can and must be dissolved the instant a better contract is available elsewhere. If those who manage these assets – the company directors – have their remuneration closely linked to the company share price, they will be brave and rigorous in trimming out fat and squeezing as much as possible from the assets. A second pressure to maximise profits comes from the stock market, because if the directors are inefficient the company's share price will sink and they will lose control, being taken over by a company and directors better able to do the job. Financial markets are so efficient that they consistently put an accurate price on a company's worth, lifting the prices of efficient companies and lowering those of inefficient companies – so takeover is an ever-present threat and the 'market for corporate control' is an essential instrument for efficiency.

But the whole narrative is shot through with intellectual and empirical inadequacies. In the first place this is an entirely economistic view of the organisation. If all contracts can be unwound at a moment's notice and reorganised around a better set of prices, this is only another way of saying that organisations have no history. In this conception, companies should be visualised as simply a peripatetic, permanently shifting network of deals between workers, suppliers, creditors and shareholders.

Loyalty, trust, the organisation's social capabilities and the capacity to learn over time count for nothing. The truth is that they count a lot, as argued in the chapters ahead.

It is an open question whether the shareholder value, free market thesis even works in its own terms. One intriguing study demonstrates that high CEO pay tends to be followed by weak rather than strong share price performance; between 1993 and 2000 the majority of companies headed by the ten highest-paid CEOs underperformed the stock market average over both one year and three years afterwards.[18] As for the efficient market hypothesis, this is the most fiercely contested theorem in economics. Despite enormous intellectual effort, nobody can prove that stock market prices accurately reflect all the information available – a vital component of the conservative theory. In fact, the evidence points the other way. Mary O'Sullivan, reviewing the evidence, insists that it is more a matter of faith than proof, and that 'anomalous evidence on the behaviour of returns is rife'.[19] Indeed, Michael Jensen, one of the high priests of the hypothesis, found no fewer than six studies showing that after a takeover share prices fell by an average of 6.56 per cent, rather than rising as they should. 'These negative abnormal returns are unsettling because they are inconsistent with market efficiency and suggest that changes in stock prices during takeovers overestimate the future efficiency gains from mergers,' he conceded.[20] Quite so.

There is a vast literature proving that, far from creating value, takeovers and mergers destroy it. McKinsey, for example, reviewing 160 mergers between 1992 and 1999, discovered that only 12 of the merged groups succeeded in lifting organic growth above the trends before the merger; the other 148 failed.[21] Another management consultant, KPMG, found in a survey of over 700 cross-border mergers between 1996 and 1998 that only 17 per cent added value, while as many as 53 per cent actually destroyed shareholder value, with the remaining 30 per cent of deals making no difference.[22] Mergers and takeovers, in short, do not work. The marrying of two different organisations with disparate cultures and people systems cannot be performed as the by-product of a shotgun wedding to appease the financial markets; companies are more complex than the doctrine of shareholder value ever comprehends.

That has not stopped the tidal wave of takeovers and mergers which since 1994 has seen a cool $5 trillion change hands. There were 5000 mergers in 2000, double the level of a decade earlier. They may destroy value and lower growth, but each CEO believes that he or she will be different – and investment banks, chasing the fees, do nothing to disabuse them. The authors of the McKinsey and KPMG reports do not conclude that there is something structural about mergers that makes them very unlikely to work; for the consultancies see the opportunity for fees in trying to facilitate the impossible. The whole culture produces deeper economic weakness. Success in a takeover demands that the predator be in favour with Wall Street; the predator's market valuation must be higher for every dollar of profit than the potential victim's, so allowing the predator to pay for the bid by the market accepting more of its shares. AOL could never have succeeded in its bid for Time Warner, for example, had Wall Street not valued its shares at absurd levels, with the price more than a thousand times the annual earnings apportioned to each share.

This pressure intensifies the already acute competition to maximise shareholder value, so that economies in research, investment or the workforce are immediately rewarded in higher short-term profits and a higher share price. It also implies a worrying trend to manipulate financial accounts so that they show a consistently rising upward movement of profits – a concern voiced by no less an authority than the chairman of the New York Stock Exchange.[23] And when in November 2001 the energy trading company Enron turned from Wall Street's darling into the US's largest ever corporate collapse, it transpired that the principal cause was a series of chronically loss-making and imprudent off-balance-sheet deals not disclosed to either the authorities or investors – and apparently undetected by the auditors. The chief executive behind Enron's growth, who had resumed his position as CEO months before the company's collapse, was Ken Lay. He had been a passionate advocate of deregulation, shareholder value and the uselessness of all forms of public intervention – a posture from which Enron directly benefited as it expanded into areas hitherto the preserve of publicly owned or regulated utilities. Now the subjects of federal and congressional investigations into their conduct, including potential fraud, he and his company are emerging as one of the very best examples of why the philosophy he championed is so suspect – and why, despite the pleas of business, there remains a case for regulation. In the wake of Enron's demise there is growing concern that much of corporate America's balance sheets and profit statements cannot be trusted.

The new emphasis is not conducive to innovation achieved by research and development; corporate spending on research fell consistently by some 1 per cent a year in constant dollars over the 1990s. Instead, as the leading authority on US industry outlines, companies look to short-term, low-cost adaptions and accommodations, exploiting partnerships with government-funded research at universities or ideas generated by alliances with foreign companies.[24] US companies, in short, have invested in tactical product development – spending more and more on this over the 1990s in the attempt to shore up market share – or tried to take over other companies to achieve market leadership and with it the power to set prices and operating margins. The number one in a sector consistently makes higher returns than the number two, and the number two more than the number three. Hence the struggle, by fair means or foul, to be number one.

So it is, with US companies looking for higher returns over shorter periods than their competitors,[25] that the US has less invested capital for every hour an employee works than Germany (around 75 per cent) and France (85 per cent) – despite a decade of rising investment. American companies compensate, however, by insisting that their workers work longer hours (28 per cent more than German workers and 41 per cent more than French workers[26]) to maintain comparable levels of production. The quest for economies is relentless; the National Bureau of Economic Research has found that half of all firms each year have gone through a wave of downsizing with results we will explore in the following chapter. But the lack of invested capital means that, despite all this effort, the output per hour worked is not only lower than the US's main competitors but until the mid-1990s was consistently growing less rapidly. Even since 1995, properly measured, US productivity growth has been only marginally higher than in Europe, even falling back in 2000[27] – and, as we will see in the next section, it is disputed how much of this increase is attributable to the improvements generated by ICT, and how much to the long American boom.

For the US did enjoy a remarkable decade over the 1990s – but it was not driven by the rise of shareholder value and the alleged disciplines of Wall Street, as the conservative consensus insists. The sustainability of the recovery, given its extraordinary imbalances, has been discussed earlier, as have its sources in financial deregulation, the credit explosion, cheap money and cheap oil. It was within this extraordinarily benign environment that corporate America prospered, helped by the problems of the opposition. Japanese competitors were flattened by the decade-long stagnation of the Japanese economy, while European rivals were hindered by the restrictive economic policies operating in the EU as member countries prepared to meet the demanding criteria for European monetary union.

Moreover, American companies enjoy one great advantage over any of their competitors. They operate in the world's largest single market; the US is the highest-income region that has such deeply unified markets for goods, technology, capital and labour. It is inevitably a testbed for new innovation, allowing scope for experimentation and failure that no other national market can offer. This combination of exceptional natural resources and a continental market has been identified by economic historians as the core of US competitive advantage[28] – despite the impediment of the stock-market-based financial system. The 1990s thus saw the world's largest market growing consistently for close to ten years – its longest ever sustained period of expansion. Against this background the surprise would have been if American companies had not performed relatively well. Indeed, from the rest of the world's point of view, it is just as well that the US has disabled itself with its financial and corporate structures and their accompanying culture.

And there is a third, unsung advantage that US companies enjoy: the powerful role of federal spending, especially on research, through the massive university system, and the competitive advantage that accrues through US regulatory agencies. David Mowery reports that by 1995 universities accounted for 61 per cent of all basic research, which was largely paid for by federal funds.[29] The research has a remarkable pro-business bias, too, with the universities having set up over 500 research institutes seeking to support business interests. This is a mobilisation of free research effort no other country can match. American economists have demonstrated that the returns to such pure university research are phenomenal, much higher than for private research, because they are freely available to the business community – and that every dollar spent on public research provokes another four dollars of private research.[30] This US research network, as we have seen, is one of the country's formidable competitive advantages; in the past it has created world leadership in a number of key sectors and it is one of the drivers of the new 'ideapolises'. Yet for conservative theorists this is the truth that dare not speak its name. For it is work performed by the public sector.

Seventy-three per cent of US patents cite publicly funded science as the basis for the invention; yet in a national discourse dominated by conservatives, federally funded frontier research has declined. To turn this situation around, said the US Competitiveness Council in its report for 2001, the US must increase national investment in frontier research, strengthen support for fundamental disciplines that have been neglected, expand the pool of US scientists and engineers, and modernise the nation's research infrastructure.[31] The federal share of national R&D dropped from 46 per cent in 1985 to 27 per cent in 1999. US research facilities are falling into disrepair. In 1998, a majority of research institutions claimed that they had had to defer necessary construction or repair programmes because of a shortage of funds. As matters stand, the report continued, the US will be unable to meet the demand for scientists and engineers in coming years. By 2008 there should be jobs for 6 million scientists and engineers in the US, but it looks unlikely to be able to supply them. Forty-one per cent of PhDs in science and engineering awarded in the US go to foreign students, many of whom return home afterwards. While conservative economists try to prove the efficient market hypothesis – really trying to justify what we already know to be the irrationalities of Wall Street – the US is allowing the true source of its economic strength to rot on the vine.

Unsung public support for the economy does not stop with R&D. America's regulatory agencies are gatekeepers to the world's largest market, and their approval is essential not just for new products in the US, but for producers seeking access to the rest of the world. The Food and Drug Administration's tough tests for new drugs, for example, have become a world gold standard, forcing every pharmaceutical company to have a strong research presence in the US – witness GlaxoSmithKline's decision to move its research headquarters to America, as reported in chapter 1. The flow of foreign companies wanting to undertake R&D in the US has become a tidal wave, and most seek US partners – so that US companies wanting to limit R&D costs to boost short-term profits have a ready supply of collaborators.

These advantages have only partially offset the new Wall Street inspired priority accorded in corporate strategy to financial considerations, which has hastened the dumbing down and hollowing out that began in the 1980s and continued over the 1990s, even if its worst effects were masked by the boom and the impact of IT. As the painstaking work of Michael Porter at Harvard University has demonstrated, the US has surrendered technological leadership in a wide range of sectors – and the key driver in the process has been the priorities and business objectives set by Wall Street. Even the much-vaunted productivity miracle, discussed later in this chapter, is of much less dramatic proportions than claimed. The US has enjoyed a boom which its conservative ideologists have wholly misinterpreted; and by doing so they have undervalued and further undermined the country's sources of real advantage. As the economy enters more uncertain waters and the stock market bubble deflates, the tenuousness and fragility of America's economic success are becoming more obvious, extending even to the jewel of the 1990s crown – information technology and the New Economy. This was supposedly the ultimate proof that conservative economics worked. Now we are learning otherwise.

So what about US leadership in the New Economy?

Such a critique will surprise many readers. Surely America's powerful stock market and accompanying 'equity culture' are meant to lie behind its recently established leadership in the New Economy, which is now lifting productivity growth back to the rates of thirty years ago? Critics may moan about short-termism and the rest, but surely America's highly developed and liquid stock markets are fundamental to its success? They make it easy to buy and sell shares in quoted companies and encourage savers to part with their cash because they know they can quickly realise their investment whenever they want. Without this structure, along with the preoccupation with shareholder value and a willingness to take risks to get above-average profits, the flow of venture capital – $90 billion a year at its peak – to high-tech start-ups and dot.com companies would never have taken place. The New Economy would never have happened.

The stock market permitted the development of the market in young, unproven companies that became an indispensable part of the dot.com revolution, allowing venture capitalists to release their initial investment in high-tech start-ups as the companies were floated on the stock market as Initial Public Offerings (IPOs). Even the sour taste left by the recent stock market collapse can never obliterate the scale of the achievement over the 1990s, which left the world with one of the great waves of innovation and re-established America's technological leadership. As Michael Mandel, economics editor of *Business Week*, has written, 'The stock market is not simply an innocent by-stander in the New Economy. Rather, with the rise in risk capital, the market has become the critical nexus of economic growth and innovation.'[32]

Mandel is right; but, as even he concedes in his prescient book *The Coming Internet Depression*, the intimate connection between the stock market and the New Economy can be as much destructive as creative. The argument goes further. It is obviously true that the boom in high-tech stocks helped foster new start-ups and greatly accelerated the pace and penetration of IT development – but it did so at staggering cost. The whirlwind of hype that surrounded the New Economy was created by a vicious feedback loop in which the stock market was an essential transmission mechanism. It delivered extraordinary gains and, by boasting about them, helped to spread the fevered message that something very extraordinary was going on, so that not only the US but soon every Western and Asian stock market suffered a collective suspension of rational judgement. Wall Street's appetite for short-term gains in share price that had proved so counterproductive for companies like Boeing, undervaluing the patient commitment to business-building that is at the heart of any successful enterprise, had now been magnified hugely into an epic stock market bubble. Its implosion is not only having calamitous effects for the American economy but has exposed the weakness in the way the New Economy was constructed.

Information technology and the internet are important, but in any ranking of the great technological developments of the twentieth century they still rank below the impact of, say, electrification or the car – although as ICT becomes used more pervasively the chances are that it will rank alongside them. Thus, although American productivity growth did improve between 1995 and 2000, it is probably still too early to explain this entirely in terms of New Economy effects. Professor Robert Gordon of Northwestern University, the US's leading guru on productivity, argues that two-fifths of the productivity spurt is wholly explicable in terms of the usual upturn that comes at the end of an economic recovery, and the rest of the growth has been focused on the 12 per cent of the economy engaged in the manufacture of IT and IT-related durables which benefited from the doubling of computer investment after 1995, which is unsustainable.[33] Beyond that there has been little or no increase in underlying rates of productivity growth. Half of US investment spending in 2000 was on high technology goods, up from 15 per cent in 1992 – a position that will plainly fall, especially as much of the investment has failed to produce a return according to an important report by management consultants McKinsey.[34] The authors show, in confirmation of Gordon's findings, that most of the increase in US productivity growth after 1995 – much as it is – was focused on only six sectors (three of which were semi-conductors, computer manufacturing and telecommunications) and that the other 70 per cent of the economy recorded little or no increase. The evidence for a transformational increase in US productivity that is sustainable as high tech investment falls back to normal levels is scant.

Gordon sees little prospect of IT making the same impact on productivity as the great clusters of inventions ranging from chemicals and oil to water sanitation, but on this the jury is still out. My own view is that ICT will ultimately make all organisations more porous, permeable and thus networked – opening up a potential for cost reduction and change in organisational structure the scale of which we can only guess at. But that is for the future. For the purpose of the present argument, all we need to note is that the idea that any transformation was happening of the scale and speed which the stock market was explicitly indicating during the late 1990s, given the prices IT shares achieved, was for the birds.

Here the new conservative ideology reinforced the market's inherent desire to believe fanciful stories to justify incredible short-term profits. In the past, technological innovation had always been driven by large corporations and government; now the media, new IT moguls and stock market hucksters all agreed that, as it was being propelled by hungry venture capitalists and fast-moving ICT-created networks, it had to be faster and better done. After victory in the Cold War there was a new triumphalism in the air – 'We're bullish on America,' screamed Merrill Lynch – and the death of inflation together with the benefits the IT revolution brought in train seemed to justify claims that America had entered a new era.

Wall Street's own enthusiasm thus created a self-fulfilling prophecy and apparent virtuous circle. Because the markets believed in the privately led, entrepreneurial economic transformation they were prepared to deploy vast sums of private risk finance in the service of technological innovation – and this very enthusiasm created and sustained the buoyant markets in which the start-up dot.coms could be sold for a fortune, so justifying the initial support. As venture capitalists found themselves habitually making returns on average 7–10 per cent higher than the rest of the equity market, that became further evidence that the New Economy was something special – and inflated the bubble further. So, however out of control and absurdly valued it became, the stock market was essential to the hi-tech revolution – and the hi-tech revolution was equally essential to the bubble.

So far, so good. But the fatal difficulty with the role of the stock market is that of time horizons. There is a tension inherent in any stock market between the financial community's desire for liquidity, so that it can keep its options open, move money from underperforming to potentially higher performing assets and take profits at will, and businesses' desire for commitment over time and their need for investors to stick by them in tough times and not get too excited in good times. All stock markets tend to value short-term profits more highly than long-term profits,[34] with some estimates suggesting that cash flows more than five years in the future are discounted at twice the rate of shorter-term flows. Economies can live with this irrationality as long they have some countervailing capacity, either through some part of the shareholder base being committed to them whatever the share price (family owners, employee owners or cross-shareholdings, for example) or through a system of corporate governance that protects them from the markets' worst excesses. The US system offers little such countervailing power; indeed, the stock market is at the heart of the financial system. So when the market lost its head with enthusiasm for the New Economy – rather as seventeenth-century Dutch investors were seized with enthusiasm for tulips, or nineteenth-century British investors with zeal for railway companies – not only did it simply run away in a classic asset price bubble that represented a collective madness, the consequences poisoned the heart of corporate and investment decision-making and ultimately threatened the sustainability of the New Economy itself.

The old dictum of John Maynard Keynes, the greatest British economist, is that the object of much stock market investment is to buy, hope the upward momentum lasts and then sell – an exercise in guessing the state of average opinion about affairs rather than what the affairs actually are. Or, as foreign exchange dealers put it more succinctly, the trend is my friend. In the US of the late 1990s this principle was taken to extremes. The markets' permanent short-termist tendency was exaggerated by a matrix of cultural and psychological factors into the most colossal irrational feedback loop of modern times, brilliantly described by Yale economist Robert Schiller in *Irrational Exuberance*. Keynes said that the best way of conceptualising much stock market investment was as a classic game of musical chairs with the players circulating around the chairs at ever greater speed, hoping that when the music stopped they would find security in the form of a safe chair by selling – and another player would be left holding the losses. In the first few months of 2000 it seemed that the entire US – from 37,000 investment clubs and tens of thousands of day-traders to ordinary Americans sharing the belief that markets naturally produced amazing returns – was playing musical chairs in the hope that someone else would be left holding the losses when the bubble burst. It proved a delusion.

For, as the bubble approaches bursting point, the only assessment that

counts is whether it will last long enough to make a turn in the few trading hours ahead and pass the vastly overpriced security to a fool greater
than you. Prices reach stratospheric levels. Cisco Systems, for example,
was valued by the stock market at $160 billion in 1998, more than thirty
times its sales; put another way, even though its sales and profits grew by
150 and 120 per cent respectively throughout the 1990s, its share price
rose at an annual rate of 2000 per cent over the same period. Its fall to
earth, along with the rest of the high-tech sector, was inevitable. The
apologists argue that this willingness to support companies at such high
prices was tribute to the stock market's long-termism; the lie to that was
the average length of time hi-tech shares were held. At one point at the
peak of the boom Yahoo! shares were held on average for no more than
eight days and Amazon shares for seven days. By contrast, shares in Coca-
Cola are held on average for twenty-six months and GE for around thirty
months – hardly a statement of commitment by the standards of serious
technological development, which can take up to a decade, but an age
compared with dot.com norms. The markets had become hyper-myopic,
with the consequence that the real prospects for hi-tech companies were
irrelevant.

Rationality ceased to play any role. Companies that offered little more
than on-line specialist retailing, following the apparently successful example of Amazon and its selling of books and CDs, were valued at levels
that were simply crazy. Hundreds have simply folded. Even Amazon
itself, enjoying all the advantages of early entry and a global brand, has
proved to be founded on an economic model that delivers little profitability. The discounts at which it buys have to be passed on to
customers, leaving it with woefully thin margins to cover its overheads;
it makes just 2 per cent on every book sold, compared to 30 per cent for
Barnes and Noble, the US's leading bookseller. It has relied on a mad
share price both to raise cash and to offer incentives to its workers; but
share options are worth less as shares plunge. Workers have found that,
rather than enjoying a position as flexible 'owners' at the cutting edge of
a technological revolution – which is how they were instructed to think
of themselves at the peak of the boom with their share options – they are
now working up to seventy hours a week at poor hourly wage rates. And
even those terms are under threat from competition in the low-wage

parts of the US or Asia to which Amazon is moving as unhesitatingly as any other US company under pressure to deliver share-price performance. Motivation has plunged, and at the time of writing, despite the elimination of flexible working and aggressive rounds of redundancy, Amazon has just registered a tiny and fragile profit, notwithstanding its once fantastic stock market valuation. Ravi Suria, leading IT analyst at Lehman Brothers, doubts its position is sustainable.[35]

To point this out is not to decry the inventiveness or importance of the companies at the heart of the ICT revolution; rather, it is to observe that the stock market that once succoured and nurtured them is now their enemy. The search engine and internet portal Yahoo! is a remarkable company by any standards, even if it was never worth the $150 billion or more at which it was once valued. And the essential role of Microsoft in developing user-friendly software to exploit the net cannot be over-estimated. But even these companies have been caught out by the reversal of the extravagant valuations of the market and the greed it fostered. Not only executives but many core staff insisted on being paid in stock options, so their loyalty and commitment lasted only as long as the high-tech bubble. As the bubble has deflated and the stock options become worthless, the dot.com and IT companies have found it impossible to hold on to their staff, with turnover rates of 50 per cent or more in a year commonplace. Yahoo! lost three chief executives of its regional operations; and when the chairman relinquished the overall chief executive role in February 2001 as advertising revenue plunged, it was almost impossible to recruit a successor. Venture capitalists have found that the organisations they created to float on the stock market disintegrate no less quickly; directors and key staff simply walk away from companies whose sole objective was to make their backers overnight fortunes. Even the mighty Microsoft, which privileged its early joiners with generous stock options, has found it necessary to hire successive rounds of new employees on a temporary basis with none of the rights of the core staff in order to keep costs low and profits growth high – thus dividing the workforce against itself.

Much of the real performance of the IT sector was itself dependent on the capacity of other IT companies to raise cash on the bubble market. Yahoo!'s revenue came from other dot.coms advertising on its web pages; as they imploded with the collapse in stock market values, so they cut their spending. The chance of an early turnround in Yahoo!'s fortunes is negligible – and so, consequently, is the chance of any CEO making a fortune through share options. What the stock market had given, so it took away.

Indeed, the collapse of the stock market forces the mirror-image process of severe contraction upon companies as aggressively as it once permitted growth. All companies in a market economy suffer retrenchment when sales and profit growth falter – but when a share price falls to a tiny fraction of what it once stood at, retrenchment turns into rout. Marchfirst, an internet consultancy with a turnover of $1 billion, saw its share price dive by 92 per cent; 2000 lay-offs, a third of its US labour force, followed within three months in November 2000 as it struggled with the financial consequences of being unable to raise further stock market cash. By April 2001 it had filed for bankruptcy. Telecommunications manufacturer Lucent was tempted by the prospect of ephemeral stock market gold to try to turn itself into a digital, web-based provider of internet access equipment and software, using its own ludicrously high share price to acquire a succession of internet companies. But it could not make the transition, and it has decimated its workforce in the struggle to recapture profitability – its own sales having been sharply affected by the rash of bankruptcies among dot.com companies themselves. Lucent was not alone: high-quality companies like Xerox and Kodak felt the compulsion to digitalise their operations quickly and rashly, and have incurred massive losses as a result. The whole bubble has led to a massive misallocation of resources and managerial effort in the quest for instant riches.

The cutbacks that follow from these mistakes become self-perpetuating. Bankrupt and ailing IT companies themselves cut back on demand, and that causes a fresh round of retrenchment and loss of confidence – and contingent, temporary workers are the first to be made redundant. Traditional companies tempted into the morass find themselves having to unravel their mistakes. The hope is that the current recession will be short-lived, but the structural weaknesses of the IT sector do not permit a rapid recovery. The dot.com boom has proved, in the words of technology consultant Mark Anderson and editor of the Strategic News

Service,[36] to be little more than a scam – but one in which the pension funds who were the ultimate providers of risk capital to the venture capitalists have lost billions. The US may have launched the IT revolution, but its financial system is disabling it from maintaining its leadership. A casino is not the best platform on which to grow long-term investment and innovation.

The bursting of the dot.com bubble and the repercussions of the closely associated frenzy in telecommunications (explored in chapter 6) have left the American financial system facing the most extensive losses since the 1920s stock market crash. As American consumers retrench and the financial system tries to stitch back together its tattered balance sheet, the US economy looks floored, facing years of depressed growth, however shortlived the 2001/2002 recession may be. The productivity miracle has proved a mirage. Great economic assets, from the American banking structure supportive of small and medium-sized enterprises to its infrastructure of R&D investment, have been neglected and run down. Nor are the costs only economic. This episode has been the backdrop for a massive social experiment – the tolerance, indeed promotion, of extraordinary inequality along with the privatisation of the public domain – whose social implications are only just becoming apparent. The worst of it is that the rest of the world is willy-nilly drawn in. American conservatives have a lot to answer for.

5
To those who have shall be given

America is the most unequal society in the industrialised West. The richest 20 per cent of Americans earn nine times more than the poorest 20
per cent, a scale of inequality half as great again as in Japan, Germany
and France. The US has more of its population living in poverty – 19.1 per
cent – than any other Western industrialised country;[1] worse, the bottom
10 per cent of Americans, even though they live in a richer society, are
poorer than their counterparts in Europe, Canada and Japan[2] – only the
poorest British rank below the poorest Americans. And at the very top of
American society, incomes and wealth have reached stupendous proportions. The country boasts some three million millionaires, and the richest
1 per cent of the population hold 38 per cent of its wealth – again, a concentration more marked than in any comparable country.

Ever since the early 1980s this already unequal society has been growing more unequal. Average household incomes have fallen as blue-collar
wages in real terms have fallen, a trend particularly marked in the bottom
fifth of the population. Salaries for those at the top, meanwhile, have
exploded – a trend that has if anything accelerated over the last twenty
years and which in terms of disposable income has been powerfully reinforced by the structure of first Reagan's and now Bush's tax cuts. It is true
that as unemployment fell in the later stages of the economic recovery
after the mid-1990s the wages of blue-collar workers began to rise in

149

real terms for the first time since the late 1970s; but elsewhere middle Americans' incomes were held back by waves of corporate downsizing. The rate of growth of inequality between the top and bottom may have slowed down, but the gap between the middle and the top has widened further.

This inequality is the brutest fact of American life, a standing offence to the American expectation that everyone shall have the opportunity for life, liberty and happiness. Plainly those at the top have very much more liberty and material grounds for happiness than those at the bottom. But equally, while this may be a rampantly commercial society, it genuinely subscribes to the view that everyone must have opportunity. Birth, race and gender should not obstruct the chance for upward mobility. There are no titles in America; it was the founding fathers' profound belief that the US should escape the flummeries and nuances of class evinced by the aristocratic hierarchy of titles. The republic even banned the aristocratic idea of primogeniture: land should not be handed down through the first-born, but repeatedly split up so that the individualism of every American would be supported by access to property, whether they were born first or last.

Every immigrant who became and becomes a citizen should be able to boot-strap themselves up by their own hard work, and the country's most repeated story is of how those who have made it have done so by individual merit and effort. To support this morally correct and socially imperative urge, education should be universally available, and a commitment to this principle seemed to be borne out in practice: a university was one of the first institutions each new state established as the west was opened up. Even in 1800 the US had more universities than England. The US invented the scholastic aptitude test (SAT), purporting to give the most objective view of every American student's intelligence, so that advancement in the education system would be – and would be seen to be – by merit. The interwoven conception is that all Americans have equal chances of advancement, as befits the citizenship the constitution confers, and that social mobility is the reward to all who work. The founding fathers and John Locke cast a long shadow.

However, the reality of extraordinary inequality makes a mockery of this account of American life, an account which is integral and essential to the conservative story. It discredits the entire conservative belief system: in the face of this reality, a just society cannot be conceived as an aggregation of morally pure individuals pursuing their own liberty with minimal taxation, minimal government and minimal welfare. It suggests, at the very least, that John Rawls's argument for an infrastructure of justice to facilitate the access of everyone to opportunity and provide some minimum underwriting of basic needs is more than justified. There is a role for government. Individualism alone does not suffice to deliver the outcomes that the framers of the constitution intended and American culture seeks.

This is why conservatives expend so much effort in attempting to explain away inequality, dispute the figures and redefine the argument. If the American way has only the insecure understanding of what drives wealth generation outlined in chapter 4, and produces the unfair social outcomes suggested by the existing degree of inequality, then the whole conservative intellectual and political edifice is exposed as a mere sham to justify the position of the rich – and a fundamental betrayal of the idea of America. It also means that the Europeans who want to copy the US need to think again; a more self-critical America might find that after all it has something to learn from the Europe it spends so much time decrying and mocking.

The key element in the conservative retort to protests at inequality is that the pattern of rewards is essential to keep the American economy dynamic, and that the same dynamism is socially expressed but hidden in the static inequality figures. It may be that at first sight America appears unequal, but what is disguised is that there is an enormous rotation upwards and downwards, so that individuals are swapping places in the income hierarchy both from year to year, and over their lifetime. They may begin their career on a low income, but they finish it on a high income; they may be born to poor parents, but they end up rich. Here is Milton Friedman joining battle to defend inequality in the early 1960s:

Consider two societies that have the same distribution of annual income. In one there is a great mobility and change so that the position of particular families in the income hierarchy varies widely from year to year. In the other, there is great rigidity so that each family stays in the same position. Clearly, in any meaningful sense, the second would be the more unequal society. The one kind of inequality is a sign of dynamic change, social mobility, equality of opportunity; the other of a status society. The confusion behind these two kinds of inequality is particularly important, precisely because competitive free-enterprise capitalism tends to substitute the one for the other.[3]

The difficulty for Friedman, and the many conservatives who repeat this argument, is that, as we will see, while they need this argument to be true, it is false. America's social rigidities are as embedded as – and worse than – those in Europe.

The polarised society . . .

US society is polarising and its social arteries hardening. Inequality is producing an ever more pronounced social stratification. Uppermost are the privileged top 20 per cent: an educated, propertied class whose incomes and wealth are steadily rising and whose grip on the great institutions of upward mobility – the elite universities, the law and business schools – is growing more secure by the year. Then there is the middle 60 per cent of the population, whose household incomes are stagnating, who had a surprisingly small stake in the share price boom, who are now severely indebted and whose working lives are increasingly at risk with little to compensate. And then there are the bottom 20 per cent, who are locked into low-wage, low-skill jobs, are served by chronically indifferent schools, have scant access to health insurance and are trapped in their circumstances, with fewer avenues out of poverty than the poor in other industrialised countries. *The State of Working America*, described by the *Financial Times* as the most comprehensive independent analysis of the American labour market, reports, for example, that the poor in the US are less likely to exit poverty in any one year than the poor in Canada, Germany, the Netherlands, Sweden and the UK – and if they do are more likely to have re-entered poverty after five years.[4] Whatever else this picture suggests, it hardly corresponds to the conservative vision of a country whose social mobility is so much higher than other countries that it can justify having the highest inequality.

The polarisation is taken to the extreme at the top and bottom. At the very top an overclass is emerging that increasingly is opting out of American life, using the conservative, anti-statist political philosophy to justify its detachment. At the very bottom there is an underclass that is also developing its own culture, one of resignation, disaffection and alienation, locked in a desperate struggle for survival and bitterly familiar with the gun violence that disfigures American life. The respective sumptuousness and bleakness of the two lifestyles represent a scale of difference in opportunity and wealth that is almost medieval in its scope.

This unease is captured by the decision of 120 billionaires, including the legendary investor Warren Buffet, America's fourth richest man, to found the campaigning organisation and pressure group, the Campaign for Responsible Taxation. Launched in the wake of the capital gains tax reduction awarded in 1997 as part of the budget deal between President Clinton and a Republican-controlled Congress, the group promised to use its tax savings to finance the pressure group's case for fairer taxation and oppose the new Bush administration's plans for eventual elimination of both capital gains and inheritance tax. Buffet's argument is that the US is in danger of developing an aristocracy of the wealthy. Just as it would be absurd to select the US Olympics team for 2020 from the children of the winners of the Olympics in 2000, he says, so it is wrong to construct a society whose likely leaders tomorrow – given the advantages that wealth confers – will be the children of today's wealthy. This does not just offend the values of democracy and equality of opportunity on which the US is constructed; it will be economically disastrous. Buffet and his fellow campaigners are right – even if they have been unsuccessful in making their case; but the pass has long been sold.

The chief means by which contemporary Western societies offer their citizens a chance to reach reasonable living standards and move up the socio-economic hierarchy is education. At first sight the US does well. In its schooling system, fourth-grade students (in British terms, the fourth year of primary school) do better than their international counterparts, and 37 per cent of its 18–21-year-olds go through higher education – one of the highest proportions in the industrialised West. Moreover, the

US's university standards, especially in the top fifty universities, are on average the best in the world. Salaries are high and the research record is excellent. So they should be: the US allocates 1.4 per cent of GDP to tertiary education, twice the proportion of Britain and significantly higher than the 1.0 per cent spent by Germany and France.

But take a closer look, using more stringent criteria. As a system that offers every young person a chance for educational achievement and the acquisition of formal academic or vocational qualifications – the key instrument for social mobility – the US structure fails. By twelfth grade (in British terms, the year after GCSE; in the US, the last year of school), American students are falling behind their international peers, especially in mathematics and science. And while in Germany, for example, 80 per cent of school-leavers go on to receive either vocational training or a degree, and all except 1 per cent receive formal post-secondary education or training, in the US 46 per cent of school-leavers gain no certificate or degree – and an extraordinary 31 per cent receive no formal training or education after leaving school.[5] The message is stark. Those Americans who do not get to college are pushed into the labour market with a severe lack of skills, education and vocational training.

And those who do get to college are overwhelmingly students from the higher socio-economic backgrounds – just as they always have been. A key study in 1965 found that two-thirds of the explanation for educational achievement was accounted for by family income, and another study thirty years later arrived at exactly the same figure.[6] The SAT test, which is the key measure of intellectual ability offering entry into the best colleges and universities, is – as Nicholas Lemann exposes in his monumental study *The Big Test* – not so much a measure of innate mental abilities as a measure of middle-class mental abilities. What the US testing system is doing is validating the middle-class grip on the university system; private coaching to help pass the test is extensive, with fees in New York ranging up to $29,000 (£20,420). It is thus hardly surprising that the most exhaustive study of upward mobility for white men since 1950 finds that there has been no net change.[7]

These historical numbers are worrying enough; but, as inequality has risen over the last twenty years, it is becoming more and more obvious that surveys of mobility in the future will more than warrant Buffet's concern about the emergence of an aristocracy of the wealthy. For the cost of going to university over the last twenty-five years has exploded. The average cost of tuition, fees, and room and board has risen fourfold since 1977 to an average $10,315 (£7264) today; the overall average masks a stark contrast between the average cost of study at private universities ($17,613 [£12,403]) and public universities ($7013 [£4938]).[8] Yet as costs have risen, federal and state support to help fund students' costs has both declined and been refocused on the middle class. In 1965 the Pell Grant, the largest federal programme for poor students, covered 85 per cent of the cost of four years at a public university; in 2000 it covered just 39 per cent of the bill.[9] The Hope Scholarship, introduced by President Clinton, provides up to $3000 of tax credits to fund university education – but it goes mainly to families earning between $30,000 and $90,000 (£21,126–63,380), whose children would have gone to college anyway. States have cut their support for college students on average by 32 per cent since 1979.

The result of this vicious scissor movement – rising costs cutting against falling state and federal support – is a calamitous drop in the chances of a poor student acquiring a university or college degree; and this in an environment where there are negligible alternative forms of vocational and formal education. Borrowing money on the scale now needed to finance college is easier for students from better-off families and expectations of reasonable earnings than for students from low-income families. As Gaston Caperton, president of the College Board, admits, the US 'is not doing a good job helping low income students succeed'.[10] In 1979 a student aged eighteen to twenty-four from the top income quartile was four times more likely to obtain a degree by age twenty-four than a student from the bottom quartile. By 1994, the latest year for which we have figures, the figure was ten times more likely. Given current trends in inequality, college costs and falling state support, this already disastrous ratio can only have got worse over the last eight years. We can thus be certain that American social mobility over the decades ahead will deteriorate below its already modest level.

As if all this were not enough, there is also a widening gulf between public and private universities. The poorer public universities are finding it harder to recruit and retain the best staff, and are locked in a vicious circle of a weakening reputation, falling funding and high student drop-outs;

only 67 per cent of students at public colleges and universities complete their degrees, compared to 83 per cent of students at private universities. To British eyes, the inequality of the American system is startling. If 7 per cent of British schoolchildren are educated privately at schools which dominate the academic league tables (98 of the top 100 schools in the *Financial Times* 2001 league table ranking A-level results are private), 11 per cent of American schoolchildren are educated privately at similarly top-performing schools. Moreover, 22 per cent of American students attend private colleges and universities, for which the average fees, as noted above, are $17,613 or £12,403 – an outlay which requires, for all but the very wealthy, a willingness to take out enormous loans. The British university system, by contrast, is almost entirely publicly funded and, for all its weaknesses, has a much more equitable system of grant assistance for poorer students.

America's private universities represent the pinnacle of the US system. Ninety-two per cent of the 1.4 per cent of GDP that the US spends on tertiary education is spent on private universities and colleges.[11] The network of private Ivy League universities in the east is world-famous, including the elite names of Harvard, Yale, Cornell and Princeton; but there are private universities of equal rank in the west (Stanford in California), south-west (Rice in Houston, Texas), midwest (Chicago and Northwestern) and south-east (Emory in Atlanta, Duke in North Carolina). The US's two leading technological universities, MIT and Caltech, are also private. Together these institutions enjoy a stranglehold on access to the top positions in American life. The total annual costs of attendance at these elite private universities can reach $35,000 (£24,640), although they are well-endowed enough to offer needs-blind admissions (i.e. so that income level should not dictate the offer or acceptance of a place), providing grants from their own funds to help support poorer students. However, the growth of endowment income, except in the richest institutions, is not keeping pace with fees, so that even this support for poorer students is weakening – and even rich universities are not indifferent to the advantage of admitting the children of rich families and the subsequent contribution they will make to the endowment fund. The way Britain's leading private schools, like Westminster and St Paul's, still manage to produce a disproportionate supply of students to Oxford and

Cambridge is reproduced in the US in the way private schools like Andover and Exeter still manage to get above-average representation at Harvard and Yale. Money talks, and the well-funded private schools and private universities are locked in an exclusive and privileged embrace.

Despite America's public attachment to the idea of meritocracy, the wealthy – just as Warren Buffet argues – ensure that their children get privileged access to the best schools, the best universities and the most influential networks. They can pay the fees. The Bush, Gore and Kennedy families are only three of the more famous political examples of how wealth begets both more wealth and influence. Five generations of the Bushes, for example, have been 'tapped' to become members of the Skull and Bones Club at Yale, whose initiates retain a commitment to the lifelong scratching of each others' backs, while never acknowledging they were members; other alumni include a roll-call of American presidents and statesmen. In itself there is nothing remarkable about private clubs of privileged insiders in private universities; it is just that the country that boasts them should be more guarded about its pretensions to meritocracy. Behind most of the Fortune 500 companies lies a rich, self-reproducing family network based on the fortunes made by the founder.

In one sense, membership of this super-elite *is* democratic; for money buys entry to the club, and new money is as valid as old money. The precondition for the rich tightening their offspring's grip on the upper echelons of American society in new dynasties, via education, is the fact of being rich and growing richer. Over the last decade the new fortunes made in the US have been spectacular, with CEO remuneration packages topping $12 million (see chapter 4). The story, of course, is that the fortunes and the incomes are essential to make American capitalism work so well; but, again as observed in chapter 4, high executive pay is closely followed by poor corporate and share price performance. Performance has little to do with reward. Rather, as Cornell University's Professor Robert Frank argues, incomes at the top are rigged by winner-takes-all effects which the better-off are only too willing to exploit even as they attempt to justify them as the returns for risk and effort.[12]

News of a winning formula or individual, for example, in any industry or sector, is more quickly disseminated in an era of information technology; and because the new drive for shareholder value makes winning more valuable, the competition to get the exclusive services of 'winners' has grown more intense. Thus from publishing to investment banking, executives with a track record of success are in a unique position of market power, which they have exploited with increasing ruthlessness to achieve staggering salary and share option deals. Robert Reich in *The Future of Success* shows how individuals in every walk of life exploit the new culture of 'putting yourself in play' to get the market to bid up the price of one's personal brand to stunning levels.[13]

And although these rewards are objectively irrational and absurd, they become a self-fulfilling need. If social standing depends on the possession of ever larger 'trophy' homes or yachts, then, as Robert Frank argues, executives need the wherewithal to buy them in order to compete with their peers.[14] Thus what drives incomes ever higher is not scarcity of talent or outstanding performance; rather, it is the market price of the luxury goods that executives need to own to show that they are part of the same executive community. This is a world in which membership fees of the right golf club can cost over $30,000, the right Patek Phillip wrist-watch up to $17,500; to compete, executives have to be earning $1 million or more a year.

Spending on luxuries – from premium cigars and wines to vacation homes – has risen dramatically faster than overall spending; between 1995 and 1996, for example, at four times the rate.[15] As argued in the previous chapter, there are no rules for the determination of executive incomes built into company law, despite the best efforts of the SEC, which has no powers to interfere in corporate governance; companies are the private property of shareholders and their directors, and if they feel the need to pay themselves extraordinarily there is no effective obstacle to their doing so. In this climate, luxury goods become disposable commodities; trophy homes are built, discarded and destroyed once their function as emblems of luxury display has been fulfilled – rather as trophy wives are divorced as their looks fade.

Yet this irrationality cannot be openly acknowledged. The elite must necessarily tell the story that wealth creation and business success require incentives on this scale. Most elite members are fierce advocates of free market economics and equally fierce critics of any form of public intervention as inevitably ineffective and self-defeating. Their incomes are to them the proof that free market economics work. Moreover, their wealth and spending power allow them to live independently of any form of state initiative, without using any facility or function delivered by the state. They can live in their own privately defended villas, mansions or ranches, insure themselves privately for private health care, educate their children privately and travel by private plane and car. In short, they can secede from the civic realm and be materially better off – proof positive that there is no need for the state and that the universe of the private is morally superior. They are simply ignorant of the condition of their fellow citizens.

In this sense the super-elite are in the vanguard of a civic secession that is spreading throughout the privileged top 20 per cent of American society. There are now some three million Americans living in over twenty thousand gated communities offering the same privatised lifestyle to better-off Americans as the super-rich can claim.[16] The gated community achieves its most extreme form yet in the new fully independent incorporated cities, like California's Hidden and Rolling Hills, where residents declare political independence; exempt from state (but not federal) taxes, they collect their own taxes and provide their own benefits. These cities are getting bigger; Green Valley in Las Vegas, to be completed in 2005, will have a population of sixty thousand. Formally known as 'homeowners associations' (HOAs), they are the most complete expression of opting out and detachment; their members need never come near public institutions or participate in wider civic life. But they are not non-political; in California, HOAs were the organised base for campaigns against school bussing and in favour of lower taxes (like Proposition 13). Their justification is not just the political and cultural need to opt out; they represent Americans' search for the ideal community and an escape from the haphazard violence of much American street life. For, as Edward Blakely and Mary Gail Snyder write, gated communities and HOAs are 'more than walled-off areas and refuges from urban violence and a rapidly changing society. They are also a search for socio-spatial community – the ideal community that Americans have sought since the landing of the Pilgrims.'[17] But in expressing that quest by founding a community from which others are kept out – the terms for admission to an HOA can include a minimum age for children and weight for dogs; intruders can be shot – and which exists as a civic bubble insulated from other citizens, the instigators and owner–members are mounting nothing less than a civil revolt that paradoxically reinforces the trends from which they are fleeing.

For the new inequality is eating at the bone marrow of American civilisation, helping to create a culture in which impersonal contract, hawkishly policed through a mountain of ever more aggressive litigation, is succeeding trust, community and assimilation as the principal form of social exchange. Patrick M. Garry, in *A Nation of Adversaries*, argues that civic secession is helping to create a litigation culture, which in turn accelerates the breakdown of American communities.[18] Between 1960 and 1997 the number of lawsuits brought annually has quadrupled, so that litigation is increasing at seven times the rate of the population. Litigation, of course, is not all to be deplored; it remains one of the great instruments ordinary Americans have with which to fight back against corporate power or abuse of political power. The difficulty lies in its intrusion into large areas of private life, so that in matters where norms, traditions and expectations of reciprocal behaviour used to define accepted practice – bringing up children, responses to death, relationships between the sexes – litigation has come to occupy a decisive role. The law has become one of the US's fastest-growing professions – since 1970 growing three times faster than the economy[18] – to the point where the US now has the highest number of lawyers per 1000 inhabitants in the industrialised world. Co-operation is giving way to a pervasive adversarialism in which confrontation and litigation, rather than community endeavour or political action, are seen as the principal means of achieving one's goals. Even to say 'sorry' after a road accident has become culturally difficult because it might mean acknowledging some liability in a subsequent court action.[19]

The Americans, as noted earlier, and as explored at length by Robert Puttnam in *Bowling Alone*, are ceasing to be a nation of participators; instead, they are turning into individualist, suspicious litigators. In Puttnam's formulation, a long civic generation born between 1920 and 1940, that voted more, joined more, and trusted more, is giving way to new generations that have become progressively disengaged from all forms of civic life. There is no one index of social capital, but Puttnam identifies the same phenomenon across the gamut of American life. Membership of unions and political parties is down; readership of newspapers and audiences for mainstream television network news are down; attendance at parent–teacher associations is down. Indeed, between 1973 and 1994 attendance at a public meeting of any local club or organisation fell by 40 per cent.[20] In 1965, 7 per cent of an individual's time was spent in community organisations; by 1995 this was down to 3 per cent.

Puttnam's work must nevertheless be treated with caution. The better American values have shown remarkable stability, as argued in chapter 2, and there are new forms of association – for example, internet chat rooms and teenage clubbing habits – that even his exhaustive work has undervalued or neglected. And while on international comparisons of trust the US may be well below the Nordic countries, it still scores significantly higher than France, Germany and Italy.[21] If American social capital is declining, it is from a relatively high base. On the other hand, mainland European countries, as argued in chapters 8 and 9, have much more vigorous public systems for underwriting and expressing community, and rely less on the informal private systems of self-help and association that traditionally have been important in the US. They have mechanisms for compensating for the deficiency of social capital that the US does not.

Even allowing for some overstatement on Puttnam's part, the evidence points in the same direction across the board. The growth of gated communities and the explosion of litigation are parts of the same pattern as the decline in joining and participating. American civilisation is becoming more fragmented, polarised and dissociated as the shockwaves of the conservative revolution radiate through the system. Students from higher-income families are increasingly more likely to win degrees; social mobility is only modest and set to decline. These trends have causes deep within conservative attitudes and policies; and the extension of the same principles into the American labour market and into the country's culture and public realm are intensifying the polarising processes.

. . . exacerbated by the flexible labour market

The magical, iconic quality in a market economy in thrall to the maximisation of shareholder value is flexibility. Indeed, the concept has come to have an almost noble connotation: flexibility implies agility, adaptability, intelligence and responsiveness. There is scarcely another word in the American lexicon that embodies so many virtues. Flexibility is what makes a market economy work. Financial capital, for example, is mobile and flexible; it has no loyalties, nor does it expect any. Its job is to chase the highest returns. Over the last thirty years, corporations have increasingly looked for the same quality from their workforces. If a company chooses to run down a branch of production, then it needs the flexibility to extract itself as quickly and cheaply as possible. When it increases output, it needs to do so in such a way that, if market conditions change, it can disinvest as quickly as the financial markets may choose to disinvest from its shares. Hiring a worker is not so much a contract with reciprocal obligations as a cash deal – one that the employer should be able – flexibly – to cancel at will.

American employment law has always been aggressive in its insistence that companies are, in the words of the precedent-setting 1884 judgement by the Tennessee Supreme Court, free 'to discharge or retain employees at will for good cause or for no cause, or even for bad cause without thereby being guilty of an unlawful act per se'.[22] The doctrine of employment at will has long been fiercely contested as Dickensian, and over the last twenty-five years most state courts have recognised exceptions to the general principle. But as the courts have decided in favour of worker rights, employers have gone to ever greater lengths to preserve the original doctrine, both in custom and in practice. More than three-fifths of employers report that they sometimes offer no form of employment contract; over half concede that they sometimes include wording in their contract specifying that the employment can be terminated summarily for any reason.[23]

The upshot is that the American labour market is characterised by impermanence, from which not even the professional and managerial classes are immune; in 1993, for the first time ever, more white-collar workers than blue-collar workers were unemployed. As the labour market tightened in the second half of the 1990s, impermanence worked to the advantage of those workers with scarce skills, who were able to bid up their wages in the 'talent war'. Even the poorest have managed to work more – though their wage rates have scarcely risen.

However, this cyclical effect does not disguise the underlying trends.

Over time the story is one of rising turnover rates, more contingent work, an explosion of the use of agencies supplying temporary workers, and longer hours. The average American now has nine jobs in a lifetime, and approaching three in ten Americans work in jobs on non-standard terms – part-time, temping, on call or day labour. In a strong labour market the essential riskiness of being permanently disposable is not so apparent, for another job can be won quickly; and in any event, in the strong labour market of the late 1990s standard employment grew as employers bowed to the inevitable and accepted more contractual arrangements and accompanying worker rights. Nevertheless, this trend cannot be expected to continue. Non-standard jobs are advantageous to employers because they lack basic entitlements. Only 60 per cent of contingent workers, for example, and a bare 40 per cent of temping agency staff, have health insurance coverage.

It should be no surprise that the most dynamic growth in the US labour market has been in temping. Growing at 11 per cent per annum over the 1990s, the sector now employs nearly 2.5 million workers; 10 per cent of all vacancies in the US over the 1990s were filled by employment agencies. Manpower, with 600,000 staff, is the largest employer in the US. The employee's relationship with a temp is the purest, flexible cash deal there can be, with no attendant worker rights. The risk of changing market conditions is displaced on to such workers, notwithstanding that they are the least well equipped to bear such risk. The same drive to minimise obligations to the workforce lies behind the desire to employ part-time, defined as any job that requires less than forty hours a week. Part-time workers do not qualify for overtime rates, for example, and their hourly wage rate is typically two-thirds of the rate for the same full-time job.

The American workforce is keenly aware that these trends are but more evidence that every employer is under growing pressure to be hawkish. What was conspicuous about the 1990s was that the pace of corporate re-engineering was sustained without let-up over the economic recovery, so that in 1995, the last year for which figures are available, 15 per cent of male American workers had lost their job in the previous three years. Between 1993 and 1995 (again, the most recent years for which data are available) nearly as many jobs were lost as during the 1981–3 recession. Between 1980 and 1995, thirty-nine million Americans were caught up in one or another corporate downsizing programme.[24]

In these conditions, even in a tight labour market workers have been wary about pushing for higher wages; the reality of downsizing, the growth of contingent work and the threat to move jobs to low-cost parts of North America or abroad (General Motors has moved over forty plants to Mexico, for example) are all parts of a picture in which work is at risk. As a result, average wages steadily fell in real terms for more than twenty years up until 1995 for all but the top 20 per cent of the workforce. It was only the boom of the late 1990s – now looking unsustainable – that reversed the trend. To compensate, those four-fifths of Americans who faced falling real wages worked longer hours over the same period and continued to do so into the second half of the 1990s, even as wage rates in real terms began to harden. On average, Americans now work around fifty hours a week, up from about forty in 1973 – more than any other industrialised country except Portugal; they also have the least paid holiday.[25]

If working life is hard for the majority of Americans, for around a fifth of the working population at the bottom, who on average have incomes of no more than half the median income (the European definition of poverty), life has become increasingly desperate. (The overall figure for this proportion of the population masks the disastrous condition of blacks and Hispanics, among whom poverty is twice as common as for whites.) Eligibility for income support and public assistance is being steadily withdrawn; cumulatively, it had halved by 1998/9 from the levels of twenty years ago.[26] Poorly educated and with negligible access to training programmes, the poor are locked into their status. Fifty-four per cent of those in the bottom 20 per cent in the 1960s were still there in the 1990s; only 1 per cent had migrated to the top 20 per cent.[27]

The journalist Barbara Ehrenreich conducted her own social experiment, spending 1998 working in a series of low-wage jobs as a waitress, hotel maid, cleaning woman, nursing-home aide and Wal-mart sales clerk. The result of her year, documented in *Nickel and Dimed*, is an extraordinary, Orwellian testimony to how tough American working life is for the bottom 20 per cent. She had absolutely no financial margin beyond paying the rent and what she needed to survive; saving or finding the time for any training to upgrade her status was beyond her. 'Most civilised nations compensate for the inadequacy of wages by providing relatively generous public services such as health insurance, free or subsidised child care, subsidised housing and effective public transport,' she writes. 'But the United States, for all its wealth, leaves its citizens to fend for themselves – facing market based rents on their wages alone. For millions of Americans, that $10 – or even $8 or $6 – an hour is all there is.'[28]

For the advocates of welfare 'reform' the absence of these supports, along with the new five-year time limit for receiving welfare, has produced the social success of lowering the number of families on welfare from 4.4 million, when the Welfare Reform Act was signed in 1996, to some two million in 2001. Many states chose to shorten the time limit even further, with Virginia, for example, offering only ninety days to find work before benefit ceases. Overall, four and a half million fewer people received welfare benefits following the passing of the act.[29] The incentive, for the states who administer welfare and the recipients alike, is to do everything to find benefit claimants work; even the unemployment rate for single mothers fell from around 40 per cent to under 30 per cent in 2001, although as recession bites numbers are beginning to rise again. In 2001, too, child poverty fell to its lowest level for twenty-one years.[30]

How much these outcomes are attributable to the simple operation of a booming economy and the investment many states made in child support, thus making it easier for many poor mothers to work, and how much to the threat of losing benefit (the object of welfare reform) is an open question. Nor is it clear, as the recession deepens and jobs disappear, how sustainable the improvement will be – or whether the American public will be prepared to accept destitution for those whose five-year welfare entitlement has expired, beginning for women in 2002. But even if welfare reform had worked as the conservatives preached – which it has not, at least not as satisfactorily as they claim – it still leaves the Rawlsian question unanswered. If, behind a veil of ignorance, we did not know whether we would be in the circumstances of America's bottom 20 per cent, none of us would willingly deem their condition as acceptable. They are not equipped with skills; their basic needs are neglected; they are trapped in their low-wage jobs; they have no ladder upwards; they are not offered health insurance; they are not provided with schools that will give their children even the semblance of equality of opportunity; if their children do win places at college or university, the costs of attendance are beyond them and state assistance is negligible and declining. The infrastructure of justice, in short, is close to non-existent. What has been put in its place is a system that relieves the middle class of paying the tax that might support such an infrastructure, in the name of a social mobility that equally does not exist. This is self-interested callousness masquerading as morality and economic efficiency.

For these conditions could partly be excused if income and social mobility in the US was high. It is not. Lawrence Mishel, Jared Bernstein and John Schmitt, the three authors of *The State of Working America*, compare the mobility of workers in America with the four biggest European economies and three Nordic economies. They find that the US has the lowest share of workers moving from the bottom fifth of workers into the second fifth, the lowest share moving into the top 60 per cent and the highest share of workers unable to sustain full-time employment.[31] The most exhaustive study by the OECD confirms the poor rates of relative upward mobility for very low-paid American workers; it also found that full-time workers in Britain, Italy and Germany enjoy much more rapid growth in their earnings than those in the US, which in this respect ranks roughly equal with France.[32] However, downward mobility was more marked in the US; American workers are more likely to suffer a reduction in their real earnings than workers in Europe. Even the OECD, high priest of deregulation, finds itself forced to conclude that countries with more deregulated labour and product markets (pre-eminently the US) do not appear to have higher relative mobility, nor do low-paid workers in these economies experience more upward mobility. The OECD is pulling its punches. The US experience is worse than Europe's.

These results are not unexpected; the surveys repeat the evidence accumulated since the war that the US, despite all the propaganda in its favour, has shown little or no difference in measured mobility compared with Europe. Lipset and Bendix, in their pathbreaking study *Social Mobility in Industrial Society*, could find no evidence in the 1950s that American men were moving any more rapidly from manual to non-manual labour than men in other industrial societies. Later studies comparing the income mobility of the US with the Nordic countries and Germany find either that there is no difference, or that there is less mobility in the US.[33] Leading sociologists Robert Erikson and John Goldthorpe found precisely the same result in a more detailed breakdown of mobility, measuring both what happens intergenerationally and what happens over one individual's lifetime.[34] Indeed, they argued, it is probable that American social mobility is overstated because the category used to define the top class – 'professional, technical and kindred workers' – is so broad that it includes workers who would be categorised further down the class hierarchy in the more tightly drawn European classifications. The mystery, as Erikson and Goldthorpe write, is why, given that there is no evidence of American exceptionalism or higher social mobility, the myth persists.

The answer is that nobody in the highly introverted society that the US has become can believe that foreigners might do it as well as or better than Americans – and the conservative intellectual ascendancy is not going to disabuse them. The point made earlier needs emphasising. The historical data already show that mid-twentieth-century America had only modest rates of income and social mobility by international standards, and that these showed no signs of improving over the postwar period. The combination in the contemporary US of flexible labour markets and reduced educational opportunity for low-income students – the great achievements of conservatism – can have only one result: in the future, mobility, disgracefully, is set to fall.

America is developing an aristocracy of the rich and a concomitant serfdom of the poor – and in so doing is laying its own economic vitality open to threat. Not only is it deluding itself, it is deluding the entire globe before which it holds itself up as the economic and social model to emulate.

The unfair bargain

However unfair the 'flexible labour market' might be in its distribution of rewards and risk, its freezing of the bottom 20 per cent into poverty and its baleful influence on income and social mobility, it is widely regarded – certainly by American conservatives – as the key to American economic success. The American rate of job generation has compared favourably with that in Europe; dig deeper, however, and the story is very different from the explanation offered by conservatives.

If flexibility is defined as the degree to which a wage is a contract that can be unravelled when employers wish, uncontaminated as far as possible by regulations, collective bargaining or employment protection, and if it is the panacea the conservatives claim, then the US should have succeeded in lowering unemployment rates across the board over the 1990s. Unemployment among poorly educated, low-skilled workers would be broadly similar to that among better-educated, higher-skilled peers, because their wages would be driven down. But the opposite is the case. The unemployment rate of the poorly skilled in the US is 4.5 times higher than that of college-educated workers, the highest ratio of all industrialised countries.[35] The American labour market, for all its vaunted flexibility, turns out to be the *least* efficient at pricing poorly skilled workers into work – despite its punitive welfare policies towards the unemployed. It is, however, very efficient at ensuring that top people's pay grows explosively.

The secret of the American job story is less its flexible labour market than what has happened to the structure of its economy as a result of a 25-year credit boom that has fuelled a sustained consumer boom, coupled, on the supply side, with the evolution of the sexual revolution and thus women's appetite and ability to join the world of work. On top of this, a consistent supply of immigrants has helped keep wage rates at minimum levels however tight the labour market has become; the US's long border with Mexico, ensuring a steady supply of cheap labour, in this respect has as much to do with labour market flexibility as lack of employment regulation. In any case, to present the US labour market as wholly unregulated is again to comprehend the world through conservative eyes: American employers have to comply with a raft of stringent rules over health and safety, along with racial and sexual discrimination. All societies, even the US, have to set limits to the degree work can be treated as a commodity and employers have a free hand.

Over the last two decades America has created the world's largest service sector, driven by astonishing consumption growth, and in turn has created forty million jobs. As Americans turned into a nation of credit-financed shoppers preoccupied with their health, so they created over fourteen million jobs just in the nation's shopping malls, hospitals and health-care centres – most of which were 'non-standard' jobs filled by women. A female army of cashiers, sales clerks, nurses, cleaners and waitresses has fanned out across America, picking up contingent work in the low-productivity service sector, their experiences so ably documented by Barbara Ehrenreich. What has driven their willingness to work is not just a new readiness to join the labour market; it has been need. The Employment Policy Institute in Washington computes that 29 per cent of families have incomes that fall below a reasonable estimate of their budgetary need; mothers simply have had to work, especially over a period in which male wages have been stagnating in real terms.[36] Americans, in short, have created a treadmill for themselves and hailed it as an economic miracle.

Even so, the growth in the numbers of two-earner families, which now constitute nearly half of all families, has not been enough to sustain living standards and spending in an era in which real wages have fallen. Americans have gone massively into debt, aided and abetted by an increasingly deregulated banking system pumping out credit. By 2000 the stock of household debt had reached an all-time high in relation to household income, driven largely by a growth in mortgage debt. But the greatest increase in debt over the 1990s was incurred by the middle 20 per cent of income earners – evidence of how the need to borrow was felt most keenly by those whose living standards were most under pressure. The proportion of income eaten up by debt service has been rising sharply for those on incomes below $50,000 – up from 18 per cent in 1995 to 22 per cent in 1998. For those at the bottom, with incomes of $10,000 or less, debt service is an even heavier burden, taking 32 per cent of their income – an extreme pressure reflected in a doubling in the number of pawnshops by over 10,000 between 1986 and 1996. Exposed to extraordinarily high interest rates on small loans, poorer Americans see their chances of being able to enter the housing market diminish as house prices in real terms escalate. These are the dwellers in the mushrooming trailer parks around the country – the flip-side of the gated communities. As Barbara Ehrenreich found, rents are so high that sometimes low-paid workers have to sleep in their vans or trucks.

The rate of American employment generation over the last twenty years remains an achievement, but it is wrong to present the American labour market as the philosopher's stone of job creation. This was a particular achievement at a particular moment of time. For example, full-time jobs in the unionised manufacturing sector have held up well over the last twenty years by international standards, tribute to the strong growth of domestic demand. Again, this has less to do with the structure of the labour market than with the performance of the wider economy. But crucially, the credit that has driven the consumption – and much of the jobs growth – has been taken on by ordinary wage-earners even as their wages have been squeezed in real terms; at the time of writing they face highly uncertain economic prospects with enormous cumulative debts. Servicing their current debts will be demanding enough, let alone assuming new debts. The great job-generating machine is coming to the end of its capacity to deliver.

As it does so, the asymmetry of power in the labour market between employers and workers will start to have more malign consequences. Even those who enjoyed the benefits of the talent war of the late 1990s as the labour market tightened, and who declared independence from large companies, making their own careers as so-called 'free workers', are finding that harsher economic times bring new insecurities. Those working for companies fear another round of downsizing from which nobody at any level is safe. Everybody is under pressure, at risk and disconnected in an economy where contingent contracts are king. The hours worked continue to climb. The alleged bargain is that this is the price that has to be paid for an efficient, dynamic economy which will deliver opportunity and mobility. But the bargain is a fraud. The conservative proposition is about to come under closer scrutiny than it has faced for twenty-five years.

The collapse of the public realm

Yet the political environment in which any debate takes place has been degraded by the same forces: the US today, in Michael Sandel's words from chapter 2, is little more than a 'procedural republic'. The ever onward encroachment of the market and its values has invaded and polluted the heart of the political process. The decline in direct citizen involvement in politics has been associated with and exploited by an enormous extension of corporate and business power as the parties compete for funds. Money, as billionaire Michael Bloomberg demonstrated by effectively buying the mayorship of New York in 2001, has become central to political success.

The cost of American elections has grown explosively as politics has grown more centralised and more reliant on the media to extend its message. The community of interest between the Republican party and business described in chapter 3 has given the Republicans an inbuilt advantage in winning campaign finance. Of those who contributed to parties and candidates in 1997, 81 per cent earned more than $100,000 and were over forty-five; half described themselves as conservative while less than a third called themselves liberal.[37] One of the side-effects of the enormous and growing inequality of American society is that the Republicans have had an ever richer base from which to raise their finance; if the Democrats try to redress the balance, that serves only to ratchet up Republican spending to stay ahead. Just to enter American politics has become prohibitively expensive.

The American political system has such effective inbuilt checks and balances that the corporations and rich individuals who furnish the wherewithal cannot buy power in a straightforward cash transaction, however much they would like to. Typically they give 'soft' money, according to the stipulation that they can support a cause but not a party or candidate. However, they have an agenda, and they look for paybacks, as we saw in chapter 1. This is the further pollution of the American political discourse. In order to compete for funds, the Democrats have found themselves being pulled in the same pro-free-market, anti-tax-and-welfare policy directions as the Republicans, so that both parties are huddled around a pro-business centrist political philosophy because that is what makes raising campaign finance easiest. Moreover, the fund-raisers – the individuals who raise money that can be directly spent on the candidates' campaigns, in contrast to 'soft money' – have become the key figures in selecting which politicians will be chosen to represent the party. If they feel they cannot sell a politician to their donors, then effectively they have the right of veto. Thus both the face of the politician and the policies espoused are effectively dictated by money.

The most direct influence of all is that of the lobbyist, directing campaign finance to those members of Congress up for re-election on the quiet understanding that the *quid pro quo* will be support for a key line change in a bill – or just to lay the ground of obligation against a future need to elicit a reply to the telephone call mustering support for an amendment or veto. Jeffrey Birnbaum, Washington Bureau chief for *Fortune*, writes in *The Money Men* that President Clinton openly acknowledged at the memorial service for the prominent Democratic fund-raiser and lobbyist Dan Dutko that without his capacity to raise money he would never have been president. Any number of congressmen and women can say the same. It is this fund-raising power that gives lobbyists and advocacy organisations like the NRA and the AARP (American Association of Retired Persons) their clout. And remember one fact from chapter 1: every presidential nomination for the last twenty years has been won by the candidate who raised the most money. If a democratic political system is meant to offer a means by which a country can engage in public and rational argument in the pursuit of the public interest, and to hold decision-makers to account through the ballot box, then the US is an increasingly dismal failure. It has the form of democracy without its content.

This deformation of the political system has consequences for the rest of the public domain. Expressing public objectives and sustaining the public infrastructure have become increasingly difficult. Federal expenditure on roads, schools and universities fell as a proportion of GDP throughout the 1990s even under a Democratic president, while few states dared raise their tax base to compensate for the fall-off in federal spending; indeed, many were more hawkish about spending cuts than the federal government. The Bush administration's spending plans are set to accelerate the process still further.

The US transport infrastructure is increasingly frayed, with endemic traffic gridlock and a decaying public transport system. The Federal Highways Administration estimates that 50 per cent of US major roads and highways are in backlog over their repairs, while the Federal Railroad Administration has not inspected more than a third of the US's highway–rail crossings for more than five years. Standards in the public education system are hardly helped by the decline in average starting salaries for public-school teachers to 97 per cent of college graduates' average starting salary – and an accompanying decline in average SAT results for new teachers. And the deterioration of the public sector extends well beyond core areas like transport and education: the Food and Drug Administration, for example, had the resources to inspect only 5000 food processing plants in 1997, compared to 21,000 in 1981.[38]

The collapse of overt public provision and public investment is only the tip of the iceberg. The quality of public debate and the fabric of American culture have become subordinate to ambitions for individual and corporate profit. Americans thus have ever less protection against the individualisation and fragmentation of American life. As work offers less structure and community less meaning to people's lives, companies have used television and the tools of mass advertising to provide alternative sources of meaning with the overt aim of increasing their turnover and profits; branding has emerged as a means to achieve the status and sense of belonging that social and economic structures no longer provide. Starbucks' marketing director, Scott Edby, captures the new intent of the corporations when he says that his company's aim is 'to align ourselves with one of the greatest movements towards finding a connection with your soul'. For Starbucks read Marlboro, Ford, Nike, the Gap, etc. A disorientated America is seeking comfort in the security of great brands.

Shoppers will have learned about the brands through advertising – most likely through TV advertising. Television is both the ubiquitous form of American communication, and central to its commercial culture. In one respect the ubiquity of television is a pleasure – available alike in the bowling alley, at the supermarket check-out and in the waiting rooms of every American airport. But ubiquity has meant increasing trivialisation. The average American watches four hours of television a day and the average home receives no fewer than forty-five channels;[39] some 50 per cent of Americans watch television during dinner – and a third during breakfast. Only 2.2 per cent of viewers watch public television; the rest watch television financed by either sponsorship or advertising. Fifteen hundred advertisements are screened daily on US television,[40] and as the rate charged to the advertiser is directly linked to the size and spending power of the audience, there is a relentless battle to ensure high ratings. With attention spans as short as they are and the remote control always to hand, TV schedulers are acutely aware that they must use every contrivance possible across the gamut of programmes – from lurid plot lines in soap and drama to highly emotional talk-show interviews – to sustain their audience's interest.

Hyper-competition in a 45-channel marketplace facing increasing diversion of limited viewer time to the internet is one driver of the character of American television; another is our old friend, shareholder value. GE, the patron saint of the doctrine, took over NBC in 1986; nine years later, Westinghouse's purchase of CBS and Disney's takeover of ABC completed the picture. The American networks' prime obligation is to sustain their owners' share price; with the arrival of cable and satellite channels having shrunk their audience share from 90 per cent to 60 per cent, the competition has become brutal – as have its consequences. 'The product of commercial television is not programs,' declared Reuven Frank, the former NBC News president. 'If one thinks of making goods to sell, the viewers are not the customers, those who buy the product. Advertisers buy the product, pay money for it. Programs are not what they buy. What they buy, what they pay for, is audience.'[41]

In the US, culture is overwhelmingly popular culture; Americans want to be entertained and diverted, and it is done with élan and professionalism. Some programmes are made with spectacular production values. *Seinfeld* and *Ally McBeal* are high-class television by any standards. But the pressing need to capture and hold attention gives rise to a relentless drive to create shows that emphasise human freakery, dramas with plots that border on the surreal. Violence and sex hold the viewer, and there is growing evidence that this skewed emphasis is spilling out into American culture – in particular among American children. By the age of eighteen the average American will have seen 200,000 acts of violence and 40,000 murders on television[42] – and America is tragically familiar with the consequences of 'acting out' such violence. The teenage perpetrators of the Columbine High School massacre in April 1999 used the media message – everything from their 'cool' hitman black coats to their laughter as they killed – to stylise the atrocity they committed.

In Robert Puttnam's view, the length of time Americans spend watching television and the content of much of what they watch are principal causes of the decline in social capital; heavy TV watchers are temperamentally less inclined to be joiners and participants, and the TV they watch leaves them more disconnected from ordinary social realities. Television and its values are a barely accountable instrument in the cannibalisation of American culture – and American democracy.

Above all, the intense competition for audience from an ever lower cost base is transforming the way television reports the news and, through discussion and documentary, creates the platform for national public debate. Television is abdicating responsibility. Quality news is expensive, and under GE's ownership the unattractive ratio of expense to audience payback has forced rounds of downsizing on NBC's news operation which have been aped by the other networks. No network has a Supreme Court correspondent any longer, and the foreign correspondent networks have been decimated – but it is not just a question of the *extent* of coverage; the coverage itself has to be either soft or confrontational if it is to hold an audience. Thus policy issues have been supplanted by 'human interest' stories: features about oddballs, scandals and celebrity profiles. The sound-bites become ever shorter, news reports more peripatetic, with rapidly changing images. Emotion rules; politics is denuded of nobility, rationality or any sense that it defines a national conversation – rather, it is reduced to a sport in which every move is about personal advancement and rivalry.

Worse still, independent investigative journalism is in headlong decline; for it is expensive and risks upsetting important sponsors and advertisers. The numbers of instances where fear of corporate reprisals has checked TV journalism are mounting;[43] for example, during the Gulf War CBS offered to cut its coverage so that every ten-minute segment ended on an upbeat note to benefit the ensuing adverts. During the war against Afghanistan, journalism suspended its critical faculties; the Bush administration was allowed an almost free hand to qualify key American liberties. Its actions might have enjoyed popular support and even have been justifiable; but ordinary American citizens would not have had the chance to reflect on any counter-arguments because none was offered. This was a democracy that had simply ceased to operate; for the owners of the channels of communication would brook no debate.

Broadcast journalists themselves, as James Fallows (himself a journalist) argues, have become celebrities, able to command winner-takes-all fees on the lucrative conference and punditry circuit; their unwillingness to bite the corporate hand that feeds them is self-evident. Fallows concludes, 'The way modern journalists choose to present the news – that the world is out of control, they are governed by crooks and that fellow citizens want to kill them – increases the chances that citizens will feel unhappy, powerless, betrayed by and angry about the political system.'[44]

Newspapers and magazines are under similar pressure; institutional share ownership, with its attendant priorities, has come to publishing as well. Fifty-seven per cent of the *New York Times* and 52 per cent of the *Washington Post* are owned by institutional investors whose priority is shareholder value.[45] The same hollowing-out of newsrooms, accent on the emotional, and growing unwillingness to offend potential advertisers and sponsors are narrowing the scope of written journalism. As a consequence, Americans are becoming less informed and knowledgeable about the world. The great American tradition of serious commentary is under an ever-intensifying siege. As one leading journalist commented, 'We're not mission driven, peopled by our propensity to inform. We're just here to entertain, to soothe. We're here to sell our wares.'[46] Neil Postman summed up the parlous situation in *Amusing Ourselves to Death*: news, as much as politics, has become a branch of the entertainment business.

The US is, above all, the country of consumption, complete with 28,500 shopping malls. Over half – 53 per cent – of all purchases are made in these scientifically designed consumption factories,[47] whose location and internal store layout are calibrated to maximise spending. Financed and in many cases owned by pension funds and insurance companies, the shopping mall is the perfect investment proposition – for rising profitability is guaranteed. From the neighbourhood mall to the super-regional mall, the principle is the same: the shopper is led through an enclosed and privately policed precinct insulated from anything unpleasant – be it the weather or the socially undesirable – and presented with a mix of shops that has been chosen to meet what extensive market research predicts to be the exact profile of the likely shoppers.

The privatisation of the spirit and the disintegration of the conception of the civic begin with the retreat of public space. American cities still throb with vitality; at their best they are great tributes to American cosmopolitanism and its democratic spirit. Successive waves of immigrants have left their mark, and there is a generosity in the city layout and size of buildings that is awe-inspiring and lifts the spirit. But little by little the downtown areas are becoming sanitised and privatised. Instead of the tumult of the urban city centre where public space – for recreation, education, sport, political meetings – interacts with the private, there is a new dominance of the private, symbolised by the corporate skyscraper and the shopping mall. The shopper does not enter a thoroughfare with public rights of way; he or she enters a private space that has been manipulated to make him or her want to spend more. Security is private. The space belongs to the landlord or shop-owners, whose objective is the maximisation of their rent and sales turnover and who accept no civic claim. As Margaret Crawford writes, 'the world of the shopping mall . . . has become the world.'[48]

For conservatives, the shopping culture, the weakness of the public discourse, the trivialisation of politics and the domination of money all help to entrench their ascendancy and limit the scope of any challenge. The myths about America offering equality of opportunity and high social mobility can be peddled without effective comeback; inequality and the very tough lives of ordinary Americans hardly enter the national public conversation. It is conservatives who protest about the corruption of Washington politics as part of their anti-government story, even as they exploit the weaknesses in the system to entrench their own position.

Yet the US is stirring. The first five chapters of this book have rested upon an extensive American literature protesting about what has happened to their economy and society. It is not just foreign critics who believe the US has not solved the age-old question of how to construct a just economic and social order – or operate an effective democracy. A growing number of Americans share the same view. The argument that Europe should copy the US is in important respects, as we shall see, the wrong way round. It is European social outcomes and democratic practice from which the US now needs to borrow; nor is the European economy as sclerotic as US conservatives like to claim. Yet it is the US – the country which has left so many of its citizens barren and ill at ease with themselves, and which itself is riven by internal concern and criticism – that is held up as a model for the world. How that has happened is where we turn next.

6

The globalisation of conservatism

This book opened with the concern that the public realm in Britain is in eclipse; that there no longer seems to exist a widely shared will or belief that the growth of inequality should be checked; and that our civilisation is being consecrated to the interests of a very particular idea of capitalism. The British live within the shadow of the American conservative conception that capitalism is a sealed, economistic world in which success follows naturally from as little government as possible allowing the maximum freedom to follow the economic imperative of buying cheap and selling dear in the service of making the highest profits. The much-invoked spirit of enterprise is defined entirely in economic terms. It should not and does not rely on any form of social organisation or context, whether the internal organisation of the company, or the quality and quantity of the intellectual, social, human and physical capital which surrounds it and in which it is embedded. The watchwords for a successful capitalism are liberty, flexibility, self-interest and enterprise. Its enemies are the 'burdens' of regulation, taxation, welfare and any form of social obligation. They may be essential to the trust and the social, human, physical and intellectual infrastructure of a market economy; but in the script of American conservatism they have no part.

This is a hopelessly one-sided account of both what creates a successful market economy and what underpins a just society. The first five chapters of this book have marshalled enough evidence at least to place a question mark over this approach as it has evolved in the US over the last twenty-five years. America's society has become unfairer; opportunities for all apart from those at the top of the pile are narrowing; its public infrastructure in the widest sense has weakened; and, as the economy comes back to earth, its underlying performance is seen to be much more modest. The American economic achievement over the 1990s rested on the build-up of phenomenal and unsustainable economic imbalances and a stock market boom whose unwinding is already having a depressive impact which, whatever the current signs of recovery, is likely to restrain the growth of the US economy for some time. Many companies have had their competitive capacities undermined rather than strengthened by the devotion to the pursuit of shareholder value. This is not to deny the record of American job generation, technological innovation and industrial restructuring, only to place it in a wider and more sceptical context.

Yet this set of – at best contestable, at worst downright wrong – conservative axioms has become the new international common sense. They are marshalled as the intellectual support for the way globalisation is advanced and justified, essentially extending the principles by which the US is run to the world. From the American perspective this has a number of advantages. It validates the American economic and social model. It acts as a crowbar, forcing others to follow the American lead and open up their markets on American principles, thus giving American companies an inherent advantage in the global struggle for market advantage. And it justifies the US's instinctive unilateralism and reluctance to compromise any economic and political sovereignty in multilateral institutions and processes. The US can portray itself as an exceptional civilisation, with a sacred obligation both to itself and to the world to be the custodian of the only true way. It has successfully fought fascism and more recently communism. Its obligation is to remain an unsullied beacon of what is possible through consecrating an economy and society to the pursuit of liberty.

In both economic and social terms this uncritical and introverted stance leads to a remarkable lack of self-knowledge. This is an environment in which the former chairman of the US Stock Exchange could recently say that 'in matters of finance and politics, if not culture, we are becoming the world and much of the world wants to become us'; or a former minister that 'Americans should not deny the fact that of all the nations in the history of the world theirs is the most just, the most tolerant . . . and the best model for the future' without any trace of embarrassment or qualification.[1] The national stock-taking after the dreadful acts of 11 September 2001 has been all the more difficult because so much of the American national conversation is wrapped up in this self-congratulatory guff. 'We're the brightest beacon for freedom and opportunity in the world,' said President Bush, trying to explain the attack to his compatriots.[2]

It is not just that the rhetoric gets in the way of the US comprehending how others might see it; fundamentally, it gets in the way of the US understanding its own strengths and weaknesses. America, as we have discovered, is *not* the brightest beacon for opportunity in the world. To make this point is not to fall into crude anti-Americanism or to criticise the entire gamut of America's complex relationships with the rest of the globe; for example, there is no doubt that the US was correct to respond to the terrorist networks in Afghanistan in the way that it did and that the world will be safer rather than riskier as a result. Rather, it is to highlight that the triumph of American conservatism has entrenched an uncritical acclamation of what is by European standards an eccentric and particular view of what makes capitalism work over time – and that a more rounded conception of what delivers a just economic and social order, built around markets and the profit motive, would be not only in the American but the global interest.

Consider the debate in Britain. It has taken two landslide general election victories by New Labour finally to convince the political class that it should take seriously the electorate's settled belief that public services need to be improved. For example, at last there is a recognition not only that health expenditure must be lifted towards the European average, but that one way or another funding it will necessarily involve an increase in taxation or in social insurance or some combination of both – and that while private capacity, acumen and expertise may be helpful, even vital, as a change agent in improving public delivery, this does not excuse the state from finding additional resources. If we want better education, health and transport we need public initiative and public taxation. Equally, there are limits to how much individuals can provide for their own retirement through individual saving, which is hazardous and insecure. There is a dawning realisation that growing inequality has serious social effects – in the housing market, for example, where desirable districts are out of the reach of even moderately well-paid families, or in education, where rich private schools dominate the league tables of academic excellence, making a mockery of equality of opportunity – that in the medium to long term will give rise to intractable social tensions.

Why has it taken the Labour government so long to respond to the voters? Because, for twenty-five years, public policy in Britain has faithfully aped the conservative axioms dominant in the United States, consigning critics to the political margins. UK income tax was last raised in 1977. Labour market regulation in Britain is even lighter than in the US. Public investment has fallen to new lows. The rail system was privatised, with disastrous results. The litany is familiar. These developments are undoubtedly attributable in part to the British political vulnerability to conservatism and in part to the inability to construct a viable social democratic settlement that culminated in the experience of the 1970s; together, these gave Thatcherism its political opportunity. *Laissez-faire* nostrums seemed an attractive way out of stagflation and low productivity, and dovetailed neatly with many cultural totems, just as they did in the US. But they would not have become so entrenched if the American right had not won such complete control of the economic and social agenda in the US, if the propaganda offensive arguing that the US model offers so many apparent advantages had been challenged more strongly, and if globalisation had not taken on the character that it has.

The British experience has been echoed in Europe, where, as we shall explore in later chapters, American conservative principles have begun to encroach on liberal social democratic foundations. The European social contract as represented by the welfare state is under fire, blamed for high unemployment by conservative American critics and their converts in Europe; Europeans are being advised to reorganise their financial systems and approach to company law around the American example. The European welfare system has defects, certainly, and there are important shortfalls in European systems of corporate accountability, which often lack transparency. But the attack is one-sided. It takes no account of the benefits the European system produces in productivity, now as high as in the US (in some countries, higher), and in social outcomes that are incomparably better, in Rawlsian terms of fairness and equality of opportunity. Europe should not seek to refound itself on American principles; rather, its own principles should be defended while the processes are modernised. In any case, high unemployment in some parts of Europe, the chief excuse for criticism, has much more complex roots than the structure of Europe's social contract.

The international application of the American way, via the integration of financial and trade flows around free market 'Washington consensus' principles, is supposed to be the avenue to global wealth creation. But, in the world as in the US, wealth creation is not naturally accompanied by its fair distribution. Just as inequality within the US and Britain, and in the majority of OECD states, has risen over the last twenty years, so it has grown internationally on seven out of eight possible measures. As the international economist Professor Robert Wade argues, the distribution of international income now represents a champagne glass, with a wide shallow bowl at the top, representing the richest 20 per cent who have 82.7 per cent of the world's income, and a long stem at the bottom. Astonishingly, 60 per cent of the world's population enjoy a mere 5.6 per cent of its income.[3] The same low commodity prices that helped the US to experience its ten-year boom by permitting low inflation and cheap money have entrenched much of the rest of the world in grinding poverty, and borrowing on the private capital markets to lever themselves out of their situation incurs the risk of financial crisis and massive capital flight. Winner-takes-all effects make matters worse; technological innovation and investment flow to – and are created by – richer markets. Without intervention, debt relief and aid transfers it is difficult to see how the condition of the less developed world is likely to improve relative to that of the first world; and while there is not a simple relationship between this prospect and the creation of third world terrorism networks, plainly it not unreasonably provokes an immense feeling of injustice which the West needs to address. Yet American conservatism rules otherwise, for to do so would offend its canons. The same indifference pervades global attitudes to inequality.

It is easy to interpret this new world order as a form of American empire; after all, the US has been indisputably the world's leading capitalist power ever since 1945 and the world's only superpower ever since the collapse of the Soviet Union in 1991. It is palpably self-evident that, if it had wanted different outcomes, it had the power to will them. Yet such an analysis fails to capture the complexity of what has happened, the compliance of other countries in the creation of the world system and the real benefits that some – notably Japan and the Asian tiger economies – have experienced as the result of how it works. Nor is Washington politically structured to deliver the sustained and coherent policies that can create and manage an empire; it is cross-cut by different conceptions of the national interest held by the various departments of state and political parties, and above all by the Senate, House and President, which in turn superintend a continental economy with a vast array of different and competing interests. American manufacturing and its workforce, for example, actively oppose the Wall Street view of what constitutes an appropriate US economic and foreign policy.

While it is wrong to characterise the US as monolithically and single-mindedly building a world order around a coherent strategic plan, it is equally wrong to characterise globalisation as some politically neutral force springing from ICT and the anonymous forces of trade and financial liberalisation – as, for example, leading globalisation theorist Professor Tony Giddens of the London School of Economics tends to do.[4] Globalisation has been politically shaped by the US deploying three simple guiding principles in an ad hoc but increasingly determined fashion. First, the US looks to exercise its power unilaterally rather than have its autonomy constrained by international alliances and treaty obligations. Second, it focuses aggressively and unilaterally on promoting the interests of those sectors and companies that plainly benefit, because of their ascendant market position or technological lead, from globalisation – notably financial services, ICT and, latterly, those with leadership in intellectual property. Third, it instinctively looks to market solutions and remedies, both as a matter of intellectual and ideological conviction, and because over a period these render it more likely that American interests will prevail. The bigger and more powerful tend to succeed in 'free', unregulated markets.

These three predispositions have always been present in the United States as an autonomous continental great power, supported by its own conviction of its special destiny as an exceptional civilisation. But as conservatism has grown in influence and the various countervailing, international checks to the deployment of American power have fallen away, so each has become more marked. The world could certainly have a more threatening and malevolent power at its centre, and if this power is to have an overweening ideology, better the advocacy of liberty than the fascist and communist ideologies that disfigured Europe in the first half of the twentieth century. That does not mean, however, that the particular economy and society that the US has become represents the acme of a just economy and society. If we care about the public realm, equality and the importance of the social contract; if we wish to promote fairness and equality of opportunity; if we believe that these values should underpin the global order, then US conservatism needs to be challenged and the country needs to be repersuaded that even America depends on others for some things and that forms of multilateral co-operation are in its interests. There is only one source of countervailing power and values: Europe. This is where the argument next leads; but first we need to understand how the modern world has been shaped by those three American predispositions – and how the rise of conservatism has made them more acute.

Unilateralism, power and free markets

Power politics are always rough and tough, and there has never been a period – nor should one be expected – when the US has somehow subordinated its perceptions of its own interests to some idea of the global public good. All states at all times prosecute their interests. What is true, however, is that for twenty-five years after World War II the US chose to prosecute its interests through a web of multilateral treaties and alliances – albeit always as first among equals – through which it believed its interests could best be served. In the great war against communism there was a common Western interest, and the US knew that if it was to lead the West there needed to be common rules of the game which were accepted by itself as much as by lesser powers, although it was careful to entrench its own leadership position. What has changed since the collapse of communism and the triumph of conservatism is that the

US increasingly believes that there is one set of rules for it and its nationals, and another for the rest of the world. Thus every country can extradite and sue the perpetrators of terrorist acts as long as they abide by international law in their courts – except the US, which reserves the right to try by American military law. Thus the extraordinary period in the aftermath of the Afghan war during which the Bush administration unilaterally decided to suspend the rules of the Geneva Convention for captured Al Quaeda and Taliban fighters. This was only partially reversed under intense international pressure so that Taliban detainees enjoyed the conventions – but neither group prisoner of war status.[5] This is an assertion of exceptionalism that stretches across the board, from financial regulation to how the US should organise its security.

In the years after World War II the story was different. As the war came to an end urgent negotiations took place between the Americans and British about how to prohibit the beggar-my-neighbour trade and competitive devaluations of the interwar period when countries had tried to export their economic problems, provoking the implosion of trade and credit that turned recession into the 1930s depression, and which became the seedbed of fascism. Instead, world trade and finance were henceforth to be conducted within a framework of universal rules that favoured economic openness and internationally agreed responses to individual economies' difficulties. Under the system agreed at Bretton Woods in New Hampshire in 1944, every member currency was pegged to the dollar, whose value in turn was pegged to the price of gold and freely convertible into it. To join the system, states undertook to adjust their domestic economic policies to sustain their exchange rate, and to devalue or revalue only after consultation and agreement with the International Monetary Fund (IMF) – which would in turn advance them transitional loans in vital hard currency, dollars, in exchange for their implementing austerity programmes while they traded their way out of unfinanceable trade deficits. The World Bank, established at the same time, was as a multilateral institution to channel aid and loans to support third world development. Three years later the General Agreement on Tariffs and Trade (GATT) was signed pledging to work for progressive reductions in the postwar legacy of protectionist tariffs.

The system worked, underwriting the postwar economic boom. The

Europeans became steadily more confident about lowering tariffs and opening up their borders as they began to earn trade surpluses convertible into dollars backed by gold – and there was always the reserve option of an organised devaluation to adjust their international balance sheet if they hit the economic rocks. Trade grew explosively as tariffs fell by 73 per cent between 1947 and 1961. The counterpart of the surpluses established by Japan and Europe – with the painful exception of Britain, which still ran deficits – was a burgeoning American trade deficit. The prosperity the US had wanted to foster was coming into being – and in a multilateral context.

At the negotiations in 1943 and 1944 the US had insisted, in an exercise of raw power, that the dollar (backed by gold), rather than a new international currency, bancor (again backed by gold), should be the international unit of account, for which Keynes had pressed. Moreover, the US gained decisive voting rights in both the IMF and the World Bank. But this was a power play within a multilateral framework. In philosophical terms America's New Dealers accepted that the new system should operate along liberal, Keynesian lines. 'Strong', creditor countries should be under just as much obligation to adjust their economic policies as 'weak', debtor countries; and government management and regulation of national economies was accepted as inherently vital to achieve more income equality, employment and economic stability. Harry Dexter White, the chief US negotiator and treasury secretary, fought off Wall Street pressure for the system to be run with no capital controls, agreeing with Keynes that controls were imperative if national governments were to control domestic interest rates to achieve full employment – even if they might inhibit the growth of Wall Street internationally. Thirty years later, no such inhibition on US financial interests and autonomy of US action would be acceptable. But the 1940s was the time not only of the IMF, World Bank and GATT, but of full-hearted American support for NATO and the UN.

From the American point of view, the Bretton Woods system had one chronic defect. It might make the dollar the effective world monetary standard, so permitting the US to pay for whatever it wanted worldwide with its own currency; but the *quid pro quo* was that the dollar should hold its value against gold. The US could never devalue, and that set a constraint on American economic policy. Eventually the dam would break. Not even the giant American economy with its legendary productivity could permanently underwrite the value of the dollar in terms of gold – and from the late 1950s and over the 1960s American gold reserves steadily fell.

No great power can sustain its position for long unless it can pay its way, and the first great assertion of conservative US interests and harbinger of the consequent recasting of the world economic order was the American refusal between 1971 and 1973 to continue its role as banker of last resort to the world financial system. This ranks with the collapse of the Soviet Union in 1989 as a pivotal event in postwar history.

There were two potential solutions to the problem of America's haemorrhaging gold reserves. The first was to reform the system multilaterally with international agreement and even go so far as creating a new world paper reserve currency, which would relieve the pressure on the dollar and would be managed by a strengthened IMF as a kind of world central bank. Or the Americans could throw down the gauntlet, insist the rest of the world revalue their currencies so that the dollar could have the same relationship with gold – and if it refused, simply scrap the system and create a de facto world dollar standard. Throughout the 1960s the Kennedy and Johnson administrations tried successive administrative and regulative wheezes to support the dollar – notably imposing restrictions on American companies' investment overseas through capital controls, together with voluntary restrictions on US bank lending to foreigners – and so keep the international bargain America had struck. But so large were US demands for foreign capital that they could only delay the ultimate reckoning.

As banks fled the US to escape the controls and the financial pressure mounted, criticism from Wall Street was reinforced by a vocal group of articulate conservative economists, famously including Milton Friedman and Alan Greenspan. Together with economists from Chase Manhattan, Morgan Guaranty and First National City Bank of New York (all chafing against capital controls) they unashamedly advocated the unilateral option as, in 1969, the US Treasury canvassed opinions on how to react. The world's currencies should float against the dollar, they argued, which had no serious rival, and the US should stop guaranteeing that the dollar was worth a fixed amount of gold. Such a system of market-based float-ing exchange rates would work better than the government-managed system of Bretton Woods. Exchange rates would quickly find the correct natural market rate; the system would be stable, and the outflow of American gold would stop immediately. Moreover, America could scrap all its controls on movements of capital so that the US government, financial institutions and corporations could spend as freely as they liked. Instead of the US having to make any kind of economic adjustment, the rest of the world could adjust to America's ambitions. As it was shoul-dering the burden of defending 'freedom' worldwide against the ambitions of communism, it was a fair deal. The world, after all, was lucky to have the US.

And that was what happened. In the eighteen months up to August 1971 the strain of financing both the Vietnam War and the US trade deficit obliged the US government to insist that foreign central banks bought over $40 billion (over $100 billion in 2000 prices) to balance America's international books – a potential catastrophic liability if they insisted simultaneously on converting their dollars into gold. In May 1971 a European block, lead by the Germans and including the Netherlands, Austria and Switzerland, decided to let their exchange rates float upwards – detaching the fixed link with the dollar – rather than be forced to reflate their economies to relieve pressure on the dollar which they considered inflationary. As described in chapter 11, this was the end of a grim two-year battle to hold European exchange rates in a pattern consistent with plans for European integration and even monetary union. The Europeans saw themselves as bearing the brunt of America's fiscal and monetary indiscipline; the Americans saw the Europeans as ungratefully pursuing their own advantage.

In an atmosphere of gathering crisis President Nixon struck back. He simply suspended the convertibility of the dollar into gold and slapped a 10 per cent surcharge on all imports into America. Over the next two years the US, resisting any attempt by the rest of the world to persuade it to accept any economic constraints in the reconstruction and potential reform of the system, arm-twisted and bullied its way to the establish-ment of a world financial system in which the dollar would necessarily be the number one currency against which other currencies would float.

When the last attempts to gain agreement on a multilateral system were shattered by the quadrupling of oil prices in the autumn of 1973, the world moved from a gold exchange standard managed by international agreement to a dollar standard in which the US accepted no obligations whatsoever in the management of its own currency. Treasury secretary John Connally, co-author with Nixon of the policy, captured American indifference to others' views: 'We had a problem and we are sharing it with the rest of the world – just like we shared our prosperity. That's what friends are for.'[6]

Connally's hard-headed assessment that, whatever complaints America's 'friends' – Europe and Japan – might make, the US could and should do just what it liked, laid down the essential tramlines of American foreign economic policy for the next thirty years. The US needed to appropriate 80 per cent of the industrialised West's current surplus for its own strategic and military purposes, as Nixon told the German Bundestag two days after he had suspended dollar convertibility into gold.[7] If its allies would not agree to this voluntarily, the US would find another way to deliver the same result.

On New Year's Day 1974 the US lifted all its capital controls. The dollar fell sharply, but that was of little consequence; it had no rival. American free market conservatives, the Wall Street financiers and their allies in government, schooled in realpolitik, had claimed their first major scalp: the international economic order was to be built unilaterally around American interests. And it was the conservative ultras who had provided the intellectual underpinning for this démarche – even if they had no clear idea of where it might lead.

The first immediate impact was evident in how the US approached the build-up of dollar surpluses in the Arab oil-producing countries as the oil price quadrupled, and was kept high by the Organisation of Petroleum Exporting Countries (OPEC) making production cutbacks. The multilateral approach of the postwar period would have been to organise the deposit of the OPEC dollars with the IMF and World Bank so that they could be recycled into the Western industrialised countries and third world alike in an orderly and predictable way, financing the trade deficits that emerged everywhere as a result of the oil shock and so averting a synchronised recession as demand fell everywhere simultaneously. With capital controls lifted on the dollar alone, another option was created. The petrodollars could be deposited with US banks and recycled as loans to national governments and corporations wholly through the private American financial sector; as the US no longer had any capital controls, dollars held anywhere were part of the same vast pool of dollar liquidity. Between 1976 and 1981 US banks increased their overseas assets from $80 billion to $300 billion, lending largely out of London, where the remaining American rules on interest rate ceilings on deposits did not apply. Bank lending to national governments, especially in the less developed world, exploded, rising sixfold over the decade.[8] National governments do not go bankrupt, wisecracked Walter Wriston, the buccaneering chairman of Citicorp, as the proportion of his bank's profits made from overseas transactions soared to 80 per cent.[9]

As Leonard Seabrooke describes in US Power in International Finance, increasingly the New Deal apparatus of financial regulation began to creak at the seams. In 1980, to keep the petrodollars flowing into New York after the second oil shock, the Americans decided to allow banks to create 'international banking facilities' in the US without any interest rate ceilings nor any requirement to lodge a proportion of the cash with the US Federal Reserve as a so-called reserve requirement. Now, not only was there an indivisible dollar market at home and abroad, but dollars everywhere carried the same interest rate free from any regulatory inhibition. Going it alone around market-based solutions was proving the biggest shot in the arm the US financial system had had for fifty years; its deposit base and lending ambitions were moving beyond the US to become global.

Nor was this the only advantage. Since the early 1970s the US has run a large and growing trade deficit while simultaneously financing a steady build-up of overseas direct investment, cumulatively worth at the end of 1999 some $1.1 trillion, and sustaining its vast military operations overseas. Nixon's target of winning 80 per cent of the industrialised world's current account surplus has been achieved comfortably. When there have been strains, the US has responded with further acts of market-based 'liberalisation' to step up the vital inflows of dollars. In 1984, for example, Ronald Reagan abandoned the tax deducted at source on interest and dividends paid to foreign holders of American financial assets – withholding tax – making it more attractive for foreigners to finance America's burgeoning deficits. The US then complemented that action by twisting its partners' arms to relax and indeed abandon their capital controls, making it easier for other countries to export capital to the US. In 1988 the Basle Accord was signed, under which banks had to raise the levels of core capital in their balance sheets to underwrite their lending; it was deliberately aimed at raising the demand for US government securities, which counted as part of banks' core capital. Japanese banks alone, reports Seabrooke, as a result had to buy over $20 billion of US treasury notes and bonds after Basle.

By 1989 every major European economy had been forced to drop capital controls, as powerful offshore markets in marks, francs, pounds, lire, guilder and kroner developed – all created by the US's decision to have no capital controls so that there was an offshore foreign exchange market in each currency; and the boundaries between the domestic and offshore market were impossible to police. So it has continued. As the pool of dollar liquidity has increased yearly with the size of the US trade deficit, so US banks have wanted to exploit the pool to lend more, both at home and abroad, and break down regulatory barriers to the growth of their business. Thus in 1991 the Fed allowed J. P. Morgan to become the first bank to underwrite issues of public stock since 1933 – the forerunner of the bonfire of financial controls over the 1990s described in chapter 4.

Liberalisation, by integrating the world's principal capital markets but around a dollar standard, has thus served US interests twice over: it has enlarged the dominance of US financial institutions and made financing the US trade deficit much easier. In one year alone, 1995, foreign central banks bought $70 billion of new US treasury securities – half the total issued.[10] Foreign exchange turnover has grown exponentially, as have flows of capital and bank lending. Investment in finance and insurance now constitutes a third of all American investment overseas, with Citicorp, Prudential of America and State Farm Insurance leading the charge. American banks' share of the world financial services market has doubled in the last twenty years.[11] Goldman Sachs, Morgan Guaranty and Merrill Lynch now dominate investment banking in London, an American takeover that is a by-product of the developing monetary system.

At times it has been the Europeans (as in the late 1990s) and at other times the Japanese (as in the late 1980s) who have shouldered the burden of providing the US with its necessary dollar inflows, through a mixture of direct and indirect investment. From the American perspective, the identity of the source of the investment has not mattered, any more than the switchback ride of the dollar has mattered. What *has* mattered is that the system is constructed to maximise US economic and financial autonomy. The dollar's value has alternated from periods of extreme weakness, as in the mid-1980s, to extreme strength, as in the late 1990s – but with little impact on US economic policy, which has been set wholly around domestic priorities. When George Bush senior was asked about the dollar, at that moment declining, he signalled the insouciance of every US president since the break-up of Bretton Woods in his reply: 'Once in a while I think about these things, but not much.'[12]

Thus the capacity to finance the enormous trade deficits of the 1990s without any constraint on the evolution or growth of the US economy has not been a happy by-product of something technical and anonymous called 'financial deregulation'. The stock market boom and the role of the financial system in attracting inward flows of capital on a vast scale have been the results of a series of consistent policy choices over thirty years reflecting those essential US reflex predispositions towards unilateralism and markets. Nobody in the 1970s could accurately foresee what might happen; but by pushing the scope of US financial autonomy outwards, enlarging the role of the New York markets as financial intermediaries and insisting on the pivotal role of the dollar, the US has created an environment in which essentially the rest of the world adjusts to US economic choices – and becomes enslaved to the prevalent US financial and economic ideology. And that is not liberalism.

Handmaidens of the new conservatism

The transmutation from a liberal to a conservative world order is most obvious in the transformation of the two great Bretton Woods institutions – the IMF and the World Bank. Originally cast as liberal custodians of a global public interest, they have become de facto agents of the US

Treasury in its quest to sustain American financial hegemony and policy prescriptions irrespective of the consequent contradictions and strains.

The collapse of Bretton Woods in the early 1970s removed the liberal rationale for both institutions. There was no longer a system of exchange rates to be policed and managed by the IMF; if countries wanted short-term credit, they could negotiate terms with American banks now freed from the controls that had inhibited their lending – a trend that under-mined the importance of the World Bank just as dramatically. Countries at any stage of economic development could borrow directly from Wall Street, or from international banks operating in the eurodollar market in London. This market in vast sums of expatriate dollars had sprung up during the 1960s as governments, central banks and multinationals bor-rowed and lent the dollars they had acquired from the US offshore in London, free from American controls. As mentioned earlier, once capital controls were lifted, American banks rushed to capture the markets they had lost to London, and pushed their lending aggressively.[13] But the loans, denominated in dollars, carried American interest rates, which went up and down as the US Federal Reserve changed American mone-tary policy to suit the needs of the US economy. A disaster was waiting to happen.

It duly occurred in 1981. Paul Volcker, the incoming chairman of the Fed, following the prescriptions of the Chicago school, doubled US inter-est rates to check the growth of American money supply. Less developed countries suddenly found that their debt service requirements doubled too, and in August 1982 Jesus Silva Herzog, Mexico's finance minister, announced what Walter Wriston had said was impossible. Mexico simply did not have the financial wherewithal to service its $94 billion of debt; it was technically bankrupt. Worse still, the American and European banks that had been so ready to lend in 1981 and the first half of 1982 simply turned off the tap. The privatisation of the world financial system was exemplifying the volatility against which Keynes and the New Dealers had wanted to guard when they founded the Bretton Woods system in 1944.

The situation could not be left unaddressed. If Mexico was not bailed out, then the loans made largely by American banks would be worthless; they would have to be written off, imperilling the banks' own creditworthiness and their capacity to support the US economy. Loans to Mexico and Brazil alone equalled 90 per cent of the total capital of America's top nine banks.[14] There had to be a rescue package. But Mexico in 1981 was not confronting the US of Harry Dexter White, Roosevelt and Truman. The conservative revolution described in chapter 2 had now embedded itself in Washington under Reagan's presidency, and it intended to extend the gains it had made abroad as much as at home. If Mexico, or any other indebted borrower, thought it could change the terms of the international system so that it could protect employment and growth at home – the essential underpinning, after all, of Bretton Woods – then it had better think again. Nor should there be any symmetry of adjustment, with the US accepting some responsibility for the situation – it was the US banks, after all, that had pushed their lending so aggressively. In the moral universe of the US conservative, it was the borrower, not the American lender, who had displayed moral turpitude, and there would be no indirect support for Mexico by helping American banks. Mexico had to accept that the rules of the international game would remain exactly the same, and that if it wanted to borrow from private banks in the future it would have to earn that privilege by imposing an extraordinarily tough austerity package right now. Only then would the US support any international bail-out; and, given the US veto in the IMF, this was the precondition for any negotiations.

Imprisoned by the new US intransigence, the IMF began to jettison the notions of balanced adjustment and non-interference with the political philosophy behind national economic policies. Instead, it required not just austerity but detailed changes in Mexico's policy, changes that were to foreshadow the 'structural adjustment' demanded of applicants for loans and aid in the late 1980s and throughout the 1990s. This was a pseudonym for a raft of policies that went well beyond the legitimate requirement to tighten monetary and fiscal policy in order to free resources for export while cutting imports – the only path any capitalist economy can take to restore financial probity, whether it is run on conservative or liberal principles.

Mexico, along with the rest of Latin America, had to accept the medicine; for there was no alternative. In exchange for an IMF support package, Mexico, and latterly Brazil and the rest of indebted Latin

America with similar arrangements, had to accept swingeing cuts in public expenditure and structural adjustment programmes imposed with increasingly ideological fervour: basic programmes of health, education and poverty relief were regarded as wasteful and extravagant – and thus were savaged. And because most of Latin America was retrenching simultaneously under IMF guidance, the knock-on consequences were multiplied; recession spread across the continent. In Mexico, where half the population had no running water, per capita incomes were to fall 40 per cent between 1983 and 1988. For Latin America as a whole it was a lost decade, precisely the kind of economic and social disaster that the liberal designers of Bretton Woods had tried to avert – but a disaster that American conservatives, now in control of the system, were prepared to countenance as the price of US dominance.

Calls for reform of the system, for an orderly approach to debt relief and for a return to a more managed system of exchange rates, were brushed to one side. It was not just that they demanded a willingness to exert some control over the now gigantic financial markets, with an explicit loss of autonomy for the US; any such control went against the mantra that free markets worked perfectly – certainly better than any comparable system managed by government. But as the 1980s wore on, it became clear that the predictions of conservative ideologues like Milton Friedman, that floating exchange rates would tend to produce stable currency values, were wildly wrong. The foreign exchange markets became a byword for market irrationality, with exchange rates experiencing prolonged periods above or below any reasonable judgement of their sustainable level – pitched to excessive heights and depths by a succession of speculative short-term bets that once a trend had been established it was more likely to continue than to break. Speculation on the basis that 'the trend is my friend' reinforced the misalignments, wholly against the predictions of market theorists that it would be against such absurd valuations. But while the overvaluation of the yen, for example, in the late 1980s and early 1990s would be an important cause of the long recession of the Japanese economy, periods of dollar overvaluation had no parallel impact on the US economy. The US was a continent in which exposure to international competition was less significant, and in any case the system was constructed to permit it to run large trade deficits with no consequences for its domestic economic policy

Over the 1990s the characteristics of the system became yet more exaggerated. Foreign exchange turnover continued to grow exponentially as new and more innovative techniques were developed to hedge against individual risk – although the system could not insure itself against the risk that the system was at fault. Distressed borrowers or those who wanted US trade and assistance had to submit to the new canons of the US right, embodied in the now hardened-up version of structural adjustment: they should lift controls on their financial system; they should lower taxes generally, but especially on corporations and the rich; they should privatise; they should open up to foreign investment; they should deregulate; they should reassert private property rights; they should cut back spending on welfare, health and education; and they should place price stability as the top economic priority. In short, they should adopt the same economic programme that the American Business Roundtable and the Chicago school had recommended for the US. Equality of opportunity, the sharing of risk in a social contract, the redistribution of income, investment in social, physical and human capital, and any attempt to manage capitalism or develop public enterprise should be forsworn.

Pressure on all countries to pursue this 'Washington consensus' mounted – in particular, pressure to open their financial systems to American participation under the rubric of liberalisation. Thus, for example, between 1990 and 1993 over $90 billion – a fifth of net capital flows to developed countries – migrated to Mexico in search of the high interest rates to be found by investing in Mexican securities denominated in dollars.[15] In December 1994 the dollars threatened to leave the country in days as US investors and mutual funds worried about Mexico's capacity to service its debts. The 'Tequila crisis' prompted a second joint US Treasury–IMF bail-out, demanding in return for $40 billion an aggressive structural adjustment programme. The IMF's dependence on, and synchronisation of its actions with, the US Treasury was now open. But this was not a bail-out of US and Western banks, as it had been in 1982; it was a bail-out of US investors who had wanted the 14 per cent interest rates available on Mexico's dollar assets rather than the 5 per cent on US Treasury bills, but were unprepared to accept the consequential risk.

Again Mexico had to swallow its reluctance; it floated the peso, which halved in a matter of weeks, while interest rates doubled in two months. But US investors got their money back in full, in part from the US Treasury and in part from the IMF.

As the 1990s wore on the IMF became yet more subsumed under the US Treasury, with more damaging effects. Their joint response to the financial crisis in east Asia between 1997 and 1998 was another calamity, echoing the experience of Latin America in the early 1980s but involving much greater volumes of debt. The financial deregulation in east Asia pressed for by the US in the early 1990s had sparked credit booms and escalating trade deficits across the region; but these interacted with the pegging of Asian exchange rates to the dollar both to ensure price stability and to minimise the risk of exchange rate losses to American investors. The fixed exchange rates were impossible to hold and became irresistible targets for foreign exchange speculation. One by one the so-called Asian tigers found their exchange rates devastated by speculative attacks, and looked to the IMF for assistance.

But the IMF was now totally in hock to the US Treasury. Compared to the size of the speculative flows, the sums it could raise from its own resources were trivial; so it needed the firepower of the US to support its lending programmes. This was a position of weakness that the US happily exploited. Korea, Indonesia and Thailand had not only to undertake the austerity programme demanded of Latin America in the early 1980s, but also to restructure their economies around American conservative principles. For example, journalist Paul Blustein describes in *The Chastening* how in Korea the US and IMF teams checked into the same hotel, the US team insisting that the IMF extract further drastic reforms from the Koreans even as it negotiated in tandem with the Korean ministry of finance.[16] In the fire sale of assets to pay off debts, American multinationals picked up a whole range of companies at knock-down prices: US firms spent $8 billion on Asian businesses in the first half of 1998 alone. Asia pledged to accelerate its Americanisation. The result of the austerity programmes imposed simultaneously across east Asia was a regional depression, making the recovery plans of individual countries harder rather than easier to achieve – precisely in accordance with Keynes's dictum that recession in one country reinforces recession in another.

Yet apart from criticism in Japan and by some liberal American economics professors like Harvard's Jeffrey Sachs and Princeton's Paul Krugman,[17] the IMF got off largely scot-free for what was by any criteria a massive policy mistake. The American financial establishment had been bailed out – again – from the results of its imprudent lending. Abroad, the adjustment was borne by the peoples of the countries to whom it had lent, and on terms that would lead to a greater opening to American capital in future. The system could continue. It had the protection of the US Treasury. Those who argued that it was flawed because smaller countries simply could not cope with the consequences of violent inward and outward flows of freely flowing capital got short shrift; all that was required was more transparency and information for the market to make its judgements, and all would be well. After all, markets worked perfectly if allowed. Yet in 2001 greater transparency did not prevent Turkey and Argentina suffering sudden capital flight on just the same scale, and with the same consequences.

It is not that there is no viable alternative to the current system; it is that any alternative would qualify American hegemony and reduce the benefits the US enjoys from the current structure. And anyway, the new conservative orthodoxy insists that the IMF and US Treasury have been right to focus on austerity and structural adjustment, and not to be concerned with the wider economic, financial and social consequences of what they do – even on the occasions when these consequences impinge on the New York banking system. The bail-out of the hedge fund Long Term Capital Management, led by the New York Federal Reserve in September 1998, with some $200 billion of off-balance sheet liabilities and a chief executive, John Meriwether, as gung-ho about free markets as Enron's Ken Lay, might have prompted some reappraisal about the risks of running the international financial system as it was. Nothing of it. The bigger game was and is to attack statism and governmental influence wherever it is found.

The transformation of the IMF's role was mirrored over at the World Bank, which over the 1980s was progressively invaded and influenced by the new right. Its annual *World Development Reports* became more conservative as the right's grip on Washington tightened; in 1987 the Bank argued that the very interventionist principles upon which it had been founded were now disruptive for private sector growth.[18] Its 'structural adjustment loans' matched the thinking of the IMF as reflected in its structural adjustment programmes, and indeed the Bank became as fervent an advocate of the conservative cause as the Fund.

Then in 1995, under its new president, James Wolfensohn, the World Bank began to strike out in a different direction – arguing for debt relief, and insisting that good government, education and health were as important as adhesion to the Washington consensus in promoting economic development. But it was fighting the tide. In November 1999 Wolfensohn's chief economist, Joseph Stiglitz, resigned – evidence that in any attempt the World Bank might make to return to its liberal roots, its scope for manoeuvre was very limited. Stiglitz had been restless about the Washington consensus throughout his tenure of office, arguing in a 1998 lecture that the obsession with price stability is counter-productive and that economies can tolerate a low level of inflation without it accelerating, as the consensus argued.[19] Recessions, he argued, need to be countered by allowing automatic stabilisers to work; and the financial system, far from being accurately characterised as a market, is an economy's 'brain', and is impaired rather than improved by deregulation. Stiglitz further insisted that privatisation would fail in the absence of investment in the institutional framework of an economy – its legal system, for example. He later explained that he fought against the IMF austerity programmes in Asia, on the grounds that they would lead to a synchronised Asian recession, but to no avail.[20] If anything, the IMF wanted to be more severe.

Stiglitz's criticisms are right, and come from inside the belly of the beast. But the system has built up too much momentum to give way to such rationality, which in any case for the conservatives is beside the point. The point is to entrench the dominance of the dollar, now accounting for 77 per cent of all international loans and 83 per cent of all foreign exchange transactions[21] – proportions as large as in 1945, even though the relative weight of the US economy in world GDP has shrunk since then. Stiglitz might complain that 'all too often the dogma of liberalisation became an end in itself, not a means to achieving a better financial system,'[22] but this was no irrational economic dogma. It was the dogma of the expanding superstate. The international financial system has been shaped to extend US financial and political power, not to promote the world public good. And that is what it has done. In the process it has opened up a bridgehead that has created opportunities for many more US corporate interests besides those of finance.

Globalisation as Americanisation

As early as 1974 it was becoming clear that the character and structure of American capitalism were changing. For twenty years American prosperity had been consistent with a growing trade deficit; as long as the rest of the world accepted dollars and workers in the displaced industries in the US moved on to find work elsewhere, the deficit seemed of little lasting consequence. Trade unions and the industries affected protested loudly, but the overall balance sheet was plainly good for most American consumers and the Fortune 500. Indeed, as half of all US imports were from the affiliates of US companies abroad that had sourced production overseas to boost profits, the deficit was the inevitable concomitant of profit-maximising US multinationals tending to manufacture in low-cost countries – and as such a positive benefit to corporate America. What was beginning to matter was less the location of factories and nationality of workers than the intellectual capital embodied in whatever was being produced and the necessary access to overseas markets which delivered the extra sales and profits growth that were crucial given the saturation of the US market. In 1970 IBM had emerged as the world's largest computer company with its 360 series; Texas Instruments was the world's leading manufacturer of integrated silicon chips; AT&T was the largest corporation in the world by turnover. Over the 1970s US leadership in the new information industries strengthened, so that by the early 1980s Microsoft, Apple and Intel were already well established. In January 1983 *Time* magazine gave the personal computer its 'man of the year' accolade; the IT revolution had begun in earnest, and what the US wanted was to open the world to its lusty high-tech champions.

For if intellectual property and control of information flows were beginning to matter more, that in turn meant that market access to service industries like finance and telecommunications began to rank alongside market openness in conventional manufactures as a prime policy concern. A new hierarchy of priorities was emerging in which sustaining leadership in the information economy and opening up the service sectors – notably finance and telecommunications – of the world's principal economies became at least as important as ensuring free trade in commodity manufactures, where in any case the US hardly had a comparative advantage.

Again, it is hard to argue that there was any blueprint. The US simply threw its weight behind those companies and sectors that it felt could exploit trade openings and used free market, free trade theory as the intellectual lever to achieve its strategic ends. It could allow its transnational corporations to locate production according to their best judgement on profitability, and as long as the dollar was the world currency it was of no concern if the resulting pattern of production meant US trade deficits. In any case, if the US could dominate services, IT, the flow of information, telecoms and intellectual property rights, then it controlled the framework in which all trade flows took place.

From the launch of the first American satellite in 1962 the US had been alert to how this new technology would equip its companies to take the lead in controlling and disseminating information; the 1962 Communications Satellite Act allowed private companies to take stakes in NASA's direct broadcasting satellites for commercial usage, and provided for AT&T to extend its monopoly on long-distance communications into space. The company's Telstar made the first transatlantic satellite transmission of television later that year. The US shrugged off attempts by the French in 1970 and the Russians in 1972 to establish a multilateral framework for the use of satellite broadcasting and telecommunications within which the prior consent would be required of nations that would be impacted from space; the US refused to accept any infringement on its sovereignty. Rather, it became more interested in how its nascent and unchallenged grip on the new communications technologies could be exploited to support the growth of its overseas economic interests. The Hollywood studios had build up an unrivalled distribution network in the first half of the century that had entrenched their global leadership of the film industry; now the same possibilities were opening up for American television, IT and telephone companies. If government control of television and telephone services in Europe and

Japan could be broken down, the US would dominate the new information age as it had the twentieth-century industrial age. The pivotal year
was 1974, when the Trade Act empowered the US government for the
first time to include services in the industries over which it was mandated
to negotiate tariffs and access, and also empowered the US to act unilaterally – the infamous 301 clause – in defence of particular trade interests.
When the US had to choose between loyalties to multilateral arrangements such as GATT and equipping itself to act unilaterally, already the
US was unhesitatingly coming down in favour of the latter.

Over the next three decades the same predispositions that had been
deployed to recast the world financial system would be used to recast the
world telecommunications and information system – and used ever more
aggressively as US power and the conservative ascendancy grew. This was
globalisation led by the US pursuit of its interests. Financial liberalisation
and telecoms deregulation went hand in hand. American financial expansion abroad relied on the new IT and telecoms technologies; if US banks
were forbidden from using them they could not create their 24-hour
global financial networks. By 1985 Citicorp had linked its offices in
ninety-four countries, and was trading $200 billion daily in the foreign
exchange markets; without satellites, PCs and a dedicated global telecommunications network such turnover would have been impossible. It
needed telecoms deregulation as much as capital market deregulation to
pull off the coup. Between 1972 and 1985 the 1000 largest US banks
increased their dedicated spending on telecommunications from 5 to 13
per cent of their total operating expenses.[23] Over the 1980s and 1990s a
parallel axis to that between the US Treasury and the IMF and World
Bank grew up between the US Department of Commerce and first
GATT and latterly the World Trade Organisation – and for similar reasons. The multilateral institutions' choice was stark – if they did not
accommodate the US's unilateral ambitions then the US would achieve
its ends without them. So, better keep some multilateralism than have
none at all. The GATT could no more launch a round of tariff reduction
negotiations without US support than the IMF a bail-out, and when the
so-called Uruguay round of tariff reductions and market opening began
in 1985 the US insisted that intellectual property rights, service sector
trade and in particular telecommunications were on the agenda – thus

bypassing what the Reaganites saw as the statist International Telecommunications Union (ITU), the intergovernmental agency which regulated international telecoms business. Four years later the ITU agreed to take part in the GATT talks, recognising the reality that the US was going to drive through telecoms liberalisation and that its only chance of saving even minimal public interest obligations was to work through GATT. In 1990 GATT ruled that American multinationals should have access to all the service markets of GATT's signatory states. Four years later the US used GATT to compel the European Union to agree to open all its voice communications (post, telephone and telegraphs) to competition. In 1995 the US forced through GATT a framework agreement on trade-related intellectual property or TRIPs, protecting the enforcement of intellectual property rights, with the result that the US Patent Office – as the gatekeeper controlling the exercise of patents in the world's largest market – would become the de facto upholder of all advances in the information age. In April 1996, by which time GATT had been succeeded by the World Trade Organisation (WTO) the US delegation walked out of the WTO talks, declining to take further part unless telecoms liberalisation was made global; a year later the WTO gave in and opened up seventy countries to US telecoms companies on American terms. With the World Bank and IMF insisting on telecoms deregulation as the price of every structural adjustment programme, the US was succeeding in deregulating global telecoms in the 1990s as it had finance over the 1970s and 1980s. By the early 1990s the US trade surplus in services had quadrupled to $60 billion a year.

To capitalise further on these hard-won openings the US telecoms industry needed to reorganise and consolidate at home. It pressed hard for deregulation that would allow it to form new domestic groupings and alliances as a platform for expansion overseas – and it wanted to move fast. New Deal and liberal notions that access to telecommunications should be universal and that there were public service obligations associated with information dissemination in general and broadcasting in particular had been undermined throughout the 1980s as part of the conservative grip on US thinking. Conservative appointees to the key Federal Communications Commission (FCC) repudiated notions of the public interest and social equity in determining communications policy, insisting instead that information should be structured as a market-place.[24] The Democrats, swept up in enthusiasm for the New Economy, became apostles for liberalisation – hoping vainly that they could create a genuinely competitive marketplace which would deliver an information-based economy free from overwhelming corporate power with only light or minimal regulation. They should have thought again. In any case, the now vastly expanded role of money in American politics meant that if they wanted to receive the largesse of the PACs or political action committees (see chapter 2), they would have to talk the language of deregulation and liberalisation. By 1995 AT&T was the largest single PAC donor, and the lobbyists for deregulation were the cream of former White House staff from both main parties.[25]

Before the onslaught of lobbying and assertive private interests there was no defence, and the 1996 Telecoms Act was the inevitable result. Democrat congresswoman Marcy Kaptur called the process leading up to the act 'living proof of what unlimited money can do to buy influence and the Congress of the United States'. That did not trouble Citicorp any more than AT&T. The telecoms companies wanted less regulation, they wanted the right to build their own self-standing networks and they wanted to use their allocations on the terrestrial spectrum as free as pos-sible from public service obligations; long-distance carriers wanted to enter local markets; all wanted cross-ownership rules relaxed. All that they wanted, they got. In contemporary Washington, dollars, informed by the self-righteousness of the new conservatism and aided and abetted by lobbying, buy anything.

The Telecoms Act was the trigger for the most infamous financial bubble in world financial history, which would ultimately waste, according to the *Financial Times*, $1000 billion of real cash around the world in absurd investment – and yet more trillions of dollars in falling telecoms share prices.[26] The deregulation of the financial system in the 1980s followed by the forced opening up of the world telecoms market in the 1990s were the preconditions of the madness; every semi-privatised or wholly privatised telecoms company in the world could become a player, borrowing money on global financial markets to finance its global ambitions to be the owner of as many complementary networks as possible. All bubbles are ani-mated by a big idea, and the telecoms bubble's big idea was that in the new knowledge economy waves of digitalised information would be pumped through a multiplicity of broadband cable networks; the notion that each country needed only one network, giving universal access, was old-fashioned socialism. There would be enough information for many networks, and private enterprise would show that competition would deliver what old state-owned telecoms companies could not. This was American conservatism's gift to the globe. It was to prove a total disaster.

The first-round effect of the Telecoms Act was an orgy of takeovers in the US; in the first half of 1998 136 merger deals worth $120 billion were announced between US telecoms companies. Long-distance carriers merged, and paid extraordinary prices to buy local networks; one such carrier, Worldcom, paid between six and nine times the value of the telecoms infrastructure of two local carriers (MFS and Brooks Fiber) in order to construct a national network. It now faces dismemberment as its debts overwhelm it. Cable companies merged with telephone companies; AT&T paid $44 billion for the cable giant TCI. Simultaneously a wave of mergers and conglomeration hit the providers of all the digitalised software that would allegedly be pumped through the new networks. Time Warner, already a presence in terrestrial, cable, digital and satellite TV, film, music, books, newspapers and online publishing, merged with the internet portal and search engine AOL to gain dominance of every possible piece of the converging markets in digital information. Disney bought ABC for the same reason. And once they had captured market share in the US, all had eyes for the new opportunities opening up in Europe and Japan – whose companies themselves began to consolidate in anticipation of the American advance. A fifth of all mergers worldwide in 1999 were initiated by global telecoms companies.

The consequences for American consumers have been baleful. Although long-distance call rates have fallen, local telephone and cable rates have soared. Absurdly, some 60 companies emerged as aspirant network builders and carriers in an industry which, even in a continental economy like the US, is a natural monopoly: there is no more reason for rival cable networks than competing road networks. Telephone companies have been 'slamming' (signing up customers without permission) and 'cramming' (billing customers for services not provided) with impunity; a million people a year have been signed up without their agreement, and millions more are charged for services they have not used. Only 2 per cent of US telephone lines are served by new competitors. A mere 6 per cent of American consumers are connected to the internet through broadband networks. Educational programmes for children have virtually disappeared; low-power television stations to serve ethnic minorities have been neglected and their programme standards have fallen; community-based broadcasting is disappearing.

The catastrophic effects did not stop there. There was a global frenzy as telecoms companies all tried to ape the American lead, combining the ownership of cable networks, mobile phone networks, communication satellites and sometimes even the manufacture of equipment: there would be enough traffic to support many competing networks outside the US as well. All paid absurd prices to realise their ambitions, offering ridiculous sums in Britain's auction of the radio spectrum for third-generation mobile phones, for example, or making acquisitions at ludicrously inflated prices. Global stock markets chased up their share prices, encouraging everyone to join in the game. But there never was the avalanche of digitalised information, and when the dot.com bubble burst it was followed inevitably by the end of the telecoms boom – in which trillions of dollars were at stake. We are left with vast overcapacity, threatened bankruptcies and a massive debt overhang in which only a fraction of the capital invested is remotely recoverable. British Telecom, Deutsche Telekom and France Telecom were by the autumn of 2001 saddled with $160 billion of debt compared to combined earnings of $40 billion. Share prices have been decimated. In Britain, new cable operators like NTL and Energis are engulfed by debt and struggling for survival: again, the notion that there would be sufficient traffic to justify the business model of companies competing in an industry which is a natural monopoly was ridiculous. Equipment manufacturers like Marconi, as described in the following chapter, have been sucked into the disaster – all chasing that other icon of the US conservative revolution, shareholder value. The US Securities and Exchange Commission is even investigating sham transactions between rival telecommunications carriers, including British companies, set up to inflate revenues. And despite it all, no country can boast a complete broadband cable network. If the public sector in the leading industrialised countries had spent a fraction of the lost cash in each building one public network, the spread of the information economy would have been faster by years. That was forbidden by the conservative orthodoxy.

The act and its consequences have been a global fiasco, just as IMF structural adjustment and austerity programmes have been. But to conservative America that does not matter. The greater game lies elsewhere. The global system has been constructed to disallow government autonomy and give the maximum freedom to business, whatever the irrationalities and extravagant waste. The object is not to promote notions of equity, the social contract, equality of opportunity or the public realm. The object is to promote the autonomy of action of American transnationals in general, and American control of the global financial and information technology systems in particular. Others can join in the system the US has done most to create, and benefit if they can. But with 62 per cent of global information technology business originating in the US and American companies owning 75 per cent of the global software market, there should be no illusions over who are the winners. One hundred and eighty commercial satellites orbit in space; all but half a dozen are American-owned. The US controls the information age as it does the world financial system. American conservative ideology has served its purpose. The question is whether it serves anybody else's purpose – and how the world might be different.

7

Britain in the American bear-hug

Britain's intellectual and political history over the last twenty-five years has mirrored America's remorseless drive to the right. Because Margaret Thatcher was such a formidable conservative force, it is easy to characterise the rise of British conservatism as a purely British affair, drawing on Britain's conservative traditions to contest the products of British socialism and the labour movement. But hers was a conservatism that always had one eye on the other side of the Atlantic – inspired by it and looking for ideas from it. 'The fundamental strength of the American economy is the underlying enterprise culture of the American people,' she said in a speech in the mid-1980s. 'It is, therefore, vital to secure in this country that same enterprise culture.' It was an oft-repeated mantra.

The same sentiment has been expressed in almost the same tones by both Tony Blair and Gordon Brown, who, no less enthusiastic about US economic dynamism, equally uncritically accept the American explanation of how its 'success' has been achieved. 'In the 1980s Margaret Thatcher rightly emphasised the importance of the enterprise culture,' wrote Gordon Brown in the *Wall Street Journal* in June 2001, 'but this did not go far enough.'[1] Brown wants to extend this culture to ordinary people as an instrument of individual advancement. The British political class accepts the American success story, as much as its account of high social mobility, on its own terms, with little challenge; there is little investigation into whether these claims are true and even less into the associated costs and deficiencies.

Yet the 'success' and ideas so many British leaders want to copy are, as previous chapters have made clear, not only very contentious but – and increasingly – no less than the successes and ideas of American conservatism. This very particular doctrine has had a huge influence in Britain over the past quarter-century, challenging 'one nation' Conservatism and Labour's social democratic tradition alike. The depiction of taxation as an unparalleled economic burden and moral offence could never have happened, for example, without the ammunition supplied from the US, just as the 'flexible' labour market could never have reached its iconic status. The lazy way in which American conservatives identify any activity of the state with socialism has been imported wholesale, so that British conservative writers can pitch the British Post Office on a continuum of statism/socialism that culminates in the Soviet gulag.[2] As the entire American political discourse has moved to the right, Britain's has faithfully followed.

Britain is peculiarly vulnerable to trends in American politics. The British relationship with the US is necessarily more complex and unique than that of any other country. The original thirteen colonies were, after all, British; the war of independence was fought against Britain; the two countries not only speak English, but share the same philosophical roots. Neither country's economic development was state-led; Britain's industrial revolution happened as spontaneously as the US's industrialisation. In both countries, the state's contribution was primarily to provide the over-arching framework within which private property based capitalism could flourish, whether by setting tariff walls (which both countries paradoxically did aggressively until they became the dominant economic power) or by defining a powerful legal framework in which contracts could be enforced. Neither country deliberately set about building a financial, educational and scientific infrastructure – as did France, Germany and Japan – in order to industrialise. Development and its institutions were market-led.

Nor is that all. If over the nineteenth century both Britain and the US grew similar models of capitalism justified by the same essential philosophy, over the twentieth century both shared the same enemies – fascism and communism. As its economic power waned in the first half of the twentieth century, Britain increasingly took the view, dramatised as the US army proved the decisive influence in settling the World War I, that its international interests were best served by defining itself as a partner, if increasingly a very junior partner, in a relationship whose aims were shared. Britain has actively sought to enmesh its military, financial and economic decision-making with that of the US, accepting that while this brought important losses in sovereignty, they were more than offset by the gains.

This 'special' relationship, affirmed once more during the war in Afghanistan in 2001–2, allows Britain to define itself as the representative in Europe of the English-speaking Anglo-Saxon model – a stock market based capitalism, complete with a minimal welfare system and flexible labour markets, which has both global ambitions and thus necessarily global defence and security concerns. Britain may have some of the features of the European model, but the more it can behave like the US the more efficient it will be. Euroscepticism is presented as a noble assertion of the country's real roots and values.

Think back to chapter 2. Of the four clusters of values that define Europe's distinction from the US, Britain is unambiguously European in its attitude towards the social contract, equality and the public realm. The British are firmly in the European camp in their attitudes towards the reasonableness of the state acting to provide a basic income to the disadvantaged and maintaining the social contract. Just a casual glance at the World Value Survey (a detailed survey of values in forty-three countries) identifies Britain as a member of the European camp over attitudes towards areas as disparate as religion and work. For example, 36 per cent of Britons, 30 per cent of West Germans, 29 per cent of French and 37 per cent of Spanish say that 'life is meaningful only because God exists'; in the US, the proportion is 61 per cent.[3] Equally, the British would no more abandon universal health provision or their welfare state than any European.

It is on attitudes towards property, the financial system and the market economy that British values and institutions are closer to the American – John Locke, the apostle of private property, and Adam Smith, the apostle of free markets, have left their indelible mark on both countries – but even here the proximity is overstated. The British do not believe in the absolutism of proprietorial rights as strongly as the Americans. Processes that qualify property rights – taxation or planning laws – are fundamentally more legitimate in Britain, and there is much less tolerance of inequality. In the latest *British Social Attitudes* survey, 81 per cent of respondents thought the gap between rich and poor too wide, with 73 per cent arguing that the government had a responsibility to narrow the gap.[4]

Yet while the patrician Tory one nation tradition has been happy to accept Britain's essential Europeanness and take what in Europe would be characterised as a liberal, Christian democrat position towards the social contract and regulation of capitalism, another strain in British conservatism has wanted to identify more completely with the US. As American conservatism launched its ideological counter-offensive against American liberalism, this brand of British conservatism rose in tandem – importing the whole paraphernalia of anti-state ideas that have been outlined in the last half-dozen chapters. But if these concepts have had a malevolent impact on the US, they have had a doubly malevolent impact in Britain, distorting our national conversation and preventing us from understanding who we are and how we work. In the process the Tory party has been wrecked, British social democracy compromised and an endemic Euroscepticism allowed to flourish. Nor has underlying British economic performance notably improved with productivity lagging, or our Rawlsian infrastructure of justice been protected. It is not a happy story.

The story begins

It is no accident that the British free market think-tank the Institute of Economic Affairs was set up in the same year, 1955, as the American Enterprise Institute. From its foundation the IEA, which drew upon the increasingly frenzied output from the University of Chicago, the public choice school at the University of Virginia (who argue that all public agency is self-defeating because it is captured by vested interests) and the great US right-wing think-tanks, was one of the principal conduits by which American conservative ideas were introduced into British conservatism and the right-wing press. Over the 1960s and 1970s the IEA was to parrot the great US conservative causes, from the rise of monetarism to the application of free markets as a universal economic panacea. At the high-water mark of British social democracy it canvassed private rather than state pensions, education vouchers and the privatisation of state utilities. In 1974 the dedicated Conservative party in-house think-tank, the Centre for Policy Studies (CPS), was established; and in 1977 the Adam Smith Institute followed, completing a fateful trio of free market propagandists, all looking to the US for ideas and inspiration.

The decisive moment came with Mrs Thatcher's general election victory in 1979. Thatcher was at heart a simple, right-wing Tory with a gut hatred of trade unions and nationalised industries together with a powerful belief in the virtues of the English middle class, whose privileges she set out to defend and enlarge. What the new think-tanks gave her, relayed straight from their American conservative mentors, was an intellectual rationale to justify her instincts. Her grip on the high theory of monetarism and free markets was never very solid, so that the inconsistencies, say, in wanting to roll back subsidies to nationalised industries in the name of markets while retaining them for farmers and home-buyers never troubled her. What she wanted was a justification for attacking traditional Tory enemies and helping traditional allies, both of which she did with gusto. Moreover, she was at home in the US; she liked its lack of unions, nationalised industries and welfare state, and bought the proposition of American conservatism that liberty meant enterprise.

Much of the Thatcherite programme should be seen as a twofold mission: to pull down the social democratic settlement and to construct in its place a simulacrum of the US. Thus the nine employment acts that made the UK the least regulated labour market in the OECD. Thus the accent on tax cuts for the rich and incentives for enterprise. Thus, as her government grew more confident, the constant insistence on 'market' and 'private sector' solutions. Thus the great drive towards financial and telecoms deregulation. Thus the creation of planning-free zones as a tool of urban regeneration. Thus the tougher and tougher approach to the welfare state – a case study worth exploring in a little more detail.

The great social achievement of the Labour government elected in 1945 had been finally to lay to rest the distinction between the deserving and undeserving poor that had disfigured a hundred and fifty years of British social life from the industrial revolution. The nineteenth-century workhouse and the twentieth-century means test had rested alike on the pitiless view that the poor were poor because of their moral deficiencies, and did not deserve to be treated as potential fellow citizens. In establishing a strong welfare state in which welfare benefits were available as a matter of right, Labour broke with this entire tradition.

This departure was never likely to appeal to Margaret Thatcher. In 1987 a London conference of American dependency theorists – the avant-garde of the American right – was held at the instigation of the CPS to put the argument that welfare caused poverty by undermining the moral character of those who depended on it and thus made them unable to escape welfare – one of the key tenets of American conservatism, whose lineage, as we have seen, can be traced back to Leo Strauss. This is part of a wider argument in which to be poor and accept welfare is characterised as a personal choice arising from moral weakness – marking out the undeserving poor. One of the contributors, Charles Murray, had gone further, claiming to demonstrate that welfare directly created a dependent and self-generating underclass – and his theories were uncritically celebrated in the *Sunday Times*. America's underclass is largely black, and its plight is impossible to understand outside the particular history of American slavery and racism; equally, the idea the poor choose to be poor flies in the face of reason. This was the theory of the workhouse in modern guise. But none of that mattered to the British conservative propagandists. They wanted to undo Labour's settlement, and were happy to make use of any ammunition.

The policy conclusion was that welfare should be made contingent on a willingness to work, the underlying assumption being explicitly that the poor are feckless and do not deserve to be treated as equal citizens. By 1987 Department of Employment ministers had made six official visits to the US to examine welfare to work programmes,[5] and the conference was but another step on the journey. Over their eighteen years in office the Conservatives were to make welfare benefits increasingly contingent on the willingness of the unemployed to look for work – an approach directly modelled on the US 1988 Family Support Act (FSA) and various state welfare-to-work initiatives – and progressively to reduce unemployment insurance as a citizen's right. But while the FSA did not compel workers to come off welfare if they could show they would be worse off as a result, and required states to increase their training investment, Thatcher's initiatives made no such concession; they were more punitive even than the new American system.[6] By the end of the Tory period in office, unemployment insurance for twelve months had become the jobseeker's allowance, available as a non-means-tested citizen's right for only six months – under tight scrutiny – and its value in real terms fell as increases in the rate were linked to inflation rather than the growth of average earnings, which rises faster than inflation. As a result, those living on welfare became progressively poorer in relation to those on average earnings.

The notion that the proper objectives of an active labour market policy, including helping the disadvantaged to find and hold work, were perfectly consistent with the maintenance of social insurance as an entitlement and reasonable levels of welfare benefit that did not pauperise the recipients, together with even greater investment in education and training passed the conservatives by in both Britain and America. It was not until New Labour's New Deal that a more enlightened conception was launched with a guaranteed commitment to training. The introduction of the minimum wage meant that all those who came off welfare were better off. But enlightenment was limited. While insisting that recipients of unemployment benefit and income support be aggressively tested for their willingness to look for and find work – a fair enough *quid pro quo* for receiving benefit – actual benefit levels remained niggardly. There was no substantive improvement to their level or structure, which remained means-tested and indexed to the lower growth in retail prices rather than the growth in average earnings. The revival of social democracy did not dare challenge the heartland of conservatism; the poor had better stay poor.

The American imports did not stop there. In health, an eccentric paper by the conservative Alain Enthoven of Stanford University in 1985, suggesting that 'there seems to be no substitute for competition and consumer choice' to improve the dismal performance of the NHS, which was deemed to be 'frozen by an excess of egalitarianism', was adopted wholesale in the NHS reforms of 1990, with disastrous results. Ignoring the fact that health outcomes had improved remarkably over the 1980s while costs had remained stable – between 1980 and 1988 NHS hospitals increased inpatient treatment by 16 per cent, emergency treatment by 19 per cent and day surgery by 73 per cent, without a significant real increase in costs – Enthoven argued for an internal market to improve responsiveness, punish the weak performers and reward the effective. He suggested that health authorities should essentially contract with each other and with GPs for business.[7]

Enthoven's ideas were not even given a trial run; they conformed to the conservatives' prejudices, and thus were legislated for on the basis of only a computerised simulation of what the impact might be. The break-up of the NHS into elements that contracted with one another in a quasi-market, as Enthoven recommended, immediately lifted costs by creating an expensive bureaucracy through which the contracts were audited. More seriously, access to treatment became dependent upon the bargaining skills of doctors and hospitals, with no parallel system for allowing successful units to invest and expand or unsuccessful units to turn themselves around. A two-tier system was created, entrenching health inequalities and jeopardising the core principle – universality of access – upon which the NHS was founded. New Labour was to abolish the internal market; but again the reform was incomplete. The NHS remains structured around a balkanised network of trusts and primary care groups that have to contract with each other to produce health care. The notion that the NHS must be respected as a social organisation with a unique culture is in danger of being lost.

The greatest bequest of American conservatism was its assault on taxation and the ludicrous advocacy of the Laffer curve (described in chapter 2), purporting to show that the incentive effects of low tax rates were so great that they produced a greater overall tax take than higher rates. British Conservatives took up the battle cry of Reagan's Republicans with even greater enthusiasm. It became part of the accepted wisdom that high taxation is a massive economic disincentive and source of wider economic underperformance (which at absurdly high marginal rates it is; but beyond that there is no economic proof of any disincentive – indeed, there is some evidence that the higher the overall tax burden the better economic performance as a result of a stronger public infrastructure[8]), that it is no solution to 'throw money' at severely underfunded public services and that public spending is definitionally inefficient and wasteful. The only direction for income tax rates is downwards; as more taxation has been raised from indirect taxes that impact more heavily on the poor, so the system has become less progressive. To tax and to spend became the greatest sins in the lexicon, even though British public services and the quality of the British public infrastructure were to become among the worst in Europe.

So it was that Thatcherism owed its intellectual inspiration to the conservative movement in the US. Even the apparently home-grown initiative of privatisation would have been less intellectually defensible had it not been launched at a time when the US economic, business, financial and political establishments had become converted to a purist conception of the efficiency and creativity of the market. Privatisation merely took the logic of deregulation, already well-established in the US, to its logical conclusion.

The passionate belief in the efficacy of markets had its most complete expression in the recasting of the British financial system, which has become almost an exact replica of New York, but within the European time zone. Its financial assets are as freely tradable; there are no controls on the international convertibility of sterling any more than there are on the dollar; regulation is minimal. In the stock market, individuals own only 20 per cent of the shares; the rest are held by institutional shareholders – just over half by British pension funds and insurance companies, and some 30 per cent by foreign, mainly American, institutions.[9] The value of shares held by institutional investors represented 197 per cent of British GDP in 1998 – 176 per cent in the US.[10] The same investment and business philosophy, the maximisation of shareholder value, prevails; the same investment banks and management consultancies who promote the doctrine in the US operate in almost exactly the same way in London. Takeover and the deal are king, facilitated by the same domination of share ownership by financial institutions.

This is no accident. London's role as an international financial centre, waning as the sterling area and empire became progressively irrelevant, was reinvented during the 1960s as the intermediary where offshore dollars could be deposited, re-lent and invested in the new eurodollar and eurobond markets – driven by the process outlined in chapter 5. When in 1980 capital and exchange controls were lifted, following Nixon's example, and then in 1986 membership of the stock exchange was opened in the so-called Big Bang to international banks and investment banks that could buy the existing stockbrokers, the process was complete. London was wide open to any bank or financial intermediary that could pass the Bank of England's undemanding creditworthiness tests; shares and bonds could be traded between banks in an electronic, screen-based market – with foreign banks and bankers enjoying a light tax and regulatory regime designed to attract Americans.

Against this background New Labour has struggled to establish even a moderate strain of social democracy. It has not dared to challenge the doctrine of shareholder value or the system of corporate governance, as economic historians Richard Roberts and David Kynaston outline in their honest assessment of the entrenched dominance of the City of London and its values, *City State*. Its attempts to improve the quality of working life through regulation have been modest and voluntaristic; it has proudly defended the least regulated labour market in the OECD. It spent four years resisting the introduction of the EU directive requiring British companies to inform and consult their workforces over key decisions, and accepted the directive only grudgingly in the immediate aftermath of a second landslide electoral victory. It has promised not to raise income tax rates for a second successive parliament. It has been carefully selective in raising welfare benefits only to the 'deserving' poor – lifting income support for children and devising a tax credit for working families. It has presided over the fall of public investment to its lowest proportion of GDP since 1945, and permitted gross underspending of even modest plans. It has carried on the means-testing of the welfare system, extending it to incapacity benefit. Its loss of confidence in public enterprise and need to justify public spending by demonstrable efficiency gains is evident in its rigid commitment to public–private partnerships and the financing of public investment through the private finance initiative – even in contexts where the gains are dubious, like the London Underground and hospital building in the

NHS. Under the London Underground Public Private Partnership, it will, astonishingly, be 2008 before the first new trains – twelve in total – will be introduced, an abrogation of the public interest that tests new limits.

New Labour has made gains, but famously they have been either by stealth or very cautious. A large increase in public spending that began in 1999 is beginning to turn round two decades of public neglect. The government has dared to open a debate about how an improved NHS is to be paid for, but without openly calling for more taxation. In the criminal justice system it is committed to the rehabilitation and education of prisoners and has softened British drug laws. There are signs of significant improvement in educational performance. Britain's aid budget is to be increased.

These are all important signs of movement; but in its essentials, Britain's economic and social model remains profoundly shaped by conservatism. The great themes of our age – the rise of inequality, the over-riding priority of business and the decline of the public realm – have not yet been intellectually and politically challenged, nor has any popular narrative been developed that might do the job. Conservatism's grip may be weakening at the margins, but it remains ascendant.

The world gone mad

Yet the benefits of this marriage to the precepts of American conservatism have been at best qualified, at worst illusory. Britain's inflation and employment performance has certainly improved, both absolutely and relatively, and this is trumpeted as proof that Britain is making better progress towards emulating American 'success' than other European countries;[11] but the gains are only modest. Historic data from 1999 and projections up to 2003 assembled by the OECD (the Paris-based club of government economic analysts and forecasters) suggest that Britain's growth in GDP and employment will be lower than France's and only fractionally higher than Germany's; even Italian employment growth will be higher. It is true that Britain's unemployment rate will have been markedly lower than all three over the period, but the economic slowdown in 2002 and 2003 will see a similar proportional rise.[12] After decades in which Britain was unambiguously the worst-performing economy in Europe its recent improvement is cause for relief, but hardly so stellar as to support the argument that its progress towards Americanisation should be followed by the others – or that pursuit of the US model has brought unadulterated rewards.

Indeed, drill a little deeper and the results are profoundly disappointing. After more than twenty years of importing the nostrums of American conservatism Britain is no nearer developing an 'enterprise culture' – if that is to be measured by the growth and level of productivity, new patents and presence in new technologies – than it ever was. The British government's own survey of business investment shows that the top 500 British companies invested only 7.9 per cent of their revenue, while the top 500 international companies invested 9.6 per cent of their revenue. Only 44 British companies ranked in the top 500 international companies; if they are excluded, the other 456 British companies invested a paltry 5.8 per cent of sales.[13] Moreover, while the top 500 international firms raised their investment by 12 per cent per year, the British 500 managed only 10 per cent. So it is that while France, Germany and Italy have dramatically closed the productivity gap with the US, Britain's relative improvement has been slight; the gap, although narrower than it was, is still yawning. Output per hour worked is 32 per cent higher in France, 29 per cent higher in the former West Germany and 21 per cent higher in the US,[14] and on current investment behaviour it will widen.

Britain has an American-style deregulated labour market, weak trade unions, indifferent social protection and a fierce market for corporate control to keep the management of quoted companies, as the conservatives would argue, on their toes. It has, as a survey in *Management Today* reported in July 2001, rewarded its chief executives more handsomely than other European countries, so that in 1999 and 2000 executive pay rose by 29 per cent to an average annual salary of £509,000 compared to £382,000 in France and £298,000 in Germany. Meanwhile, ordinary workers' pay was the lowest of the same countries. With these advantages, if the conservatives are right the British economy should be clipping along. Instead, its performance is only modest.

For the zealots – rather like ancient druids or the cargo cult islanders – this is proof only that something is wrong with their rituals and they must redouble their efforts; not that their whole belief system may be awry. Others do not acknowledge the reality at all. The *Sunday Times* Business Section's economic columnist and conservative zealot Irwin Stelzer is a classic of the breed, who rehearses his prejudices as the truth, selectively choosing his facts while omitting others, week after week – a tendency, as we have seen, that extends to conservative academics like Alain Enthoven. In Stelzerland a 'sclerotic' Europe has lagging productivity generated by a 'eurocracy' that delights in setting burdensome regulations that 'drive entrepreneurs mad'. His view is that European governments set tax, cost and regulatory burdens that are the sole cause of uncompetitiveness; his hero is the individualistic entrepreneur chasing the next idea, rightfully worth billions, and that America's pro-enterprise approach can be relied upon to beat all other economies over time. He has no interest in any social capabilities that might create organisational creativity or support high-performance companies; that is 'corporatism'.[15] The notion that output per man-hour might be higher in the former West Germany and France than the US is plainly preposterous, as is the idea that, apart from one or two exceptions, the European corporate sector is anything but deadbeat. Yet Stelzer's partisan effusions go unchallenged in a way impossible for anybody who takes the alternative view. Offered a platform in an American-owned newspaper (in addition he writes for the *Sun*) to propagandise the Washington consensus and the new conservatism with no health warning, he is part of the internationally accepted common sense. Typically, he was a member of an advisory council for the now-bankrupt Enron, where his constant advocacy of minimal regulation in exchange for more than useful remuneration helpfully contributed to an intellectual climate supporting Enron's fraudulent operations. He is an adviser to the Smith Institute, a think-tank close to Gordon Brown, where he rehearses the familiar free market litanies. He also advises Rupert Murdoch, acting as a key intermediary with the British government: during the negotiations over the relaxation of Britain's media ownership laws in 2001 and early 2002, for example, the ministers concerned were obliged to offer him any access he wanted where he pressed his anti-regulation case. At the heart of the economic, government, media and business establishment he can get away with consistent presentation of unsubstantiated ideology as the truth – and does so regularly.

It is an analysis that infects the entire economic and consultancy establishment. The McKinsey report into productivity, commissioned by the chancellor Gordon Brown soon after the 1997 election, reveals just how deep the prejudices go – and how perverse the recommendations are that flow from such flawed and ideologically informed 'analysis'. McKinsey starts its report with the unashamed and explicit view that the benchmark economy is the US, and that the puzzle for Britain is how to import more American best practice. It adopts the unconventional view that the core of the British problem, far from lack of investment, is land use planning: 'regulations governing product markets and land use in corporate behaviour, investment and pricing'. These, it concludes, are the 'pervasive explanation' for lower British productivity. A shake-up in overly restrictive British planning rules to allow firms more freedom to expand and enter new industries along American lines is the single most important contribution the British government could make to lifting productivity.

At first sight this seems an innovative idea – until the evidence is examined closely, when it plainly becomes batty. McKinsey's 'insights' were foreshadowed in the early 1980s by the Adam Smith Institute, which inveighed against the 'planning class' and cited Houston as an example of the benefits of a *laissez-faire* approach to planning: the only American city then without politically authorised zoning, it was growing rapidly.[16] However, it is now clear that Houston's growth in these years was part of a much wider renaissance of the southern and specifically Texan economy – which proved limited when pollution and toxic waste grew over the decade, choking its growth; a trend accompanied by the quiet relegation in order of priorities, even by American conservatives, of the notion that planning laws inhibited growth. McKinsey had not read the literature. Nor had the authors of the report broken down the sources of productivity growth to identify correctly the importance of the emergence of new firms in contributing to productivity. If they had done so they would have realised that the ideological assumption upon which they based their analysis had wildly over-estimated the role of firm entry. The OECD has demonstrated that firm entry and exit is relatively trivial as a cause of productivity growth, and that notwithstanding British planning laws, firm entry is considerably easier in Britain than in the US, where in any case it makes a negative contribution to productivity growth.[17]

In fact, most productivity growth in both countries is achieved within the firm – as it is in every country the OECD surveyed. McKinsey might make grandiloquent boasts about how its judgements are informed by global experience, but in truth it – like Irwin Stelzer and Alain Enthoven – is a simple propagandist of the conservative Washington consensus, right or wrong. There is even an argument that planning laws, by generating higher-density urban areas, help to increase productivity by clustering skills in close physical proximity so that there is a much greater chance of inter-firm and inter-employee learning. But this is not what McKinsey's brand of economics teaches, and so the point is not even considered.

Indeed, in assessing the causes of productivity growth, conservative economics looks in entirely the wrong direction. Conservatives want to prove that markets are economically and morally superior to all other forms of organisation. Economic efficiency, for them, is about the permanent freedom to complete the most cost-effective contract and to move on to another if there is a better opportunity; in this world, the aim is to allocate resources effectively through buying cheap and selling dear. The assumption is that productivity is delivered by firms being able to exit from costly contracts, whether with their workforce or their sub-contractors, and enter new ones quickly and flexibly; that production is simply a matter of combining workers, machines and technology in the best technical configuration through top-down managerial direction; and that the optimal production configuration is self-evidently obvious once costs and prices are known. The organisation in which these choices take place is beside the point. Its history, the quality of its leadership and internal organisation, and the uncertainty in which it makes strategic choices about what to do and how its market might evolve are abstracted out of the account. These 'soft' issues are not allowed to muddy the 'hard' message: productivity is about entrepreneurial freedom to cut deals independent of any consideration other than cost minimisation and profit maximisation.

Yet, as the OECD has established, the heart of productivity growth is what happens inside the firm, and firms are human organisations. Mary O'Sullivan, assistant professor at INSEAD, Europe's leading business school, argues persuasively that innovation cannot be conceptualised within the market contracting framework, for it is an organisational quality that flourishes better in some environments than others. In the first place, organisations cannot be scrapped and rebuilt at will; they develop cumulatively over time and what they have been determines in part what they can become. A major steel or chemicals company cannot easily transmute into a bank or insurance company if it believes that might maximise its profits; it has sets of skills and competences that are unique to a particular industry, even to that firm. Its directors, managers and workers know what to do to make that particular firm function in that particular industry, and they will necessarily be at a disadvantage if they try to migrate wholesale to a different industry or economic function. Their success depends on their ability to innovate within their organisational capacity, and that in turn depends on their learning capacity – on their ability, at every level, to move on. Even if managers choose to command and control in a top-down way – as on occasion they must – they have to act on information that is passed up to them, and that in turn demands that the organisation operates as a successful social process. Information is collectively gathered and synthesised by the organisation as a whole, and necessarily account has to be taken of competitors' strategies. Put bluntly, this is a social and leadership process which too much reliance on individualistic market contracting obstructs. The more conservative economics rules, the less innovative the organisation.

The evidence marshalled by O'Sullivan shows that across countries, industries and firms there are certain golden rules conducive to innovation. The directors who make decisions over investment need to be closely aligned with and understand those who are at the competitive front line; they need to be close to their key managers and operators, who need to be constantly feeding back to them information about market conditions and new technologies. Equally, there needs to be a shared loyalty to the organisation's goals; and this is easier the fewer individual members break away to sell their own skills on the open market. And finally, there needs to be a consistent commitment to continue to make investment – in skills, knowledge and physical assets – over time, so that obsolescence is counterbalanced by new resources. Planning restrictions, regulatory burdens and high taxation are seen for what they are: at most, second-order problems; at worst, intellectual red herrings because they obscure the real drivers of innovation. Just to enter this universe is to realise how feeble the McKinsey/Stelzer/conservative approach to understanding enterprise and innovation is. They are not even at first base.

For what becomes immediately apparent is that conservative economics, with its emphasis on maximising shareholder value and market flexibilities, is actively inimical to innovation and productivity growth. External shareholders impose their view on what constitutes appropriate investment, setting criteria and goals that are inevitably distant from the organisation's competitive coal-face. Moreover, the company with a quotation on the London or New York stock exchange faces a shifting and volatile base of owners, always ready to sell the company to a predator if its performance falls below their expectations – sometimes a judgement that is made after just two or three quarters' poor results. Moreover, if directors, star managers and key income earners are always ready to put themselves on to the labour market to maximise their incomes, then their loyalty to the organisation over time is necessarily weakened. Individual wealth generation comes before that of the organisation. In the world created by conservative economists, innovation becomes more difficult.

McKinsey, for example, uncritically accept that Britain's capital markets are good for productivity because they are market-based and flexible. Wrong. The increasing emphasis in Britain's capital markets, like those in the US, is not on increasing investment and innovation; rather, it is on trading financial assets for immediate financial gain, so that the focus continually transmitted by the markets to the corporate sector is on the need to increase profits – by whatever means. If the result of some historic innovation has been to deliver the desired financial return, then the markets readily welcome it – but no more than they would welcome increased profits achieved by any other means: redundancy, asset-stripping, a clever deal, tax avoidance or even smart manipulation of the corporate balance sheet – although, as the markets have discovered with Enron, sham traffic between telecoms companies and hideous fraud in the financial sector, when the process of manufacturing profit by any means goes too far it is self-defeating. Indeed, as I argued in *The State We're In*, the perennial problem in capital markets structured as they are in Britain and the US is the commitment problem. The innovative organisation needs a platform of committed owners prepared to delegate the scale and priorities of investment decision-making to the managerial insiders similarly committed to the organisation over time – but that is precisely what the Anglo-Saxon capital markets, as they have evolved over the last quarter of a century, do not do.

British and American companies do not in general have a multiplicity of small owners (a structure in which the influence of any one shareholder is tiny, offering collective stability) or a small core of committed owners, either of which might provide such a platform; instead, the bulk of their equity is owned by some twenty or thirty representatives of collective savers – pension funds and the like. No single pension fund or insurance company is large enough to reap the rewards of offering a committed platform to innovative companies; to do so risks suffering poor investment performance while others exploit more appealing short-term opportunities – and savers migrate to them because their marketing literature can boast that they have outperformed whatever share prices on average have done in the short term. So because the large financial institutions cannot be organised collectively, insisting that they must have the same rights to buy and sell as freely as any other shareholder, however small, and because they are at the same time very powerful, major companies have an unstable and demanding ownership base. In reality, of course, the principal investment institutions are too large to sell all their shares in the top 200 companies, because prices would collapse if they did so; but they reserve their right to do so, thus condemning the system to the worst of all possible worlds: the appearance but not the reality of liquidity. That appearance makes corporate organisations more peripatetic and short-termist in their business strategies in order to appease their short-termist owners. One result is the phenomenally high proportion of after-tax cashflow that companies pay out in dividends (an average of 50 per cent in both Britain and the US) or in buying back their own shares to support the price.

The markets' priorities get into the quick of corporate decision-making. In the US, the story of Boeing and the rise and fall of the dot.coms are salutary enough; and Britain has its own share of disasters from applying the doctrine. The demise of GEC, one of Britain's leading manufacturing companies, as a result of the interplay of shareholder value and the financial markets' fads is one of the saddest. At the beginning of 1999 it sold its defence operations to raise a war-chest to fund its transformation into what the financial markets at that time considered the fashion – a focused high-technology company. In order to justify the markets' expectations, it had to buy companies quickly rather than grow organically – and in April 1999 it splashed out £2.8 billion on buying the most fashionable company of all, an American producer of internet switching equipment called Fore Systems. In May the chairman, George Simpson, told an investment conference that he would double GEC's value in three to five years, and in October the group was renamed Marconi.

The demands of the capital markets were overtly dictating Marconi's strategy, so that it was buying overpriced companies in the middle of the world's biggest financial bubble to assuage its shareholders' expectations. Research, creativity and innovation were subordinated to one overarching aim: to double the share price. As the dot.com and telecoms bubble deflated, Marconi's orders fell – but worse, the companies it had bought proved worthless. In November 2001, two and half years after it was bought, Fore Systems was judged valueless and £2.8 billion was written off. By now Simpson and two other senior executives had left the company (with Simpson insisting on an extravagant golden goodbye as reward for his disastrous services), but the damage done was irreparable. By following the injunctions of maximising shareholder value and obeying the markets' wishes, Marconi has cast its very future into doubt.

Marks and Spencer is another sorry story. For decades the company had been a byword for value for money and quality in British retailing; it had a close relationship with its supply chain and state-of-the-art high street stores. The priority was the customer. But over the 1990s the gangrene of shareholder value began to infect this great British institution. The City wanted ever higher margins and ever greater commitment to growth; M&S should do deals and it should squeeze its assets harder. Creativity and commitment to organic growth were downgraded; lifting the share price became the endgame. Instead of investing to be at the frontier of fashion, in 1997 the company paid Littlewoods £182 million for nineteen large city-centre stores which would cost another £450 million to refurbish. The City liked the signal of commitment to growth through deal-making – but in fact it was symptomatic of a set of strategic priorities that would lay the company low.

Judi Bevan, author of *The Rise and Fall of Marks and Spencer*, writes that 'a little at a time they [the executive directors] sacrificed the founding family principles of value, quality and service in the dash for profits.'[18] Eventually the gradual loss of competitiveness and failure to invest in high-quality, fashionable products had their inevitable result: sales and profits fell. Three years of restructuring and shrinkage were to follow, involving the sale of the company's European and American operations. The new priorities were clear: the new executive chairman had a performance bonus closely linked to the share price, and the object was to shrink the company, selling sites at home and abroad, to raise £2 billion to give to shareholders. Twenty-five years of growth shuddered to a halt. If Marks and Spencer is now starting to recover, it is from a shrunken base and with its former commitment to creativity and quality much damaged. Shareholder value had again reduced a creative company to a dismal creature of profit maximisation – paradoxically less capable of delivering high margins and profits than it had been when committed to the customer and a conception of quality. The fixation with increasing the share price enters the warp and woof of the organisation. It becomes the fulcrum around which every facet of the company turns, dictating how budgets are set and negotiated, how performance schemes are established, how the human relations functions are discharged, the priorities of research and development while setting demanding criteria for new investment with short payback times.

Corporate problems like these are never connected to the structure and culture of the capital markets by the conservative economic mainstream. McKinsey's report – and Stelzer's columns – are quintessential examples of this blindness, celebrating the 'flexible' Anglo-Saxon capital markets as handmaidens of risk-taking and enterprise, which reach their quintessential expression in the rise of venture capital. Yet, as O'Sullivan points out, there have been 3500 venture-backed public offerings on the New York Stock Exchange since 1993, and even before the stock market fall in the spring of 2000 over half of them were trading below their offer price – an indication that many were essentially frivolous or brought to market too early. But on this, as on the structure and behaviour of the financial system in general, there is a blind spot. Venture capitalists personify 'enterprise'; they are part of a market-based financial system; therefore they are simply beyond reproach, and there can be no shortcomings in the way they function that they themselves would not recognise and correct. In McKinseyland we must look to government and regulation for the sources of productivity weakness, not to the way the markets themselves are functioning – unless they are working 'imperfectly', i.e. because of government and regulation. The European conception of organisations as critically having social capabilities and needing to balance the interests of all their stakeholders in order to achieve high performance and innovation is not even on the radar.

Resurrecting the public realm and discovering Europe

The conservative consensus spills over into the way public debate is conducted and defines what are considered to be the reasonable options of public policy. It has led the Conservative party to be characterised as hostile to society, disconnected from its own country. New Labour, for all its earnest desire to marry economic disciplines with genuine social progress, is locked into the same paradigm.

The Blair government certainly wants an improved range of social democratic outcomes, as do those who voted for it. It wants improved public services and more social cohesion. It wants less discrimination in every walk of life. It wants to promote a just capitalism in which companies take their obligations to their customers and workers more seriously while becoming more innovative and productive. It wants a stronger social safety net. More controversially, it also recognises that Britain needs to be an active member of the European Union, because Britain as a European power needs to be part of an emerging continental market and party to the evolving European political conversation. None of these aims can be seriously doubted.

The problem is that it is attempting to achieve them while respecting the canons of American conservatism; for that is the route, it thinks, to relegitimising the centre-left while building a new coalition with the centre. Thus it can make suitable obeisance to the new conservative common sense while trying to make stealthy social democratic advances. But there is more to it than that. Both Tony Blair and Gordon Brown have come to believe that there is enough that is correct about the conservative propositions to make it unnecessary to challenge them. So the political project at the heart of the third way is the attempt to marry two incompatible value systems – American conservatism and a modernised European social democracy. It is an exercise doomed to failure. Already there is a growing disconnection between the leadership of the Labour party and its natural constituency; without a change of course, the gap could become unbridgeable.

For the universe of ideas that supports notions of the enterprise culture cannot be made to serve a declared public interest or purpose; its very objective is to celebrate the primacy of markets and individualism over public endeavour and social goals. It is to substitute the private for the public. Business should be untrammelled and have no social claim or regulatory 'burden' placed upon it. The third way reply does not dispute this point; rather, it argues that in practice business can be made to serve a public purpose, and that no reasonable person should object on principle to a service being owned publicly or privately. As long as the end result of public delivery is ensured, all that should matter is that the means is efficient and cost-effective.

It is a delusion. The advocacy and defence of the public realm is important in itself. This is an idea that should not be scrambled up and killed along with ideas of socialism and collectivism. It defines a universe of belonging, membership of which allows individuals to relate to society and society to them. It is this philosophy that opens up the notion that business is not solely about the exercise of property rights in the service of wealth creation; instead business has social capabilities and a social dimension which it must respect. It is through recognising these facets that a different and richer conception of enterprise is opened up, one whose values connect to social democratic social goals. Put another way, this European conception of enterprise is underpinned by the same value system that underpins the establishment of the social contract – a value system epitomised by the Rawlsian idea of an infrastructure of justice.

This crucial idea of the public has been corrupted by the socialist legacy. Just as each act of nationalisation was portrayed as another building-block in the full scale socialisation of the means of production via 'public' ownership, so each act of privatisation is now hailed as a retreat from socialism and advance towards full-blooded capitalism. This ideological discourse prevents straight thinking about the attributes some economic and social functions must have if we are to construct a just civil order.

The case for public education and health clarifies the point. The universal provision of education to every child and access to health of every citizen, irrespective of their capacity to pay, builds on the core Western belief that some institutions and processes in society must be universal in their scope – not as a precondition for socialism, but as part of the foundations of a humane civilisation. European socialism did not choose to make this distinction, lumping together the establishment of universal education and health with the public running of natural monopolies like water, gas and electricity networks and the nationalisation of, say, coal, steel and airline industries – all as uniform elements of the same socialist advance. They never were. Now that socialism is receding, American conservatism and the Washington consensus are trying to make the same claim in reverse. Just as socialism bundled a collection of disparate activities under one rubric, so privatisation does the same; everything can be privatised. But it cannot. There are some activities that are irreducibly public in their scope and need to stay public.

This distinction is what is absent from New Labour's approach. It has accepted the proposition that publicly owned and run activity is necessarily inefficient, and that by moving to the McKinsey universe of free contracting and managerial direction incentivised by profits it will gain more value for every pound spent. It believes that, as long as the elected government of the day can specify the outcomes it wants, then it can preserve the public character of what is provided through regulation or clearly specified contracts.

In some areas, of course, this proposition holds. There is little public interest in the public ownership of a steel company. But this is not true in the building and sustaining of a national network – like rail or even broadband cable – where there are no immediate profits to be made and even long-run trading losses to be borne, but where the public interest demands that the network be universal in its reach, first-class in its quality and equitable in the way it treats its users, who definitionally constitute the entire population. A national postal service must serve every household, wherever located; a national rail network must offer every citizen the ability to travel; a national broadband network must offer every user the same opportunity to be 'wired'. The privatisation and fragmentation of British Rail and the inability to build a broadband cable network through private initiative both reveal the same truth. The character of some forms of enterprise requires public engagement, public direction and even public ownership.

The case of the rail industry and the collapse of Railtrack is important, for it shows that the formula of public regulation of a private company to achieve a public interest has failed. The narrow quest for operational efficiencies by thinning out layers of management, scaling back the workforce, lowering wages and eroding skills has hollowed out the rail infrastructure and made it less safe – witness the accidents at Paddington and Hatfield. The fragmentation of the industry into contracting parties – over twenty train operating companies and Railtrack – raised costs as contractors sought to lift profit margins. On some estimates the cost of building and maintaining new track has trebled; the electrification and upgrade of the west coast line is costing £16 million per mile – three times as much as similar upgrades undertaken by British Rail.[19]

Railtrack, charged with investing in new rail infrastructure, never had a sufficiently large capital base to allow it to take on the billions of debt necessary to finance rail modernisation. It needed continual government grants; yet after receiving them, its first obligation had to be to sustain its creditworthiness and stock market rating by paying dividends to its shareholders. It failed both as an innovative company and as a company discharging the public interest. Its collapse in September 2001 and replacement by a public interest company with no obligation to pay dividends to shareholders was a seminal moment. By ensuring that the new company has the capacity to borrow and invest, and to direct the re-integration of the rail infrastructure with the train operating companies, the government is ensuring that the public interest is protected. This is not renationalisation; it is securing the public realm and universality of provision in an economic activity where it would otherwise be lost.

A similar intervention is now required with the private finance initiative (PFI). This is an allegedly technical means of introducing private finance and management into the construction and maintenance of public assets – hospitals, prisons and schools – in return for a fee paid over a thirty-year period. The argument is that the state gets better-managed assets that are funded off balance sheet; the means justifies the end. But, as the left of centre think-tank the Institute for Public Policy Research pointed out in a critical report in 2001, *Building Better Partnerships*, the means *changes* the end. The report usefully identifies three criteria that define 'publicness', to which PFI contracts must, it argues, conform if they are not to change the character of the public service they are providing. They must be accountable to every citizen; they must protect social equity, so that they continue to maintain universality of access; and their improved efficiency must be won not at the expense of the terms and conditions of public sector workers, but through genuine organisational innovativeness brought by a private sector approach.[20] Judged on these criteria, very few PFI contracts in the NHS would have gone forward. They offered little or no genuine increased efficiency to compensate for increased financing costs – indeed, on some calculations construction costs were almost twice the original estimate.[21] Most hospitals were smaller than the publicly owned and funded hospitals they replaced, and tended to have none of the 'expensive' attributes – like accident and emergency departments or beds for the long-term sick – of publicly run hospitals because those would menace the financial returns the PFI contractors sought. Organisational innovativeness has meant no more than brutal cost minimisation. The means had changed the ends. In some areas of the public service, notably prison provision, standards had fallen so low that the PFI has produced improved outcomes. But this cannot be taken as the axiomatic, general truth to which the Washington consensus and its faithful followers in London lay claim.

Once policy-makers enter the conservative paradigm, none of these subtleties is admissible. Rather like McKinsey recommending a relaxation of planning laws to boost productivity because it defines all problems in the terms of American conservatism, New Labour has trapped itself into conceptualising the problem of public service delivery as how to introduce as much private enterprise as possible into the public sector while preserving its public character. But the real question is different. It should be how to organise the public sector so that it is organisationally creative, rigorously run, well led and properly funded. The private sector might be an effective agent of change or subcontractor to help achieve these ends, but it cannot and should not be expected to become a surrogate public sector. That is not what it is set up to do.

The same conflict infects New Labour's social policy. The great fight in the first half of the twentieth century was to win citizens a basic income so they could avoid destitution in the face of life's hazards – unemployment, sickness and incapacity – and the certainty of old age. This was portrayed as a social citizenship right to match the political rights so hard fought for over the previous century. The goal was to offer every citizen the opportunity to participate in the life of society, whatever his or her circumstances. This was described as the welfare state; the collective underwriting of risk to ensure that everyone could express their humanity.

Here again ascendant American conservatism has spread its baleful influence. The social contract should not, it insists, be expressed as a system of social insurance which brings entitlements to all citizens. Instead, entitlements should be conditional, means-tested and meagre. In Britain the principle now spreads from incapacity benefit to pensions; do not expect a basic income from the state to support you without some form of means test to ensure you are deserving. The notion that as a citizen you have a right to participate in society through being offered a basic income is dead; it is too expensive for the exchequer, implies higher taxes and might undermine your moral character. Where possible you should undertake your own provision in the private sector, which will necessarily be more efficient.

It is not. Take pensions. One of the proudest boasts of Britain's political class is that Britain, unlike mainland Europe, is not sitting on an expensive pension time-bomb. Future pension funding is going to prove expensive if the retirement age remains the same as the population becomes proportionally older. Historically, Britain has shared the costs of provision among the state, the corporation and the individual. As understanding has grown about future funding problems, both the government and companies have been withdrawing their support. Britain is avoiding the pension time-bomb only because it has largely privatised the problem and is prepared to accept relative pensioner poverty.

The government is allowing the basic pension gradually to wither away, indexing it only to the increase in retail prices rather than to average earnings; all the government will engage to do is to provide a safety net for the poor in retirement, pitched at a level well below the standards of living available as a citizen's entitlement elsewhere in Europe. To ensure a decent retirement income each individual must save and invest through a company pension fund or private pension plan managed by an insurance company. The pensions thus provided depend on share prices remaining buoyant to drive up the value of accumulated savings, along with interest rates staying high so that the annuities bought with the investments provide a solid income. Neither precondition holds, so that if the current cohort of savers want to achieve the same pension as those retiring today they will have to save twice as much.

But that is not the state's concern. People must look after themselves, even if the insurance company through which they might save – like Equitable Life – turns out not to be able to honour its promises. The Equitable cut its pension benefits by 16 per cent for 900,000 savers as a result of a miscalculation it made in the mid-1980s; others will doubtless do the same as investment returns fall generally. The number of companies operating pension funds in which they promise to pay a pension linked to final salary has fallen by three-quarters in just seven years; they are too expensive given low interest rates and modest investment performance. This is a devastating collapse that will have a disastrous impact on the income of future British pensioners for which they are completely unprepared.[22]

Not only are companies closing their final salary pension schemes; they are lowering their contributions to the replacement schemes in which pensions are completely dependent on the performance of the stock market and interest rates. To compensate, individuals need to raise their own contributions by 10 per cent or more if they want reasonable retirement incomes – equivalent to lifting the basic rate of income tax by 10 pence in the pound. If they are saving wholly by themselves, they should be putting aside at least £15 out of every £100 they earn for their entire working life – and even then their pension will be very modest and unpredictable, dependent on the vagaries of the stock market and interest rates.

Yet in the Panglossian world of the conservative, none of this should be happening. Only the state does not keep its promises; the private sector always does, and it is morally better for individuals to act for themselves rather than act collectively. New Labour is at least attempting some improvement of pension provision by offering a minimum retirement income guarantee, so that those who have no savings or private pension at least do not have to rely on the now impossibly low state pension; yet this minimum guarantee, in proportion to average earnings, is still well below what is offered in mainland Europe. Worse, it penalises those pensioners who, on low incomes, have saved all their lives but whose resulting private pension only brings them up to the guarantee level. They get nothing. But the state is not interested in fairness, or offering a square deal to its citizens; it wants to save money.

What would be fairer and more cost-effective, and offer a predictable pension, would be a nationally run social insurance system to co-exist with private saving – exactly like the scheme hammered out by Barbara Castle in the mid-1970s. This was the use of the state to improve the condition of the people in a social contract – now deemed impossible, intellectually, ideologically and financially. The British state has avoided the pension time-bomb only by displacing risk, misery and poverty on to the next generation of pensioners. If the Europeans have a problem, it is because they plan to treat their pensioners properly.

Yet Britons want to retain their social contract; they even want to improve it. If they understood the pensions issue, they would want a European-style pay-as-you-go state pension rather than the lottery they are offered. They want improved delivery of all public services, and understand the limitations of asking the private sector to assume public responsibilities. They certainly want an improved public transport system, and are beginning to ask hard questions about why Britain seems incapable of providing it. They are, in short, very European.

And, as the debate about raising British productivity and economic performance rages, it is worth noting that few European companies are suffering the calamities that have afflicted Marconi and Marks and Spencer. Europeans have economic and social structures that create more high-performance, world-class companies and many fewer disasters. Yet all this is only insecurely and uncertainly understood in either Downing

Street or the wider British business, economic and financial establishment. The British campaign, almost laughable in the circumstances, is to persuade the mainland Europeans to emulate the British and recast their economies and societies along the lines preached by American conservatives so that Britain can live with EU membership more easily – and the EU can improve its economic and social performance.

To mock this stance is not to argue that every aspect of the European model works perfectly. Yet if Britain is to make reforms they should conform to core European values and principles that, as I will show in the next chapter, demonstrably work better than our own. Only if this is grasped wholeheartedly can Britain make a success of its membership of the EU and of shaping its own economy and society in the way that our people and our history require. For we share our distinct values with our fellow Europeans.

The march of the American conservative right and the eclipse of American liberalism have helped to undermine our own distinct conceptions of the public realm, citizenship and the proper relationship between the market and society. It is time we recognised that Europe has something very important to offer – something much better than the US.

8

Europe works

British and American commentators have been administering the last rites over the European economic and social model ever since British and US unemployment began to fall in the early 1990s while Europe's stayed stubbornly high, falling only towards the end of the decade. European 'stakeholder capitalism' is being gradually dismantled, runs the argument. The vital disciplines of the stock market are being gradually imposed through an enlargement of their role and adoption of the principle of maximising shareholder value, while over-expensive, featherbedding welfare states are scaled back. The European model is being compelled to converge with the American model both because of the remorseless logic of having to match the latter's economic efficiency and because of pressure from global investors, notably pension funds, insisting that if European companies want access to capital on the same terms, then the rules that favour them in the US and Britain will have to be reproduced in Europe. Above all, change is necessary to lower unemployment, the price Europeans pay for ignoring the injunctions of *laissez-faire* economics and persisting with their inflexible labour markets and rigged capital markets.

It is true that European companies today are taking the interests of shareholders more seriously than formerly, whether as a result of the Vienot report in France, arguing for more transparency and fewer defensive cross-shareholdings,[1] or of the new 'Eichel-law' in Germany, that will allow the disposal of cross-shareholdings without incurring capital gains tax. British mobile phone firm Vodafone's successful hostile $200 billion takeover bid for Mannesman in 2000 was hailed as further evidence of the trend. Equally, budgetary pressure and persistent unemployment are forcing retrenchment of the welfare state, and most European countries are focusing on tax, benefit and training policies that make work pay, closing down the scope for individual workers voluntarily to remain unemployed for sustained periods. American conservatives contentedly assure themselves they are winning the argument.

But what is actually impressive is less the unequivocal march towards the American model, and more the degree to which Europeans are updating the best of the old in new conditions and discarding only what is plainly redundant. The social contract conception remains at the heart of the European attitude towards employment regulation and the character of the welfare state. And while more care is being taken not to disadvantage shareholders in a globalising capital market, European businesses still fight to retain the notion that the interests and capabilities of the entire business must come first, and that shareholders should not become an overprivileged sectional interest group. Moreover, as we will explore later in this chapter, high unemployment originates more in lack of overall demand than in the price of labour market regulation.

The value of shares quoted on European stock markets may have risen strongly over the 1980s and 1990s, with British and American pension funds and insurance companies increasing their ownership – but there is nothing like the same 'market for corporate control' that exists in the US and the UK. Nor is there likely to be; for what is striking is that European companies retain their commitment to organic growth rather than financial engineering along Anglo-Saxon lines. Over the 1990s there were only nine hostile takeovers in France, and seven in Germany; dividend distributions remain low; and comparatively little money is raised directly from the stock market. Mannesmann was uniquely exposed to takeover – it courted foreign ownership of its shares, so that 40 per cent were held by overseas institutions; no other German company approaches such a high percentage.

Europe's economic and social model lives. Certainly it is under continuing pressure from both the capital markets and conservative propagandists, and part of Europe's business and financial elite is increasingly attracted by the glittering universe of American capitalism with its dazzling incomes for senior executives and glamorous deal-making. Yet again, what is remarkable is how much stands in the face of pressure and temptation alike. For example, the aligning of the interests of executives and shareholders in share option schemes, now developing in both France and Germany, is much more modest in scope – and the criteria for earning such benefits are much more long-term and demanding than in the US.

The distinctive European approach to capitalism is deeply embedded, and Europe's economic and social institutions and values are widely respected – even venerated. The various countries of Europe have outwardly different structures of capitalism, but what they hold in common is far greater than what divides them. And what they all have at their core is the high-investment, high-performance enterprise.

European enterprise at work

Volkswagen should be a basket case. It manufactures cars and trucks in high-cost Germany. It has a highly unionised workforce who work a 28.8-hour week for up to £23 an hour. Its largest shareholder is the state government of Lower Saxony, which owns 18.6 per cent of the company's shares. It has a cumbersome supervisory board on which both the trade unions and the regional government are represented. Its directors have only a small number of share options, and its chief executive is paid under $1 million a year – a tiny fraction of the $32 million and $22 million made by his opposite numbers at Ford and General Motors. The total value of stock options available to every VW employee in 2000 in aggregate was $1.7 million; when Jacques Nasser ceased to work as CEO of Ford he alone had over $16 million of unexercised share options. Worse, VW shareholders' voting rights are limited to 20 per cent, so the company can neglect to promote shareholder value, allowing it to become sclerotic and uncompetitive. It is under no threat of takeover unless its system of voting rights is changed.

There is scarcely a canon in the conservative free market rule book that Volkswagen does not offend. It was only in 2001 that it prepared accounts conforming to international standards, and although it acknowledged that it was going to change its focus from sales maximisation to achieving the highest possible stock market value of the group, this was not done because it believed in the primacy of shareholder rights; rather, it was because in a world in which creditworthiness and even reputation are so closely linked to the markets' judgements, having a higher share price was better than having a low share price. It pays only 16 per cent of its post-tax earnings as dividends, retaining the rest to support its enormous investment in R&D, which at 4.8 per cent of turnover is higher than Ford (4.0 per cent) and General Motors (3.6 per cent).[2]

Yet Volkswagen remains Europe's largest car maker and has increased its market share from 16 to 19 per cent since 1993 – largely at the expense of Ford and General Motors. Even in the US its market share has jumped by 2 per cent over the same period. It is the most internationalised car company in the world. It has revived the near-bankrupt Czech car manufacturer Skoda. Its Passats and Golfs, redesigned VW Beetle and range of new cars are the envy of its rivals. Its engineering prowess and innovativeness are streets ahead of its American competitors: the VW Golf, Bora, New Beetle, Audi A3, Audi TT, Seat Toledo and Skoda Octavia all have the same A4 platform, sharing a single chassis, engine, gearbox, power train, gearshift and air-conditioning system – a degree of engineering excellence well ahead of its American competition.[3] According to the predictions of American conservatives, none of this should be happening. VW should be down and out.

Or take tyre maker Michelin in France. This is a firm that, 112 years after it was formed, is still dominated by the family whose some 250 members own around a third of the shares; its current chief executive, Edouard Michelin, is the son of another Michelin, François. It has to deal with the communist trade union, the CGT, and to operate within the allegedly crippling confines of the 35-hour week, recently introduced in France. Like Volkswagen, it pays its chief executive and directors a fraction of the salaries of their American competitors at Goodyear. And, like Volkswagen, it has not given top priority to the promotion of shareholder value; its declared aims are to be at the technological forefront of tyre manufacture and to sustain its market position. Dividends were only 26 per cent of depressed earnings in 2000, with the more typical ratio well below 20 per cent. It invented the first car tyre in 1895 and the first radial tyre in 1946, and its latest contribution is the Pax – a tyre that can function even when punctured. Michelin tyres are used by five of the eleven Formula One Racing teams; when Concorde needed a new fool-proof tyre after the disastrous crash in Paris in which all the crew and passengers died, it turned to Michelin to find an answer. Michelin spends 4.2 per cent of turnover on R&D compared with Goodyear's 2.9 per cent.[4] What should be another basket case is the technological leader of world tyre manufacture. Before Goodyear bought Sumitomo, it was also the world's largest tyre manufacturer; it remains the largest in Europe. Yet according to conservative theorists it should be on the road to competitive extinction.

And then there is Finland's Nokia, the world's leading mobile phone company. This is another corporation that should not exist, and has dared to challenge the principles of capitalism as set out by the ideologues of the enterprise culture. Originally a wood-processing and rubber-boot company, Nokia started the 1990s worrying about how its toilet-paper sales would hold up in its main market – the former Soviet Union. High levels of Finnish taxation should have dampened this company's ambitions from the start, and if that didn't trap it, powerful trade unions should have finally sealed its fate. Nearly half of its 60,000 global labour force work in high-wage Finland, a country encumbered with monstrous charges – in conservative eyes – to finance its generous and incentive-depleting welfare state. Nor does it pay especially high executive salaries which, even with share option schemes on top, are severely reduced by penal Finnish tax rates on high earners. Chief executive Jorma Ollila was paid $1,250,000 before stock options in 2001; G. R. Wagoner Jnr, his opposite number at Motorola, the number two in the mobile phone market, received over $2.5 million with some $9 million in unexercised stock options. Yet Nokia has managed to keep together the senior management team that over the past decade has directed the company's exponential growth.

Nokia's success is legendary. It has 35 per cent of the world mobile phone market – more than twice its nearest rival Motorola – and its track record for innovation, commitment to design, and effective management of its 150 subcontractors is second to none. Dan Steinbock in *The Nokia Revolution* quotes one key Nokia manager as saying: 'Using traditional financial measures is liking driving a car by looking at the rearview mirror . . . for us there are three basic critical success factors: customer satisfaction, operations efficiency and people involvement.'[5] Steinbock adds that at Nokia innovation is not thought of as the preserve of the R&D or product development departments; 'instead, it has been thought of as something that can and should pertain to the entire value chain.' Yet for an ideological commentator like Irwin Stelzer the company should have no right to trade at all, let alone successfully.

These three companies are representatives of three of the more distinct of Europe's economic and social models – the German social market model, the French statist model and the Scandinavian social democratic model (all discussed in chapter 9). The cities in which they are headquartered, Wolfsburg, Clermont-Ferrand and Helsinki, are recognisably German, French and Finnish, and each company culture resolutely reflects its country of origin. Yet each is a global force with a superlative track record of technological and organisational creativity. And each challenges the precepts for successful enterprise as defined by American conservatism. They are largely insulated from takeover except on their own terms; their executive teams are not fully aligned with shareholders' interests; unions are powerful and workers are protected; taxes are high, and the working week is short and regulated. Nor are they alone. The same success story could have been told in relation to a leading German chemicals company (Bayer) or a French industrial gases company (Air Liquide); representatives abound across Europe – as they must, given the region's astonishing record in investment and productivity growth. Nothing should be less surprising given the build-up of European investment over the past thirty years; while the US capital stock grew a mere 65 per cent between 1965 and 1991, Italy's grew 130 per cent, France's 150 per cent and Germany's 175 per cent.[6] On the basis of trends in investment over the past ten years, the differential will remain the same or widen. European capitalism has a vitality and dynamism wholly disallowed by the conservative consensus.

But Volkswagen, Michelin and Nokia are not goody two-shoes. They are unambiguously capitalist. Michelin has halved its workforce in Clermont-Ferrand over the past fifteen years and has not hesitated to close factories or rationalise production when necessary; when it announced 7500 redundancies after a profit increase in 1999 it was condemned by France's socialist prime minister, Lionel Jospin, for its capitalist insensitivity. Volkswagen has bargained toughly with its workforce to hire new workers on considerably poorer terms than its existing German employees in order to stay competitive, while Nokia will not be able to survive the downturn in mobile phone sales without redundancies and retrenchment. Each is mindful of the need to sustain profits and avoid losses. The notion that they are in any way 'socialist' is risible.

Yet, as capitalist enterprises, they conduct themselves very differently from their American competitors, each embodying the European sensibility that its job is to remain faithful to the organisation's fundamental mission – in these three cases, respectively to make the best cars, tyres and mobile phones – and it is prosecuting that mission by integrating all their stakeholders into the whole that will enable their organisations to grow sustainably and make profits over time. Their shareholders are but one vital part of the organisation – not the masters to whom every part of the company must be subservient – and, moreover, they and the directors have wider obligations to the society of which they are part. Although each company comes from a different society and culture, they all provide similar answers to the basic question whether property rights in a capitalist society should be exercised wholly self-interestedly and autonomously. The answer, in all three countries, is a decisive No. In each, laws of corporate association have developed, along with a network of supportive financial institutions, that permit the interests of the whole organisation to come before the sole interests of the property-holders – the shareholders.

Moreover, that formal requirement is supported by a corporate and managerial culture personified in each case by the chief executive and senior management team. Volkswagen's chief executive from 1993 to 2001, Ferdinand Piesch, Nokia's CEO from 1992 to the present day, Jorma Ollila, Michelin's Edouard Michelin – each is steeped in the organisation he leads and in what is required to sustain its technological and market leadership. These are not chief executives on the US model, holding

office on average for four years or less, charged overtly above all to maximise shareholder value; these are chief executives who set out to
husband their companies to a position of sustained market leadership
over time, and who are buttressed in that objective by their countries'
rules of corporate governance, legal structures and banking systems.
They want to make profits and can be as hard as nails; and the organisations they lead are as capable of cutting corners, manipulating markets
and lobbying for special favours as any other capitalist enterprise. That is
the nature of the beast. But the structures and cultures in which they
operate drive them towards business building rather than financial engineering. Robust and sometimes painful decisions are taken in the service
of the organisation and the communities in which it is embedded – not
primarily in the interests of the shareholders.

The first precondition for this approach lies in the way shareholders
interpret the rights attached to property ownership and how those are
shaped by law. Essentially, in each of the three systems highlighted here,
the institutional, legal and cultural framework permits managers to put
the needs of the organisation – constrained, obviously, by the competitive exigencies of the marketplace – before the demands of any one
stakeholder group, notably those of shareholders. This offers each enterprise a twofold advantage. First, it defines an overall ownership culture
which new shareholders, including those of British and American pension funds, must accept in the act of buying shares. Dividend
distributions, for example, are set in terms of the overall financial needs
of the company rather than driven by the need to conform to shareholder priorities. The pay-out ratio of dividends to earnings for these
three companies varies between a fifth and a third – around the
European average, and a fraction of that among their American counterparts, where the average is close to 80 per cent (see below). Corporate
law erects legal obstacles to the process of hostile takeover bids; in
Germany voting rights may be restricted, for example, and in France the
freedom for holders of bearer sharers to remain anonymous may make
it impossible for a hostile bidder to assess the chances of success in a bid
because he or she does not know the identity of the shareholders and
whether they support the incumbent management. Again, French company law permits companies to reward loyal long-standing shareholders

with a double vote, or to give the founding family or trust a golden share with over-riding voting rights; more than two-thirds of the top 200 French companies allocate double votes to long-standing shareholders.[7] Without the support of the president director general (PDG), a successful hostile takeover is very difficult to mount.

Second, the existence of this institutional, cultural and legal framework allows the organisation to manage its shareholder structure to give it a stable platform on which it can rely in good times and bad. Both Volkswagen, with the stake held by Lower Saxony and the 20 per cent limit on shareholder voting rights, and Michelin, taking advantage of the French corporate law which allows it to be established as a *compagnie générale des établissements*, with a third of the shares held by the family and also operating shareholder voting right restrictions, can thus ensure that a critical mass of shareholders will stay invested in the company for the long term. At different times in the 1990s the trading prospects of both Michelin and Volkswagen would have made them vulnerable to takeover had their corporate governance and share structure been organised along American lines; both retained their independence and have subsequently flourished. Until 1998 Nokia took advantage of Finnish company law that allows voting rights to be restricted to a privileged group of friendly shareholders; but with some 90 per cent of its non-voting shares held by overseas investors and under pressure to cater to Wall Street's prejudices this became untenable, and now it has one class of share with equal voting rights. However, the company's embeddedness in Finland, its unique managerial culture and track record, and its market leadership provide it with a strong bulwark against takeover. It is now big enough to argue that its own style gives shareholders the value they seek – but it needed Finnish protection to reach this position of strength.

The conservative consensus attacks this approach across the board. The first criticism is that, because being a shareholder in such an enterprise is unattractive compared to other investments, European companies will progressively suffer from a shortage of willing investors so they have to pay a premium to attract them. Their cost of capital will rise. Nor is it easy for them to engage in big international takeovers, because shareholders in target companies – especially in Britain and America – will prefer to sell to companies who take their obligations to shareholders more seriously. Worse still, the lack of threat of hostile takeover and complacency about the need to make profits will featherbed senior directors and managers. They will not hunt aggressively for deals and efficiency in production. They will take the soft option in negotiations with powerful unions. They will be less hungry and enterprising.

This is a naïve view about organisational productivity, as argued in chapters 5 and 7, and plain ignorant about the sources and cost of external finance. Over the last two decades the American stock market has been a trivial source of capital for American enterprise. Between 1952 and 1995 in the US, for example, 90 per cent of capital expenditure in non-financial enterprises was financed internally by the companies themselves rather than raised through issuing shares. Between 1981 and 1996 US non-financial enterprises actually bought $700 billion more in shares through share buy-back programmes and takeovers than they issued to finance investment. And the stock market makes a huge claim on profits; between 1990 and 1995 firms paid out 78 per cent of their after-tax profits in dividends.[8] Whatever else it does, promoting the interests of stock markets and shareholders does not deliver cheap and plentiful capital.

Indeed, as argued in chapter 4, it does the opposite. The paradox of creating a market in which the direction and management of companies can be contested through hostile takeover is that it creates an increasingly insupportable burden on companies. Internally generated funds are largely earmarked for shareholders as dividends or share buy-backs. Payback on investment has to be fast. Overall investment levels have to be lower. When an economic downturn occurs or the company faces a competitive challenge, it has to place the shareholders' interests before the organisation's – holding up dividends but cutting investment, for example. Neither Volkswagen, nor Nokia, nor Michelin could have established and maintained its technological and design leadership in an American context, any more than Boeing has managed to do.

For the stock market–shareholder value nexus raises the cost of capital and compels the company to make its top strategic objective keeping the share price as high as possible. Recall, too, the evidence marshalled in chapter 4 about the terrible record of failure following takeovers and mergers. One of the reasons plausibly advanced for Europe's high productivity is that the 'market for corporate control' is so undeveloped.

Thus the only reliable way to buy a company is to secure the agreement of its directors and senior managers – the precondition for the successful marriage of cultures that is difficult enough to achieve when integrating any two companies, and virtually impossible if one company has been the prey of the other in a hostile takeover. Restructuring is driven by economic need rather than deal-makers' expectations of fast profits.

Independence from the stock market is not just about the ownership structure; it is about companies' capacity to look to the banking system for long-term finance. European companies, like their American counterparts, raise the vast bulk of finance for expansion through their own internally generated cashflow: over 80 per cent of German investment is typically financed from internal funds. Supplementary long-term finance is raised from the banks, which in France, Germany and Scandinavia have played a crucial role – augmented in the German case from the vast pool of saving built up as the in-house pension reserve, safeguarded from Maxwell-type fraud by compulsory reinsurance with the great German reinsurance companies. These banks are prepared to offer long-term committed loans, financing gaps and allowing European enterprises to capitalise upon being relatively free from takeover and take a longer-term developmental approach to building their businesses.

European companies plainly watch their share price, but they do not see it as the key driver in determining their fortunes. For example, Volkswagen's memorandum setting out how it intends to organise its internal financial control system to maximise the Volkswagen share price is revealing. The company assumes that a 13 per cent cost of equity – no more and no less – is reasonable, given shareholders' expectations, and says that in future it will organise its pricing and investment strategy to offer this return – but adds, 'It is not intended to adjust the cost of capital continuously to short-term fluctuations in the financial markets.'[9] This is not the pursuit of shareholder value as understood in the US. Volkswagen seeks, as an international company in an era of financial deregulation and globalisation, to offer shareholders a better deal to reflect their growing power; but only as one group among many key stakeholders whose interests have to be balanced in the interests of the organisation as a whole. They should expect 13 per cent; no more, no less. The expectation in Britain, by contrast, is to earn 20 per cent.

All three countries' banking systems were developed to support the growth of industry and commerce, and again, although the relationships are loosening, they still exist. France's big bank groupings have historically had a close relationship with the French state, and were even nationalised after World War II before being subsequently privatised in the 1980s and 1990s, while Germany developed a more complex relationship of public savings and investment banks at regional or *Land* level, with an industrial refinancing arm – the Kreditanstalt für Wiederaufbau – at national level. With a commercial arm that has built close relationships with its customers in order to develop confidence in their borrowing policies and supported the relationship by taking shares, Germany's banking system has been a ready supplier of long-term finance to business on a scale even greater than its counterpart in France. Despite all the talk of reform and a greater equity culture, only 18 per cent of the liabilities of German companies is owed to shareholders today – exactly the same proportion as twenty years ago.[10] The Nordic countries' industrial banks follow the German model: for example, the Swedish government still has a 25 per cent stake in MeritaNordbanken, the largest commercial bank, which was established in the nineteenth century explicitly to channel Swedish savings to industrial development, and still retains that culture.

All three banking systems strive to create long-term relationships with business borrowers in order to serve each client's credit needs as an organisation; this provides a more reliable market for the bank, allowing it to build a portfolio of loans in which it has confidence, and provides a crucial financing ally for business. The more the company can borrow paying predictable interest rates and the less it has to rely on issuing shares where it has to pay a risk premium, the lower its overall cost of capital – and the more investment it can undertake. Moreover, if it has a platform of stable ownership it can take a strategic view of its direction, knowing that there will be a powerful pay-back from its investment in research and people alike. Together, these are the institutions and processes that support a culture of production and wealth creation, in sharp contrast to the American conception of wealth generation as primarily about deal-making and pure buying and selling in markets. It is a profound dichotomy.

Airbus – a case study

Airbus represents perhaps the quintessential expression of European attitudes towards production and technology – and also the point at which the gulf between the European and American approaches is most public and uncomprehending. From the US point of view this project is the creature of protracted government subsidy and protection – yet for Europeans it embodies their distinct approach to enterprise. In 1967 the French, German and British governments committed themselves to a long-term vision of building an organisation dedicated to civil aerospace production and technology, which Europe needed as a counterweight to the de facto monopoly supplier Boeing, and whose ownership structures and managerial culture were to be designed to serve the organisation rather than maximise short-term profits. Now, in the first decade of the twenty-first century, the Europeans are reaping the fruits of a commitment sustained over more than thirty years.

To design, build and develop a fleet of state-of-the-art civil aircraft was always going to be a long-term task. It would require shareholders prepared to defer their returns for perhaps decades. It would require, as the American aerospace industry had received through defence contracts, billions of dollars of grants to support the public interest in possessing an aircraft manufacturer that the markets could not create spontaneously themselves. The time horizons for the returns on equity investment and private bank debt are extraordinarily short-term compared to the time needed to develop an aircraft business. It was only the capacities of the European enterprise model that allowed Airbus to be contemplated for a moment – capacities that the British never understood, thus condemning them to the smallest role in the enterprise, one which even then they very nearly forfeited. In 1969 the British pulled out of the consortium, re-entering only in 1978 when Airbus had successfully made its first American sale to Eastern Airlines; the ideological and political wobble reduced its stake from an equal third to only 20 per cent. Yet even that minority holding has proved a good investment.

To get Airbus started required a corporate structure that would not enthrone the interests of private shareholders and which could mix flows of grants and loans freely in order to serve the needs of the organisation.

249

French corporate law provided the answer in the idea of a *groupe d'intérêt économique* (GIE), a form of incorporation whose overt purpose is to grow an organisation rather than produce returns for shareholders – a constitutional impossibility in the US. Ever since the foundation of Airbus the American criticism has been that massive subsidies, together with the French and German governments' insistence that Air France and Lufthansa respectively buy Airbus planes, have given the consortium a protected market. In the late 1980s the Gellman Research Associates report commissioned by the US government alleged that since its foundation Airbus had received $13.1 billion in 1990 prices from its government shareholders and that it had repaid only $500 million of $25.8 billion of loans that it has raised over its life.

The numbers were probably exaggerated, even if correctly signalling the broad scale and nature of the support, and Airbus's deliberately opaque accounts did not permit an authoritative rebuttal. However, if Airbus has received a subsidy, so have Boeing and McDonnell-Douglas. Between 1978 and 1988 the US firms received over $10 billion of research grants from the Pentagon and a further $13 billion in indirect support. Boeing's defence contracts alone, with their guaranteed profit margins, were worth $40 billion over the 1980s. Without some form of government subsidy, aircraft production and development, which can take decades to become profitable and where upfront costs can run into billions, is impossible either side of the Atlantic. The Americans chose to offer their subsidy through an ongoing relationship between defence contractor and government which they considered legitimate; what they consider illegitimate is to give a subsidy in such a way that a business plan that the markets would not sanction becomes operational.

Boeing's dependence on subsidy was thrown into sharp relief by the success of its lobbying efforts after 11 September and the consequent sharp fall in demand for civilian airliners. Its Washington office, headed up by Rudy F. de Leon, former deputy secretary of state for defence under Clinton, went into overdrive. Congress agreed a $20 billion deal, leasing 100 new wide-bodied unsaleable 767s to the US air force; there will be a major military aircraft renewal programme after the campaign in Afghanistan; Boeing is pressing for corporate tax rebates; and new R&D work is being undertaken on military prototypes, in particular unmanned aircraft. Boeing is as much a client of government as Airbus, if not more so.

At the heart of the dispute are the twin issues of time horizons and the character of corporate sustainability. Airbus, after thirty years, has dropped its GIE status and become a single corporation with publicly quoted shares. It prepares accounts to international standards and makes a profit. Its family of civilian aircraft are technologically advanced and, as Ivan Pitt and John Norsworthy say, offer airlines around the world 'lower operating costs, a new generation of technology, spacious cabins and on-board avionics'.[11] By providing competition, in future it will prevent Boeing from charging the same monopoly prices for new aircraft that it set on the jumbo, the 747, throughout the 1970s, 1980s and 1990s. Its capacity to operate independently of the time horizons of the capital markets means that it can find the $12 billion it needs to build the A380, the superjumbo, offering airlines and passengers technological possibilities for cheap air travel that would otherwise not exist. It has enriched the technological depth of the European aircraft industry. US suppliers also benefit; Airbus spends $5 billion a year with American subcontractors.

In production and design style Airbus is fundamentally different from Boeing. The US company, as described in chapter 4, has been unable to husband its workforce, design capacity and production infrastructure before the demands of Wall Street. It suffers from production pinch-points as a result of reducing its overheads to provide the required short-term returns. It has had to lay off risk, contracting out production to other suppliers and thus weakening its central productive capacity; the long-distance version of the 777, for example, part of which was built in Japan, was late into service because of difficulties in co-ordinating the size of the plane with the necessary aero-engines – and as a result lost further ground to Airbus's A330 and now A340. Meanwhile Airbus, because it has the necessary financial muscle, can retain control of the central production process and collaborates around a central purpose to gain knowledge, skills and expertise. This, it believes, is the key to its success. Like Volkswagen, Nokia and Michelin, it is dedicated to production and engineering excellence, and its wider constitutional structures support this mission.

In order to achieve its success it has had to take a thirty-year rather than three-year view of profitability; and that in turn has meant a declaration of independence from the criteria for liquidity and profitability set by the capital markets. It has had to put the interests of building planes, fighting for orders and pleasing customers before the demand for dividends. In the conservative discourse this subsidised aircraft manufacturer, free from the disciplines of the financial markets, should be a failure, along with Nokia, Volkswagen and Michelin. On the contrary, Airbus is the most successful aircraft manufacturer in the world. Europeans can be proud, and look their tormentors in the eye. Their system works.

So what about European unemployment?

The overwhelming blight on Europe's record, undermining its self-confidence and seeming to validate the conservative critique, is its indifferent performance over the 1990s on increasing employment and reducing unemployment. But, as mentioned in chapter 7, in the late 1990s job generation in France, Italy and Germany began to contrast favourably with trends in both Britain and the US, disproving the notion that there is something intrinsic about the European labour market that condemns it to never-ending high unemployment. It is wrong to conceptualise joblessness as resulting purely from Europeans' mistaken desire to extend ideas of the social contract to the labour market, burdening it with charges and regulations so that it cannot sustain high employment. The OECD, for example, finds that the degree of European employment protection 'has little or no effect on overall unemployment' and, to the degree that it has any impact, affects the demographic distribution of work rather than its overall level.[12] Another study finds that the non-employment rate for men aged between twenty-five and fifty-four over the period 1988–95 was 11.9 per cent in the US (excluding the very high US incarceration rate in prison) and averaged 11.7 per cent in Germany, Italy and France.[13] Where the US has scored over Europe has been in the generation of female jobs; but, as argued earlier (see chapter 5), that has more to do with the sexual revolution coming earlier to the

US than Europe, so that women's desire and willingness to work, along with society's structures and attitudes, are more advanced. Moreover, many American women have gone to work because of household need, and strong consumer demand has created the opportunities.

None of the conservative explanations for unemployment holds water. For example, leading German economist Fritz Scharpf, in the definitive study on the relationship between the welfare state and unemployment, proves that unemployment is unconnected to the level of social spending.[14] While it may be true that the US and Japan have achieved high employment with low social spending, it is also true that the Nordic countries have achieved high employment with high social spending and generous levels of income support for the unemployed. More significantly, if the sectors of the economy which are exposed to international competition are isolated, his study still shows zero correlation between level of social spending and unemployment. In fact, in those sectors, the US has the same employment rate as France, and a lower employment rate than Austria and Germany! Therefore, the size of a welfare state and generosity of unemployment benefit have no impact at all on employment, and lack of international competitiveness is not the cause of European unemployment.[15] If anything, writes Scharpf, 'the countries with the highest levels of employment in the internationally exposed sectors of the economy are characterized by stakeholder-oriented forms of corporate governance and by cooperative industrial relations that differ significantly from American (and British) forms of shareholder-oriented corporate governance and deregulated labour markets.'[16]

Next there is the commonplace assumption by many American critics that the pattern of demand in the new knowledge economy favours skilled rather than unskilled workers, that the burden of regulation and strong unions borne by Europe has prevented its unskilled workers from pricing themselves into low-paid jobs – and that this is the chief cause of high unemployment. Scharpf refutes this thesis, too – and so does almost every scholar who examines the figures closely. Professor Stephen Nickell of the LSE, a member of the Bank of England's Monetary Policy Committee, finds in an important paper that European unemployment afflicts unskilled and skilled workers to almost the same degree – and that

Germany in particular does not suffer from especially high unemployment among its unskilled workers.[17] (He also points out that Germany's strong system of education and training means that even workers in the 'unskilled' category are grounded in basic skills that make them eminently employable.) Nickell's finding is confirmed by John Schmitt and Lawrence Mishel, who report that unemployment rates for poorly educated adults at the margins of the labour force are only marginally higher in France and Germany than they are in the US. But this is precisely the category for whom any form of employment protection should – if the conservatives are right – weaken their employment prospects still further. The ratio of the college-educated unemployed to those with no qualification is, as reported in chapter 4, high in the US compared with Europe, again suggesting that the European labour market works quite well in pricing unskilled workers into jobs.[18]

One more piece of proof. The claimed 'flexibility' of the US labour market implies that job turnover rates should be higher, and that this helps to generate jobs; in fact, they are lower than in highly protected Italy and the same as those in France. The lowest job turnover rates are in Britain, whose unemployment record is the best among the big four European economies.[19]

The only impact welfare seems to have on differential unemployment and employment rates relates to the strictness with which access to unemployment benefit and income support is associated with a demand that applicants undertake training, look for work actively and/or participate in government work schemes. Thus unemployment has fallen rapidly in France, Sweden and Finland, where over 10 per cent of the labour force has entered active work programmes since 1998,[20] and remained low in Denmark and the Netherlands, which accompany generous unemployment benefit with a strict requirement that the unemployed search for work. But, importantly, these trends are independent of the overall level of labour market regulation, extent of unionisation and generosity of welfare payments.

The lazy charge that European unemployment is the fault of unions, regulation and social charges does not bear serious scrutiny. Employment generation has system-wide roots, and the role of demand is at least as important as the character of the labour market – or so conclude

Scharpf, Nickell, and Schmitt and Mishel. The more telling characteristic of both the US and Britain is that both economies and labour markets have benefited from a sustained rise in personal consumption, which would not have been possible without financial systems that permit consumers to assume enormous amounts of personal and mortgage debt. In effect, the American and British economies have enjoyed the benefits of a long-term, privatised reflation.

Over the five years up to 2000, for example, private consumption in real terms rose by 4.5 per cent per annum in the US and by 3.9 per cent per annum in the UK, compared to 1.7 per cent per annum in Germany and 2 per cent per annum in France – and this in turn has helped support a burgeoning service sector in both Britain and America, with the accompanying job generation.[21] Relatively depressed growth in private consumption in France and Germany has not been offset by buoyant public consumption; in Germany, public consumption has grown by 0.5 per cent per annum in the five years to 2000 and in France by only 1.8 per cent per annum. In Britain and America, by contrast, it has grown by a useful 1.6 per cent per annum in real terms – underwriting the growth in private spending so that total spending has grown handsomely over the five-year period.[22]

The combination of financial market deregulation and a financial system organised to canalise credit to consumers has been the critical component in generating this demand growth, which France and Germany have been able neither to reproduce nor to compensate for by an orthodox Keynesian public sector led reflation. Both countries have been compelled by their obligations to the Maastricht Treaty creating European monetary union to keep their economies on a tight rein in the run-up to and launch of Europe's single currency; and on top of this, Germany has been transferring some 4.5 per cent of GDP every year during the 1990s to the former East Germany,[23] forcing it to take even more of a hair-shirt budgetary approach. In a climate of economic austerity in which no risks could be taken with inflation lest it imperil the chance of creating and then joining the single currency, neither country was able to initiate a major programme of financial deregulation – with the accompanying chance of a credit and consumer boom – even had it wanted to.

The policy task is self-evident. It is to guard what is good while lifting the growth of public and private demand to American and British levels; if that can be done, together with bringing a greater supply of women to the labour market, there is no reason why the European economy should not experience similar rates of growth and job generation to those America has achieved over the past twenty years.

In any case, Europeans have viewed their financial systems in a different light – as having a primary role in the long-term development of their economies, rather than as marketing money to generate personal consumption. They may need to modify this approach, as I have suggested; but they should not simply discard it, for the character of the financial system is fundamental to how property rights are exercised, and that in turn is fundamental to the creativity and productivity of their corporate sectors. The European system – the cluster of approaches to property, equality and the social contract, and the public realm – works as an integrated whole. It offers high productivity, quality workers, organisational creativity and high social protection. Nor does it have to pay for these advantages with high unemployment, as the conservative consensus insists; rather, unemployment is the short term by-product of the shocks that the European economy, and especially the German economy, have suffered and the constraints that have been placed on the growth of consumption. It can be ameliorated by greater demand and by adopting more activist policies towards getting the unemployed to search for work – while preserving the scope and generosity of Europe's welfare state. Europe's future, if it guards what is best about its model, is bright.

9
Siblings under the skin

Europe is a collection of countries replete with ancient enmities, united by no common language or culture. If the United States, built on immigration from Europe and with English as a lingua franca, can organise only a limited cultural fusion around the lowest common denominator principles of liberty and free markets, and has had little success in sustaining a consensus to provide a continent-wide social contract or public realm, then what chance has the continent from which its founders came? So runs the daily cry of Britain's army of Eurosceptics. What unity of economic and social purpose is possible that might underwrite its new single currency, the euro? What European public is conceivable in which European political institutions might be rooted and by which they can be held to account? The only Europe that is sustainable, runs this sceptical argument, is a Europe that has no more ambition than to trade with itself peaceably while guaranteeing capitalism and democracy; one that makes no incursions on the sovereignty, institutional structures and cultures of its member states.

It is an argument all the more powerful because it seems grounded in European reality. Even if EU members succeed in achieving similar inflation, interest rates and fiscal policies to qualify for entry into the euro this is only surface convergence, for which in any case a high price has been paid by some in lost output and unemployment. The underlying economic and social structures of the EU states still vary hugely. There is an academic industry devoted to classifying and reclassifying European countries into any number of models, depending on the character and relationships of their trade unions, companies, welfare systems, labour markets, regulatory regimes, financial markets and governments – fortifying those who can see only differences and obstacles to the European project. Moreover, each of these elements hangs together with all the others as part of an interdependent national whole; weaken any one to serve the cause of building Europe, goes the argument, and you do so at your peril.

There is, though, another argument. In the first place, the big economic indicators of Europe's performance are much closer than commonly realised; the differences in inflation, interest rates and budget deficits are now minimal for countries in the single currency area.[1] Patterns of taxation and public spending are also converging towards similar levels. This is not surface convergence. Moreover, this parallel economic performance is matched by common values and purposes that lie beneath the apparently irreconcilably different matrices of institutions and systems. Those clusters of values around property, the social contract, equality and the public realm surface and resurface across the continent. Europe does have an approach to capitalism that is distinct from that of the US, and although there are different variants across Europe, more unites than differentiates them.

By now it should be clear how this European brand of capitalism manifests itself at the level of the company. But the same value system extends beyond the corporate environment to constitute the platform for building a society-wide contract in which risks are collectively shared, incomes for the unemployed, sick and retired are pitched generously enough to allow them fully to participate in society, and powerful education and training systems attempt to give each individual the opportunity to maximise his or her individual potential. The reason why Europe compares so favourably with the US in respect of social and income mobility is that every European state sets out to offer equality of opportunity to all its people; the American neglect of the bottom 50 per cent in the name of individualism is not reproduced in Europe. And this social capability is supported by a conception of the public realm whose underwriting of public science, public transport, public art, public networks, public health, public broadcasting, public knowledge and the wider public interest gives European civilisation its unique character while offering many of its enterprises competitive advantage. These are the structures upon which European companies base their innovativeness and creativity, and which have allowed them the extraordinary rates of investment and productivity growth that have enabled them to begin to overtake their US counterparts. Each variant of European capitalism may have elected for different means; but the ends they want to achieve are undergirded by the same values. There may be different varieties of European capitalism, but they are siblings under the skin. Far from its being impossible to build a European Union with a common public and common values that could hold its institutions to account, the avenue is open to us if we choose to take it – a proposition we will explore in the next two chapters. But first we need to understand just how much Europe holds in common.

What the European models hold in common

The most famous of the European models is 'Rhineland capitalism' and its associated social market economy, which prevails in Germany, Austria and the Netherlands, extending in part to Belgium. This is the universe of the decentralised state, consensual labour relations and the stakeholder company which overtly sets out to establish itself as a self-standing, associative organisation rather than the creature of its shareholders. Profits are reinvested in the enterprise and dividends are proportionately low. A company's shares tend to be owned by other companies, banks and insurance companies that have trading relationships with the business and are well-disposed towards it rather than regarding a rising share price and swelling dividends as the supremely important objectives of their shareholding. The system of corporate governance provides for representatives of the shareholding groups to join representatives of the workforce and unions on supervisory boards that set the overall strategic direction of the company. It is difficult to mount a hostile bid successfully without the agreement of the supervisory board. Article 76 of German company law requires managers to run their business in the interests of the entire organisation and prohibits the supervisory board from detailed intervention.

Despite globalisation, the fulcrum of German industrial relations and wage setting remains the agreements and deals reached between industry-wide trade associations and industry-wide unions – more than two-thirds of wage agreements formally or informally are set by collective wage agreements in this way[2] – but the unions behave as responsible business partners because as stakeholders they are integral members of the organisation. The reputation that the overall system has for constructing high-performance, co-operative workplaces is so good that it is very hard for companies to undermine and break up the unions without occasioning a public relations disaster. In 1995, for example, the metal industry employers' association, Gesamtmetall, tried to face down the industry-wide union, IG Metall (the second largest union in the world), to achieve job flexibility; but the consequent strike so threatened the image of constructive co-operation that individual firms broke ranks to show solidarity with their workers. Gesamtmetall backed down.[3]

The crucial intermediary is the works council, which by law has to be represented in corporate decision-making – but which is, conversely, prohibited from initiating strike action.[4] Thus the council is deliberately set up to be the intermediate, neutral forum where union and employer can work out their relationships and manage tensions without the risk of precipitating industrial conflict – an agency for constructive conversation and communication within the organisation. It was Volkswagen's work council that suggested a pay cut and the 28-hour week to the management in response to its threat to lay off 30,000 out of a 140,000-strong labour force in the mid-1990s; and the works council again that was central to Volkswagen's recent ability to hire new workers at lower wage rates than the existing workforce. The system is central to Germany's ability to arrive at co-operative solutions to competitive pressures.

German workers have high levels of education and training – a commitment that has its roots in the medieval guilds – so that workforce and employer alike have an investment in long-term organisational growth. Companies voluntarily participate in a national training system which offers apprenticeships of at least three years in 370 accredited training courses – and the training system is integrated into the educational system, so that students move seamlessly from schools into training colleges or company-based apprenticeship systems.[5] Sixty per cent of German teenagers are engaged in some form of vocational training, which carries little of the social stigma it still bears in Britain, where it is seen as a second-class option for those unable to pursue formal academic qualifications. Readers will recall that in the US 46 per cent of school-leavers receive no form of educational or vocational qualification (see chapter 5).

This combination of high skills, high investment and commitment to long-term organic business growth is at the heart of the German productivity miracle, endowing the German economy with its capacity to build companies, large and small, that are extraordinarily adept at diversifying and upgrading production while maintaining high quality. American conservative critics portray the expensive system of training, lack of threat of takeover and high union involvement in management as inhibitions on productivity, but German defenders of the system reject such arguments. Wolfgang Streeck, for example, argues that the combination of high costs and what American conservatives would describe as an excess of skills forces German companies to be more creative and compete on their capacity to be innovative in their product ranges – and that high skills and capability to invest become instruments of competitiveness. 'Excess skills make possible an organisation of work capable of flexibly restructuring itself in response to fast-changing, highly uncertain environmental conditions.'[6] By operating in an environment in which economic and social obligations are intertwined, the firm paradoxically finds itself more competitive than if it aimed only for economic benefits.

This stress on the importance of the social spills over into the generous German welfare state. Employers' and employees' social security contributions together tend to be very high, and are clearly differentiated from the tax system as a system of social insurance.[7] Benefits, however, reflect varying contributions, a demand made by postwar Christian Democrats as the price of their support for the system; as a result there is a wide range of benefit levels, especially in pensions, rather than equal entitlements for every citizen. The middle class thus have as much of an incentive to belong to the social insurance system as the poor. The society-wide social contract and its explicit reflection in business organisation could hardly be more evident – and the result is a high-wage, high-productivity, production-oriented economy characterised by a commitment to quality and technology.

The conventional account is that this social market economy is on the ropes in the face of the encroaching influence of the stock market and its priorities. Share prices on the German stock market have more than quintupled over the last two decades, and three financial market promotion laws have sought to make trading in shares easier and cheaper – culminating in the recent decision to make the disposal of large strategic cross-shareholdings free of capital gains tax. Companies are taking more interest in their share prices and their shareholders' views, introducing investor relation departments; directors' remuneration rose by 66 per cent between 1996 and 1999 as performance-related pay kicked in.[8] These developments, together with the announcement by the leading car manufacturer Daimler-Benz that its prime objective is now the pursuit of shareholder value, and the transformation of the giants of German banking, notably Deutsche Bank, into global actors, are meant to sound the death knell of the traditional system of finance and corporate governance. And, as this is the linchpin of German social market 'Rhineland' capitalism, offering the stable ownership and financing which underpin the whole fabric of long-term planning, industrial relations and workforce development, the whole edifice is said by its critics to be about to fall.

However, the continuities in the picture are more striking than the differences. Martin Hopner at Cologne's Max-Planck Institute, in the most exhaustive survey of how German corporate governance is changing, concludes that far from abandoning its traditional model, Germany is rather combining it with elements of the Anglo-Saxon model.[9] Only 26 per cent of German shares are held in dispersed ownership, he writes, and while shareholder value is admired in Germany its injunctions are not followed; the fact that executive pay is rising and more foreign institutions own German shares does not mean that Germany has a market for corporate control, or that the legitimacy of trade union associations and works councils has been reduced. Indeed, paradoxically, it is trade unions and external investors in alliance that are pressing for more transparency of accounting standards.

German banking, too, should be seen in this way – as combining its traditional German approach with the new opportunities offered by globalisation. As Richard Deeg argues, German banking has always been profoundly segmented into local, regional, national and international operating units, both by regulation and by the desire of the German banking community to build strong business relationships – which requires being embedded in local and regional business.[10] The segmentation remains, but has become more marked. The international arm of German banking has become more globalised and more strongly oriented towards the capital market, while the local and regional segments of German banking have continued to play their role as relationship bankers to German business. The institutional matrix of savings banks, co-operative banks, the regional *Landesbanken* and the industrial lending banks are all still pumping out long-term bank loans to businesses they know intimately, just as they always have.

Thus, although German banks have been unwinding their single large shareholdings, so that today there are only two bank shareholdings exceeding 25 per cent in the top fifty companies, that pattern has been replaced by one of a number of banks with smaller shareholdings. Companies, especially in Germany's highly competitive small and medium-sized business sector, still look first to the public savings and co-operative banks for finance rather than the stock market. Bank debt still constitutes some three-fifths of the capital employed in German business, and equity remains at just under 20 per cent, as it was twenty years ago.[11] As a result, businesses that in the US and Britain would feel they had to have a stock market quotation can in Germany remain controlled by the founding family or its network and be supported by the local and regional banking system; there are 650 public limited companies in Germany, compared to over 2000 in Britain and 7000 in the US – but business overall has higher rates of productivity, innovation and investment in Germany than in either of the other two. The banking system created by state and national government to support German business remains as important as ever, even though its international operations have changed their character; and even that change has been embraced only in order to serve German business better. Thus the heart of the stakeholder enterprise and social market economy remains intact – supported by a powerful consensus that it should remain intact.

So attractive is this model that it is overtly copied by the post-communist societies in eastern Europe. They have tried to sustain the same stability of private ownership through German-style cross-shareholdings and investment funds owned by banks.[12] They have constructed banking systems – underwritten by the government – to supply long-term loan finance to enterprise as cheaply as possible. Hungary's Underwriting Company, for example, guarantees long-term loans exactly as Germany's industrial refinancing arm did after World War II. The welfare system is necessarily less generous, but it remains universalist in its ambition; education and health are seen as public goods to be provided by the state.

The second variant is that practised by the social democratic Nordic countries. These are more overtly collectivist and egalitarian, and the influence of Christian Democracy, especially in its concern to match social benefits with social contributions, is less strongly felt. Union membership rates are very high, ranging from 70 per cent of the workforce in Norway to over 95 per cent of the workforce in Finland.[13] Welfare is based on universal entitlements and is very egalitarian; there is virtually no means-testing, even though the welfare system is substantially funded by taxation rather than social security contributions. Income tax, as a percentage of gross wages, is the highest in Europe; social security contributions are no more than average.[14] The state actively sponsors training, job mobility and job search, while paying high levels of unemployment benefit. There is also a powerful commitment to support the family, with long periods of maternity and paternity leave. Besides the generous welfare state, there is high-quality provision of public health and education, important sources of employment in their own right.

These are important differences; but the outcomes are very similar. Benefits are as high as in social market Europe – unemployment benefit varies from 58 per cent of average earnings in Finland to 90 per cent in Denmark – and the schemes are combined with training programmes.[15] There is huge investment in human capital. And companies, although not organised along formal stakeholder lines, have the same commitment to sustaining associative organisations through integrating and balancing the demands of unions and shareholders. Hostile takeovers are made very difficult by companies being allowed to allocate voting rights to friendly shareholders, so that in Sweden, for example, one share can carry as many as 1000 votes.[16] Dividend distributions are low, and bank finance is preferred to stock market finance; the banking system still has a high degree of state involvement to ensure support for business. National trade unions reach accommodations with national employers' associations. Wages are high, but so are productivity levels, buoyed up by high levels of investment and social peace. Regulation is extensive. The state plays a more active role in the name of the collective social will, but the character of the resulting capitalism is very similar to that in social market Europe.

Then there is Catholic southern Europe, where the legacy of fascism and military dictatorship still casts a long shadow – Italy, Greece, Spain and Portugal have all had direct experience of one or the other, some of both. These are more corporatist countries, where relationships between big business and the state remain close. Organised labour is more overtly political, oppositional and distrustful of private enterprise, but equally is less powerful; union membership ranges from only 11 per cent of the workforce in Greece to 26 per cent in Portugal. The social contract is still discernible, however. Employment protection is the highest in Europe, maintained at these levels to minimise worker discontent and head off grievances that might spark trade union recruitment;[17] and care has been taken to build a welfare state that will offer care from cradle to grave, although there is not the ideological coherence that defines the welfare systems of social market and Nordic Europe. Provision in the south tends to consist of a mish-mash of universal payments, especially pensions, together with more means-tested, targeted and conditional benefits.

Capitalist firms in this model have the same organisational template as the two north European models, although this owes much more to the role of family and state than to a compact between unions and share-holders. Family enterprise remains immensely important; this is especially so in the dynamic small and medium-sized business sector, but even leading firms like Italy's Fiat can still be dominated by the founding family. Over three-quarters of the top thirty Italian firms quoted on the Milan stock exchange are each controlled by one shareholder with a majority stake, usually the founding family.[18] Where the family interest is absent, direct state ownership and regulation achieve similar results. Again, the stock market is less important than banks in financing enterprise, and the state is ready to step in to cushion and manage industrial change. Economic development can be uneven, with substantial disparity, for example, between the south of Italy and the north, and markets tend to be regulated to favour particular interests and client groups. The state – in all cases a post-1945 creation – has much less legitimacy than in the north, and the traditions of social citizenship and political participation which inform northern Europe are much less firmly embedded, but southern Europe has found its way to a capitalism and social contract that perform in similar ways.

The final two models are each represented by a single country: France and Britain. Both are long-standing nation-states with powerful central governments and traditions of weak regional autonomy; but their approaches to economic and social organisation could hardly be more different. France, with its Napoleonic code and tradition of state support for industry that goes back to Colbert, remains dirigiste and statist despite recent 'liberalisation' – but over and above that it has elements that resonate with the southern, social market and Nordic European models alike. It has a generous universalist welfare system paid for by social security contributions along social market principles; and it has a profound commitment to public health and education along Nordic lines. The proportion of students taking the *baccalauréat* has risen from 28 per cent in 1980 to approaching two-thirds today.[19]

However, the close relationship of its large corporations to the state, even though loosened by fifteen years of privatisation, and the adversarial and politicised trade union movement are more southern European in character. Union membership, at 9 per cent, is the lowest in Europe; but French companies, like their northern European counterparts, accept that employee–employer agreements should apply to all their workers; so that collective bargaining agreements cover more than three-quarters of the workforce. Employment protection legislation is stronger than that of every other European country outside southern Europe.[20] The French, like other Europeans, have struck a recognisable social contract. And if the state owns less than it once did, it remains a powerful regulator and driver of French economic and social life; any company, for example, considering significant redundancies has to produce a social plan explaining how it will help the redundant to re-attach themselves to the labour market. In addition, the government has been among the most interventionist in Europe, supporting early retirement programmes for the over-55s, and more recently promising to create up to three-quarters of a million jobs for young people. The configuration of elements may be different, but the end result is a degree of protection and welfare for French employees similar to those in Scandinavia and social market Europe.

As in Germany, there has been a significant transformation of the economic model over the past two decades. For some, the retreat of the traditional state influence in planning, the financial system and direct ownership of industry is evidence that France is in the throes of becoming fully Anglo-Saxonised or modernised (the two terms are seen as interchangeable by French business); others see as much continuity as change.[21] At first sight the scale of change is certainly extraordinary. The privatisation of the banking system and the scrapping of the entire mechanism that allowed the government to direct loans and credit to favoured companies has implied a massively significant move to a more market-based financial system. The sell-off of state-owned business, along with the phasing out of state subsidies to the business sector, have removed another traditional state instrument of economic direction. Foreigners now own some 40 per cent of the equity of the top 100 French companies,[22] and as we have seen there have been moves to match the corporate governance rules of Britain and America.

Again as in Germany, however, the movement towards a more market-based financial system has not meant the surrender of the core, long-termist, business-building attributes of French enterprise, which remains recognisably stakeholder in character even if the means by which it pursues these ends are very different. French company law states, echoing German company law, that management should pursue the company's social interest (*intérêt sociale de l'entreprise*) or social capability; in other words, the shareholder interest is only one of several that need to be balanced to serve the organisation as a whole.[23] The president director general (PDG) is formally entrusted with enormous executive power to prosecute and represent the interests of the entire organisation, and although the old system of *bancassurance* in which financial holding companies held friendly cross-shareholdings is rapidly unwinding, French PDGs can accord differential voting rights to their shareholders depending on their longevity and loyalty so that they can always secure a majority of friendly votes in any hostile takeover bid. As noted in chapter 8, shareholding in France, as in Germany, tends to be concentrated, with the majority of shares being owned by a few groups or individuals, typically including the founding family; on average, 48.2 per cent of the shares of the 416 largest French companies are held by the five largest shareholders, all of whom will have a long-term relationship with the company.[24] They will have voted in the PDG, who can thus expect their support. In short, if the supervisory board is the gatekeeper to controlling a business in social market Europe, the PDG plays a similar role in France.

This allows French businesses to take a similar broad view, encompassing the whole associative organisation, of its long-term needs as its German counterparts. Like them, French companies tend to look to the banking system rather than the stock market for finance; dividends are low, and the accent is on retaining profits to invest in research and development. French output per man-hour, like that of the former West Germany, now exceeds that in the US – and French capitalism, while remaining distinctive, is converging towards the European norm.

And then there is Britain. This is Europe's outlier – the economy and society regarded as nearest in Europe to the American model. At one level this is self-evidently true: no other European economy has financial markets as powerful and international as those of the City of London, nor a business environment – supported by a web of company law and institutional practice – dominated by the notion that the sole obligation of companies, policed by the savings institutions and investment banks, is to maximise shareholder value. Hostile takeover is easier and more prevalent than anywhere else; in Britain bank support for business tends to be contractual rather than relational, and lending is very short-term. Employment protection is the weakest in Europe,[25] and business regulation and all forms of taxation are fiercely resisted by the business establishment as a 'burden'. The cultural aversion – embedded in the state and business community alike – to intervening in the operation of the market has been reinforced by the recent intellectual and political ascendancy of conservatism, in particular under the Thatcher and Major governments.

The consensus view is that this 'Anglo-Saxon' structure has brought the British economy many benefits, notably the lion's share of inward investment flowing into Europe, on which Britain is uniquely reliant; but the bitter truth is that on almost every measure of true competitiveness (productivity, investment, innovativeness, research and development, market share, new patents) Britain lags behind both Europe and the US. The reliance on inward investment for so much growth and innovation is in one sense a sign of economic weakness. Britain has been fortunate that since the pound's forced exit from the European exchange rate mechanism in 1992 the management of the economy has been benign, and since 1997 positively good. The independent Bank of England established by Chancellor Gordon Brown in that year has proved adept at setting interest rates judiciously to meet its target for inflation while the framework of rules for setting public spending, taxation and borrowing has proved robust and effective, and the economy has enjoyed nearly a decade of sustained growth. But this has not compensated for deep-seated structural weaknesses in its approach to capitalism which continue to plague its performance.

Britain's difficulty is that despite sharing with the US a common language and many common approaches to finance and corporate governance, the same values that underpin European capitalism are embedded in Britain. The doctrine of shareholder value is more controversial in Britain than it is in the US for this very reason. Despite more than twenty years of being lectured by the political class on the need to celebrate business and enterprise and give thanks for having capitalism, Britain remains firmly European in insisting that business has no right to insist on special privileges, and that it should rather earn the right to trade in British society through the integrity of its commercial relationships and the quality of its service. Britain has had four codes of corporate governance over the past decade – the Cadbury, Greenbury, Hampel and Turnbull reports. These are not isolated, unconnected attempts to assuage the concerns of a temporarily aroused public that business should respond to its wish to see more ethical behaviour. Rather, they are a response to a persistent and growing demand for better standards, more rigour in the transparency of decision-making and clear rules for conduct at the highest level in companies. The business community and business associations have needed to show that they are prepared to consider change as the decade has unfolded exposing successive shortcomings in the way companies are run, notably over the setting of executive pay. British business has urgently needed both a code of practice and a narrative to fend off the accusation that its practitioners behave little better than cowboys.

The rise in executive pay, though trivial by American standards, brings stormier criticism every year, and British institutional investors are compelled by public opinion to intervene – or at least be seen as intervening – to make sure that executives and directors do not pay themselves over-extravagantly. Their interventions may be feeble, but that in turn creates more criticism. Unlike American business, British companies operate in an environment heavily influenced – as in the rest of Europe – by the legacy of feudalism and notions of the common good, expressed alike in one nation Toryism and socialism. To hold property, including corporate equity, is a privilege that comes with attendant reciprocal responsibilities. Capital gains tax and planning laws carry more legitimacy in Britain than they ever could in the US. But instead of understanding this and turning the culture to the service of building a more long-termist, innovative capitalism, Britain is still seduced by the possibility of becoming more like America as the route to capitalist success – unwilling to accept the reality of its core European beliefs or recognise how rich the rewards of the European capitalist tradition have been in promoting productivity and innovation. The British are so fixated with what happens across the Atlantic that they cannot see the merits of what is happening across the Channel, and how it might be adapted to deliver the productivity growth that business, government and society want and need. Instead, Britain sticks stubbornly to an organisation of capitalism that is at odds with its fundamental values and which works poorly even in its original American context – let alone a British European one. For there is much less that is American in Britain's success than the US likes to boast – its achievements have been won by a more European approach to capitalism, whether or not it understands this itself; and even if Britain wanted to reproduce the mores and attitudes of the US, as a deeply European country it simply could not.

Where Britain is unambiguously European is over the idea of the social contract. The British variant may be increasingly fly-blown, but it exists none the less – and the population remains fiercely attached to it, to the despair of the political class. The provision of health care free at the point of use by a tax-financed, publicly owned National Health Service is a political imperative no politician can escape. Although the welfare system is by European standards mean and limited in its scope, it remains the lineal descendant of Beveridge's system of social insurance and impossible to abandon. Support for health and education spending remains high, with 63 per cent of respondents in the latest social attitudes survey reporting they would increase tax to spend more on education, health and social benefits,[26] and trade union membership still encompasses a third of the working population. The axiomatic assumption that Britain is more American than European, and that it could not hope to sit easily within the European Union and its economic and social model, is misplaced. In trying to Americanise itself, Britain has lost its way. It is through the rediscovery of what it holds in common with Europe that it can heal its psychosis – looking to America while being European: a dislocation that enfeebles its effort to build a creative capitalism and a just society. Britain needs to rediscover and reassert the European value system at its core.

Europe's welfare states, trade unions, labour market regulations and belief in the husbanded or stakeholder enterprise – along with the role played by government – are not economic and social aberrations. They arise from its feudal, Christian past, its tortured experience of industrialisation and urbanisation, and the searing clash between fascism and communism as attempts to establish a universalist response to the moral crisis posed by the inequities of income, wealth and power created by capitalism. Europe's economic and social model is everywhere the result of the reconciliation of these tensions, and Europe's social democratic and liberal parties on the left and Christian Democratic parties on the right have become the twin custodians of core European values and the European settlement. They define Europeanness. They are non-negotiable European realities.

Thus the attempt to build an ever closer union in Europe is less far-fetched than it might seem. The builders of Europe should be more confident, less in awe of the boasts of conservative America and less

ready to accept that their continent is plagued by irreconcilable differences. For even the pro-European consensus accepts that if Europe wants
to build a single market and single society, then its only route is to copy
America as far as it can. The EU has allowed itself to define its task as 'lib-
eralising' and 'deregulating' – what Fritz Scharpf describes as 'negative
integration' (see chapter 10) – in accordance with the consensus view that
there is little to be done in Europe except build a single market because
its varying economic and social models are impossible to integrate. In
today's conservative climate, this is the new common sense.

Indeed, the pro-European consensus insists that if Europe wants to
exhibit the same alleged economic and social dynamism as America,
then it should go further still down the negative integration route. Its various economic and social models, with their 'burdensome' rules that
protect trade unions and shield companies from takeover, should be dismantled to reproduce America in Europe; taxes and social charges that
limit the rewards to risk-taking and undermine the so-called enterprise
culture should be lowered; and so on and so on – by now the reader
should be familiar with the dreary litany. This will produce the win–win
outcome of unleashing economic dynamism and promoting integration
simultaneously. It may turn the EU institutions into agencies that are hostile to key European values, losing legitimacy and support in the
process – but this is the only realistic option.

It is not, of course. The choices Europe has made are more than reasonable. They produce efficient outcomes, embody profound economic
and social priorities that have a great deal in common with one another,
and are currently modifying themselves to the forces of globalisation
rather than capitulating in wholesale abandonment of their core values
and principles. There is thus is a different approach to building Europe.
It starts with the same shared commitment to democracy, human rights
and market capitalism. From that foundation the EU could go further
and assert that the European model is distinct and valuable, and that it
wants to set out to help rather than hinder European states as they try
to reform their systems – rather than abandon them – in the face of
globalisation. It would underline that Europe's commitment to the
social, so far from being a source of inefficiency, is a source of competitive advantage, and while it should be modernised to reflect global

economic changes it should not be abandoned. In short, Europe should work to build itself up – to integrate positively – around a much more self-confident belief in the merits of its distinct approach to capitalism and the social contract.

The social contract works . . .

The very success of the European model is tribute to the robustness and effectiveness of its settlement. The chief characteristics of European capitalism are the innovativeness and creativity of its companies, and a relatively higher growth in output per man-hour over the past two decades than in the US. The relatively stronger position of labour in Europe, secured either by trades unions or through regulation together with ownership structures that oblige shareholders, bankers and managers to husband companies, has led to a much denser, thicker and more complex conception of organisational efficiency, adaptability and productivity built upon high trust and high skills. This system's advantages may have been temporarily clouded by the superior growth of American employment and the so called New Economy miracle of the 1990s, along with slow overall growth in European employment in the backwash of German reunification and European preparation for monetary union, but even if core European beliefs did lead to the inefficiencies portrayed by conservative critics, they would still be defensible. Europe's social contract produces valuable social outcomes – a reality frequently neglected within the barrage of criticism.

This is important. As we have seen, each European economic and social model is characterised by a combination of income redistribution, social insurance, means-tested social benefits, and provision of public health and education that make taxes and social security contributions higher than in the US – and a combination of employment protection, labour market regulation and higher trade union representation that buttresses the rights and powers of Europe's workers more than those of their counterparts in the US. As demonstrated in the last chapter, these mechanisms do not create higher unemployment, nor have they damaged Europe's powerful record on enterprise and productivity. What they have done is to produce an array of social outcomes which on every important measure are significantly better than in the US.

In the first place, it is worth recalling some of the findings set out in chapter 5. The widespread view in America, shared by many in Europe, is that this immigrant society, where millions came to better themselves, is much more socially mobile and less class-bound than any in Europe. This was not supported by any evidence even in the immediate postwar period, and more recent surveys of income and social mobility have shown that it is no better than that in Europe – and at its worst significantly poorer. The grip of the rich on the upper echelons of the education system has grown while the lack of skills and education among the bottom 50 per cent of the US population is increasingly trapping them in low-wage, low-skill jobs from which their rate of exit is much worse than in Europe. For all its record of employment generation, it is the US that is the more sclerotic society in terms of measured mobility.

Moreover, the US is much more unequal, and notwithstanding its higher overall per capita incomes, its poor are absolutely worse off than their counterparts in Europe. Capitalist economies generate inequality; typically, if there are no interventions and social transfers, between 20 and 30 per cent of the population will have incomes that are at least 50 per cent lower than the median disposable personal income, the definition of poverty used by the OECD and EU. The issue is how societies should respond to alleviate this situation. The American approach is minimalist, except only in provision for its elderly. As economist Timothy Smeeding has shown, the US welfare system, even before its scaling back during the Clinton years, raised the incomes of the poor sufficiently to reduce the proportion of adults in poverty only moderately, from 26.7 to 19.1 per cent.[27] In Germany, France and Italy social transfers are dramatically more effective; using the same benchmark, only 7.6, 7.5 and 6.5 per cent of their adult populations respectively live in poverty. And while 24.9 per cent of American children live in poverty, the proportions in Germany, France and Italy are 8.6, 7.4 and 10.5 per cent respectively. Whatever other boasts it may make, the US can hardly claim to be compassionate or more efficient than Europe in its attitude to the relief of poverty.

Britain, as the Anglo-Saxon representative in Europe, should be expected to produce similar results to the US. It is true that with 14.6 per cent of its adult population and some 18.5 per cent of its children living in poverty, its social outcomes lie somewhere between those of mainland Europe and the US. However, because the British starting point is the most dire on either side of the Atlantic – 29.2 per cent of its population live in poverty before any intervention or social transfer – the proportional impact of its social security system in reducing poverty is much closer to Europe than to America.

Here again, what stands out is not the differences with mainland Europe, but the similarities. The key benchmark for adults of working age is what happens when they are made unemployed. Britain's system is built around means-tested and qualified benefits rather than a comprehensive and universal system of social insurance; but if as a result unemployment benefit is wretched by European standards, this is partially compensated for by generous contributions to help with rental payments (housing benefit). The so-called 'replacement ratio' – the aggregate support provided by the government to unemployed workers, expressed as a proportion of their former earnings – is 64 per cent for a British couple on average earnings with two children, within shouting distance of the 74 per cent ratio in France and Germany.[28] And, as workers' incomes fall to two-thirds of average earnings, the British system of means testing offers a robust safety net (rather than social insurance) that produces outcomes that compare reasonably with other European countries – and contrast sharply with what happens in the United States. The replacement ratio for a couple with two children on this lower income rises to 83 per cent, higher than Germany's 74 per cent and in the same area as France (86 per cent), the Netherlands (90 per cent) and Sweden (90 per cent). This is why the British system, even though allegedly much closer to the American approach, is nearly as effective as the Europeans in alleviating poverty. The US replacement ratio for a couple with two children on two-thirds of average earnings is 51 per cent – much lower than any European country except Italy and Greece – which is why the US is so ineffective at reducing poverty. The conservative theory is that this makes its unemployed more keen to find work. But again, to recall Fritz Scharpf's findings outlined in the last chapter, there is no relationship between the replacement ratio and the generosity of the welfare state and unemployment. The Netherlands and Denmark, for example, have higher proportions of their workforces in employment than the US, but also greatly higher replacement ratios, taxation and social spending.

All western countries act aggressively to limit poverty among the elderly – those aged over sixty-five. The US social security system lowers the proportion of the elderly living in poverty from 58.7 per cent before transfers to 19.6 per cent after transfers – an intervention which reduces the prevalence of poverty by a cool two-thirds. But even here the Europeans outperform the US. Germany, France and Italy all spend more than 10 per cent of their national income on pensions, twice as much as the US and the UK. As a result it is hardly surprising that only a tiny proportion of their elderly live in poverty – 7.7, 4.8 and 4.4 per cent respectively – and that they all lower pensioner poverty by around 90 per cent through state intervention. The country with the highest proportion of pensioner poverty is Britain, where a whopping 23.9 per cent of the elderly live below the poverty line. Britain may be able to boast that of all five countries it is the only one in which spending on the elderly will be lower in 2050 than in 2001, so that it has no impending budgetary crisis; but the other side of the coin is that its elderly are in the most acute financial circumstances. There is no such thing as a free lunch.

Once more, all is not as it seems. While the US is debating the privatisation of its social security system to compel individuals to save and invest on their own account for retirement, Britain's Labour government is working within its own means-tested conception of the social contract to offer pensioners a minimum retirement income guarantee over and above the British basic state pension. Poor pensioners, if they have no other form of income, qualify for this guaranteed retirement income, which is 25 per cent higher than the state pension. This measure may not be part of a Nordic or social market Europe system of social insurance, working instead within the British means-tested social safety-net tradition, with all the disadvantages catalogued in chapter 7; but it does none the less represent an attempt to address pensioner poverty within a social contract framework. In any case, with France, Germany and Italy all trimming pension benefits and extending minimum contribution periods because of budgetary pressure,[29] there is some sign of convergence – but the social contract approach for all stands. As the privatisation of pensions proves to have greater and greater shortcomings, the British reaction will not mirror that of the US administration; for public pressure will demand an improvement in government-provided pensions and a strengthening of the social contract framework.

European electorates are profoundly committed to publicly led social transfers and institutions, which they recognise directly benefit their lives and living standards. The most obvious of these, apart from various forms of income support, is health care. Germany led the way with the introduction of compulsory health insurance for industrial workers in 1883, and fifteen years later France had established a system of near-comprehensive insurance – both pre-dating the rise in socialism. Britain's system of health insurance followed in 1911, but eligibility was confined to those in work. Thus before World War I Europe's big three states had already put in place one of the building blocks of the social contract in health – but built around the insurance principle.

Since then there has been a divergence of how health is financed; but each European country has become committed to providing health care available to every citizen free at the point of use (although some require small nominal payments from citizens, with the poor protected by means-tested assistance if they cannot pay) and provided on the basis of medical need. France, Germany and the Netherlands have built on their original foundations and made health insurance compulsory and comprehensive, while Britain, Spain, Italy and the Nordic countries have developed health systems financed by general taxation. But whether tax- or insurance-based, all the systems are unambiguously public creations. Health insurance funds are not privately run by profit-making companies quoted on stock markets, but have overtly social aims and have been established explicitly as non-profit-making bodies to provide the public goal of universal health insurance. French employees, for example, insure through the Caisse National d'Assurances Maladies des Travailleurs Salariés and mutual insurance companies, while in Germany, with its social market tradition, the task is left to closely regulated mutual insurance companies supplemented by sickness funds, whose boards – like those of its companies – include both worker and employer representatives. Their tariffs are negotiated with government, and the terms on which they do business with hospitals, clinics and doctors are also closely regulated. As Richard Freeman comments in his account of European health systems, 'social insurance systems are clearly not public systems in the way that national health systems are, but nor can they be said to be "private". Finance and delivery are organisationally separate but publicly mandated: these are public systems with prices, not private systems with elements of regulation.'[30]

The American system, based on private insurance with profit-making insurance companies and supplemented by Medicare for the old (which still needs topping up with private supplementary medical insurance to pay surgeons' and doctors fees'!) along with Medicaid for the 'categorically needy' on or below the federal poverty line, rests on very different philosophical foundations. This is not a social contract in which access to health care is guaranteed whatever your income; the US is prepared to allow 16 per cent of its population – some 43 million people – to live without any form of health insurance. A quarter of those earning less than $25,000 (£17,850) have no insurance, while only 8 per cent of those earning more than $75,000 (£52,800) are without insurance.[31] This is the social expression of a market society in which the same patterns of inequality of income are allowed right at the centre of one of every human being's most important aspirations – the right to health, even to life.

The US system is not only socially unjust but also calamitously economically inefficient. Despite around 14 per cent of GDP being spent on health, American life expectancy is lower than in the four big European countries – and markedly lower for men. Male life expectancy in France is 74.2 years, in Germany 73.6, in Italy 74.9 and in Britain 74.2: all are higher than in the US, where it is 72.7.[32] Infant mortality is lower in Europe. Eight babies under a year die for every 1000 births in the US – significantly more than in France (4.9), Germany (5.3), the UK (6.0) and Italy (6.2).[33]

What inflates American health expenditure is the inevitable desire of the privately insured to pay whatever is needed to restore themselves to health – and the medical profession's readiness, given that there is no budget constraint, to offer whatever they can to their patients. For the better off, the system provides very high-quality health care indeed, dragging up certain average health outcomes. American survival rates for breast and lung cancer, for example, are better than in the UK, and only

10 per cent of patients wait more than a month for non-emergency sur-gery, compared with over half in Britain.[34] However, American performance is not especially better than that of mainland Europe, where expenditure runs at two-thirds of American levels. And as dissatisfaction mounts in Britain about the low level of health expenditure and indiffer-ent health outcomes, the US is explicitly not the model held up for public admiration. New Labour is pledged to lift public health expenditure to the European average by 2005 and has dared to begin to argue that as this cannot be done within existing financial resources more will have to be found – and that the best route is taxation. Even the Conservative party openly cites the social insurance model of France, Germany and the Netherlands as being more likely to increase the resources devoted to health, deliberately avoiding the political mistake of copying the US model. Britain, its political parties are finding, is very much a European country with European attitudes.

... and a vibrant public realm supports a vibrant economy and society

Nor is belief in public agency confined only to creating and sustaining a social contract. It is, as argued in chapter 2, part of a much wider value system that sees the public realm as a means of establishing, expressing and working towards common economic and social goals that cannot be achieved by individual interests but are none the less intrinsic to any society's well-being. The universe of political debate and government action, critical to a democratic society, is but a subset of the wider public realm and dependent upon it for its vitality. Citizenship is not just about the exercise of votes or the right to live under the impar-tiality of the law; it is about participation in the totality of public choices, economic, social and cultural, that confront any community. The public realm is where communal choices are examined from the point of view not of individual but of public advantage – and where political options are framed, as far as possible, impartially and disinter-estedly. This in turn requires a public space in which information can be publicly and freely gathered, exchanged and disseminated – through channels ranging from newspapers to scientific debate – which is thus the precondition for a vibrant culture of citizenship. Broadcasting, scientific research, the process for making public appointments – all are parts of a sphere of attempted impartiality dedicated to serving the common good. This sphere becomes the basis for public initiative to create opportunities through government action that could not be created by private economic and social actors alone. The public is larger than the narrowly political, and it both demands and accords the widest definition of citizenship – economic, political and social.

The concern to uphold this broad conception of citizenship rights to serve a common interest runs through European civilisation like a golden thread. Thus there is a public interest in every citizen being well educated, because the social whole benefits from high average levels of educational attainment. There is a public interest in every citizen having access to good health care, not least because infectious disease knows no boundaries. There is a public interest in every citizen having access to impartial news and information, without which there is no chance of participating in public debate on some broadly equivalent basis of knowledge. There is a public advantage in the dissemination of scientific knowledge so that its veracity can be tested and so that it is universally available as a basis for material advance for all. Every citizen should have access to a telephone network. And so on.

These notions of the public good entail profound economic and social choices that are distinct in character from those made by the US. They are, as we have seen, the moral underpinning of universal health care provision and measures for poverty alleviation more comprehensive than those attempted by the US – but they also extend to economic initiatives such as establishing the Airbus consortium or ensuring the banking system provides long-term credit flows. When European states are sufficiently far-sighted this readiness to establish common public rules can have not just useful social results but rich economic paybacks too. When, for example, Finland, Norway, Denmark and Sweden came together in 1983 to form the Nordic mobile telephone network, they paved the way for the European standard bandwidth which Nokia and Ericcson so successfully exploited in the mobile phone business – and which is now set to become the global standard. Rather than allow market forces to establish a common bandwidth, the route the Americans have followed, the Nordic countries acted to produce the win–win outcome of rapid mobile phone development for consumers – and industrial success for mobile phone producers.

This idea of the public and the legitimacy it accords to the state is analytically distinct from socialism – although European socialism has drawn upon it to justify its philosophy, and by conflating socialist and collectivist aims with public interest aims has helped to discredit both. Plainly there are occasions when the collective and the public are the same; for example, clean air and drinkable water can be regarded as both public and collective interests. Collective ownership of a particular industry may not be in the public interest. In other circumstances, it may be necessary to establish public ownership of, say, a rail system, in order for it to be run effectively or indeed at all; but the public for whom this transport is created includes the wide array of private and individual interests that constitute society – not an egalitarian collective. Collectivism and the public realm are not interchangeable concepts.

This confusion stands as a barrier to American understanding of what is going on when Europeans justify government initiative with reference to conceptions of the general or public interest which Americans too readily interpret as socialist. For while socialism as a philosophy demands that the interests of private capital be subordinated to some expression of an egalitarian collective or community, the public interest is an idea that co-exists with markets and private property – and indeed can be put to their service. Thus the 1957 Treaty of Rome provides for a liberal, market-based European economy that entrenches private property rights, free trade, competition and openness, but also specifies the duty of the European Economic Community (as it was then) to protect the general interest. It is not that the US does not have a public interest tradition itself – Madison argued that the federal system of government was designed to uphold the public interest, and the consistent appeals to bipartisanship are an appeal to this tradition – it is that it has become so degraded by lobbying, pork-barrel politics, campaign finance and the ideology of individualism that it has lost any relationship to the core principle.

This is most obvious in the two civilisations' respective approaches to information and ideas, always present over the past fifty years but becoming more important as ICT and the 'knowledge economy' become driving forces of economic and social progress. In the infancy of the ICT age every European country acted to ensure that a national public broadcasting organisation was established, bound by law to disseminate politically balanced news and information – a determination reinforced by the disastrous experience of communist and fascist control of television and radio. It is a tradition that has continued. The quintessential expression of this European conception of public service broadcasting is Britain's BBC, obliged constitutionally to attempt impartiality in its coverage of news and current affairs, but beyond that to entertain, inform and explain to every citizen. The Netherlands ensures that broadcasting time is allocated to all social and political groups proportionate to their size in a patchwork quilt of religious and political channels, while Germany's public broadcaster, the ARD, has a complex system of rules ensuring that senior appointments exactly reflect the balance of political forces in Germany. France's TFI and Italy's RAI are under the same obligation to attempt impartiality and public service broadcasting. In the hurly-burly of real politics, parties and governments jockey for advantage while the public broadcasters themselves, under proliferating competition from television delivered terrestrially, by cable and by satellite, have had to popularise their schedules – but the underlying mission survives even in Italy, where the politicisation is most acute. There is a public interest in ensuring that each citizen has the opportunity to be informed and entertained by a broadcaster with that mission, rather than profit maximisation, at its heart.

European governments and the EU are aggressive in their regulation of broadcasting content. The public interest demands that advertising is not openly misleading. Racist expression is banned. There has to be clear separation between programmes and any sponsorship. There are guidelines about how much content can be foreign-made – entrenched in article 4 of the 1989 EU broadcasting directive – and broadcasters should allocate 10 per cent of their budgets to support programme makers 'independent of broadcasters'.[35] While American broadcasters plead the first amendment's commitment to absolute free speech, making public interest regulation almost impossible, Europe acts to ensure that television and radio conform to public interest criteria. In particular, there are tough laws on media ownership and cross-ownership; Germany prohibits the granting of national broadcasting licences to any group in which one individual has more than a 50 per cent interest, while France forbids any company or individual to control more than 30 per cent of total newspaper circulation. Even Britain, which has been ineffective in preventing concentration of newspaper ownership, only allows newspaper groups with less than 20 per cent of national circulation to control TV stations with up to 15 per cent of the market. Even if this rule is relaxed, as seems likely at the time of writing, rigorous rules on the content of schedules will be maintained or even strengthened.

The thinness of American conceptions of the public interest has been accentuated by the ICT revolution. The tradition that information is essentially an economic commodity in which corporations trade, and that attempts to assert a public interest are essentially statist, has been deployed to full effect by the corporations of the New Economy to privatise the access to information that in Europe is regarded as a public good. As a result of intense lobbying by the US's giant media and ICT companies, in 1998 the US passed the Digital Millennium Copyright Act, making it a criminal offence either to break a copy protection mechanism or to circumvent any control designed to prevent access to information – in essence a giant step towards privatising the internet. But by the same token, US legislation protecting individuals in respect of how information about them might be traded and used without their knowledge is extraordinarily weak – so that insurance companies and credit rating agencies can swap data they have collected without any obligation to tell the individual concerned. There is deemed to be no public interest either in maximising access to potentially public knowledge and information or in offering individuals privacy.

The Europeans, by contrast, have attempted – albeit weakly – to protect a conception of the public interest. The EU's copyright directive attempts to balance the proper desire to secure intellectual property rights with reasonable exemptions for what might be copied. While the US bans the breaking of any encryption code in any circumstances, the EU permits reproduction and the breaking of codes if there is a presumption this might advance the public interest. The 1998 EU data protection directive, moreover, details exactly what companies can and cannot do with data in their possession; in particular, they cannot pass it on to a third party without the consent of the individual or company concerned. Nor can companies gather any information about individuals' sexual behaviour, race, religion or health without their express consent. To add insult to injury from an American perspective, the directive prevents companies from transferring data and information to countries where there is 'an inadequate level of protection' – which under current law includes the US. American Airlines lost a lawsuit in which they tried to defend transferring information about their Swedish customers to the US.

The same concern to advance – or at least protect – the public interest has informed the EU's approach to telecoms liberalisation, in contrast to what has happened in the US. Readers will recall that it was under intense US pressure that the EU established an internal market for telecommunications in the late 1980s and early 1990s, importantly specifying that public telecommunications contracts should be subject to competitive tender. This opened up the European equipment market to American manufacturers while giving private companies the right to built telecommunications networks. While the US 1996 Telecoms Act paid due lip service to the principle of universal telephone provision, it set in train such powerful forces balkanising the US telephone system with such weak regulation that the declaration made little practical sense. By contrast, the 1993 EU green paper declared that telecommunications are a matter of citizenship. Telecoms operators should accordingly provide public phone boxes and directory enquiries services; and the need for universal provision meant that even if some services were unprofitable they should be paid for by all service operators. The aim, it said, 'should be to provide consumers and businesses with a diverse offering of quality telecommunications at competitive prices whilst guaranteeing universal access to basic telecommunications services for all citizens'.[36]

American critics regard this concern as antediluvian, costly and an inhibition of liberty. Yet it is the Nordic countries that are in the vanguard of developing the New Economy, aided by the public realm concern to implement a system of broadband cable with universal reach, mirroring their establishment of a universal bandwidth for mobile phones. As the telecoms bubble bursts, leaving in its wake a trail of bankrupt companies and incomplete networks, it is plain that the preoccupation with promoting private interests in the hope that the public interest would spontaneously emerge (as Adam Smith predicted) has proved a false compass. And if democracy and the good society are underpinned by the maximum access to information, its privatisation in the US will in the long run surely undermine the vitality of its civilisation.

Europeans, in keeping with their values, have fought to keep the remarkable findings of the human genome project in the public domain for the benefit of all humankind; the US, in keeping with its values, is prepared to permit their privatisation. If this clash over the importance of protecting a public realm is at bottom a moral argument, the Europeans win hands down. The promotion of the corporate bottom line cannot be allowed to dictate the codes and values by which we live – in the US any more than in Europe. It is time to draw a line in the sand; and for that we need a European Union with a clearer sense of what it can and should be doing – supported by members who understand that alone they have little chance of sustaining the values and principles they hold so dear.

10

The idea of Europe

Today's European Union is a remarkable, if still incomplete, achievement. Its founding six members have been augmented by another nine, and up to ten additional countries in eastern Europe, as well as Malta and Cyprus, now want to join.[1] The formerly communist countries want to guarantee their commitment to democracy and the market economy through EU membership in the same way that Spain, Portugal and Greece did twenty years ago. Europe at last has reached agreement on its core principles, and has constructed the institutional and security apparatus peacefully to protect them. If it seems that contemporary Europe could never again repeat the mistakes of the past, it is the fact that the postwar generation and its visionary leaders – men like France's Jean Monnet and Robert Schuman, Belgium's Paul-Henri Spaak, Italy's Alcide de Gasperi and Germany's Konrad Adenauer – had the courage and foresight to lay the cornerstones of what has become the contemporary European Union that makes it probable if not certain that Europe will never again go to war with itself. It is an achievement that, given Europe's tormented past – and the ethnic conflicts that overwhelmed the former Yugoslavia in the 1990s – is worth consolidating and protecting to the last.

The open question is what this European Union really is and what it could become. Its Eurosceptic critics and some of its supporters see it already as close to a surrogate federal state, and determinedly moving further in that direction. Jean Monnet, the moving force behind the first attempt in European integration that resulted in the European Coal and Steel Community in 1952, three years later became the president of the Committee for the United States of Europe – hardly disguising his ambitions for what Europe might be. But what the EU has become by early 2002 suggests that its ultimate destination will be very different from a federal state; indeed, it has had elements of both a club of sovereign member states and a new supranational entity since its beginning, and the two sit in permanent tension. It is nearer a United Europe of States – a muddier, complex and less clear-cut political conception than a new federal European state; but workable, legitimate and potentially extraordinarily powerful as a champion of European values and interests.

The difficulty is that some of the manifestations of the contemporary European Union seem to indicate that it is something it is not. European federalists can point to the EU's parliament, its supranational quasi-civil-service-cum-European-directorate in the European Commission, an infant rapid reaction force that gives it a nascent military capacity, its new single currency and a body of law adjudicated upon by its own Court of Justice as evidence that the building blocks of a new state are in place. And the EU also has, as British Eurosceptics repeat ad nauseam, its own flag and anthem to complete such aspirations to statehood – along with European treaties that demand that their signatories accept the higher sovereignty of the European Union's institutions. Indeed, the judgements of the European Court of Justice have quietly built up a body of case law building on the EU's treaties that does constitute a form of de facto constitution.[2] Enthusiasts and sceptics alike can see evidence for what seems to be an emerging new federal state.

But to take this view is profoundly to misunderstand the real political possibilities of these Europe-wide institutions and processes, and the purposes to which they are put. Since the EU's foundation Europe's grand aspiration and the jealous guarding of national interests, sovereignty and sensibilities have co-existed in sometimes creative, sometimes destructive fashion. Jean Monnet saw his planned European Defence Community vetoed by the French parliament because of its infringement of French sovereignty – and the same concerns have run through every European initiative to the present day, culminating in the complex horse-trading of the Nice summit in December 2000 over member states' voting rights in an enlarged 27-member EU. The European Union may have the trappings of a state, but it is a state without its own public realm. It is a state whose ability to act proactively is inhibited both by its nation-state members and its own constitution, which has formidable power to knock down national rules and regulations but very constrained power to build them back up on a European level.

The apparatus of European institutions was built to create a common market; member states have ceded the sovereignty necessary to achieve this by treaty, but going beyond this aim has always been difficult. And even then member states have properly wanted to keep political control of the market integration process – a role accorded to ministers meeting in European councils, and in particular to the six-monthly meetings of the European Council of heads of government. As a result, decision-making in the EU more closely represents diplomatic negotiations between the member states themselves, the Commission and the parliament than an openly political process with clear mechanisms of accountability. Moreover, the boundaries between supranational and member state authority vary across the three pillars of European competence – justice and home affairs; foreign, defence and security issues; and economic and social affairs – so that the procedures and processes by which any decision gets taken shift constantly.

Even if Europe's decision-making structures could be made properly transparent and accountable, its institutions would still suffer from a democratic deficit. There is no European public realm, nor a European 'demos' – an electoral community with a shared European idea of citizenship – that can hold European institutions, processes, officials and politicians genuinely to account. English may be emerging among Europe's elites and burgeoning middle class as its de facto lingua franca, and its political parties may more closely consult and copy from each other; but this is a far cry from a continental polity and public realm united by language, political parties and media.[3] Despite the ICT revolution, the live public realm remains firmly rooted within national boundaries. If Europe's fledging 'state' is to be democratically legitimised by the conception that it is governed by the people, then Europe's supranational institutions fall at the first hurdle; for Europe's peoples remain firmly organised in their nation-states.

For Eurosceptics, this means that Europe is doomed to illegitimacy and that there must be a freeze on all further integration and an unscrambling of what already has been achieved – but that is far too pessimistic a judgement. The constituent parts of Europe do have core values in common. If it wants to protect its associative, stakeholder capitalisms and their accompanying social contracts before the march of globalisation it needs to be able to find a continental political voice to do just that; and it is already some way towards that goal. It is perfectly possible to design a more politically accountable system of European governance in the here and now, building on what we have, but respecting the principle that as far as possible government authority should be close to the people in the member states. It is also possible to develop a constructive agenda of building up Europe rather than tearing down barriers to trade. And while it is obvious that Europe at present does not have a European public to hold it to account, that does not mean that such a public will never be attainable; it may take more generations, but European peoples themselves harbour ambitions for themselves and their continent that suggest that, far from Europe being the top-down enterprise that Eurosceptics depict, what is happening reflects deeply felt urges and sentiments. One poll, for example, shows that approaching three-quarters of Europeans would like at some time in their life to live and work elsewhere in Europe – compared to the 0.4 per cent who succeed in doing so. Moreover, the revelation of the extent of US military power in the Afghan war, and the cavalier disregard by the Bush administration of its treaty commitments and European views, has prompted a growing awareness within Europe of its common values, attitudes and interests. A United States of Europe is eminently buildable, not least as a countervailing power to the United States of America. Indeed, the peoples of Europe need it sooner with the passing of every month.

The long march

If Europe in the early years of the twenty-first century is plagued by ambiguities over how it is to reconcile the traditions of statehood of its members with its ambitions for collective action, this was no less true in the 1950s as Europe's founding fathers tried to find a way through the logjam of nation-states to some formula that could bind the continent together and above all avoid another destructive European war. Jean Monnet's strategy was functional – attempting to identify positive initiatives around which Europe could construct supranational entities – and in 1950 was the driving force behind the famous plan of the French foreign minister, Robert Schuman – mentioned above – to pool the running of the French and German coal and steel industries under common regulations in a coal and steel community that other European countries could join. Italy and the Benelux countries duly did so, and in 1952 the European Coal and Steel Community was born. For the Italians and Germans this was manifestly as much a political as an economic commitment; a means of binding their countries into the West. Monnet saw it as the forerunner of more supranational arrangements for other industrial sectors like aerospace, airlines, transport and especially civil nuclear power – Euratom – through which Europe could be taken forward on a functional sector-by-sector basis. But despite the success of the ECSC there were no takers for more; Germany's free market Chancellor Konrad Adenauer was wary of ceding sovereignty over too much German industry to the protectionist and statist French, and the overtly political avenue was closed down when France vetoed the defence community in 1954.

Thus the only way forward was the lowest common denominator conception of a Europe that pledged itself to promote free trade in a customs union: the European Economic Community or EEC – the title it retained until it became the European Community with the passing of the Single European Act in 1987 and then the European Union after the full ratification of the Maastricht Treaties in 1994. (I shall follow the treaty descriptions – EEC to 1987, EC to 1994, EU thereafter). It was to be managed by a supranational body (the EEC Commission) answerable to a council of heads of state, each with a right of veto, together with its own Court of Justice, and was to begin with a twelve-year period in which trade barriers would come down gradually in order to allow France time to adjust. On this basis, the original six members of the EEC – France, Germany, Italy, Belgium, the Netherlands and Luxembourg – were able to sign the Treaty of Rome in 1957. Maurice Faure, France's negotiator, talked a suspicious French national assembly around by insisting that France was no longer a great power; it would be Europe, he said, that would take its place alongside America, Russia and China by the end of the century.[4] The possible ambitious political consequences of the customs union were already being touted – but the EEC was the beginning of a long, tortuous and still uncompleted road.

For if the political ambition was large, the attempt to establish a consensus in favour of what the renowned German political scientist Fritz Scharpf calls 'positive integration'[5] – creating Europe-wide institutions, policies and processes – was difficult if not impossible right from the beginning. By agreeing that the object of the European Economic Community was trade liberalisation to create the desired four freedoms of movement of goods, capital, people and services, and then giving Europe's nascent supranational institutions the sovereignty over nation-states to secure this end, the Community's founders bestowed upon the project of European integration a curious if not bizarre bias from its very inception. Pulling down rather than building up became institutionally entrenched. The structure of the new EEC, with its Commission, able to prosecute for failures to comply with the Rome treaty, and its Court of Justice, authorised to make binding legal judgements on member states, meant that the always painstaking business of building a coalition for positive action among member states – positive integration – was infinitely harder than the negative integration which the new institutions had been founded by treaty to complete: the removal of tariffs, quantitative restrictions, and barriers to trade and competition.

In other words the difficulties Monnet had found in organising positive integration were actually embodied in a treaty and a process that would unleash European integration, but largely in the negative context of agreeing not what to do to create a customs union, but rather what *not* to do. And even building a customs union was to require unanimity among member states, agreement of the parliament, Commission and Court – and no opposition from key constituencies across Europe. In any case, before the launch of the EEC a committee of experts from the International Labour Office and the ECSC had decided that comprehensive social and labour market policies should not be part of the economic integration process. As one leading observer commented, 'to have gone further would not have been politically acceptable at that time for each member prided itself on its advanced welfare system, its union traditions, its dedication to social progress, and to have asked them to dismantle their cherished edifices would have met with no response.'[6] Thus, until the late 1980s when Commission president Jacques Delors offered a decisive change of gear, Europe's story was one of largely failed social action plans, discarded directives aimed at harmonising best practice in employment or environmental policy, and only small-scale efforts at directing funds towards areas of social distress and backwardness – efforts for which the Rome Treaty had grandiloquently called. The fifth directive on company law, aiming to establish German style co-determination across Europe, simply died. Even the EEC's safety and health division sought only to standardise the regulation of products; to extend the EEC's remit to working conditions, at least until the 1989 social charter, was beyond both its capacity and its ambition. As for reform of the Common Agricultural Policy, arguably the one institution that, for all its warts, represented a positive integration of Europe, that was beyond the system's capabilities.

Thus over the first years of the EEC's life, the battle lines that would determine its evolution became firmly drawn. It was not Britain but France that first felt acutely the threat to national sovereignty, insisting in the famous 1966 Luxembourg compromise that any nation-state could block a proposal made by the European Commission if it threatened an interest of supreme national concern – a check to the supranational ambitions of the Commission and Court, which were already using their new powers to accelerate the construction of a genuine common market and creating a fledgling system of European governance. The Common Agricultural Policy, agreed in the Rome Treaty, was launched in 1962, and in 1967 each member state agreed to cede a small proportion of the VAT it raised to the Commission to support the spending of the tiny social fund in backward regions and deprived social sectors. What was to be today's EU was hesitantly taking shape.

The new European institutions suffered palpably from a lack of democratic accountability and real political community. President de Gaulle was the national leader who saw this most clearly, arguing that Europe could only be a community of nation-states because only they had legitimacy – even while Europe engaged in the painstaking business of building the political community it lacked. In the Fouchet plan drawn up under his insistence, the French proposed that European integration proceed as largely an intergovernmental affair, and that the institutions of the EEC be placed firmly under the political authority of the member states. The Fouchet plan was rejected because the other five members were reluctant to give up their supranational idealism and accept Gaullist realism over the power of nation-states. None the less, they all took de Gaulle's lessons seriously by re-engaging with the EEC and thus lending it legitimacy. They sought to breathe more life into the European parliament, and insisted that the European Commission retain its emerging role as guardian and advocate of a European public interest. More importantly, during the 1960s the concept of 'building Europe' – whatever its democratic shortcomings – began to win ground as an end in itself in all the member states, each of which was able to justify European integration as an important national goal, albeit for very different reasons.

As the 1960s wore on, the French became less critical of the EEC and more protective of their effective political leadership of this dynamic new economic grouping – or, as one French minister put it when France vetoed Britain's belated application to join for a second time in 1967, it kept an EEC of 'five hens and one cock'.[7] With Germany bound to pacifism by its constitution and reluctant to assume an activist international role, the Europe of the six was set to become Greater France, with the Brussels Commission an effective adjunct of the French civil service. For Germans, terrified of their past, this was a European coalition that locked their country into a commitment to liberal democracy and market capitalism while offering it a legitimate means to exercise non-threatening influence on the development of Europe. Indeed, so great was its willingness to put European interests before its own that Germany agreed to pay for the French-inspired CAP, thus committing itself to underwrite the prosperity of French agriculture – a position that has been sustained for forty years.

For Italy, preoccupied with resisting the advance of its powerful communist party, the EEC implied a commitment to democracy and capitalism that its own domestic politics did not guarantee – and the EEC's impartial bureaucracy was a great deal less corrupt than its own.

The Benelux countries, over-run in two world wars, now had an institutional framework that allowed them to develop the sovereignty of their parliamentary democracies, offered them leverage over European policy that had not existed before and again – especially important for the merchant Dutch, with their long free trade tradition – established a Europe along free market principles. As economic growth boomed, the Common Market shared with Japan the distinction of being the most rapidly growing part of the world. Its prestige reached new heights, and questions of legitimacy and what it might do positively became less pressing issues.

Once the birth pangs were over and the new structures had bedded down, each of the original six had important reasons for regarding 'Europe' as a powerful force for good in its own right – even if this Europe was to put pressure on each of them to establish a free market, roll back their regulations and limit their social ambitions to a greater extent than any of them might have chosen freely.

The struggle for Europe's heart – American or European capitalism?

Over the 1970s and into the mid-1980s the EEC continued as a largely uncontroversial customs area, any ambitions for more social and economic regulation checked by its constitution and the ambivalence of its member states. The British reversed their early refusal to join, and took up membership in January 1973 validated by a referendum in 1975. The most potent argument in favour of the move was economic – if Britain had enjoyed EEC growth rates since the mid 1950s, argued the pro-Europeans, it would have been a much richer country. But as Greece joined in 1981 and Spain and Portugal followed in 1986, what became newly important about the Community was less its own internal workings and more that, to become a member of the club, each state had to sign up to a basic framework of democracy, the rule of law and market capitalism. The dictatorship of the Iberian fascists and the Greek junta could not be repeated if Spain, Portugal and Greece were to sustain their membership. The EEC was becoming the guarantor of democracy, liberty, prosperity and markets in a continent that had been plagued by authoritarianism, fascism, communism and every variant of command and control economics. This alone justified its presence.

The exception to the general lack of momentum towards integration was the launch of the European Monetary System (EMS) in 1979. The teaser facing Europe's builders during the 1970s was how to maintain the pace of economic growth after the collapse of the Bretton Woods system of exchange rates and the subsequent quadrupling of oil prices. The structures that had been created in 1957 did not offer an effective vehicle for any pan-European economic policy, but it was obvious that an era of floating exchange rates coupled with benign neglect for the dollar was hitting Europe in two ways. Not only did European exchange rates tend to appreciate against the dollar, thus damaging competitiveness (especially for Germany), but they did so at different rates, thus upsetting the pattern of exchange rates within Europe – not least by making currency relationships volatile and unstable. Germany's Chancellor Helmut Schmidt, sharply critical of the impact of American policy on Germany and Europe, forged an alliance with France's Giscard d'Estaing to try to recreate the exchange rate stability that had helped propel growth from the end of World War II to the early 1970s – *les trente glorieuses* (the thirty glorious years). The EMS was born. Britain, as in 1957, was inevitably sceptical about such a grandiose European scheme, and its monetary experts predicted the system's immediate collapse.[8] Britain did not join, and the EMS prospered.

The EMS was a classic way of pushing Europe forward through essentially negative integration while respecting national sovereignty. Members of the EMS had to organise their economic policies so as to keep their currencies within the permissible margins of manoeuvre; thus they gave up the freedom to float their exchange rates but without constructing any binding supranational authority to superintend their national economic and monetary policies. They consulted and informed, and sought permission from the council of European finance ministers to make currency adjustments. If their currency came under speculative assault, they could turn to the network of European central banks to lend them hard currency to support their exchange rate – inevitably deutschmarks, lent by the now even more powerful German central bank, the Bundesbank – but only around an agreed policy of economic stabilisation.

The election of the Mitterrand government in France provided the infant system with its toughest test; there was massive speculation against the franc in financial protest over Mitterrand's ambitious 'socialist' programme of reflation and nationalisation, and by 1983 the French had realigned – or devalued – three times in three years and suffered a massive haemorrhage of their foreign exchange reserves. But although Mitterrand flirted with pulling out of the EMS, the French stayed in – and embarked on a policy of 'socialist rigour' designed by finance minister Jacques Delors to lower inflation and move towards budget balance at home and trade balance abroad to keep the franc within the EMS's limits. It was a landmark moment in the relationship between France and Germany, in French economic policy and in French attitudes towards Europe. Whatever France's pretensions to European leadership, its economy was exposed as palpably less powerful than the German. Moreover, just twelve years of floating exchange rates since the collapse of Bretton Woods had generated such exponential growth of private capital flows that it was impossible for one country to declare independence from the new conservative consensus about the appropriate conduct of policy. After the inflationary 1970s the financial markets had become converts to the monetarist proposition that the number one evil was inflation, and that any policy that threatened to increase it – whatever its potential economic and social benefits – was irresponsible and to be castigated. They would sell the currency in question, so making any planned economic expansion largely self-defeating.

If France was to challenge German economic pre-eminence and sustain its European leadership, then it would have to change tack. It would have to pursue budgetary and counter-inflationary rigour, while at the same time reframing the context in which its capitalism did business around the market principles of the Treaty of Rome. The old instruments of dirigisme and state direction were plainly outmoded. If French productivity – and indeed, mainland European productivity in general – was to match that of the US, one of the preconditions was the establishment of a continental-scale market to match. Europe had to move from being a customs area to a genuine single European market, and beyond that to become a more united economic and political force. 'I've always believed in the European ideal,' said Jacques Delors in an interview in October 1983, 'but today it's no longer a simple question of idealism, it's a matter of necessity . . . Our only choice is between a united Europe and decline.'[9]

The French conversion to this cause coincided with the second term of Margaret Thatcher's government in Britain, and the beginnings of more vocal business lobbying, notably from the European Roundtable (ERT) of industrialists, for the elimination of trade barriers and harmonisation of regulations in a genuine single market. In January 1985, just after Jacques Delors became president of the Commission, the ERT chairman Wisse Dekker ratcheted up corporate Europe's demands in a blueprint for a European single market entitled 'Europe 1990: An Agenda for Action'.[10] Delors and the Commission seized the moment as the cue for the next round of integration which they had been waiting to set in motion, and launched it with the demand that, as constructing a single European market was such an urgent priority, decision-making should proceed on this task on a basis of majority voting, to make progress more timely and efficient. It was a classic moment of political entrepreneurship in which the Commission demonstrated its capacity to set the European agenda – and integrate the very different preoccupations of the member states into a coherent whole.[11] While Britain saw the single market as the further cementing its programme of economic liberalisation at home, France saw it as the platform for regaining competitiveness now that other policy options were ruled out – and Germany continued to back the extension of the market in which so many of its own firms were pre-eminent.

What was being created was a Europe in which common positions on welfare, health, education, industrial relations and above all economic policy were as far off as ever. While each individual European state had developed complex mechanisms to manage and regulate capitalism, now collectively they were engaged in an enterprise either to deregulate or even drop them in the name of constructing a single European market – while putting little in their place. As Renaud Dehousse commented, the EU was set up as a market, so that member states' regulatory capacity had been 'severely constrained' by membership;[12] moreover, even when areas like consumer and environment protection had been included in treaties, the provisions did little more than legitimise what states were already doing – and 'the very concept of a common market did not provide guidelines for how regulatory policies ought to be conducted and what levels of protection sought.' Even if the EU had been more determined to act supranationally, the democratic deficit and lack of political community of which de Gaulle had complained twenty-five years earlier were as acute as ever. The European enterprise was becoming ever more an exercise in extending free market principles, while doing little to protect the values and practices that, as described earlier, so much define European civilisation.

Cometh the hour, cometh the man. Jacques Delors had seen the Single European Act not as an isolated measure of further economic liberalisation, but as part of a game plan to rejuvenate what had been a stagnating European process; he inserted a chapter in the act calling for European monetary union. Just as importantly, his establishment of the principle of qualified majority voting to advance the single market was a masterstroke, creating a precedent that could be extended into other areas. Delors was ambitious to give Europe the social, political and cultural dimension it lacked – and to use every ploy possible to drive through a positive integration process including qualified majority voting. 'The creation of a vast economic area, based on the market and business cooperation, is inconceivable – I would say unattainable,' he declared in the year of the Single European Act, 'without some harmonisation of social legislation. Our ultimate aim must be the creation of a European social area.'[13]

Delors understood well that by unleashing a powerful single market, the EEC would also unleash countervailing forces that would want to constrain it at a European level. The single market needed the balance of an active European social and labour market policy; the redistribution of income to the poorer European regions would be required in earnest. Nor did his ambition stop there. As French finance minister he had encountered at first hand the constraints of the financial markets, and he understood completely that if the EMS was to become more than a deutschmark zone with the Bundesbank acting as the de facto European central bank it would have to be Europeanised into a single currency. In

April 1987 Tommaso Padoa-Schioppa, a senior Bank of Italy official, warned in a report that the complete freedom of capital movements envisaged by the Single European Act would threaten the EMS's capacity to continue, and over the next year pressed the case for a single European currency as the only effective response – convincing the already half-convinced Delors that Europe should move quickly to adopt that aim.[14] Delors understood that France had only two realistic options: either to opt for floating rates, in which case European integration would be irrevocably damaged and the Bundesbank's position would remain unchallenged; or to opt for full monetary integration. And what was true for France was true for Europe.

In 1988 Delors moved on all three fronts – social, monetary and regional. At the Hanover summit he won agreement that a committee of central bankers and experts under his chairmanship should produce a feasibility report on a European single currency – but only after the EC had passed a directive insisting that every EU state move towards full liberalisation of capital flows. Delors was playing a double game. Capital market liberalisation was a medium-term threat to the EMS, to which he had become convinced a single currency was the only answer; but his twin-track approach of simultaneously furthering capital market liberalisation allowed him to keep the central bankers onside for his larger political project.[15] That same year he won agreement to double the funds available for a European regional policy – the so-called cohesion fund – so that Spain, Portugal, Greece and Ireland began receiving EC capital inflows of between 2 and 4 per cent of GDP, equivalent in scale to Marshall Plan aid flows, which underwrote an acceleration of economic growth in all four countries. Further, he promised the European Trade Union Federation a European charter on social rights; this 'social charter', delivered at the Strasbourg summit in 1989, set out twelve fundamental social rights – and every member state, except Britain, accepted it.[16] For the first time since its inception the EC had moved from negative to positive integration.

Delors' conception of Europe as an 'organised space', together with his capacity to use the Commission to further his ends, was visionary; it created the possibility for Europe to realise its potential for collective action beyond market liberalisation. The authority to make these changes could come only from intergovernmental action, and Delors was fortunate that both Germany's Chancellor Kohl and France's President Mitterrand were committed to European integration. Delors cleverly presented his Catholicism to Kohl and his socialism to Mitterrand as a means of enlisting them both to the cause of regulating capitalism on a European scale. And by offering them the bait of a yet more market-based Europe he was no less careful to win over the 'choir' of vested business interests – the ERT, UNICE (Union of Industrial and Employers' Confederations of Europe) and EC Committee of American Chambers of Commerce (AmCham) – so they too supported the cause. At the Madrid summit in June 1989, Delors, supported by the French and German governments, won approval of his plan for monetary union – a progressive movement in three stages towards a single currency managed by an independent European central bank with greater powers for the EC Commission to run Europe's economic and financial policies. It was an extraordinary coup.

The fall of the Berlin Wall in November that year suddenly gave the project even more political urgency. The prospect of a reunified Germany and the collapse of the Soviet threat transformed the international framework in which the EC had been built. It threatened to undo all that the French political class had been attempting for the previous thirty years. A reunified Germany would be more populous and wealthy than France; the deutschmark, already the linchpin of the EMS, would become further consolidated at its centre; and the highly conservative German central bank, the Bundesbank, would in effect become Europe's central bank. If France wanted to shape European economic policy and at least to share leadership of Europe with Germany, it had to act fast and turn the Delors plan into a formal treaty obligation.

Thus the Maastricht Treaty. For Germany, given its history, Maastricht had two important attractions: it bound the country firmly into the Western community, now that Germany's eastern horizons were opening up again; and it secured the support of France for German reunification. As long as the economic terms were as rigorously anti-inflationary as Germany's own, Germany would accept the plan. The French, though, had another agenda. The single market and single currency would create a complete European economic space sufficiently large to host a challenge both to the dollar and to the conservative ideology of the financial markets, and so create the possibility of the kind of expansionary monetary and fiscal policy that both Delors and Mitterrand – from their experience in the early 1980s – knew was impossible for any single European economy.

In December 1991 the European Council met at Maastricht to sign the act creating European economic and monetary union, including the famous social chapter whose directives Europe would follow by qualified majority voting – the precedent set by Delors and now deployed in a new area of EC policy. The Germans were insistent that besides a single currency and an independent European central bank there should be accompanying moves towards strengthening the European parliament and more collaboration on defence, foreign and interior policy. If the European Council had consisted only of the original six heads of government, the bargain that would have been struck between France and Germany would have been remarkable. In essence, Germany would have ceded the Europeanisation of economic and monetary policy, but only if France was willing reciprocally to extend the constitutional framework of the German Republic and the principles of the social market economy (set out in the early drafts of the social chapter) to the whole of Europe. In speeches since Maastricht, for example that of German foreign minister Joschka Fischer in May 2000, urging rapid progress towards a fully federal Europe,[17] leading German pro-Europeans have continued to regard the Germanification of the European political constitution as the answer to its democratic deficit.

But the European Council in 1991 did not consist only of the original six. It included Britain. In the tense negotiations the British used their veto to maximum effect. Not only would they block the single currency and social chapter if they were not given an opt-out, they succeeded in watering down the bold plans for political union. What was left was still significant – increased powers in decision-making for the European parliament, the commitment to develop a common foreign and security policy, and powers for the EU Commission to initiate action on positive integration in consumer affairs and 'trans-European networks' (transport, telecoms and energy) – but it was far less than what Germany had hoped for in its grand bargain with France. The

Germans won a commitment to rename the EC as the European Union together with limited European citizenship rights, but the progress towards political union in no way matched the giant step represented by the single currency. To advance the cause even moderately Germany would have to wait until the Amsterdam Treaty in 1997 and Nice four years later to push its agenda marginally forward.

Despite Delors' guile and Franco-German support, pulling down at national level had proved immeasurably easier than building back up at European level; but the first efforts had been made. The social chapter was now a legally binding social charter that would extend information and consultation procedures, social partnership, and health and safety standards to all member states – except Britain; the Commission had extended its capacity for action; majority voting had been spread to social matters. However, Europe's political arrangements fell far short of the framework that would make sense of its ambitions for economic governance with a single currency. Delors' political subtlety had rebounded on him. In his original conception for a single currency he had wanted structures to co-ordinate European fiscal policy, but there was no agreement on the proposal at Maastricht. Instead, Europe locked itself into a highly conservative monetary regime with surprisingly little capacity to correct it with fiscal policy or put in place robust social interventions. The financial markets agenda had trumped that of the president of the Commission.

Yet the achievement of Maastricht remains significant. It was the first concrete attempt since the Treaty of Rome to change the trajectory of European integration, and it partially succeeded. It produced a vital European settlement in the wake of the collapse of the Cold War. Ten years later, Europe does have a single currency and single market, and the social charter is being implemented around the continent on a basis of qualified majority voting – with, despite its dilution, considerable impact on Britain when in 1997 the Labour government signed up to the charter from which its Conservative predecessors had negotiated an opt-out.

This is a far cry from the fully fledged social Europe imagined by Delors back in 1986; but for British workers now set to receive rights for consultation and information with the acceptance in 2001 (after a four-year battle to resist it) of the information and consultation directive that otherwise would have been inconceivable, it is none the less a gain. And Delors' cohesion fund has been a critical element in underwriting economic growth in Ireland, Spain, Portugal and Greece, where living standards are now approaching the European average. Delors' achievement, in short, was to begin to give a distinctive European face to Europe's capitalism; the stipulation, for example, that every company in Europe with more than 2000 workers must form a works council, and inform and consult with its workforce, is a substantial support to Europe's associative, stakeholder capitalism. But even a president of the Commission as powerful as Delors, with solid support in France and Germany, was unable to marshal support for a social Europe on the same scale of ambition as monetary union; he transformed Europe, but his achievement was lop-sided.

After Delors

The vital question that remains is: how is European capitalism to retain its character before the march of the market that the EU itself is dedicated to further? The issue dogs Europe. At successive summits since Maastricht the European Commission has kept nagging away at deepening the consolidation of what Europeans hold in common, trying to maintain the momentum begun by Delors towards seeking positive rather than negative integration. It continues to argue that Europe cannot simply copy America and needs to recognise its own values. It also acknowledges that there needs to be a genuine democratic process at the heart of European decision-making if the EU is to begin to legitimise itself. But progress is desperately slow.

What is lacking is not aspiration or rhetoric; it is the mechanisms and political force to achieve the desired results. The core of the problem is that there is no agreed narrative about what Europe is for and how it should get there. The most obvious problems facing the continent are its continuing high level of unemployment and its inability to match American growth rates. As argued throughout this book, recent US employment and growth levels are very particular and unsustainable achievements; but, without an agreed narrative and a real belief in Europe's economic and social model, that has not prevented a collective psychosis settling on European leaders. To deliver alleged American dynamism they feel they need Europe to be more like America, accepting the tidal wave of propaganda from the US that the European way is at heart wrong, and that what Europe must do is to be Americanised. There is thus a fundamental disconnection from reality. The European political class finds that it cannot champion and celebrate European values and institutions as a seedbed of productivity and social justice – assets which, however they might need to be modernised and overhauled, are in essence worth preserving. It finds instead that, while making ritual obeisance to Europe's difference, it then proceeds to champion the Americanisation of Europe – quoting tendentious figures about the role of small business, lack of enterprise, need for more risk capital, the costs of regulation, poor productivity and so on. It can hardly be any surprise when member states then resist the consequential policy initiatives and try to hold on to the mechanisms that have served them well. They are right. But in the process there is an impression of stasis and a growing distrust of the European project among individual European electorates as they see Europe knocking down structures that have served them well while offering little or nothing to put in their place.

Thus at the Lisbon summit in 2000 the European Council signed up to admirable targets on promoting enterprise, innovation and liberalisation whose intent was to make the EU 'the most competitive and dynamic knowledge based economy in the world by 2010, capable of sustaining economic growth, with more and better jobs and greater social cohesion' – declaring that Europe could not be like America and must deepen its commitment to social inclusion. Amen to that. But when the commitments are looked at in detail, they come straight from the canons of American conservatism and the Washington consensus. Social inclusion turns out to have nothing to do with any social contract, but instead is an invocation of the importance of jobs in relieving all social ills – jobs whose growth is arrested, Lisbon says, by social contract measures which support worker incomes and inhibit mobility and job search. And if you hoped for any understanding of the complex relationship between the physical, technological, human and intellectual infrastructure and the corporate dynamism that is at the heart of European and indeed the best of American enterprise, you hoped in vain. The Lisbon document is littered with references to the need to give business 'freedom', to ease the regulatory 'burden' and to promote 'risk capital'. To protest against such simplicities is not to argue that every fragment of European regulation and finance works well; it does not. But it is to argue for some recognition of context and some acknowledgement of Europe's strengths. Not one of the authors of the Lisbon summit text can have known about the growth in European productivity over the last twenty years or how European income and social mobility is now set to overhaul American – or how any of this has happened. They have simply regurgitated American conservative propaganda as truth.

It is yet another instance of the depressing way in which repeated attempts at building consensus around initiatives over employment and social affairs become emasculated. The 1997 Amsterdam summit, for example, was to herald a new commitment to employment for all Europeans; instead, all that was achieved was watered-down, lofty statements of intent that would be implemented through the business-friendly commitment to competitiveness, flexible labour markets and reduction in the tax burden – the policies advocated by the corporate 'choir' of lobbyists in Brussels. The agreement that each country would make an annual report on employment policy involved no commitment on what the content of that policy might be. The employment clauses were little better than tokenistic in the face of an emerging problem of potential beggar-my-neighbour rounds of competitive tax cuts and weakening social protection to gain a competitive edge over other European countries. This is not to argue that the interaction between some EU member states' welfare policies and their labour markets is not destructive: there is powerful evidence that incentivising the unemployed to look for work while offering them training has an important impact on lowering unemployment. This, with joint European action to remedy demand shortfalls as argued in chapter 8, would have a remarkable impact on EU joblessness. Yet establishing this simple consensus is as remote as ever.

And yet – Europe's leaders are not unaware of the values they hold in common which set them apart from the US. At both the Amsterdam and Lisbon summits unemployment was at least put forward as a concern to rank alongside achieving more market liberalisation; and making formal reports on progress and mutually examining one another's employment policies raise both the salience of the issue and the state of European best practice. At the Nice summit in 2000 a charter of fundamental rights was agreed, setting out a framework of commonly held European values and minimum rights. Like this book, the charter identifies the social contract as one essential component of the European value system, and it lays out a body of rights – to education, health, worker representation, decent working conditions, social security benefits and social services – that all Europeans hold in common. It also acknowledges the distinctive European approach to property, affirming the right to private property but qualifying it by accepting the need to regulate property rights 'insofar as is necessary for the public interest'.[18] The problem is not the ambition represented by the charter, or its statement of the kind of European values identified in this book; the problem is making it live as an over-riding European political narrative embodied in a feasible and practical economic and social programme.

The failure to do this is matched by the growing belief among the peoples of Europe that the EU is increasingly a creation of its political and business elites around their own agenda. The belief that national publics have little purchase or influence on the EU's machinations and that it does not relate to their concerns – notwithstanding important initiatives like the charter of fundamental rights – has led to growing apathy and sometimes overt disillusion with the European process. Even a decade ago the French voted by only the slimmest of margins – 51 to 49 per cent – to support entry into the euro. Germany did not risk a referendum on the subject, but the ruling of its constitutional court that the European central bank needed to be accountable to European political institutions, and that they in turn needed to be embedded in a European political community, only told Europe's political and official class, such as it is, what it already knew. Subsequently the Danes have voted against the euro and the Irish against Nice.

In a post-Cold-War Europe, the old national stories that reconciled member states to European integration are no longer as effective as they were, especially as Europe's wider economic performance is more modest. Embedded nationalism, never far from the surface, has bubbled back into view. A reunited Germany, at last confident in its democracy and its commitment to capitalism, does not seek the legitimacy conferred by a

European community as it once did. Nor can France, now evidently second fiddle to Germany, lay claim to lead a Europe with fifteen members; after enlargement to twenty-five members, whatever Europe is becoming it is not Greater France. The last pretensions to French leadership were shattered when, after Britain and Italy were forced out of the EMS in 1992, France succumbed to overwhelming foreign exchange speculation the following year; shadowing high German interest rates following reunification had created a deepening French recession. The tight bands that the EMS had operated were relaxed to allow France to remain a titular member. Every European economy was now a bigger or smaller moon revolving around the German sun.

But, as in 1983, the French did not think of leaving the EMS or abandoning the Maastricht Treaty. Rather, they intensified their commitment, taking the view that there was no other option. Over the 1990s France redoubled its efforts to ensure that its interest rates, inflation and fiscal stance were sufficiently conservative to meet the demanding criteria for single currency membership. Rather than remain a monetary moon circling around the sun of the Bundesbank, the French were intent on creating a European monetary sun of which they would be part – even though, for ordinary French citizens, as for those all over Europe, the pain associated with the attempt was more obvious than the benefits. Europe, paradoxically, headed towards the launch of its single currency in 2002 in a state of mounting crisis over its legitimacy and purpose.

The stakes could hardly be higher, both for itself and for its place in the world. The US is becoming more assertively unilateralist and conservative, while to Europe's east there are ten former communist states that need to join the EU to seal their commitment to democracy and capitalism. Germany, as the EU's paymaster, insists that they be offered the realistic prospect of joining the Union within a reasonable timetable, both as a matter of principle and as one of self-interest – Germany's need for a stable, peaceful eastern Europe is obvious and acute. Britain has welcomed enlargement for similar geostrategic reasons, but its political establishment also knows that it makes the task of constructing any form of political Europe much more difficult.

The British are short-sighted. Enlargement is desirable and in the medium term a matter of right for the applicant countries; but the addition of ten new states in the 'big bang' admission to which the EU is committed will throw the current EU structures into chronic dysfunctionality. The new applicants have demands for agricultural and regional support that will wreck the EU budget; much of their government structure is corrupt, which will further discredit the EU process. On the other hand, admission to the EU is a spur to reform. If the EU remains committed to admitting them at once, rather than in successive waves – which would be wiser and easier – then it must address its internal problems with even more speed and urgency. Without successful reform, the danger is that an enlarged EU will regress to its roots as a customs union protecting democracy and capitalism in principle rather than in detail because of the sheer logistical dilemma of co-ordinating and marshalling the interests of up to twenty-five member states. The Nice Treaty that was drawn up as a response to the challenge posed by enlargement, with its extraordinary mix of population weights and voting rights, is barely comprehensible even by insiders; as an exercise in enfranchising Europe's peoples or constructing a genuine political community it is an abject failure.

The EU must do better, and the imperative could hardly be greater. The single currency and single market, if they are not organised as an economic and social space around European values, uniquely expose European capitalism to its de facto Americanisation – with all that implies in terms of asking Europe's employees to accept greater risk, an enfeebled social contract, wider inequality and a challenge to the stake-holder routes taken by European enterprise to raise productivity. Europe's increasingly lightly governed economic space has come into being just as globalisation has taken wing, endowing corporations and financial markets alike with yet more autonomous power at the expense of the traditional state. Each individual European country finds itself trying to protect its own system, with the EU offering scant support. This Europe, with its democratic deficit, dedicated as it is to enlarging the four economic freedoms – free movement of goods, capital, people and services – while building a single currency and single market is, despite itself, developing as an engine of the conservative right and a friend of corporate Europe. This is not what the founding fathers had in mind at all; it is a trend that must be checked and reshaped if Europe is to be true to itself.

The search for a new legitimacy

If the EU did not exist, the crisis of democratic legitimacy in Europe would be no less great – and the villain of the piece much more obvious. The capacity for autonomous action by individual nation-states is being curtailed by monumental forces outside their control. The reverse faced by the Mitterrand government over its expansionary policies of the early 1980s is only one of many occasions over the last twenty years when the financial markets have established their priorities over those of national governments. And the constraints go far beyond the financial. A government of a European state could not now move to rebase its electricity generation on nuclear power, any more than it could insist on giving its fishermen complete freedom over the sizes of their catches, without massive protest not only from its immediate neighbours but from the international community. Democracy is meant to be rule by the people for the people with no qualification, but in an era of globalisation the elected representatives of the people can no longer without constraint do anything that their people within their territorial jurisdiction vote for – nor can they produce the benefits the people want solely by action within their own borders. This may not be desirable within the conceptions of democracy to which we are accustomed, but it is the contemporary reality. Democracy within nation-states *is* constrained.

This is a much larger issue than simply the degree to which the electorate can hold their elected representatives to account and the degree of scope governments have to reflect their electorates' wishes. These questions encompass just one, albeit critical, component of the public realm – not its totality. Democratic politics and a political community do not emerge spontaneously; they are rooted in the wider public discourse of exchange of ideas, argument and information. One of the other facets of globalisation is that it has generated its own 'common sense' world view underpinning its advance; namely, that economic and social policy should be run according to the canons of the Washington consensus.

Thus the issue is not just that the financial markets have awesome power; it is that they have generated their own ideology, which is not subject to scrutiny, debate or any form of accountability; it should be part of the public realm but it is not. The economists at the great investment banks can write economic circulars insisting that a particular currency is to be bought or sold using whatever criteria they chose – but they are not held to account for the consequences of their deliberations. Equally, the directors and senior managers of the leading transnational corporations may have highly conservative views about what constitutes the appropriate economic and social order – usually one that accords them the maximum freedom to manage and reward themselves highly, on the grounds that the resulting wealth will trickle down to those below them – but what in effect is a public argument within what should be a public discourse goes unchallenged. This is not to deny members of the corporate establishment the right to hold whatever view they like; that is their privilege and right in a free society. What is unacceptable is that these views go uncontested, whatever their consequences, because there is no wider public realm in which such debate can take place, and more importantly no political entity that could act to challenge or qualify them. Some of the disaffection among Europe's electorates is plainly rooted in the knowledge that voices within national communities increasingly count for less and that there is no vehicle for them to count for more – and so they take revenge on what is to hand. Paradoxically, the object of their ire is the European Union even though European institutions, correctly conceived, are among the remedies.

And so we return to where this chapter began. For the foreseeable future, hopes that Europe can reconnect itself to its public directly by the democratic process, as if it were or could operate as a nation-state but at a Europe-wide level, are crippled by the lack of a European public realm, a European civil society and a European electorate bound together by language and common debate. Democratic legitimacy still resides with the nation-state, even though that legitimacy is receding rapidly as belief in public initiative and the social contract is overwhelmed by the tide of American conservative beliefs imported into Europe. The state exists to further the cause of business, markets and the rich. There is what the German social theorist Wolfgang Streeck calls a historic coalition among the nation-state, nationalism, free market liberalism and the negative integration of the European process[19] – all combining to claim that there is little or nothing that political action can do to contain or manage the market economy, and indeed that to do so would be actively harmful.

There is a collusion to be as minimalist as possible about upholding and developing the social contract and public realm, and this collusion delegitimises both the European and the national political processes alike.

An effective Europe, delivering at European level what nation-states cannot perform at national level, through political processes that were accountable and transparent, would help to relegitimise politics and democracy alike. It would do two things. The act of delivering something that could not be delivered at national level would be proof positive that Europe has a *raison d'être* that warrants the support of its citizens. It would be government for the people. Second, it would, as Jürgen Habermas argues persuasively, begin to identify Europe not as a nation-state in the sense of having a common descent, language and history, but as a civic community that volunteers to have a collective expression in Europe-wide actions.[20] It would be the first step in creating a European civic society which might ultimately be the foundation for a functioning European democracy.

For the time being, this collective action will continue to be taken through the combination of intergovernmentalism and supranationalism that, in one form or another, has been the hallmark of Europe since its inception. However, the decision-making process must become more accountable. This is what the preparatory convention on the future of Europe, set up at the Laeken summit in 2001 and charged to report to the intergovernmental conference in 2004, must square up to. The Laeken declaration of December 2001 is a hopeful sign that Europe's leaders are at last beginning to deal with this reality. The declaration talks both of enlarging the role of national parliaments and repatriating some powers to member states and also of finding ways of increasing the legitimacy and powers of the European Commission and parliament in those areas that are generally agreed to be European in their scope. It was a land-mark moment.

To win more popularity and legitimacy among its citizens, as the Laeken declaration also recognises, Europe must do more to identify and do things in concert that will better their lot. Yet notwithstanding its fine words, Laeken continues the tradition of Amsterdam, Lisbon and Nice; Europe still hankers after trying to import the American model. It is wrong. What it must do instead is find ways of returning to Jacques

Delors' agenda of positive integration around a social Europe and of organising a European economic and social space. In short, it has to find ways of defending European values and the best of the European economic and social model – and to be proud and self-conscious in what it is doing. In an age of globalisation, the priority is no longer negative integration to establish a single market; that job is largely done and has its own powerful momentum. The new injunction is to protect and further the interests of Europe's citizens in an age where the market is king, creating a vibrant and distinct European capitalism that incorporates its history and the views of its peoples. It must use the instruments that it has – notably the single currency – and develop others to serve Europe's interests. Above all, it must believe in Europe. It must do so urgently, not only for itself but for all those who believe in multilateral action to create international public goods – a process which Europe is trail-blazing for the globe.

11
Fighting back

To win much needed popular legitimacy, the EU urgently needs to show that collective European action improves the lives of its individual citizens, and that acting together paradoxically re-empowers individual member states and national political processes – even while ways are found to increase the influence of nation-states on European decision-making. The drive to improve Europe for its citizens needs to be organised explicitly around the three clusters of values that define European civilisation: the stakeholder view of property, the belief in the social contract and the commitment to a vital public realm.

What Europe can do for Europeans

Above all, any expression of these intentions has to be made concrete in ways that individual citizens can trust. For example, one obvious initiative in the wake of 11 September is the promotion of security. The system of mutual recognition of member states' search warrants for suspected terrorists was a major step, putting justice and home affairs – for long the most jealously guarded heartland of member state interests – at the vanguard of integration. It should be hardened into a European anti-terrorist police system to ensure there are as few as possible co-ordination and information failures in the drive to eliminate terrorist cells. There should be a Europe-wide system to ensure airport and airline security is performed to the highest standards across the continent with no weak spots; airport security should be in the hands of salaried, highly trained officials working for a pan-European airport policing network with a commitment to investing in state-of-the-art technology. All Europe's external borders should be patrolled by a European border guard of immigration officers working to common guidelines. Any European country is only as strong as its weakest link: there is a collective interest in acting together.

Security is but one way of offering something tangible to the EU's citizens. Europe should be the sponsor of a more prosperous future, and it should associate itself with imaginative ideas that redefine national options. Few European universities match the standards of the top twenty or so American universities, so that the burgeoning of 'ideapolises' is not happening on anything like the same scale in Europe. The EU needs to become the initiator of the greatest programme of construction and development of world-class universities ever known on the continent, ensuring that each has a unique research agenda. Regional policy should focus first on pump-priming this infrastructure of knowledge; this should take priority over even the current accent on building up the physical infrastructure in depressed regions, which, although vital, should be conceived as supporting growth rather than leading it. Better foster a world-class university in a depressed region first than improve what without such a foundation will be under-used infrastructure.

There must also be more seriousness about the EU's commitment to the networks that support mobility, communication and energy. The 1990 Dublin summit committed Europe to build 'interconnected and interoperable networks in the fields of transport, telecommunications, energy and vocational training for the benefit of citizens, enterprises and administrations',[1] and the commitment to these so-called trans-European networks was written into the Maastricht Treaty. The 1993 white paper on growth, competitiveness and employment identified them as fundamental to future growth prospects. Yet for all this talk, seven years later the Lisbon summit could call for the most 'competitive and dynamic knowledge-based economy in the world' as if nothing of the kind had ever been suggested before. It hardly referred to the commitments articulated earlier in the decade. Instead, it blithely continued to hope that 'liberalisation' and warm words would deliver the result it wanted.

It is this coalition of governments frightened of public action and an EU Commission in the grip of the private-is-best philosophy that has paralysed any effective mobilisation. Even as it has become ever clearer that Europe's transport system is uneven and increasingly overstretched, its telecommunications system is fragmented and incomplete, and its distribution of gas, oil and electricity remains nationally bounded, little or nothing has been done to change things. Access to well-functioning public transport should be a citizen's right, and transport should be part of the realm of public service as a treaty obligation. The EU must work to create a single European market in these still overly protected sectors, establishing baseline standards for performance; and where national systems fall below this standard, then national transport ministers should have to submit a plan detailing how their system is to be brought up to common European standards and a timetable in which this is to be done. The same approach should be applied to every form of universal network, so that, for example, the EU commits itself to the establishment of a Europe-wide broadband cable network by, say, 2010.

Nor can Europe's system of agriculture, food manufacture and distribution be allowed to continue unreformed. The Common Agricultural Policy stimulates production at the expense of quality, and after the BSE scandals and foot and mouth epidemic it is clear that the interpenetration of European markets demands a parallel system of European regulation. Few national publics now trust their national governments to police food standards adequately; equally, the growth of trade in food and agricultural products requires that regulation and policing have to be more robust. Europe needs to move away from industrial farming and its hazards, and towards a system of high value-added agricultural production with a greater emphasis on organic farming, tougher standards at all stages of the food chain – and a tough system of policing them, based on the models being developed for counter-terrorism and airport security. The system of guaranteed prices for basic commodities has to be scrapped and replaced with guaranteed prices for produce with higher added value (like organic food).

Over the wider economy, defensiveness should be abandoned. There should be recognition instead of the genius and distinctiveness of European capitalism – and of the values and processes that have lain behind its success. Indeed, there are signs that Europeans are beginning to recognise that there is a European approach to enterprise that works and is different from that in the US: for example, Romano Prodi, President of the European Commission, writes that the European model is at once innovative and socially engaged.[2]

European should be more discerning about what elements of the American economic and social model they choose to import, instead of regarding it as the benchmark for everything. The American approaches to university research, to attracting women into the labour market, to risk and to building a vibrant service sector are powerful signals to Europe of what is possible; less so, for example, American attitudes to finance and in particular the veneration of the stock market. Stock markets by themselves do not threaten the European enterprise model as long as they are not over-powerful – indeed, stock markets are useful indicators of a company's worth and credit rating, and also, on occasion, a useful supplementary source of finance. However, if the Europeans build stock markets on American lines, so mighty that they can enforce the idea that the only task of a corporation is to serve the short-term interests of profit maximisation, the game will be up – and Europeans will find themselves under enormous pressure to throw away their unique model of capitalism.

Individual European stock markets are already under pressure amounting to siege conditions to make their listing requirements correspond to those in New York and London. Finance and trade ministries are lobbied intensely to change national company law to enshrine and promote shareholder interests above any other. The EU Commission has even been seduced into producing a directive to make hostile takeovers and stock market-based financial engineering easier in the name of 'market efficiency', thereby establishing a European market in so-called 'corporate control'. But in 2001 the European parliament, with the support of the German government, stood against this trend and against much criticism blocked the directive. They were right. As we have seen, hostile takeovers tend to destroy value, inhibit competition and create a corporate culture in which the bottom line is the only arbiter – and thus are in tension with the tried and tested European conceptions of wealth generation. The European Commission should take heed of these findings and instead act to make it more difficult for these pressures to succeed. The evidence marshalled in chapter 4 shows that only a fraction of takeovers work. Unless very skilfully managed, with enormous care taken to marry company cultures, most mergers fail – because too little attention is paid to the ideas presented in this book. Great companies are more than profit-making machines, and cannot be arbitrarily shackled together to satisfy the ego of some CEO. Rather than surrender to the idea that hostile takeovers are somehow essential to promoting business efficiency, the EU needs to challenge this assumption with a different conception of wealth creation.

It should lead this debate, and establish a European framework for company law, company formation and stock-market listing that supports investment, growth and accountability. There will be substantial industrial and financial restructuring in Europe in the decades ahead, but it must be voluntary and driven by real market need – not by the ambitions of the great American investment banks, and their European cousins trying to ape their ways, to enrich themselves with grotesquely high fee income by promoting conglomeration for no sound business reason. The new framework should include obligations upon company directors to act as trustees of the whole organisation rather than to act as sole custodians of shareholder rights, together with an insistence that companies define their corporate purpose in their articles of association. There should be Europe-wide standards on the principles and processes of company audit so that profits and balance sheets do not get driven by the desire to appease and exploit the stock market (one of the key elements of the Enron scandal), tight rules about the creation and exercise of share options, requirements systematically to report on how corporations discharge their wider social responsibilities, and formal inclusion of worker rights to information and consultation already created by the Information and Consultation Directive. Hostile takeovers should not be impossible, but they should remain very difficult. The incentives should be targeted towards finding partners who want to throw in their lot together rather than victims to be swallowed to appease the financial masters.

Such an approach is a vital condition for Europe's maintaining its distinctive approach to capitalism, and for meeting the growing demand for accountability from its citizens. This is a demand that has been swelling for some time, fed by greater education and more discerning consumers and workers, the transparency that more intense media scrutiny brings and the movement of business into areas hitherto dominated by the public sector. These trends alone have made it clearer that corporate behaviour has social and moral consequences to which society cannot be indifferent. Today, if Western capitalism is to sustain its legitimacy before a sceptical globe in a battle for hearts and minds in the wake of the terrorist attacks, the need to respond to these concerns is even greater. The American conservative idea that we should be so grateful for business enterprise that society should allow it to trade on whatever terms suit it was never easy to translate into Europe; after 11 September it is harder still, both for the EU and in global terms. Business must have formal mechanisms by which it holds itself to account for its actions. This notion is much easier for European enterprise to accept than much American enterprise, because it dovetails with its wider stakeholder approach to wealth generation. Ownership confers obligations, and the successful organisation is one which acknowledges that its economic success depends as much on how it works as a social institution as on its efficiency as an economic mechanism – and this is as true for its relationship with its markets as for that with its employees. Only business in thrall to shareholder value is unable to accept the idea that it has to earn a licence to trade through the broader legitimacy of its conduct, both internally and externally.

This approach to corporate governance, social responsibility and accountability needs to be Europe-wide. There can be no indulgence of particular member states who want to take a more lenient view of the responsibilities attached to incorporation, rather as the US indulges Delaware as a state in which companies can incorporate with minimalist standards; that will only generate lowest common denominator corporate practice and a race to the bottom. Against the criticism that such an approach is unenforceable, the EU can now point to the twin aces of the euro and the sheer size of the European economy. It can insist that financial contracts denominated in euros are legally enforceable within the euro area only if both contracting parties have fully observed EU law; in other words, those companies that do not observe EU law risk not being able to enforce contracts. One member country taking this stance would risk a possible investment strike or capital flight; but no significant company, bank or investment house would want to risk being excluded from operating across the whole of the euro area. An individual country can be held to ransom by contemporary companies; a continent with a single currency cannot.

The ambition must extend to reframing Europe's international financial relationships. The euro is destined to become a second reserve currency to match the dollar, and the relationship between the two could serve as an axis to restabilise the international financial system – provided the US is prepared to engage with Europe on such terms. The European Central Bank and the Federal Reserve have the joint financial firepower to sustain the euro–dollar exchange rate within a predeclared range, especially if they jointly introduce the 'Tobin tax' to slow down the growth of speculative short-term trading of currencies in the foreign exchange markets. Both France and Germany have signalled their readiness to explore this innovative notion. The idea is that a tiny tax, perhaps a levy of no more than 0.1 or 0.2 per cent of the value of each financial transaction, will be a trivial charge for any long-term investor but will completely upset the hair's-breadth margins on which much speculative short-term trading in the capital markets is based – and so destroy its destructive rationale. Indeed, if the US refuses to be a partner in such an endeavour, the euro area is large enough to introduce the tax on its own. The penalty for avoidance would be the same as that just mentioned in the context of company law: miscreants would be unable to enforce contracts in European courts.

The power of the euro and the size of the European economy will allow Europe to act to counterbalance some of the developments that have taken place over the last thirty years when it had no such power. One of the features of contemporary globalisation is that countries, mindful of the danger of highly mobile companies switching location if corporate taxes are too high and simultaneously bidding for new investment by offering tax concessions, have steadily reduced taxation rates for companies and increased those for labour and consumers to compensate.

On average, the tax rate on employed labour in the EU rose from 35 per cent in 1980 to 43 per cent in 1996, while taxation of capital fell from 42 per cent to 35.6 per cent over the same period.[3] Everywhere in Europe the limits of politically acceptable taxation are being reached, constraining the scope of welfare states and making old and unskilled workers, who incur the same high social charges as more productive workers, less attractive to employ. This latter trend is especially marked in countries with social insurance systems of welfare finance, which have been required to compensate for the corporate tax flight by requiring employers to step up their social insurance contributions, thus deterring them from employing marginal workers. While the European employment rate for men between twenty-five and forty-nine stands at 90 per cent, the same as in the US, demand for older male workers and young people is depressed by the requirement to pay very high social insurance contributions for them. The overall level of employment at the core may be stable, but the distribution of employment is affected at the margins. The EU needs to establish minimum rates of corporate taxation that prevent companies from playing one country off against another and so setting the whole dynamic in motion. This would underpin the tax and social insurance base that supports welfare, education and health expenditure throughout Europe – and stop the drift away from taxing capital towards taxing labour.

Every European country wants to sustain its social contract if it can. Individual European states choose to structure their welfare systems in different ways, as we saw in chapters 8 and 9, even while their desire to have a universal welfare system springs from the same set of values. Harmonising these structures is probably impossible and should not be attempted; they result from different histories. What are required instead are rules that harmonise lowest tax rates and a social treaty that sets minimum outcomes for social policy; it can be left to individual states to find ways of achieving those outcomes congruent with their own welfare structure. By providing them with the wherewithal in underwritten minimum tax rates (there should be no constraint on high tax rates) and thus a secured tax base, along with commonly agreed outcomes, collective action at the European level can empower member states to offer their citizens a better social deal. There will still be a range of taxation: those states that tax more will be able to – indeed, will have to – demonstrate that higher taxation produces better public infrastructure and social outcomes. But as reported in chapter 7, there is already evidence that competitiveness increases with a rising tax burden – up to certain reasonable limits. The EU will allow states to exercise this choice, rather than condemning them willy-nilly to join in a race to the bottom.

One of the most important contributions the EU can make to the life of its member states is to revive the notion that public action works, and that participation in a live public realm is worthwhile and pays dividends. Here Lionel Jospin's proposal for a new European directive setting out a legal framework that would define the provision of public services across Europe is extremely attractive;[4] it would constitute a definition of the key attributes that define public provision, ranging from accountability to universality of access, and spell out which services would have to meet these criteria, extending from health to education, so that the limits of a market society would be drawn and the rights of citizenship clearly delineated. It would translate the values in the charter of fundamental rights into a codified approach to public service, and so set a framework for the participation of the private sector in public service provision. In the British context this would be an important mechanism for ensuring that private sector providers of public services would know what constituted the benchmark for standards of public provision. Above all, it would establish the importance of sustaining a public service ethos across Europe.

The euro zone already represents a sixth of world GDP. For the first time since World War II, the US confronts an economic grouping approaching it in size and cohesion – and one which, if and when Britain joins, will broadly equal it. The stakes are now very high indeed. It is evident that the terms of the pax Americana that has served the world so well since 1945 are changing significantly; as it overtly becomes more unilateralist, the US is no longer the trusted guardian of a world interest. The liberal order that was constructed after 1945 has been eroded by the growth of private corporate power and the failure of the international rules of the game to adjust to new realities and new demands for justice – whether over the environment, agriculture, debt, aid or trade. The organisation of these areas along lines that suit US corporate and financial interests is proving self-defeating. The triumph of American conservatism at home has imperilled the liberal order abroad on which the peaceful co-existence of the globe depends.

With the euro, the EU now has the weapon with which to fight back. EU contributions to the Bretton Woods institutions now exceed the dollar contributions made by the US; while the US has 17.78 per cent of the votes the EU has some 28 per cent if it chooses to vote as a bloc (around 23 per cent for the euro countries, plus Britain with its 4.98 per cent vote). So the EU can start to insist that its ideas on the appropriate international financial regime are taken more seriously. The IMF in particular needs to reframe its approach to policing the international monetary system, devising a system of wider exchange rate stability; it needs to take on board European preoccupations about the importance of constraining free capital flows, so that less developed countries in particular are allowed the opportunity to control capital outflows in crises, while avoiding the simultaneous implementation of savage adjustment programmes across whole regions. Enlightened debt relief should move higher up the international agenda. If America opts out, the euro has the capacity to become the world reserve currency and the EU has the financial wherewithal to give the World Bank and IMF the capital they need.

The EU can now argue much more forcefully for its own interests, over everything from international accounting standards and the regulation of financial institutions to rules over patenting – and can insist that the criteria that it adopts within the EU are reflected in global rules and practices. The rest of the world will no longer be Uncle Sam's backyard, and the vital transatlantic engagement that is needed to build a more just world economic and social order can be recommenced on more level terms. In areas as disparate as the environment, the arms trade and trade policy the US will have to start to make its case in debate with the rest of the world, rather than unilaterally setting the benchmarks that others have to follow. Europe can develop its own alternatives.

One important area, for example, is space. The EU showed its readiness to stand up for its interests when, at the March 2002 Barcelona Summit, it agreed to launch the $2 billion European Galileo satellite positioning system, dedicated to civilian use (unlike the US's GPS system which was constructed for the military). The European system will allow any users, including planes and ships, to locate themselves within a metre without any danger that the signals may be unilaterally suspended for US military use (as with GPS). Fiercely lobbied against by the US, who wanted a complete monopoly of such satellite ground positioning systems because an alternative might interfere with the US radio signals – as the ultra hawk Deputy Defence Secretary Paul Wolfowitz wrote to NATO – the EU stood its ground not just for European but global interest. In the run-up to the decision France's President Chirac warned that US domination of space 'would inevitably lead to our countries becoming first scientific and technological vassals, then industrial and economic vassals' of the US.[5] The EU's decision is an important declaration of common interest and an assertion of technological superiority alike: Galileo is a better system than GPS.

As the EU takes a harder position, the balance of argument in Washington, at present so heavily tilted in favour of conservative interests, will necessarily have to change. It will no longer be so easy, for example, for the US to define Western interests if the EU further consolidates its position as the major source of aid. Already the EU provides 55 per cent of the development assistance in the world and two-thirds of grant aid; if it raises its aid contribution further towards the agreed but never achieved target of 0.7 per cent of GDP, it will necessarily become undisputed aid paymaster, determining collective Western interests in world hot-spots, whether geographical, like the middle East, or ideological, like radical Islam. In March 2002, before the Monterrey conference on aid, trade and development, the EU committed itself to raising aid contributions by an extra \$7 billion a year by 2006, while the US offered an increase of only \$5 billion spread over three years from 2004. The gap between EU and US aid contributions is growing formidable. The US may have the B-52s, but if the EU has the cash its views will have a force that Washington has to reckon with.

Moreover, if Europe can start to co-ordinate a collective foreign policy and offer a rationale for the development and operation of its rapid reaction force, then it can also start to have a role not only in defining its own foreign policy interests but in policing them. This was already a developing imperative before 11 September – witness the importance of the EU being able to lead interventions in the Balkans where it has a vital interest in maintaining peace. But after 11 September there is no choice.

Future conflict is not going to be about formal wars between the principal states; rather, it is going to be about interventions to contain the spread of internecine but highly localised wars and the locations of international terrorism. No European state has the financial resource or military capacity to respond alone.

In short, the members of the EU need to act in concert; sometimes with the US, at other times as a counterweight, but always in the service of a more enlightened view of the global interest. At home, it is the only plausible vehicle for protecting Europe's distinctive approach to capitalism and the social contract; abroad, it is the only plausible countervailing force to American conservatism's attempt to shape the world in its own image. The EU must act forcefully, collectively and coherently to build its vision – and to persuade the US that it must change tack.

And so to the euro

The successful launch of the euro on 2 January 2002 is the EU's most important initiative, both for itself and for the world beyond. This was the biggest ever currency conversion the world has witnessed, and as an exercise in sheer logistics – introducing a new currency for twelve countries – it was astonishingly successful, and perfectly executed. That the peoples of a dozen European countries are all now using the same currency is in itself a remarkable achievement; its impact on accelerating the economic, political and cultural integration of Europe will be enormous. It is a declaration of unity and solidarity, and also an assertion of Europe's desire to create a monetary system that serves its own interests rather than accept a framework set up to work to American advantage.

For monetary union is not a quixotic act, putting Europe's disparate economies in an economic straitjacket, as Britain's Eurosceptics and even the governor of the Bank of England like to argue. It is a deliberate assertion of economic sovereignty in a global monetary system that for thirty years, ever since the collapse of Bretton Woods, has increasingly ceded power to the judgements of the international financial markets. The clinching argument for each of the countries that have joined is that in today's financial environment monetary and exchange rate sovereignty

is a rapidly diminishing capability even for comparatively large countries – and that reclaiming it via a single currency will in the long run
make their economies and citizens richer, though it has been a hard slog
preparing for it. Over the medium to long term this will prove the most
tangible expression yet of Europe acting to improve the lot of its peoples
in a way that no single country could do by itself. It not only opens up the
possibility of sustained low interest rates and the decades of comparatively high private and public sector demand that the US has enjoyed; it
creates a genuine continental-scale economy that, if managed well could
become the world's economic hot spot.

The conviction that a single currency offers these benefits has grown
in Europe over thirty years of experiencing the choices and dictates of
the markets. The emergence, charted in chapter 6, of American economic and financial unilateralism in the late 1960s as the US became
unwilling to accept the disciplines of the Bretton Woods system, gave
Europe its first taste of monetary destabilisation. The weakness of the
dollar forced a revaluation of the mark and corresponding devaluation of
the franc – despite a battery of measures to avoid both, with Germany
offering rebates to importers and imposing taxes on exports, and France
imposing draconian exchange controls and massively subsidising
exports.[6] Even in an environment where capital flows were only a tiny
fraction of today's, the measures did not work.

The fear was that Europe's young Common Market could not develop
into a fully integrated economic area if such brutal and unexpected dis-
ruptions to the carefully constructed balance of advantage woven into its
trade patterns and infant structures like the Common Agricultural Policy
were to continue. In 1970 the EEC of the six adopted the Werner
Committee's recommendation that the only viable response was to set
up a European economic and monetary union to protect the Common
Market from competitive devaluations. The initial aim was to complete
the process by 1980; but in May 1971, only five months after the Werner
Committee's recommendations were accepted, it became obvious that
the combination of France's and Germany's then radically different economic philosophies, along with the sheer scale of financial pressure, was
going to make any orderly progress towards monetary union impossible.
Germany, the Netherlands and Belgium had to close their foreign

exchange markets temporarily to stop the flight from the dollar from destabilising not just their currencies but their entire economic policies. There were two ways forward as the Bretton Woods system collapsed. Either Europe's currencies could jointly float against the dollar, or Europe could attempt to fix its exchange rates and police them behind exchange controls. Germany favoured the former, and statist France favoured the latter. The Werner plan collapsed.

The issues that had prompted it continued to dog Europe. The 1970s were years of high unemployment, high inflation and low growth, and the pace of European integration stagnated. The fears that had prompted the Werner plan seemed amply justified. By 1979 (as described in chapter 10) the French and Germans felt compelled to have another attempt at creating a stabler exchange rate system in the EMS; but this attempt was made harder by the rapidly increasing scale of capital flows. The American lifting of capital controls in 1974 had given a further stimulus to the growth of the eurodollar markets, so that increasingly currency was held offshore in sterling, franc and deutschmark markets convertible into dollars and each other, growing freely outside any one country's system of controls. And the supply and demand of currency within the eurocurrencies inevitably had a knock-on effect on the official exchange rates managed by the central banks. As we have seen, by 1982 not only Britain but Germany and the Netherlands had given in to the logic of the markets and lifted their capital controls. The size of the foreign exchange markets and thus the volume of accompanying poten-tial speculation were growing exponentially, developments brought home forcibly to France with its currency crises between 1981 and 1983 – and it was Jacques Delors, the architect of the euro, who as France's finance minister during the early 1980s had to fashion France's austerity programme in response. It was a bitter lesson in contemporary reality.

The accelerating expansion of the foreign exchange markets contin-ued. As late as 1983 the five major central banks (of the US, Germany, Japan, Britain and Switzerland) could between them muster $139 billion of foreign exchange reserves compared with daily foreign exchange turnover of some $39 billion dollars; but by 1992 the balance of power had been reversed, and their combined reserves stood at $278 billion compared with $623 billion of daily trading activity.[7] In 2001 they have

$653 billion of reserves ($404 billion in Japan) compared with a daily turnover of $1.2 trillion.[8] The markets could overwhelm the central banks if they chose.

As a result, without capital controls, the EMS had to resort to fiercely conservative economic policies in order to maintain the system. Essentially, members had to shadow German interest rates, inflation and budgetary policy if they were to have a chance of staying within the grid. It was this experience that convinced France that it had to opt for a single European currency even before German reunification made the case politically as well as economically pressing. In 1993 its third financial crisis – after 1969 and 1981–3 – when the franc was again the object of an irresistible wave of speculation, marked the moment when France became completely convinced. In a world in which neither floating nor fixed exchange rates offered sovereignty, the only course was to establish a single European currency.

The British have had no less eventful a ride. In the early 1980s the unstoppable and crazy rise in the pound was the chief cause of the deep recession, and over the 1980s the Tory government tried a variety of ploys to stop the same thing happening again – finally joining the EMS in 1990 at too high a rate in a desperate last effort to achieve some currency stability. The speculation that forced sterling out of the EMS in 1992 was mountainous, reaching $20 billion on 'Black Wednesday' alone – a financial tidal wave of a magnitude similar to that which would provoke the Asia crisis later in the decade. After its exit the pound fell from DM2.78 to a low of DM2.24 in 1995. Then it climbed steadily back, reaching a peak of DM3.46 in May 2000, before falling back to around DM3.15, where it has rested until early 2002. The gain in relative value and consequent loss of competitiveness, measured in real terms, is stunning. The conversion of Britain's unit labour costs into those of the euro zone at the prevailing exchange rate gives a consistent measurement of competitiveness; compared with the average rate of the seventeen years between 1980 and 1997, it gained a 15 per cent competitive advantage at its low point in 1995 – but at its peak in May 2000 it was at a 40 per cent competitive disadvantage.[9] This is the worst ratio since the war.

The heart of the matter is that it is not possible simultaneously for any one country to permit free movement of capital over its borders, and control its exchange rate and interest rates as it wants. It can do one, but not both; and even then the experience is unstable, insecure, and capable – as with Britain over the last five years – of delivering prolonged periods of exchange rate overvaluation (and potential undervaluation). Every European country has faced the dilemma of how to conduct economic policy in an environment in which seismic flows of capital can move across its borders at will, imposing constraints not only on interest and exchange rate policy – but on budgetary policy as well. The purposeful management of demand as countries choose is one of the fundamental instruments of economic policy; it has been a crucial element in American economic success over the last decade. The brutal reality is that no single European country by itself in an era of floating exchange rates has the same autonomous capacity to manage demand. That can only be regained at European level.

The dilemma over monetary policy can be spelled out in detail. Suppose a country wants to fix its exchange rate either against a matrix of currencies, like the old EMS, or against an anchor currency, like the dollar in the old Bretton Woods system. Immediately that commitment entails moving interest rates to support the exchange rate the country has chosen – but then today's vast capital flows enter the equation. As capital can move freely, quickly and on a huge scale, interest rates are driven upwards or downwards as the markets' exuberance or exaggerated fears put impossible pressure on the fixed currency rate.

Indeed, given the volumes of currency that accompany trade flows in today's world, with the high proportions of GDP represented by exports and imports, exporters and importers have simply either to bring forward or delay the normal pattern of currency exchange to put upward or downward pressure on the exchange rate. Markets never behave calmly for long. If money is moving into a currency, interest rates will have to be lowered to reduce investors' appetites to stop the rate from being forced upwards; if money is moving out, interest rates will have to be raised to persuade investors to stay – independently of whether such interest rate moves are good for the economy. And money does not move gradually; it now moves in such avalanches that the movement in interest rates has to be dramatic, amplifying the malign side-effects even more. In the end the country gives up, and allows its exchange rate to go in the direction the markets want. Thus Britain in 1992, France in 1993, the Asian economies pegged to the dollar in 1998 and 1999, Brazil in 1999 and Argentina in 2001.

Alternatively, a country can set interest rates to support its domestic economic objectives for, say, low inflation or economic growth and allow its exchange rate to find its own level freely as a result of supply and demand – but then it has to suffer directly the markets' irrational enthusiasms and despairs. Currencies can be valued high or low in relation to their underlying value for years, with episodic bouts of frenzy that typically culminate in a final sell-off or burst of enthusiasm that defines the end of the trend. The one thing we have learned about financial markets is that they are not stable. That in turn forces adjustment of the interest rate to relieve the pressure at some stage in the process – so that again the country has controlled neither its interest rates nor its exchange rate. Sooner or later the pound's current overvaluation will end, but it will not happen calmly; some event will provoke an unwanted and explosive sell-off, and at a moment when it is least wanted.

The beauty of the single currency is that it solves these dilemmas at a stroke. It allows member countries to choose the interest rate they want for the economic area as a whole and stick to it. Interest rates will be predictably lower, allowing business to undertake more investment and long-term borrowing, confident that it won't run into periods when interest rates will rise suddenly as a result of some fevered currency speculation. Moreover, it also permits interest rates to be decoupled from those of the anchor currency – the hallmark of any exchange rate system (the dollar in the current system of floating rates, the deutschmark in the EMS). The anchor's interest rate inevitably becomes the benchmark rate below which other countries cannot allow their own interest rates to fall for anything but a very short period. This imperative reached absurd levels in the EMS, for example, when member countries had to shadow high German interest rates during reunification, because not to do so risked a run on their individual currencies – but the same effect had operated during the EMS in the 1980s and back in the 1950s and 1960s with the dollar in the Bretton Woods system. A single currency allows the interest rate to be the appropriate rate for the entire economic area rather than that of the anchor exchange rate country, while simultaneously removing any interest rate risk premium that non-anchor currencies have to pay over the benchmark, anchor currency interest rate. It produces, in short, the lowest possible interest rate.

There may be occasions when the interest rate is inapplicable for the condition of one country's particular economy; but these will be infrequent, as generally most members countries' economic cycles will be broadly synchronised around broadly similar inflation and growth rates – one of the preconditions for membership. But if there are moments when a government has to use fiscal policy – government spending, taxing and borrowing – more than it would normally do to achieve the economic results it wants because it cannot support its stance with interest rates, then this is more than compensated for by the long-run benefits of a stable, predictable environment.

This advantage reinforces the benefits of Europe's progress towards establishing a single market, opening up the possibility of producing on the same continental scale as the Americans, with all the implications for boosting productivity. Europe without a single currency has been and would be a patchwork quilt of different currencies whose exchange rates could change violently at any time, a risk against which all producers have to guard by taking out expensive insurance policies – a 'currency hedge', in the jargon – to protect themselves against the possibility that the currency in which they are selling will devalue against the currency in which the goods or services are produced. It may not even be possible to hedge at any reasonable price if the risk extends for twelve months or more – in which case the risk of incurring a loss would deter many from doing business at all.

A single currency removes these risks and the accompanying costs – not least the simple transaction costs of changing one currency into another, which the European Commission has estimated at some 0.4 per cent of GDP.[10] And because the euro is a continental currency representing, on its current membership, some sixth of the world's output, it will tend to be stabler against the other world currencies – the dollar and yen – than individual European currencies could be.[11] Thus over time European businesses get a double benefit. They will be able to extend their production runs, more confident that the profits from their sales across the single market will not be hit by unexpected currency movements; and they can build up their productive capacity with cheap money, more confident that the borrowing they undertake will not suddenly become prohibitively expensive because interest rates are driven up by some currency shock. If their estimated risk premium falls by just 0.5 per cent, economists calculate that over time production would rise by between 5 and 10 per cent more than it otherwise would – more if the risk premium is reduced further.[12] Just as these benefits are available for business, so every consumer and individual borrower can enjoy the advantages of a stable, cheap money environment.

Joining the single currency would offer Britain the same shelter from the turbulence it has suffered that it already does to the euro-zone members. The arrival of the euro cements the establishment of a continental-scale economy that will not be fractured by different currency regimes. It allows interest rates to be set for the benefit of the Europe-wide economy rather than to protect a particular national exchange rate or reflect the monetary conditions in the anchor currency. It is the friend, in short, of production, investment and employment, and is Europe's response to the currency regime established by the US in the early 1970s which has cost Europe so much. By marrying the benefits of continental scale and cheap money with the already proven merits of Europe's economic and social model, over the medium to long term the growth of the EU with a single currency could not only be greater than without it – it could be startlingly dynamic. The euro is a means of delivering to Europe's citizens.

Why Britain's sceptics on the euro are wrong

As already observed, the British economy has been quietly suffering its own exchange rate crisis over the five years up to the month this book has been completed (March 2002). The pound's loss of competitiveness has exerted a terrible squeeze on all forms of manufacturing so that there are now massive imbalances between the shrunken scale of production, high levels of consumption and an overblown service sector. The government did not want to lose this degree of competitiveness, but it was simply helpless. The growth of manufacturing output since 1995 has been trivial, and in 2001 the trade deficit in goods was more than £31 billion, up by 250 per cent in just five years. Even with Britain's traditional surpluses in services and investment income to offset that gigantic deficit in goods, Britain continues to run an overall current balance of payments deficit – but this is less significant than the underlying economic structure that creates the components of the overall outcome, for in the end international accounts have to balance.

Britain's central bank, independent since 1997, has been setting interest rates to achieve its target of 2.5 per cent inflation; and with free movement of capital, the exchange rate has gone where it will. If the result is massive loss of competitiveness and a suffocating pressure on manufacturing, with all the consequences in terms of lost skills, capacity and poverty in manufacturing regions, then too bad. Yet manufacturing supports some 20 per cent of overall British employment directly, plus up to another estimated 20 per cent or so indirectly.[13] A vibrant manufacturing sector is also strategically important for the strength of British science and technology: frontier scientific innovation needs to be embodied in manufactures in order to be tested and to lay the basis for further advance. But under the current exchange rate regime, no relief can be offered. If Britain were to join the euro, it could not only enjoy all the benefits shared by its current members, but also, provided entry were secured at a reasonable exchange rate, simultaneously give some hope to the beleaguered manufacturing sector.

None of this is good enough for British Eurosceptics, who have developed a battery of counter-arguments. They claim, correctly, that to join the single currency involves the acceptance of important economic constraints, with left-wing critics in particular claiming vindication by the lack of proactive European response to the apparent economic slowdown in the autumn of 2001. The Maastricht Treaty declares that the 'primary objective of the European Central Bank shall be to maintain price stability', which, along with the growth and stability pact that was adopted in 1997, implies demanding economic and fiscal rules. Countries' interest and inflation rates should be almost identical around a very low average to qualify them for membership of the single currency, and there were stringent rules for the level of national debt and degree of budget deficit. The stability pact insists, moreover, that economic policy should be tightly circumscribed after entry. Countries within the euro should not run a budget deficit greater than 3 per cent of GDP, except in circumstances when their GDP falls by 2 per cent in any year; otherwise they face a sliding scale of hefty fines which in the worst case can reach 0.5 per cent of GDP.

As a result, say the sceptics, Europe has saddled itself not only with the stability pact but with a constitutionally independent European Central Bank, overtly modelled on the former West German Bundesbank, that has translated the treaty commitment into a 0–2 per cent inflation target across Europe – a target that over-rides all others, notably any for growth and employment.[14] What has been entrenched, as critics like Oxford University's James Forder argue,[15] is monetarism: the belief that inflation is public economic enemy number one, and that as it is a monetary phenomenon it must be controlled primarily by the targeting and control of the growth of the money supply. In this monetarist model, independent central banks, insulated from political pressure except for politicians setting the required inflation rate and then being held accountable to the national legislature for their effectiveness in achieving it, are the best means for administering the monetarist medicine to control inflation. Even Professor Willem Buiter of the University of Cambridge, a former member of the Bank of England's monetary policy committee and favourably disposed towards the euro, described the ECB as 'the latest offshoot of a central bank tradition that views central banking as a sacred, quasi-mystical vocation, a cult whose priests perform the holy sacraments far from the prying eyes of the non-initiates'.[16] The result, argues Forder, is that both before and after monetary union Europe has suffered from a deficiency of demand because it has put price stability first. If the EU could run a pan-European fiscal policy within more flexible rules allowing for expansionary budgetary packages, then the argument against the euro would be weaker, as Forder honestly acknowledges. But, as he views such a relaxation as improbable and the required co-ordination of member states' economic policies as an infringement of sovereignty, his opposition remains undimmed.

Right wing voices join the chorus, pointing out that the ECB is less accountable to the British people than the Bank of England, and that even if Europe did initiate a more flexible fiscal policy, Britain's would be just one voice in the debate on the conduct of an economic policy that affected the whole of Europe. Also, the EU as a whole suffers from a grievous democratic deficit, and the ECB is a secretive institution within this weak democratic structure. It takes its decisions in private, and does not publish minutes explaining what it has done. Being held to account by the barely legitimate and scarcely publicised monetary committee of the European parliament is hardly sufficient as a democratic instrument. Indeed, the ECB acknowledges that one of the reasons for not publishing its minutes is that to do so would reveal the voting patterns of its central bank governor members, and that would in turn put national political pressure on them to advocate their particular countries' interests – hardly a self-confident assertion that individual national central bankers can put Europe's economic interests before their own.[17] Thus surrendering the pound and joining the euro will weaken Britain's economic options, and is an abdication of both economic sovereignty and political accountability.

These arguments seem potent, but they simply ignore the realities described earlier. Now that the euro has been established, the pound floats against the euro, the dollar and the yen – a medium-scale currency trading against the three giants. As these continental tectonic currency plates move, so the pound will be even more tightly squeezed and subject to the mercy of volatile capital flows than it has been up until now. The chronic overvaluation of sterling has already cost manufacturing dear, and it is now beginning to impact on the inward investment flows upon which Britain is so dependent, which are slowing down in the older manufacturing regions of the country. Exchange rate sovereignty is a chimera.

However, similar concerns have been gaining ground in the rest of Europe. Winning a referendum on euro membership today would be as difficult in France and Germany as it promises to be in Britain; opinion polls in both countries reveal a remarkable hostility to the concept, although this has begun to wane after the currency's successful launch. This is in part the fault of those in favour, who are not making the argument with sufficient force; but the greater problem is that a collective amnesia has settled on Europe. We seem to have forgotten what contemporary realities actually are, and what the actual experience of the last thirty years has been.

For Britain – and all the other European countries, were the euro to collapse – confronts an international financial community with an explicit view of what constitutes the correct approach to economic policy and with the power to ensure that it is followed. The Washington consensus, policed by the IMF and the capital markets, is no less restrictive in its attitude to economic policy than the Maastricht Treaty; broadly, both believe that countries should strain for budget balance in all but exceptional circumstances. Indeed, the Maastricht Treaty, with its concession that countries can run a budget deficit of up to 3 per cent of GDP with exceptional let-outs in case of a severe recession, is marginally more progressive than the IMF's view.

While it is true that the stability pact imposes constraints on fiscal policy, they are over-emphasised. As leading economists Barry Eichengreen and Charles Wyplosz have shown, there have been hardly any periods since World War II when budget deficits in European countries, including Britain, have been more than 3 per cent of GDP for longer than a year, and even those were marked by exceptional circumstances.[18] There need to be rules, and it is quite wrong to suppose that outside the stability pact the UK with a floating exchange rate would suddenly have a new flexibility over its fiscal policy – or the ability to make its own rules as it chose. In reality, states today have essentially three options over their fiscal policy. They can be ultra-conservative like Singapore, Switzerland and Canada (and countries outside the euro zone such as Sweden and Denmark[19]), and run large budget surpluses. They can have the degree of manoeuvre permitted by the euro zone. Or they can join the ranks of the also-rans – the countries in which the financial markets demand a high premium to invest. Only the US has some fiscal autonomy; but even the US government has to keep a wary eye on the judgements of the bond markets and foreigners' confidence in the dollar, given its enormous trade deficit. It is only the member countries of the euro zone, acting together, that over time have the capacity to equal or surpass American autonomy. A country outside the euro zone can have a fiscal and monetary policy as conservative as or more conservative than the Maastricht benchmark; what it cannot do is have a policy that is less conservative. And if the euro zone did not exist, the benchmark would be the Washington consensus.

The British Treasury knows that there is a narrow band of market tolerance for its fiscal policy, and it does everything in its control to sustain market confidence in the credibility of its policies by staying within these tramlines. And that means keeping policy conservative. As chancellor, Gordon Brown had to spend two years earning credibility by sticking to the very restrictive targets for public spending growth he inherited in 1997, and it was only once he had earned that credibility and established an enormously strong fiscal position – with a budgetary surplus significantly larger than that of France, Germany or Italy – that he felt able to allow public spending to grow faster than GDP for three years. Even then he was criticised by the IMF for his pains, despite British national debt, at 30 per cent of GDP, being comfortably the lowest in the G7 – and British public services palpably the worst. It will take at least another five years of rapid spending growth before British health expenditure, for example, rises as the government has pledged it will to approach the EU average. The European Commission made a mild remark about the sustainability of the British government's spending plans, suggesting it was being too ambitious in incurring modest borrowing in the third year of the potential three-year spending plan; but the IMF has deemed it important to issue regular warnings. And while Gordon Brown can challenge the EU Commission for its conservative silliness, he has no such political clout with the IMF and cannot make the same political intervention to defend his policy from stupid criticism. Indeed, while the EU has scaled back its warnings, the IMF has felt no such restraint, repeating its strictures again in the December of 2001 – when they looked particularly absurd, as Brown's spending plans increasingly appeared a judicious response to an approaching economic slowdown. In terms of the Washington consensus, Britain was being imprudent; and, like Denmark and Sweden, Britain outside the euro has to fight that international consensus even to gain a smidgin of room for manoeuvre.

This is not to argue that the particular policy stance of the ECB and the Commission – currently an excessive economic conservatism which is costing them much-needed credibility – is right. In fairness, a newly established central bank like the ECB can hardly operate with the swagger and

curious result of bad ideas driving out good, or a 'Brussels conspiracy' as they would characterise it; it was a plausible response to an acute policy crisis in the 1970s over how to respond to inflation, aided and abetted by the triumph of American conservatism over American liberalism, which then exported its ideas via the formal and informal conduits outlined in chapter 6 that are associated with US hegemony. The notion that any one European country could have resisted this intellectual advance is for the birds; France tried, and it was punished severely. Rather, monetarism made the advances it did precisely because Europe was so intellectually and institutionally defenceless.

It is of elemental importance that Europe's economic policy-makers start to argue the case for a continental economic policy that acts on hard economic problems, put in place the practices and processes to deliver it, and locates the ECB's monetary policy within those wider objectives. Only thus will the euro escape the sobriquet of being, as one currency dealer anonymously but memorably described it, a toilet currency. And only thus will Europe develop the policy responses it needs not just to deal with an economic slowdown, but with other economic difficulties in the decades ahead.

This is, of course, what the French and in particular Delors originally planned. The Delors committee on monetary union proposed close economic co-ordination of member countries' fiscal policies so that they could complement the direction of monetary policy. Its members foresaw a dialogue between the central bank and Europe's economic authorities, and a recognition that their actions were interdependent – rather like the US Treasury and the Fed, and the British Treasury and the Bank of England. The ECB, representing the case for price stability, was meant to be part of a European economic conversation that would engage with real economic problems rather than with shadows from the past.

It is bizarre that while the ECB operates on the basis of a Europe-wide assessment of money supply and credit conditions, fiscal policy is conducted by national bureaucracies – and even then is constrained by the terms of the stability pact. Fiscal policy should be Europeanised, and the rules within which it is conducted made more sympathetic to the vicissitudes of the economic cycle. An economic architecture must be created which allows the EU the capacity to counteract both shortfalls and excesses in demand, and which will in turn require member states to reflate or deflate their economies around a common analysis of the European economy.

In other words, the council of economic and finance ministers, ECOFIN, needs to be more than an economic talking shop. It needs to become a deliberative body with the power to take advantage of the single currency and organise economic policy on a continental scale, including determining the appropriate euro exchange rate against the dollar and yen. It could even have, as argued by Charles Grant, director of the Centre for European Reform, a permanent High Representative for Financial Affairs – a Mr or Ms Euroland – who would chair the council and drive the implementation of a common fiscal policy.[21] This is not to argue for the abandonment of fiscal rules or the establishment of a federal fiscal policy; of course a credible fiscal policy needs to have a framework and intellectual rationale, and, as argued in chapter 10, the operational constitution for Europe needs to be intergovernmental in character, especially over matters as fundamental as spending and taxing. But it is to argue that in today's conditions the fiscal policy of any one European country will be much more effective if it is part of a coherent Europe-wide stance. As Europe has suffered from a shortfall of demand for the past five years, the urgent European interest is that all European states – especially those in countries with an acute demand shortfall, like Germany – act collectively to remedy it.

The technical instruments for undertaking this task are comparatively easy to conceive. French economists Pierre Jacquet and Jean Pisani-Ferry (the latter a former adviser to the French finance minister) have set out what could be done in an important paper.[22] They propose an economic charter which would set out clearly the principles according to which European economic policy should be run and would address the concern that the European Central Bank is excessively worried about inflation exceeding the upper end of its target range while ignoring the risks of falling prices; the ECB, as the Bank of England has to do with the British government, should have to explain itself to the euro-zone group of finance ministers and the European parliament both when prices overshoot and when they undershoot. This would provide a more proper balance to its policy. They go on to advocate a process in which the euro-zone finance ministers would assess European demand conditions and set national fiscal policies within a commonly agreed framework for what their joint impact on European demand should be. They suggest that the British and French system of three-year planning horizons should be adopted by the EU as a whole. The group of euro-zone finance ministers would thus become the economic and fiscal authority with which the ECB would engage in a policy dialogue.

The process could go further. The Commission could be given the powers to borrow on its account to finance extra structural and cohesion fund spending as part of a wider means of supplementing demand. There could even be, as French prime minister Lionel Jospin argued in his speech on Europe in May 2001, a common economic action fund from which countries would be entitled to borrow if they encountered exceptional economic turbulence. Once policy was being conducted in this framework, many of the criticisms of the ECB on the grounds of a lack of accountability would fall away. It would be plainly part of a European economic policy conversation directed by Europe's elected leaders, playing a crucial role as custodian of a low inflation rate that Europe's elected leaders had mandated it to protect, but no longer in a position to be the only European economic policy actor.

While Jacquet and Pisani-Ferry wrestle with how to improve the powers and competence of the euro-zone group of finance ministers in order to build on the euro's advantages and complete the construction of a workable European economic policy, the British economic establishment uses the same analysis to argue that the system is irredeemably flawed and that Britain should not enter. Its attitude to these issues is curmudgeonly, second-rate, unimaginative, ahistoric and uncreative. A motley collection of ageing ex-Treasury and Bank of England mandarins, the has-been doyens of Britain's economic establishment, enjoying the singular distinction of having being wrong on most substantive economic issues since 1945, has rolled out the usual mish-mash of criticisms in a classic sceptic text, 'The Economic Case against the Euro'.[23] Its authors present the usual objections to entry (one interest rate will not fit all; the system is inflexible; etc., etc.) and add that their chief concerns about the need for more transparency of decision-making, a lower exchange rate to secure sustainable British entry and the need for yet more flexible labour markets in Europe pose obstacles so insuperable that British membership should not be contemplated. Even if all those tests were passed, they still believe that managing the euro requires such a degree of political centralisation that the resulting superstate would be a priori against the interests of Europe's peoples. They are thus opposed.

What can be said? Europe's labour markets are a great deal more flexible than the British realise; the real bone of contention is whether workers should be treated as disposable commodities, as under British law, or as assets – as in the European approach. As for the exchange rate, plainly it needs to be significantly lower than that prevailing at the time of writing in March 2002. To argue that to join at the current rate would lock in a degree of uncompetitiveness that would profoundly damage the British economy in the long run is not an argument against ever joining; it is an argument against joining at the current exchange rate. The pound needs to fall by at least 15 per cent towards the equivalent of DM2.70 if Britain's membership is to be sustainable. This is hardly an impossible objective. A government announcement that it considered the right exchange rate to be very much lower, and that it intended to sell pounds and finance its borrowing in euros until that rate was reached, would see a decisive downwards move in the exchange rate.

Of course, as I have been arguing, the relationship between the ECB and European economic policy-making needs to be reformed. This is not utopianism. There is a growing recognition of the need for reform in Europe – witness the Jacquet–Pisani-Ferry paper discussed above, and the arguments in the run-up to the French presidential election in May 2002 that the ECB needs to operate more like the Bank of England – and British entry could and should be used as the trigger for change. Even if we believe that the constitution of the ECB does not represent the acme of central bank practice and transparency, that is not in itself a reason never to join until it is changed. It is an argument to engage with it and negotiate for reform from within. There is sufficient advantage to joining as matters stand; if our entry makes improvement in the regime more likely, that is icing on the cake.

What the British sceptics are doing is throwing up reasons for not joining because at root they do not believe that they are European, that they share values with other Europeans and that they can benefit from making common cause with other Europeans. Thus the core position of even ex-treasury knights: the euro will lead to a superstate and therefore is bad. It is the same reluctance and misdiagnosis that have afflicted Britain from the time when the Treaty of Rome was being drafted. There needs to be an intellectual and cultural revolution.

This is the first decade of the twenty-first century. Even the British Treasury and Bank of England have little leverage over the exchange rate, and barely more over the interest rate. Yet it is this British Treasury that will be assessing whether Britain is economically fit for entry, and in particular whether it has passed the five economic tests set by Chancellor Gordon Brown in 1997. As long as there is sufficient economic convergence, notably over interest rates and inflation, so that business cycles are aligned; flexibility to accommodate problems and shocks; the promotion of investment (especially inward investment); the securing of long-term growth and employment; and lastly, no damage to the competitiveness of the financial services industry (the promotion of the City's interests over those of all other economic groups is a telling commentary on British priorities) – then Britain should enter.

The tests are deliberately couched in generalities, and, as the National Institute of Economic and Social Research has observed, have already been passed.[24] Short- and long-term interest rates, together with inflation, are already close to or below the average in the euro zone; Britain's public finances comfortably meet all the Maastricht and stability pact criteria; and the European and British economic cycles are closely synchronised. As for inward investment, leading Japanese and American multinationals operating in Britain have warned that unless Britain joins the euro soon they will be unable to sustain the scale of their current British operations; staying out jeopardises inward investment more than entry. Recent figures already show that France is capturing more inward investment in manufacturing than Britain.

Opinion in the City is more divided over the merits of the single currency, but the majority view is that although it has done well outside the euro, it would do even better inside, making London the leading financial centre in Europe with a massive economic hinterland.[25] The point about flexibility of response to shocks is more vexed, but to the extent that this is an explicit criticism of Europe's labour markets (criticised as inflexible) it vastly exaggerates their importance as a cause of European unemployment. This has become an almost ideological conviction in Britain; but if the argument is that the EU needs to emulate Britain, this is hardly a reason not to join the euro. In any case European influence on Britain's labour markets comes via our adherence to the European social chapter rather than euro membership; the entire issue is a red herring. And as for the promotion of long-term growth and employment, the prospect of low interest rates and exchange rate stability – as argued earlier – should tend to produce more output and employment than a floating exchange rate regime. The tests, in short, are passed.

Serious issues remain that are not covered by the five tests. As argued above, entry would have to be secured at a lower exchange rate – but this could be addressed in the ways I have described. As for concerns about Britain submitting itself to a monetary and fiscal straitjacket, those need to be set against the advantages of membership and the realities of contemporary economic policy-making set out in this chapter. There is also the argument that the cost of the monetary changeover is prohibitive – wildly estimated at up to £30 billion, even though the changeover costs in France and Italy, similarly sized economies to Britain, have run at a quarter of that figure. But to say that entry is not worth the price is to fail to acknowledge the additional revenue that Britain would enjoy from seigniorage (when central banks are in effect paid interest by the banking system in exchange for cash, needed to operate the banking system but which costs the central bank nothing to issue) through the proposed share-out of the seigniorage profit on the euro. According to one group of economists, Britain's expected seigniorage receipts would more than double by 2010 to some £4 billion, which would be paid over directly to the Treasury[26] – equivalent to the revenue raised by lifting the basic rate of income tax by two pence in the pound.

Finally, there are the shortcomings of Europe's economic policy-making machinery. Here the dilemma is classic: does one engage with solving the problem or stand aside? Britain inside the euro would find important allies – notably in France – in its desire to reframe Europe's economic constitution. Indeed there is a good prospect that much the same tactics could be used as were deployed by the Labour government in negotiating Britain's terms of entry into the EC in 1974. Certainly some EU countries would welcome the chance to adapt both the stability pact and reform the broader machinery along the lines suggested by Jacquet and Pisani-Ferry. If it were obvious that this was a potential deal-breaker, British pressure would be the occasion for reform.

Even without this potentially clinching concession, the case for British entry is overwhelming – but if it is to carry the day, the culture of official scepticism betrayed in the obstructive negativism of 'The Economic Case against the Euro' must be actively countered; otherwise the Treasury will simply retreat into crabbing caution legitimised by so-called 'pragmatism'. This requires political direction and leadership at home; but it also requires more conviction in Europe, and some demonstration that it would drive the best of the reform proposals through of its own accord without British pressure. A club which has a degree of faith in its own cause and proactively redresses its problems is an inherently more attractive proposition than one beset by doubts and uncertainty.

The EU itself needs to be less sceptical and seize the moment, not least in its own interest. Currently, each national political class avoids openly acknowledging its own powerlessness and making an overtly European case to its own electorate, fearful that an opposition party might win political advantage by criticising it for not protecting the national interest. Political parties everywhere are keenly aware of the electorate's disillusion with parties and the weakening of party loyalties;[27] they do not want to fan the flames by conceding that the disillusion is even partly justified. Italian prime minister Silvio Berlusconi's desire to assert Italian interests and French uncertainty about their relationship to the EU as it stands poised for enlargement, heralding a further weakening of French influence, are as much part of this trend as British Euroscepticism.

The lack of realism and honesty is self-defeating. Europe's member states need to begin to argue for a European interest in which they locate their own interest, rather than to regard European initiatives as something to be avoided because they are politically difficult to sell. By arguing for empowerment through Europe they can win back the legitimacy that comes with political action actually changing things. If any particular member state is suffering from a shortfall in demand, say, then its governing party needs to argue that its own national response will be more effective if it is part of a Europe-wide response. This is the real route to furthering individual national interests – and empowering governments.

And this approach would have redoubled force if Europeans were less defensive about the advantages of the European economic and social model, and more aggressive about using the single economic space that they have created to advance this model, albeit while respecting national variations. This proposition needs to be supported by saying as forcefully as possible that every member of the European Union – France, Germany, Britain, or any other European state – has values and aims that they hold in common and which they can no longer articulate as effective policies within the context of their national communities alone. That with globalisation – especially given its powerful American character – matters are not going to get any better. That together they are stronger. And that the euro offers them a sovereignty and chance of democracy in monetary and economic affairs that they are steadily losing if they do nothing.

If mainland Europeans started to argue in this way, they would quickly raise an echo not only in their own countries, but in Britain. The old way of framing the pro-European argument – we must stop doing things even if we are profoundly attached to them because this will serve the great cause of European integration – needs to give way to the argument that we must do things together because that way we will get better results. It is this argument that ultimately will win any referendum on the euro in Britain. It has to become, across Europe, a truth that hardly needs to be stated.

Democratic reform

To fulfil its new potential as a world economic and political force, informed by its own distinct strain of capitalism and relationship with the rest of the world, the structure of European governance needs to be overhauled. So there remains one last nut to crack: the charge that the EU is incapable of being democratic. Solve this, and the only arguments left for the sceptics are prejudice and nostalgia.

The whole apparatus of decision-making, and in particular the relationship between the Commission and the Council of Ministers, has become opaque and unable to refute the charge that it is undemocratic. In particular, the Commission as it is currently constituted no longer works. The loss to its prestige and authority after the devastating European parliament report of March 1999 which stated that fraud and corruption pass 'unnoticed' in some top offices and which prompted the wholesale resignation of the entire Commission, has proved difficult if not impossible to reverse. A new team of commissioners, with former Italian prime minister Romano Prodi as the new president, has launched impressive internal reforms, but the parliament report's damning conclusion that 'it is becoming difficult to find anyone who has even the slightest sense of responsibility' hangs over their efforts. The Commission is becalmed in a crisis of legitimacy, unable either to make the European case with the confidence it should or marshal support for any ambitious initiative. Its morale is at rock-bottom.

Its difficulties are not cosmetic; they are structural, especially if the new task is to build Europe rather than 'unbuild' the obstacles to creating a single market and customs union. At present the Commission simultaneously has supranational authority to build a customs union which has ambitions to become much more and to act as the civil service for the Council of Ministers. In one role it is an active political entrepreneur and play-maker in the cause of Europe, even if it feels shackled by its limited conception; in another it is the servant of the member states represented in the Council. It is this constitutional ambiguity that lies at the heart of its dilemma. It is at once the builder of a federal Europe and the custodian of a federation of nation-states. Wearing its federalist hat, it is obliged by treaty to drive integration forwards; its accountability is measured by how successfully it achieves its treaty remit, rather than by the democratic credentials of its own processes. On the other hand, wearing its hat as secretariat to the Council, it needs to adopt guiding civil service principles of impartiality and secrecy, as national civil servants do, because accountability lies with its political masters. Promoting accountability for its decisions does not rank high in its constitutional priorities.

This constitutional ambiguity is echoed by the European Council of heads of government. The Council is overtly a mechanism for the member states politically to direct something called 'Europe', an entity which is actually the Europe of states that the Council itself embodies. In other words, Council meetings are organised around the same ambiguity as the Commission; they serve 'Europe' and the member states at the same time. The democratic deficit this creates is meant to be closed by the European parliament, but cannot escape the reality that at present there is no European public realm. Everywhere in Europe there is a more democratic society which wants to hold decision-making to account. Across the EU opinion polls show mounting scepticism about the European project, distrust of EU initiatives and concern about the euro. The growing danger is that, just when it is more important than ever that Europe acts together and at a new level of integration, it will be disabled by a growing backlash across the Union. The tensions and anger this is creating all over Europe threaten to paralyse the European project.

The response must be twofold. In the short term, Europe's member-states and national parliaments – which still retain legitimacy, even if it is diminishing – have to reassert political control over the European process; and the Commission has to be seen to be under politically accountable direction. Simultaneously, Europe has to work painstakingly towards creating a 'European' consciousness and a body of opinion that thinks in European terms and will ultimately be the source of legitimacy for pan-European institutions by holding them to account. These pan-European institutions need to be strengthened – notably the European parliament, which needs to be seen as the eventual heart of European democracy. Jürgen Habermas in Germany and Larry Siedentop in Britain are both surely right when they argue that the prerequisites for a positively integrated Europe are a genuine European civil society, a Europe-wide public sphere and a common political culture.[28] Neither believes that the current lack of such ingredients should obstruct integration – indeed, the act of building Europe will help create them. But we have to be realistic about where we are now, about the need to build institutions that work within today's realities even while we aim for more in the future: realism today, while upholding the European flame for tomorrow.

The first task is to intensify the role of member states and parliaments in the governance of Europe. The European Council of heads of government should meet more frequently, at two-month intervals, and it should establish three permanent directors or high representatives to chair and represent the views of ECOFIN, the council of foreign and defence ministers, and the council of justice and home affairs ministers, who would drive forward European policy in each of these areas. Each government's minister for Europe should sit in a permanently established Council of Europe that would carry forward the work of the Council of heads of government, thus abandoning the notion that this should rotate around every individual member state. The president of the Commission would chair this permanent council, on which commissioners would also sit along with the three high representatives; it would be the executive board of the EU structure but working to a legislative and policy programme established by the Council of heads of government.

The directives and body of law emanating from the reinvigorated Council of heads of government would need the approval not only of the European parliament, but of a European senate composed of delegates from national parliaments. Europe would thus have a bicameral legislature, with more political strength, more legitimacy and more political relevance: the existing parliament, elected directly by individual national electorates, and the European senate, that would represent national parliamentary interests. There should also be clear lines of political authority marking the respective remits of national and European government; health, education, law and order, and welfare must remain largely in national governments' hands even if there may be commonly agreed minimum outcomes that each European state should attempt to meet. The areas which should be passed to European level should be transparently those where the effectiveness of action would thereby be increased, so benefiting individual European citizens.

It would not be an especially elegant constitution – but it would certainly begin to close the accountability gap. Decision-making would become genuinely political in the sense of being publicly scrutinised and tested, and much less of an intergovernmental diplomatic fix. The European parliament would be stengthened decisively. The ultimate democratic goal should be the election of the president of the Commission every five years by Europe's electorate, the principle to be established by a Europe-wide referendum. For some, the risk is that a low turnout would threaten the legitimacy of the whole operation, while others worry that majorities will be unevenly spread so that some national communities vote against a proposal only to have to submit to the majority will of the rest of the EU who have voted for it. These are significant risks; but they come from the old mindset. Europe needs to start debating with itself in order to create a democratic discourse and a new legitimacy, and the establishment at Laeken in December 2001 of the preparatory convention, charged with establishing constitutional principles in the run-up to a new EU intergovernmental conference, is a magnificent opportunity. The greater risk is incurred by constructing Europe on flimsy foundations, finessing and bypassing these crucial issues.

The arguments need to be opened up. Europe-wide political parties will eventually be one means of pitching arguments at an European level, but they will develop only when the European parliament has more power, notably over taxation. This will inexorably follow its proposed strengthening. Citizen engagement, unsurprisingly, is typically higher when the legislatures for whose candidates they are voting have tax-raising powers – a position some way off for the European parliament, but which must none the less be argued for. In the meantime, Europe-wide referenda have the advantage of forcing politicians and opinion leaders to explain what they are doing to their electorates, and the very act of making an argument in European terms – even if it is lost – begins to create a recognition that there are European interests which Europeans hold in common. The pros and antis will have to organise on a Europe-wide basis, making a tangible expression of European solidarity, whatever the result of any particular debate. As for the question of individual countries being over-ruled by others, these important differences between national electorates over policy choices do not go away if they are simply manoeuvred around by top-down decision-making, or brushed over in the hope that the electorate in question will resign itself to being part of a policy to which it objects. In any case, the same thing happens regularly in most democracies. In Britain a region or a county can vote for the losing party in a general election without wondering whether it should break away from the nation. Europe needs to move to the same degree of sophistication, and the same recognition that the collective interest in hanging together outweighs the benefits of going it alone. The only mechanism we have is that of argument, engagement and persuasion – and Europe's effectiveness both internally and externally will be enhanced if it is seen to be confident of making such arguments and has equipped itself with the processes to conduct such debate.

If these reforms can be achieved, the sometimes justified criticisms of the Eurosceptics will have been met. Yet for some, especially those in Britain, nothing will suffice. It does not matter that a remodelled, more democratic Europe will serve its citizens better, meet robust demands for improved democracy and accountability, and enlarge the political, economic and social options of its member governments. They are opposed to such an end result on principle and do not believe it is possible on *a priori* grounds; they thus oppose any engagement that might bring it about. Pro-Europeans should be emboldened. The case for Europe is good enough in terms of what it already is; it is better again in terms of what it might be. Just as we should join the single currency and argue to improve the EU's economic governance regime, so we should take the same stance with the wider European project. The argument stands either which way. It can – and should – be made with this degree of passion.

Conclusion

The world finds itself at a critical juncture. The US has emerged as the globe's hyperpower, but in thrall to an extreme brand of conservatism that offers very particular solutions across the gamut of economic, social and security issues. After its show of force in Afghanistan, in which the gap between American technological military capacity and that of the rest of the world was fiercely underlined, its conservative political class and a large part of its public feel that there is and should be no constraint to the exercise of American will. The belief that America should come first, both in its own interests and in the world's – because America has a special vocation to be the world's beacon of liberty and opportunity – has come swelling to the fore in a new surge of patriotism and unilateralism. As the Bush administration characterises the world, you are either for us or against us – and even if you are for us, be sure that the relationship we want is wholly on our terms. American security in the face of fresh and ruthless terrorism is paramount, and can be secured only by the iron fist.

It is an unlovely and a dangerous prospect. This approach to ordering the world is self-defeating, and would be so even if the US were a paragon of all the economic, social and moral virtues. For what lies behind it is the exercise of brutish power and the demand that others subordinate their interests, values and ways of thinking to a superior force. As such, it is an approach inherently pregnant with tension and ultimately unsustainable.

This is problematic enough in America's relations within the industrialised West and Asia, but in the context of the complex militant fundamentalism of the Islamic world it condemns the twin protagonists to enduring mistrust and hostility.

In any case, the US is not a paragon of all the virtues. It certainly has strengths – it is an open society, and the best of its universities, companies and institutions are genuine benchmarks for the rest of the world – but they are offset by weaknesses it does not understand or begin to acknowledge. It protests that it is the land of opportunity as the arteries of social mobility harden, crystallising a self-perpetuating aristocracy of the wealthy and serfdom of the poor that is shocking by European standards. It insists that it is the most enterprising economy on earth even as other countries' productivity surpass it. It believes that its own brand of capitalism, with its narrow focus on economic flexibilities and the maximisation of 'shareholder value' is the elixir that has made the US wealthy and will do the same for others, when the truth is both more complex and more subtle. It boasts of its commitment to democracy in a political system where elected office and policy are increasingly bought. It acts increasingly unilaterally in a world where our interdependence is never more obvious and never more important to express. This conservative America is a menace.

If the rest of the world is not careful, our future will be to accept globalisation almost entirely on American conservative terms and around American conservative preoccupations. Despite the brave talk of a new multilateralism in the wake of 11 September, the hard truth is that the US predisposition to unilateralism has been reinforced. It won a potentially dangerous and protracted war in Afghanistan in three months at the cost of a handful of American lives, and needed no help from any ally. It is minded to continue to take the war to any other state suspected of harbouring terrorist cells – President Bush's infamous 'axis of evil' – in exactly the same way, and is hardening its support for a militaristic Israel, which is considering abandoning the search for a Middle Eastern peace settlement, contemplating instead the occupation of those areas under Palestinian authority and action to root out terrorism there as the US has done in Afghanistan. It promises aggressive action against Iraq to topple Saddam Hussein, justified by the belief that pre-emptive, unilateral action against possible terrorism is justified, notwithstanding the rubric of international law. This would have incalculable consequences and ripple effects throughout the Middle East. But America no longer feels the need to uphold international law or sustain the coalition that was painstakingly built after 11 September; it is the mission that defines the coalition, as defence secretary Donald Rumsfeld has repeatedly declared, not the coalition that defines the mission.[1] In other words, the US will set the strategic goal and execute it by itself if necessary. Unilateral force rules, OK or not.

The political dynamic in the US quest for a unilateral disposition of the world's security arrangements around its own definitions of its self-interest is quickening. Notice has been served on Russia that the US will no longer abide by the anti-ballistic missile treaty as it seeks to install its own missile defence system against attack from 'rogue' states. The same unilateralism extends across the board – to the climate change talks, to agreements over chemical weapons, and to the insistence that the US reserves the right to arrest and shoot those within the US or whom it extradites whom it suspects of terrorism under military law. Those looking to the US to give a lead in establishing a new liberal framework of trade, aid and debt relief to provide some succour to the less developed world can think again. The British government's call for an aid programme on the scale of the postwar Marshall Plan to assist the less developed world falls on deaf ears in Washington. This is a country that, just as it has done at other times in its history, is looking inwards rather than outwards.

In economic terms this is especially hazardous. Economic interdependence is the inevitable by-product of globalisation. The shockwaves from the collapse of Enron, the world's largest ever bankruptcy, spread far beyond the US, just as the bubble and subsequent bust in dot.com and telecoms shares has done. Moreover, it was largely owing to the financial and telecoms deregulation for which the US pushed so aggressively that the bubble and bust were so synchronised across the leading stock markets, with the consequent loss of up to $1000 trillion. For the first time since the 1974 oil shock the world faces the prospect of a prolonged period of below-average growth with recurring financial instabilities and trade tensions, in part as the result of the stunning losses the financial system has shouldered, but with only weak institutions and processes to attempt any global policy response. The US repudiates such initiatives as an infringement of its economic sovereignty, and continues to press for the 'liberalisation' of national regulatory structures, regardless of the lack of anything global to put in their place. The world must build a market in which American transnationals and investment banks can be free, and where capital can flow without hindrance to the US to finance what for any other country would be an unsustainable trade deficit and unsustainable build-up of private sector debt.

The growing consensus among economists is that the current American economic downturn will be short-lived, and the dynamic US economy will leap back into life courtesy of cheaper oil and very low interest rates. The US will do it on its own. But the likelihood of the widely expected quick return to growth on the scale of the 1990s is severely limited by the sheer scale of the debt overhang and the size of the trade deficit, with the US's accompanying dependence on foreign capital. The financial system has taken a major hit, and US consumers and business alike are chronically indebted. As it becomes more obvious that the US is reaching the limits of its ability to exploit the current system to grow at exceptional rates, foreign capital inflows and the buoyancy of Wall Street will be undermined. The US will be forced towards an adjustment of its ambitions and living standards; it will resist; and things will get ugly. The US has already unilaterally imposed swingeing tariffs to save its beleaguered but uncompetitive steel industry, in abuse of world trade rules. More is promised in agriculture and semi-conductors, with US officials warning that America is no longer prepared to be 'a market of last resort'.[2] The EU is cautioned against any retaliation, even if within the WTO's rules. Now it's one rule for the US, another for the rest of the world. If the economy underperforms or foreigners voluntarily cease buying its financial assets, the American proclivity for protecting itself and twisting the arms of its trading partners will grow more pronounced.

It is this fragile and insecure success before which Europeans are expected to bow the knee and copy the mechanisms by which it has allegedly been produced. If the American way was as successful as the conservative propagandists claim, this might be rational – but the consistent argument of this book is that American capitalism is a great deal weaker than it likes to claim, and that American society is seriously disfigured by the results of the way the economy is run. This is a particular challenge to Europe. While the US has been able to escape – so far – the social consequences of its economic structures, both because of the commonly accepted myth of its exceptional social mobility and also because of its profound cultural attachment to particular ideas of liberty which excuse social suffering, no such avenue is open to the Europeans. Nor will European society so willingly turn a blind eye to the corruption and deformation of its democracy by the forces of rapacious inequality. Yet the character of globalisation, shaped by US policy, and the drumbeat of insistence that the American model is best invite the Europeans freely to import these conceptions into Europe or to attempt to initiate them by policy means. Thus the stress on creating labour markets as 'flexible' as they are in the US, financial markets as ready to take 'risks', and the same minimalist approach to regulation, taxation and welfare.

Yet close examination of the operation of the two systems' labour markets shows that, for all their vaunted flexibility, the American labour market works less well and European markets better than either is supposed to. American workers' chances of moving out of low-paid jobs are smaller; turnover rates are not especially high; and unemployment in low-skilled jobs relative to high-skilled jobs is higher than in 'regulated' Europe. Much of America's success in job generation can be explained in terms of the high supply of immigrant and female labour willing to work at low wage rates in the expanding service and security sectors driven by buoyant, credit-driven demand. The labour market did not obstruct this development and even helped enable it; but it did not cause it.

As for the structure of the financial system, the US is already having cause to ponder whether the dot.com and telecoms bubbles were worth the financial deregulation that spawned them. Credulous European leaders who at the Lisbon and Stockholm summits advocated that Europe should find ways to generate a similarly vigorous venture capital industry cannot have known that only a tiny fraction of the thousands of initial public offerings financed by American venture capital over the 1990s are still trading above their offer price; many have gone bust. Rarely has the world witnessed such capricious and vacuous venality dressed up as 'enterprise'; rarely have so many been gulled by such duplicity.

European regulation, taxation, public provision and welfare are attacked for their attendant economic ill-effects – but the analysis of this book has shown that the criticism cannot be supported. The ill-effects are exaggerated, sometimes non-existent; but rarely if ever acknowledged are the benefits conferred by high-quality universal education and health care, and guarantee of income for the marginalised and weak. At core, the American criticism is based on a moral stance: the idea of the social contract that lies behind these structures offends American conservatism's belief in individualism, liberty and self-reliance.

And here lies the rub. European civilisation is underpinned by values Europe's leaders could not give up even if they wanted to; for their roots lie deep and define what it means to be a European. American conservatism, having wrought contemptible damage on its own society, cannot be allowed to repeat the carnage in Europe. The European belief that the wealthy and propertied have reciprocal obligations to the society of which they are part and which cannot be discharged by charity alone goes back to early Christendom – as does the associated notion that a settled people must form a social contract to entrench their association. This in turn demands a public realm that permits the articulation and expression of what we hold in common. It is these propositions that, when turned into structures and policies, produce the high-quality social outcomes that distinguish Europe from the US, which have also begun to give it an edge in the growth of productivity and innovation – albeit obscured by the unsustainable 1990s US boom. The conservative American attack on these values, poorly challenged by liberals in the US, must be better resisted in Europe. We must turn back the tide in the name of the good society and common humanities.

European history has had its peaks and troughs. This is the continent that invented capitalism, democracy and human rights, but it is also a continent soaked in war, dark ideology and blood. Since 1945 it has rediscovered its nobler traditions, and increasingly confidently expressed a belief in and capacity to deliver democracy, human rights and the rule of law, along with a vital social contract and a highly productive capitalism. The achievement is blighted by unemployment, whose chief cause lies in lack of demand in Europe – demand which remains depressed in part because until the single currency is bedded down the EU cannot have the same indifference to the consequence of stimulating demand as America, and in part because such stimulation has been ruled out by the necessary rigours of forming a single currency. Europe cannot pretend it does not suffer political scandals, but – Italy apart – they do not define its democratic systems; in none of them can office be so systematically and flagrantly bought, or the terms of democratic debate be so explicitly defined by those with money, as in the US. In the round, Europe's democracy, social contract and capitalism work well. Europeans have much to be proud of, and much to offer. It is time to proselytise European success.

The British task

Once these realities are recognised the British political project – indeed, obligation – becomes more obvious. First and foremost it is to realise that, despite the common language we share with the US – the country that grew out of thirteen British colonies – the rise of American conservatism has disconnected US civilisation from the European mainstream. Europe is our continent. We share the same history and the same core values. The British approach to the social contract and the public realm lies much nearer to Europe than to the US, and while British capitalism is organised more along US principles than other EU countries, it has brought us scant advantage.

Inequality in Britain is scandalously high and productivity remains low; Britain's companies under-invest, under-innovate and under-compete. A decade of rising demand fuelled by a deregulated financial system has given a one-off fix in terms of reducing unemployment; but households cannot go on for ever getting into debt at the same rate, permanently fuelling ever higher consumption. At some stage Britain will have to rely on its underlying productivity – and it is this that bodes ill for the medium term. The country likes to boast that it combines the best of America and Europe. A more honest assessment is that it has developed an economic model that reproduces the worst trends in American capitalism with few of the compensations, but has been unable to build a social contract that delivers anything like the same outcomes as mainland Europe.

Indeed, the dangers of allowing inequality to approach American levels in a small island that remains so European in its attitudes are barely understood. The British will not tolerate, nor can they afford, the ghet-toisation of their cities, the emasculation of their public services and the pauperisation of their disadvantaged. It is not just a question of values that makes these conditions so offensive; we live on top of each other to such a degree that a dysfunctional society imposes insupportable costs. For example, the disintegration of the public transport system, after decades of wilful neglect, threatens to make the country's ordinary life unworkable. It is only after two landslide election victories for New Labour that the British political establishment has finally got the mes-sage: the British want higher-quality public services, properly functioning public transport and decent social provision. Self-help and individualism along American lines have their limits.

The task ahead is to begin to construct a distinctive British economic and social model under the umbrella of a much more politically account-able European Union, which has in turn a much clearer conception of the values its member states hold in common and a willingness to cham-pion and support them. Britain needs to take a long cool look at how it conceives of wealth generation, and start to recognise that the process is much more subtle than suggested by the ideas it has adopted so far from both right and left over the postwar era. The attempt after 1945 to create investment and innovation through the machinery of tripartite social democracy British style ended with the stagflation of the 1970s; but the subsequent twenty-five years of labour market deregulation, lowering marginal tax rates, hollowing out the welfare system and promoting shareholder value have made little impact on the gap between British and European output per man-hour, which remains almost as large as it was before. The welcome lowering of unemployment, as mentioned above, has had more to do with demand growth than with the package of meas-ures that have made British economic structures more akin to those in the US.

The British business lobby does not help. Publicly, business presses for eased regulatory and tax 'burdens', overtly parroting the American view that companies are nothing more than a network of contracts that need to be as flexible as possible to allow managers the permanent possibility of buying cheap and selling dear; but privately, business leaders will acknowledge that their greatest challenge is to motivate and capture the energy of their staff. A good business is much more than a network of contracts. It is an organisation – an institution – that functions best if those who work for it believe that it has a purpose and vision that will serve the society of which it is part. This is not new age mumbo-jumbo, but the hard reality of business life. James Collins and Jerry Porras showed in *Built to Last* that successful companies are visionary, guided by a core purpose in which maximising profit is but one element. The central component is a sense of purpose beyond just making money – building the best planes, mobile phones, tyres, cars, etc., etc. It is this that inspires the loyalty and excites the creativity that together lie at the heart of a successful business – a far cry from the continual bleating for regulatory and tax concessions in the name of 'wealth creation.'

Of course, no business is going to refuse lower taxation or regulation, and most are perfectly happy to allow the Confederation of British Industry and the Institute of Directors to lobby about these issues on their behalf even while they know they are not central. Some managers and directors have got ideology badly and really believe that a tax-free, regulation-free environment would be the best climate for their companies. The majority know differently; yet their silence helps to create and sustain a public discourse in which building the creative, visionary companies they want to lead is harder rather than easier. By not arguing for the social, legal and cultural infrastructure that would place the overall organisational purpose at the heart of business life, so relegating the pursuit of shareholder value and lower business 'burdens' to their proper, more modest position in the order of priorities, they make a rod for their own backs. Many directors of FTSE 100 companies would privately broadly sympathise with this book's arguments about why both Marconi and Marks & Spencer have had such hard times – but if they do not deliver the next half-year's profit growth they are in terrible trouble. They sustain an environment in which doing the right things for their business is very much harder. Here the European approach is richer than the American one, where twenty-five years of conservatism have debilitated many of its once great visionary corporations, reducing them to short-term profit-maximisation machines.

To open up this debate requires organisational and intellectual understanding, then an operable legislative programme, cultural change, and business and political leadership. Britain begins this daunting task with many drawbacks. Its deeply inbuilt scepticism towards matters European blinds it to the advantages of what happens beyond the Anglo-Saxon world, and its ready acceptance and admiration of matters American make it vulnerable to vainglorious American boasts. It wants to emulate the world's top dog. Its economic and business understanding is governed by American ideas as disseminated through the business schools, economics faculties and financial press. The dominance and structure of the City make shareholder value an easy gospel to spread. The financial elite has a massive self-interest in promoting American-style capitalism. The business lobby organisations perceive their role as lobbying for breaks for business, a task in which American conservative ideology is an easy and welcome tool. British political leadership is credulous about business, and accepts the business agenda as written by business lobbyists. There is no alternative political programme, it seems, to that of private sector wealth creation on terms established by business – even though the best of British business privately has more sophisticated and subtle ideas than those aired in public debate. But they keep their counsel and tend their own affairs.

Change there must be, nevertheless – and there are signs of hope. New Labour itself has begun to move in a European direction, although it is reluctant to recognise it. Like the Lilliputians staking down the giant Gulliver, New Labour has begun to make a series of small moves that cumulatively will begin to redefine the idea of the company and the responsibilities of property owners. A new Companies Act will require directors, like their European counterparts, to acknowledge obligations to the whole organisation they serve, rather than just to the shareholders. The result of the Myners review on institutional investors is to establish more professional pension fund trustees who take a longer-term view of the companies in which they invest. Investors are now required to disclose what their policies are towards the environmental, ethical and social stances of the companies they own. The pressure on companies to behave more responsibly in relation to the communities in which they trade is growing – and so is the access to information by which consumers, investors and workers can hold them to account. More companies are accepting the case for corporate social responsibility, and beginning systematically to report on their efforts in annual social audits – a process that will be accelerated by the new Companies Act. Include the impact of the EU information and consultation directive, which will require the inclusion of workers in the process of corporate decision-making, and British enterprise begins to take on a mainland European hue.

However, none of this has been done within an overarching political and intellectual narrative. The approach has been piecemeal and unsystematic. Many of the more ambitious opportunities have been watered down and compromised. The review of company law, for example, could have reconceptualised the idea of the company and its relationship with its shareholders – but the opportunity was forgone. Other measures, like the information and consultation directive, have been actively resisted, and only the *force majeure* of EU qualified majority voting immediately after Labour's 2001 election victory saw it grudgingly accepted. New Labour remains in thrall to the overriding importance of labour market flexibility and the business lobbyists' agenda; its initiatives outside this paradigm are small-scale and cramped. It certainly does not champion a European conception of enterprise; but then neither does the European Commission, the European business community or many European intellectuals. Against that background it is remarkable rather that so much progress has been made than so little.

This is where the European Commission, and the EU and its member states more generally, need to enter the frame. They must tell a more self-confident story about Europe – the kind of story, for example, that has been developed over the last four chapters. They need to address the major blot on the European economic and social landscape – unemployment – which makes it so hard for them to put an effective case. They need to embrace the kind of reform programme advocated at the end of the last chapter, not only for themselves but for every member state – extending from techniques of economic management which will deliver a more co-ordinated economic policy to a more accountable structure for EU decision-making. It is when these two developments are combined – a growing, successful, politically accountable EU and a distinctive narrative about *why* it is successful – that Euroscepticism in both Britain and other member states will be allayed.

For Britain this is of particular importance. Britain has been wrestling for too long with the problems of relative economic decline and its social consequences, and what its place should be in the world. The last five years have seen a period of some relative economic improvement; but it needs to be built on and developed. Our core problems have to be confronted, but free from the ghosts of dogma that have plagued our efforts in the past. And our best bet is to characterise reform as a built-for-Britain variant of what we know works well in Europe – and, where US enterprise follows the same principles, in the US.

The more the linkages are emphasised between the values that underpin a new approach to enterprise and those that support the social contract and the public realm – the twin areas where Europe can go on the offensive with no constraints – the more they will win popular support. Already the recognition that European health systems are so much better than the NHS, with even the Conservative party shopping around Europe for ideas on organisation and finance, is an important breakthrough. The same is broadly true of welfare, transport, the environment, pensions, and even education and training. In all these areas Britain needs to recognise that its instincts are European, that it wants services and delivery that match the best in mainland Europe – and that it must use the state to secure those ends. The British are also prepared, despite two decades of conservative propaganda, to move towards the redistribution of income on European lines to pay for them.

Here New Labour has made an important if hesitant beginning, starting to debate how the extra resources to finance increased health spending should be raised. For the three years between 1999 and 2002 public spending has grown above the rate of growth of GDP, and this trend is likely to be continued for another three years up to 2005 in the attempt to narrow the gap between Britain and Europe which Labour itself allowed to widen to new extremes by its excessive austerity in its first two years in office. But still it lacks confidence, allowing itself to worry about the condemnation of the financial markets, the Conservative party and business rather than vigorously arguing for what it knows the public wants. It is a timidity that extends to its attitudes to the workplace and trade unions, where its approach is again informed by conservative canons. The creative workplace is one where workers and managers engage and talk with each other; organised correctly, trade unions can be crucial midwives to the constructive conversations that define all successful, high-performance workplaces.

It is by arguing for all these processes, identifying British priorities with those of Europe, that the EU can be re-established in the popular British imagination as a continent of which they are part and from which they gain. It is the crucial backdrop against which to argue for British entry into the euro. The country cannot stand aside from this epic development, with all it implies for the future economic, social and political direction of Europe. If the case for Europe is right, then so is the case for joining the euro. Europe needs Britain in, and Britain needs to join – as part of its European vocation, and in order to share the benefits. Importantly, Britain needs to enter at a significantly lower exchange rate and with reforms to the process of economic decision-making; but as long as these caveats can be met, the pro argument is conclusive. With the issue settled, Britain can start to build its own British variant of Europe's economic and social model.

Europe's challenge

The euro is not just important for offering European monetary integration and its associated benefits. It gives Europe a world currency – the only conceivable challenger to the dollar, with all that implies, including the option of running its economy on more expansionary lines and a monetary umbrella under which it can insist that European regulations and approaches are complied with. Just as financial institutions and transnational companies comply with American rules to win the benefits of a New York listing and trading within the US, so the EU can play the same card. It can insist that globalisation assumes a European dimension. It can insist that its distinctive attitudes on company law, financial regulation, workplace consultation, environmental standards, profit disclosure, transparency over accounts and taxation are upheld as the conditions for trading within the EU. The US will face a co-equal economic partner across the Atlantic, no less confident about the virtues of its economic and social model. The US can choose whether its attitude will be one of interdependence or unilateralism.

The European Union, as it contemplates the admission in the near future of up to another eight countries in eastern Europe (excluding Bulgaria and Romania), is becoming the exemplar of what a peaceful multilateral system of governance can achieve. The range of cross-border initiatives that the EU has successfully negotiated demonstrates not only that multilateralism can work, but that it is a vital bulwark of democracy, markets, social justice and human rights. The European Court of Human Rights and Europe's commitment to an International Criminal Court point the way to the future. The EU's commitment to a social contract and high-quality, universal, egalitarian social outcomes is a beacon for the rest of the world. But above all, its ability to offer a forum in which Europe's nation-states can broker their differences, review one another's policies and adopt common economic, social and foreign policy positions is an utterly novel development in world terms. If once the United States personified the future, increasingly the EU is demonstrating how interdependence can be managed and nurtured.

This is important both for Europe and for the globe. The US is hostile to all forms of international co-operation and multilateralist endeavour. It is wedded to the exercise of autonomous power guaranteed by its military superiority; and its world view is supported and entrenched by the vigorous conservative ideology that dominates its politics and economics. As a result it is not only actively dismantling the complex web of international treaties that underpin Western security and economic interests; it is obstructing any creative development of those that it cannot attack. Without a countervailing power of sufficient strength prepared to provide finance and political muscle, the development of multilateral institutions and processes by which a rampant globalisation may be governed will cease. Only the EU has the weight in the world to assume this role.

The areas in which the EU needs to protect an idea of a more liberal, multilateralist and just order are legion. Start with finance. The world needs a genuine supranational financial institution that monitors economic performance and stands ready to provide hard currency in times of difficulty; instead it has the IMF, an adjunct of the US treasury.

Argentina's economic collapse and default on its debt service obligations at Christmas 2001 are only the latest example of the IMF being forced into an absurd posture by its American masters; it should have intervened earlier and more generously. It would have been better for Argentina to have imposed capital controls and devalued the peso earlier, rather than impose a four-year recession on itself – but that option lay outside the orthodoxy promoted by Washington. The IMF needs more financial resources and a wholesale recasting of its economic thinking; the EU, acting as a whole, needs to provide the finance and insist that the Fund's approach change. It could, in extremis, reconstitute the IMF around the euro as an alternative world reserve currency; certainly it is this threat that, above any other, might make the US take a less illiberal stance.

Nor can we any longer accept the US's lax attitude to the regulation of international financial institutions, accounting standards and tax havens; it is a green light to feral capitalism, organised crime and international terrorism alike. The globe needs a World Financial Authority that will oversee the adequacy of the balance sheets of international financial institutions, regulate international financial markets, set minimum accounting standards and police tax havens. The obstruction to this development is the refusal of the US to accept any infringement of its sovereignty; the EU should go ahead anyway and establish the authority as a complement to its own EU-wide initiatives.

There needs also to be a recasting of the relationship of the industrialised West with the less developed world. The EU needs to rethink its attitude towards agriculture; instead of protecting domestic production of commodity foods, it should move into higher value-added production and open up its markets to producers in the less developed world. Together with a generous approach towards supporting increased third world health expenditure, and reframing the international financial and trade system, the living standards and prospects of the world's poorer populations would be transformed. At a stroke they would have a market for their principal export product and a capacity to insulate themselves from the vagaries of capital flight. On top of this, they could start to attack the disease and low life expectancy that cripple economic development.

According to the World Health Organisation, 643 million people in very poor less developed countries have a life expectancy of 51, compared to 78 in richer countries; for every 1000 live births, 159 of their children die, compared with 6 in the richer countries. Another 1.8 billion live in countries where the figures are nearly as bad. If the richer countries were to allocate just 0.1 per cent of their collective GDP in grants to offer between £20 and £25 per head for basic health spending in the less developed world, 8 million lives would be saved, says the WHO.[3] That and the general overall improvement of life expectancy would raise the less developed world's income by $360 billion annually. It would be the biggest bang for our collective buck yet conceived – relieving suffering and raising growth in the same act.

George W. Bush's US lifts only a grudging finger. From a conservative perspective the WHO initiative – like ambitious plans floated by the British government to set up a massive international aid programme along Marshall Plan lines – suffers from two colossal defects. Both plans are predicated on public action to produce a global public good; and both involve the redistribution of income from the rich to the poor, even as a Republican Congress fights for a scale of kickbacks to corporate America that dwarfs what is proposed for the third world and increases US defence expenditure by 12 per cent – a stunning $48 billion. There is no central role for the private sector; and to act in this way is to recognise that market solutions have no answer. Worse, it implies the US making common cause with its allies in a supranational initiative. So the US stays aloof. The only possible alternative actor is the EU.

It is the same story across the board. There is a case for a World Competition Authority, to police the immense concentrations of private corporate power now emerging. The International Criminal Court has already been mentioned, as has the international Framework Convention on Climate Change. There is need for international agreement on genetically modified food, child labour, space, piracy at sea, landmines, chemical weapons, the environment – the list goes on. The EU is currently the only power that will engage with these issues at an international level. Nor is that where international concerns end.

Peace is a precious asset. There needs to be a credible deterrent to war – and, if it occurs, a credible means of brokering, and then policing, a settlement between the combatants. It has become apparent since the end of the Cold War that flagrant abuses of human rights, either within any nation-state or resulting from conflict between states, are no longer acceptable; the Indonesian, Serbian and Iraqi subjugations of the Timorese, Kosovans and Kurds respectively have been judged to contravene human rights, and the international community has responded with military interventions. Now there has been the American elimination of terrorist bases within Afghanistan. The threats and disturbances will not go away, and the international community is faced with a choice. Up to now, the responses to human rights abuses have been dependent upon American involvement, and after Afghanistan it is evident that the US is increasingly minded to act only when its interests are directly affected. So the world can either accept its dependence on American military might, with all the political consequences that entails; or it can build a clear, internationally agreed system of rules whose transgression would trigger an equally clear international response from a standing supranational, highly mobile military force.

Any such proposal highlights an additional dilemma. What are the mechanisms of decision-making and accountability of these global initiatives? Are they to be conceived as forms of intergovernmental collaboration, in which sovereignty rests essentially with nation-states – or are they the forerunners of genuinely global institutions that conform to new rules of cosmopolitan law, democracy and governance, and will gradually limit and redefine the role of the nation-state?

There can be only one answer to this question – and it is not the one conservative America will give. In the decades ahead the world must develop global institutions to discharge the multiplicity of global responsibilities. The United Nations, portrayed by conservative America as a nest of pink liberals and do-gooders, is rather an institutional arrangement upon which the globe must build. It needs to be strengthened, and its processes made accountable and democratised – and here the EU is the inspiration and trail-blazer. The techniques it is developing can be transposed to the UN; and it itself must offer unstinting support for the elder body. As a multilateral institution itself, it must support global multilateralism.

None of this is to deny the importance and need for American engagement. We badly need the better America back – the liberal, outward-looking and generous US that won World War II and constructed a liberal world order that in many respects has sustained us to this day. Yet the reality must be confronted. It is today's US, the conservative US of George W. Bush, that is now placing this order at risk, and menacing the world's capacity to recognise its interdependence. Even a US president whose heart was in the right place – Bill Clinton – was forced by the conservative configuration of US politics into postures he deplored. In the absence of the America we need, the EU must step into the breach. Indeed, it is only by being the apostle of not a soft but a hard liberalism – a liberalism that proclaims a universal respect for justice in its widest sense as the only context in which individuals can be fulfilled, and is prepared to take tough action to secure its ends – that the EU can hope to offer an example and succour to the best of American liberalism.

The situation is not hopeless. American conservatism may be dominant now, but it has always been contested. Notwithstanding his poor campaign, a majority of US electors voted for Al Gore in 2000. In the new 'ideapolises' a new liberalism is being incubated – centred on a belief in the importance of the state underwriting risk, in securing equal rights and in investing heavily in human and physical infrastructure – that challenges the hegemony of the right. Public service and the role of government are no longer being decried with the same venom. The self-sacrifice and sense of duty of New York's firefighters on 11 September, for example, could not be bought by any private enterprise. New Yorkers and the liberal east and west coasts, along with the liberal Great Lakes region, understand this. Moreover, it is perfectly possible to think in these terms and still argue for US military action against the terrorist networks – the essence of hard liberalism.

It is upon the renaissance of America's own brand of hard liberalism that its benign re-engagement with the world depends. This was the philosophy behind the US's engagement with the rest of the world in the wake of World War II, an engagement which is so badly needed again. The same struggle that British liberalism and social democracy have with Euroscepticism has to be joined in the US between American liberals and conservatives. The terrain may be different, but the same values and principles are at stake – and they connect the US stance at home and abroad. If three key battles can be won domestically, there is a chance of American positive involvement overseas.

The first is to attack the Wall Street notion of wealth generation as short-termist financial engineering and to advocate a more subtle and sophisticated vision of wealth creation as a social and organisational act as much as an act of heroic individualism. The second is to insist that the US too needs a robust social contract to count in the bottom 50 per cent of Americans; inequality, hardship and falling social mobility should not be countenanced in a country as rich as the US and with such noble ideals. Third, and perhaps most important of all, the US has to live up to its own criteria of democracy. It is an offence that increasingly the sole qualification for a successful bid for office is to be rich; billionaire Michael Bloomberg's victory in the mayoral elections for New York, secured by an advertising blitz which he personally paid for, is an awesome warning of where the US is heading. Without reform of campaign finance, the US might as well concede that its democracy is a hollow shell in which the public conversation and political discourse are auctioned to the rich. If American liberals can win these arguments at home, they can begin to argue for the US's re-engagement, a recognition of interdependence and an understanding that security in the West means offering hope and opportunity to the destitute of the world.

Until then, Europe stands alone. The lesson for the twenty-first century is that the fight for security, prosperity and justice can no longer be won on any one nation's ground. It is international. It requires agreement on values. It is predicated on an acknowledgement of interdependence. It requires a political narrative. It requires courage and leadership. America, for the moment, has disqualified itself from this task. It falls to Europe to undertake it. This is a challenge and a responsibility that cannot be evaded. The building of Europe has become the precondition for securing prosperity, peace and justice not only in Europe, but across the globe. We must succeed.

Notes

1: The rescue

1   Paul Kennedy of Yale University wrote in the *Financial Times* on 2 February 2002 that nothing in world history paralleled this degree of disparity of power.

2   Dominique Moïsi, deputy director of the French Institute for International Relations, is quoted in the *International Herald Tribune* (4 Feb. 2002) as saying that Donald Rumsfeld's America now threatens NATO's cohesion as de Gaulle did in the 1960s.

3   See Margaret Thatcher in *Statecraft* (HarperCollins, 2002) and Keith Marsden, *Towards a Treaty of Commerce* (Centre for Policy Studies, 2000).

4   *Chicago Tribune*, 3 Nov. 2001.

5   Professor Andrew Oswald of the University of Warwick has established a close econometric relationship between the price of oil and subsequent movements in US and world economic activity.

6   Between 1982 and 1991 the profits of US multinationals grew at 10.8 per cent a year overseas, almost double their growth rate at home; see James Petras and Morris Morley, *Empire or Republic?* (Routledge, 1995).

7   See John Kay, *Financial Times*, March 2001 and www.johnkay.com

8   Julian Callow of Credit Suisse First Boston calculates that value added per hour grew by 1.6 per cent in the US between 1991–8 compared to 1.8 per cent in France, Germany, Italy and the Netherlands. Furthermore, European statisticians make no adjustment for improvements in the quality of goods and services and tend to underestimate the growth of the high tech manufacturing sector, thus understating productivity increases. See 'Minding the Gap', CSFB (Europe Ltd, 6 Sept. 2001.

9   *Business Week* (9 April 2001) describes Exxon's 'culture of radical cost reduction'; for a description of GE's strategy see Alan Kennedy's account in *The End of Shareholder Value: The Real Effects of the Shareholder Value Phenomenon and the Crisis it is Bringing to Business* (Orion Business, 2000).

10 Kennedy, *The End of Shareholder Value*, pp. 49–66.

11 See Robert Walker, 'Why Jack Welch Isn't God', *New Republic*, 6 July 2001.

12   Quoted in Kenneth Hey and Peter Moore, *The Caterpillar Doesn't Know* (Free Press, 1998), p. 133.

13   Kennedy, *The End of Shareholder Value*, p. 54.

14   See Richard Freeman, *The US Economic Model at Y2K: Lodestar for Advanced Capitalism*, working paper 7757 (National Bureau for Economic Research, June 2000), Exhibit 4.

15   Robert Frank, in Juliet Schor (ed.), *Do Americans Shop Too Much?* (Beacon, 2000).

16   See Wynne Godley and Alex Izuricta, *The Developing US Recession and Guidelines for Policy*, Levy Economics Foundation, Oct. 2001.

17   *Business Week*, 19 Nov. 2001, p. 10.

18   The Q ratio of stock market value of companies to their net worth reached 1.92 in the first quarter of 2000, 50 per cent higher than the previous peaks in 1929 and 1969.

19   US Federal Reserve, Flow of Funds Table L107.

20   See 'Is the US Trade Deficit Sustainable?' Washington DC Institute for International Economics, 1999.

21   The University of Michigan Consumer Survey reports that consumers spent $1 in every $5 of tax rebates; see *New Republic*, 29 Oct. 2001, p. 16.

22   Michael Mandel, *The Coming Internet Depression* (Pearson Education, 2001).

23   See Freeman, *The US Economic Model at Y2K*, Exhibit 6.

24   Elizabeth Drew, *The Corruption of American Politics* (Overlook Press, 2000), p. 265.

25   Robert D. Puttnam, *Bowling Alone* (Simon & Schuster, 2000), p. 212.

26   Osha Gray Davidson, *Under Fire: The NRA and the Battle for Gun Control* (University of Iowa Press, 1998).

27   Puttnam, *Bowling Alone*, p. 221.

28   William Frey et al., *America by the Numbers* (New Press, 2001), p. 172.

29   Ibid., p. 138.

30   See Hubert Védrine and Dominique Moïsi, *France in an Age of Globalisation* (Brookings Institution, 2001).

31   Michael Crozier in *The Bureaucratic Phenomenon* defines dominance as the ability 'to leave as much leeway and freedom of manoeuvre to the dominant, while imposing the strictest possible constraints in the decisional freedom of the dominated side'.

32   Philip Augar, *The Death of Gentlemanly Capitalism* (Penguin, 2001), table 14, p. 310.

33   See the *Guardian*/Inbucon Survey for 2000, *Guardian*, 2 Aug. 2001.

34   New Bridge St survey, reported in *Financial Times*, 6 Nov. 2000.

35   *Guardian*, 13 Aug. 1999. Later disclosures showed that both GE and Enron pressed for a change of energy policy. See *Sunday Times*, 10 Feb. 2002.

36   In economics, for example, the American consensus is that markets tend to work perfectly, economic actors are rational, and market failure is due to government and unions.

37   Seymour Martin Lipset and Gary Marks, *It Didn't Happen Here: Why Socialism Failed in the United States* (Norton, 2000).

38   A good account is Robert Parry's 'So Did Bush Steal the White House?', www.consortiumnews, 27 Nov. 2001.

39   Vincent Bugliosi, *The Betrayal of America* (Nation Books, 2001).

40   ABC News national survey, 1994; ACLU/BRS national surveys, 2001.

2: Custodians of the light

1 Locke, John, *Two Treatises of Government*, ed. Peter Laslett (Cambridge University Press, 1988), II para. 34, p. 301.

2 Ibid., para. 96, p. 331.

3 Ibid., para. 27, p. 288.

4 Leslie J. Macfarlane, *Socialism, Social Ownership and Social Justice* (Macmillan, 1998), p. 26.

5 Quoted in Macfarlane, *Socialism*, pp. 26–7.

6 For example, Germany's Brother Arnold, a dissident Dominican monk, and France's Jean de Roquetaille, a radical Franciscan monk, both urged uprisings of the suffering peasantry against their duplicitous, oppressive betters – ranging from loose-living clergy to swindling merchants – to anticipate Christ's second coming. See Macfarlane, *Socialism, op cit.*

7 Leo Strauss, *Natural Rights and History* (Chicago University Press, 1953), pp. 242–3.

8 'We the People of the United States, in Order to form a more perfect Union, establish Justice, insure domestic Tranquility, provide for the common defence, promote the general Welfare, and secure the Blessings of Liberty to ourselves and our Posterity, do ordain and establish this Constitution for the United States of America.' From the Avalon Project at Yale Law School; see www.yale.edu/avalon/constpap.htm.

9 See Madison's notes of the Constitutional Convention in the Avalon Project at the Yale Law School at www.yale.edu/avalon/constpap.htm.

10 Leo Pfeffer, *This Honorable Court: A History of the United States Supreme Court* (Beacon Press, 1965).

11 For a discussion of this movement see Paul Misner, *Social Catholicism in Europe: From the Onset of Industrialisation to the First World War* (Darton, Longman & Todd, 1991).

12 Bernstein criticised Kautsky's vulgar theory of capitalist collapse. Capitalism was immensely adaptable, he argued. The socialist task was rather to embark on a never-ending process of capitalist reform, the explicit reasoning behind the Erfurt programme. See Donald Sassoon, *One Hundred Years of Socialism: The West European Left in the Twentieth Century* (I. B. Tauris, 1996).

13 Quoted in Mark Mazower, *Dark Continent* (Penguin, 1998), p. 133.

14 Ibid., p. 135.

15 See Lipset and Marks, *It Didn't Happen Here*, table 8.5, p. 289.

16 Alberto Alesina, Rafael di Tella and Robert MacCulloch, 'Inequality and Happiness: Are Europeans and Americans Different?' (Feb. 2001).

17 See his great work *The Division of Labour*: Emile Durkheim, *De la division du travail social* (Félix Alcan, 1893).

18 Philip Collins, 'A Story of Justice', *Prospect*, May 2001.

19 Alexis de Tocqueville, *Democracy in America* (Cambridge, 1864), p. 244.

20 Daniel Lazare, 'America the Undemocratic', *New Left Review*, Dec. 1998.

21 Ibid., p. 29.

22 See Michael Sandel, *Democracy's Discontent: America in Search of a Public Philosophy* (Harvard University Press, 1996).

23 De Toqueville, *Democracy in America*, pp. 183–4.

24 Richard John Neuhass, quoted by Wilfred McClay in the *New York Review of Books*, Oct. 1996.

25   See Michael Shudson, 'Was There Ever a Public Sphere? If So, When? Reflections on the American Case', in *The Power of News* (Harvard University Press, 1995).

26   Kant, 'An Answer to the Question: What is Enlightenment', *Political Writings*, ed. Hans Riess, trans. H. B. Nisbett (Cambridge University Press, 1970).

27   Hannah Arendt, *The Human Condition* (University of Chicago Press, 1958).

3: Waging war without blood: the collapse of American liberalism

1   Milton Himmelfarb, quoted in Nina Easton, *The Gang of Five* (Simon & Schuster, 2000), p. 42.

2   See e.g. Peter Diamond, 'A Model of Price Adjustment', *Journal of Economic Theory*, no. 3 (1971).

3   See D. F. Hendry and N. R. Ericsson, 'An Econometric Analysis of UK Money Demand in *Monetary Trends in the United States and the United Kingdom* by Milton Friedman and Anna J. Schwartz', *American Economic Review* (1991), 8–38. The authors were able to publish this challenge to Friedman and Schwartz only after lengthy negotiations.

4   Ruy Teixeira and Joel Rogers, *America's Forgotten Majority: Why the White Working Class Still Matters* (Basic Books, 2000).

5   David Reynolds, *One World Divisible* (Allen Lane, 2000), p. 166.

6   See Robert Skidelsky, *John Maynard Keynes: Fighting for Britain*, (Macmillan, 2000).

7   Between 1965 and 1971, the *Wall Street Journal* published an average of 20.7 editorials each year criticising the size or role of government. In the next six years, 1971–6, the average jumped to 43.8 such editorials a year. Meanwhile the number of stories about government actually declined by about 2 per cent each year. See Dick W. Olufs III, *The Making of Telecommunications Policy* (Lynne Rienner, 1999), p. 108.

8   Sidney Blumenthal, *The Rise of the Counterestablishment* (Harper & Row, 1988), pp. 51–8.

9   Davidson, *Under Fire*.

10   Jeffrey H. Birnbaum, *The Money Men: How the Media Undermine American Democracy* (Crown, 2000), p. 35.

11   Robert Dallek, *Ronald Reagan: The Politics of Symbolism* (Harvard University Press, 1994), p. 125.

12   Quoted in Thomas Byrne Edsall, *Chain Reaction: The Impact of Race, Rights and Taxes on American Politics* (Norton, 1991).

13   Paul Krugman, *Peddling Prosperity* (Norton, 1994), p. 135.

14   The classic text was Paul Kennedy's *The Rise and Fall of the Great Powers* (Random House, 1987).

15   Kenneth J. Heineman, *God is a Conservative* (New York University Press, 1998), p. 208.

16   See William Berman, *America's Right Turn from Nixon to Clinton* (Johns Hopkins University Press, 1998).

17   Education spending fell by 9.2 per cent, science by 19.1 per cent and transport by 11 per cent. See Robert Pollin, 'Anatomy of Clintonomics', *New Left Review*, June 2000, p. 25.

18   See John B. Judis, *The Paradox of American Democracy: Elites, Special Interest and the Betrayal of Public Trust* (Random House, 2000), p. 204.

19 Quoted in Easton, *Gang of Five*, p. 308.
20 See David Brock, *Blinded by the Right* (Crown Publishing, 2002).
21 Teixeira and Rogers, *America's Forgotten Majority*, p. 51.
22 See Teixeira and Rogers, *America's Forgotten Majority*.

4: Greed isn't good for you

1 See Mary O'Sullivan, *Contests for Corporate Control: Corporate Governance and Economic Performance in the United States and Germany* (Oxford University Press, 2000), pp. 123–30.
2 Ibid., p. 156.
3 Lawrence Mishel, Jared Bernstein and John Schmitt, *The State of Working America* (Cornell University Press, 2001), p. 8.
4 Mark Zepengauer and Arthur Naiman, *Take the Risk of Welfare* (Odonion, 1996).
5 Alan Greenspan was on the record arguing for the abolition of Glass–Steagall as a priority for the Federal Reserve Board as early 1987; see Leonard Seabrooke, *US Power in International Finance: The Victory of Dividends* (Palgrave, 2001).
6 Gary A. Dymski, *The Bank Merger Wave: The Economic Causes and Social Consequences of Financial Consolidation* (M. E. Sharpe, 1999).
7 See David C. Mowery (ed.), *US Industry in 2000: Studies in Competitive Performance* (National Academy Press, 1999).
8 *Business Week*, 20 Nov. 2000.
9 Robert Monks, *The New Global Investors* (Capstone, 2001), p. 69.
10 Stephen Nickell, *The Performance of Companies* (Blackwell, 1995), p. 23.
11 *Business Week*, 7 April 1998.
12 Matthew Lynn, *Birds of Prey: The War Between Boeing and Airbus* (Four Walls Eight Windows, 1997), p. 217.
13 From W. Lazonick, 'Creating and Extracting Value', in Michael A. Bernstein and David E. Adler (eds), *Understanding American Economic Decline* (Cambridge University Press, 1994).
14 O'Sullivan, *Contests for Corporate Control*, p. 196.
15 Quoted ibid., p. 194.
16 G. Baker and G. Smith, *The New Financial Capitalists* (Cambridge University Press, 1998).
17 M. Jensen, 'The Modern Industrial Revolution: Exit and the Failure of Internal Control Systems', *Journal of Finance* 48, no. 9 (July 1993), pp. 831–80.
18 See Scott Klinger, 'United for a Fair Economy', 5 April 2001, on www.theotherwide.org. In six out of seven one-year periods between 1993 and 2000 at least half the ten companies with the most highly paid CEOs underperformed the S&P 500 in the following year; in four of the five years the underperformance over the following three years ranged between 57 and 66 per cent.
19 O'Sullivan, *Contests for Corporate Control*, pp. 170–1.
20 M. Jensen and R. Ruback, 'The Market for Corporate Control: The Scientific Evidence', *Journal of Financial Economics* (1983), no. 11, pp. 5–50.
21 Matthias M. Bekier, Anna J. Bogardus and Tim Oldham, 'Is the Belief that Mergers Drive Revenue Growth an Illusion?', *McKinsey Quarterly* (2001), no. 4.

22 KPMG, *Unlocking Shareholder Value, the Key to Success*, Jan. 2001.

23 Arthur Levitt said: 'While the problem of earnings management is not new, it has risen in a market unforgiving of companies that miss Wall Street's consensus estimates.' Quoted in O'Sullivan, *Contests for Corporate Control*, pp. 203–4.

24 See David Mowery, 'Overview', in Mowery (ed.), *US Industry in 2000*.

25 Harvard Business School Time Horizons Project, referred to in ch. 1 above, p. 19.

26 Mary O'Mahoney, *Britain's Productivity Performance, 1990–1996* (NIESR, 1999).

27 See Julian Callow of CSFB *op. cit.* Figure 6. The US productivity gap calculated on net GPD to adjust for the EU's more conservative depreciation policies in national accounts is only marginally higher between 1995 and 2000 – some 0.3% per annum.

28 See the discussion in David Coates, *Models of Capitalism: Growth and Stagnation in the Modern Era* (Polity, 2000), pp. 149–57, in which he variously cites Abramovitz, Lazonick, von Tunzelman et al.

29 See Mowery (ed.), *US Industry in 2000*, p. 8.

30 See Z. Griliches, 'R&D and Productivity,' in collected papers (University of Chicago, 1998); Ci Jones and J. C. Williams, 'Measuring the Social Return to R&D', *Quarterly Journal of Economics* (Nov. 1998).

31 Michael E. Porter and Debra van Opstal, *US Competitiveness 2001* (US Council on Competitiveness, 2001).

32 Mandel, *The Coming Internet Depression*, p. 36.

33 Robert J. Gordon, 'Does the 'New Economy' Measure up to the Great Inventions of the Past?', *Journal of Economic Perspectives* (2000).

34 William W. Lewis, Vincent Palmode, Badouin Regout and Allen Webb, 'What's right with the US economy', *McKinsey Quarterly*, 2002, No. 1.

35 David Miles, in 'Testing for Short-Termism in the UK Stock Market', *Economic Journal* (Nov. 1993), showed that profits expected in five years' time are undervalued by 40 per cent.

36 In June 2001 Suria wrote in a research report for Lehman that Amazon 'showed the financial characteristics that have driven innumerable retailers to disaster throughout history'.

37 Quoted in Kennedy, *The End of Shareholder Value*, p. 65.

5: To those who have shall be given

1 Mishel et al., *The State of Working America*, p. 293.

2 Freeman, *US Economic Model*, Exhibit 4.

3 Milton Friedman, *Capitalism and Freedom* (Chicago University Press, 1962).

4 Mishel et al., *The State of Working America*, table 7.16, p. 395.

5 The Policy Information Center, the Educational Testing Service Network, www.ets.org.

6 James Coleman found this figure in 1965 in *The Equality of Educational Opportunity*; it was confirmed in 1997 by Harold Wenglinsky in *When Money Matters: How Educational Expenditures Improve Student Performance and How They Don't* (Princeton University Press, 1997).

7 Robert Hauser et al., 'Occupation Status, Education and Social Mobility in

the Meritocracy', in Kenneth Arrow, Samuel Bowles and Steven Durlauf (eds), *Meritocracy and Economic Inequality* (Princeton University Press, 2000), p. 183.

8 Policy Information Center.

9 *Business Week*, 27 Aug. 2001, p. 75.

10 Quoted ibid.

11 OECD, *Education at a Glance: OECD Indicators* (OECD, 2000).

12 Robert H. Frank and Philip J. Cook, *The Winner-Take-All Society* (Free Press, 1995).

13 Robert Reich, *The Future of Success* (Knopf, 2001), pp. 145–57.

14 See Robert H. Frank, *Luxury Fever* (Free Press, 1999).

15 Ibid., pp. 14–32.

16 See Edward J. Blakely and Mary Gail Snyder, *Fortress America: Gated Communities in the United States* (Brookings Institution Press, 1997).

17 Ibid., p. 2.

18 See Patrick M. Garry, *A Nation of Adversaries: How the Litigation Explosion is Reshaping America* (Plenum Press, 1997).

19 See Martin Kettle in the *Guardian*, 5 April 2001, reporting the *Washington Post's* lawyer's instruction to a reporter never to apologise again after a car accident in Kansas in which he said sorry.

20 Puttnam, *Bowling Alone*, p. 42.

21 S. Knack and P. Keefern, 'Does Social Capital Have an Economic Pay-off?', *Quarterly Journal of Economics*, 1997, 4, pp. 1251–88.

22 *Payne* v. *Western & Atlantic Railroad* (1884).

23 David H. Autor, *Outsourcing at Will: Unjust Dismissal Doctrine and the Growth of Temporary Help Employment*, NBER working paper 7557 (Feb. 2000).

24 Richard Sennett, *The Corrosion of Character* (Norton, 1998), p. 50.

25 OECD *Employment Outlook*, July 1999.

26 Mishel et al., *State of Working America*, pp. 316–17.

27 Michael Zweig, *The Working Class Majority: America's Best Kept Secret*, (Cornell University Press, 2000), p. 45.

28 Barbara Ehrenreich, *Nickel and Dimed* (Metropolitan Books, 2001), p. 214.

29 The 1996 Personal Responsibility and Work Opportunity Reconciliation Act abolished the New Deal Aid to Families with Dependent Children and replaced it with Temporary Assistance to Needy Families, setting a federal limit of five years over which benefit can be claimed; states may if they wish choose a shorter period. Virginia, for example, gives claimants only ninety days to find work before benefits cease.

30 *The Economist*, 25 Aug. 2001.

31 Mishel et al., *State of Working America*, p. 386.

32 OECD *Employment Outlook* 2000, ch. 2, 'Earnings Mobility: Taking a Longer View'.

33 Aarberge, Rolf et. al, 'Income Inequality and Income Mobility in the Scandinavian Countries Compared to the United States' (1996), paper presented at the NEF workshop on income distribution, 26–27 Sept. 1996, Aarhus, Denmark; R. V. Burkhauser and J. G. Poupore, 'A Cross-National Comparison of Permanent Inequality in the United States and Germany during the 1980s', *Review of Economics and Statistics*, vol. 79, no. 1 (1997), pp. 10–17.

34 Robert Erikson and John Goldthorpe, 'Are American Rates of Social Mobility Exceptionally High?', *European Sociological Review* (May 1985).

35 Mishel et al., *State of Working America*, p. 404.

36 See Economic Policy Institute, *Hardship in America* (Washington: 2001).

37 Birnbaum, *The Money Men*, pp. 65–6.

38 All figures from Frank, *Luxury Fever*, pp. 56–61.

39 Carla Brooks Johnston, *Screened Out: How the Media Control Us and What We Can Do About It* (M. E. Sharpe, 2000).

40 Ibid.

41 Quoted in Bartholomew H. Sparrow, *Uncertain Guardians: The News Media as a Political Institution* (Johns Hopkins University Press, 1999).

42 See Katherine Beckett and Theodore Sasson, *The Politics of Injustice* (Pine Forge Press, 2000).

43 Chrysler refused to advertise on ABC's *Ellen* in 1997 when the title heroine came out as a lesbian.

44 See James Fallows, *Breaking the News: The Real Story of Political Power in America* (Crown, 2000).

45 Sparrow, *Uncertain Guardians*.

46 Richard Cohen, 'The Corporate Takeover of News', in Erik Barnouw et al. (eds), *Conglomerates and the Media* (New Press, 1997), p. 32.

47 Margaret Crawford, 'The World in a Shopping Mall', in Michael Sorkin (ed.), *Variations on a Theme Park* (Hill & Wang, 2000).

48 Ibid.

6: The globalisation of conservatism

1 Richard Grasco, chair of the New York Stock Exchange, in 1997, quoted in Seabrooke, *US Power in International Finance*; David Rothkopf, Clinton's former deputy under-secretary of commerce, 'In Praise of Cultural Imperialism', *Foreign Policy*, no. 107 (Summer 1997).

2 *The Times*, 12 Sept. 2001, p. 2.

3 Robert Wade, 'Inequality of World Incomes: What Should Be Done', www.opendemocracy.com.

4 See Anthony Giddens' 1999 Reith lecture series, 'Runaway World'.

5 *International Herald Tribune*, 23–24 Feb., 2002

6 Reynolds, *One World Divisible*, p. 404.

7 Andrew Walter, *World Power and World Money* (Harvester Wheatsheaf, 1993), p. 179.

8 David Held et al., *Global Transformations* (Polity, 1999), p. 211.

9 Nicholas Guyatt, *Another American Century? The United States and the World after 2000* (Zed, 2000), p. 8.

10 See Seabrooke, *US Power in International Finance*.

11 Ibid.

12 Quoted in Barry Eichengreen, *Globalising Capital* (Princeton University Press, 1996), p. 152.

13 See William Darity and Bobbie Horn, *The Loan Pushers* (Ballinger, 1988).

14 William R. Cline, *International Debt: Systemic Risk and Policy Response* (Institute for International Economics, 1984) pp. 23–6.

15   Seabrooke, *US Power in International Finance*, p. 165.
16   Paul Blustein, 'The Chastening: Inside the Crisis that Rocked the Global Financial System and Chastened the IMF', *Public Affairs* (2001).
17   Sachs is quoted as saying, 'Instead of dousing the fire the IMF in effect screamed "fire in the theater"': John Eatwell and Lance Taylor, *Global Finance at Risk* (New Press, 2000), p. 170.
18   World Bank, *Trade and Industrialisation Report 1987*, quoted by Robert Wade in *New Left Review*, June 1996.
19   Reported 19 Jan. 2000 on the internet service Business Line, www.indiaserver.com/businessline.
20   Joseph Stiglitz, 'What I Learned at the World Economic Crisis', *New Republic*, 17 April 2000.
21   See Peter Gowan, *The Global Gamble: Wahington's Faustian Bid for World Dominance* (Verso, 1999).
22   Reported 19 Jan. 2000 on the internet service Business Line, www.indiaserver.com/businessline.
23   Reynolds, *One World Divisible*, p. 517.
24   FCC heads Fowler and Brenner argued in 1982 that the 'perception of broadcasters as community trustees should be replaced by a view of broadcasters as marketplace'.
25   The long-distance team included former Senate Republican leader Howard Baker and Marlin Fitzwater, President Bush's press officer, while the representatives of the regional companies (RBOCs) included Roy Neel, former deputy chief of staff under Clinton.
26   Dan Roberts, 'Glorious Hopes on a Trillion-Dollar Scrapheap', *Financial Times*, 5 Sept. 2001.

7: Britain in the American bear-hug

1   *Wall Street Journal*, 19 June 2001.
2   See Dominic Hobhouse and Alan Duncan, *Saturn's Children: How the State Devours Liberty and Prosperity* (Sinclair-Stevenson, 1995).
3   Ronald Inglehart, Miguel Basaney and Alejandro Moreno, *Human Values and Beliefs: A Cross-Cultural Sourcebook. Political, Religious, Sexual and Economic Norms in 43 Countries: Findings from the 1990–93 World Value Survey* (University of Michigan Press, 1998).
4   Roger Jowell et al., *British Social Attitudes; the 16th Report. Who Shares New Labour values?* (National Centre for Social Research, 1999).
5   Quoted in David Dolowitz, *Learning from America: Policy Transfer and the Development of the British Workfare State* (Sussex Academic Press, 1998).
6   Ibid., p. 57.
7   Nuffield Trust, *Reflections on the Management of the NHS* (Nuffield Trust, 1985).
8   Peter Dixon of Commerzbank finds a negative correlation between tax borders and competitiveness. See 'Taxing Questions of Growth', David Smith, *Sunday Times*, 3 March 2002.
9   HM Treasury, *The Myners Report* (2001), table 1.1, p. 27.
10   E. Philip Davis and Benn Steil, *Institutional Investors* (MIT Press, 2001).

11   Professor David Storey, head of the small business research centre at the Warwick
      Business School, quoted in the *Sunday Times*, 2 July 2000: 'If you look at start-up
      rates, attitudes to enterprise and provision of venture capital, there is no doubt
      that America wins hands down. We [Britain] are closer to America than most of
      the rest of Europe but we have a long way to go.'

12   All figures derived from OECD *Economic Outlook*, December 2001. The UK's GDP
      growth between 1999 and 2003 is projected at 2.3 per cent and employment
      growth at 0.8 per cent. For France, the comparable figures are 2.6 and 1.6 per cent,
      for Italy 2.1 and 1.3 per cent, and for Germany 1.9 and 0.6 per cent.

13   The 2001 Capex Scoreboard, DTI Innovation Unit, 2001.

14   Adair Turner, *Just Capital* (Macmillan, 2001), table 4.4, p. 117.

15   These comments are all derived from Stelzer's *Sunday Times* columns in the first
      eight months of 2001, notably those of 25 Feb., 1 July and 5 Aug. Occasionally his
      relentless anti-Europeanism and pro-Americanism lifts, but only when the US
      government – as in contesting the EU's pro-competition ruling against GE's bid
      for Honeywell – falls from grace by not sticking to its usual pro-competition
      guns (see his column of 24 June 2001).

16   See Andy Thornley, *Urban Planning under Thatcherism: The Challenge of the Market*
      (Routledge, 1991).

17   OECD *Economic Outlook*, June 2001, p. 213.

18   Judi Bevan, *The Rise and Fall of Marks and Spencer* (Profile, 2001), p. 177.

19   See Roger Ford in *Modern Railways*, June 2001. Ford calculates that Railtrack's
      track maintenance costs have risen by 35 per cent since 1997 and that major elec-
      trification projects have cost three times as much.

20   Institute for Public Policy Research, *Building Better Partnerships* (IPPR, 2001), p. 32.

21   The GMB union calculates that the cost of building the first fourteen private
      sector financed NHS hospitals will be at least £1.3 billion – almost double the orig-
      inal £766 million estimate. See *Sunday Times*, 5 Aug. 2001.

22   In 1995 the government actuaries' department identified 38,000 active final salary
      schemes; industry specialist Stewart Ritchie of Scottish Equitable estimates the
      2002 figure at 10,000. The trend is confirmed by the National Association of
      Pension Funds; see Nicholas Timmins, *Financial Times*, 11 Feb. 2002.

8: Europe works

1   The 1995 Vienot report, modelled on the UK's Cadbury report calling for codified
     and improved corporate governance, set out a voluntary code in which French com-
     panies were to become more Anglo-Saxon in their attitudes towards accounting,
     cross-shareholding, treatment of minority shareholders, presence of non-executive
     directors and separation of powers between the chairman and chief executive.

2   DTI, 11th annual R&D scoreboard, 27 Sept. 2001.

3   Ludiger Pries, *Accelerating from a Multinational to a Transnational Carmaker: The
     Volkswagen Consortium in the 1990s* (Institute of Sociology, University of Erlangen-
     Nurnberg, 1999).

4   DTI, 11th annual R&D scoreboard.

5   Dan Steinbock, *The Nokia Revolution: The Story of an Extraordinary Company that
     Transformed an Industry* (Amacom, 2001), p. 128.

6 Francesco Daveri and Guido Tabellini, *Unemployment, Growth and Taxation in Industrial Countries* (Centre for Economic Policy Research, 1997).

7 Davis Global Investors' Report, cited in *L'Expansion* 10 July 1997: 'La France améliore son gouvernement d'entreprise. Capitalistes, encore un effort'.

8 All figures from Doug Henwood, *Wall Street: How It Works and For Whom* (Verso, 1997).

9 Volkswagen, 'Financial control system' (2001), p. 5.

10 Richard Deeg, *Finance Capitalism Unveiled: Banks and the German Political Economy* (University of Michigan Press, 1999).

11 Ivan L. Pitt and John R. Norsworthy, *Economics of the US Commercial Airline Industry: Productivity, Technology and Deregulation* (Kluwer Academic, 1999), p. 23.

12 See OECD *Employment Outlook*, July 2000, p. 50.

13 Robert Buchele and Jens Christiansen, 'Do Employment and Income Security Cause Unemployment? A Comparative Study of the US and the E-4', *Cambridge Journal of Economics* (1998), 22. 'Non-employment' includes the unemployed and so-called 'inactive' workers who are not in receipt of formal unemployment benefit but are receiving other forms of income support, e.g. incapacity benefit.

14 Fritz Scharpf, *Governing in Europe: Effective and Democratic?* (European University Institute, 1999).

15 Ibid., pp. 128–9.

16 Ibid., p. 130.

17 Stephen Nickell, 'The Distribution of Wages and Unemployment across Skill Groups', in Michael Landesmann and Karl Pichelman (eds), *Unemployment in Europe* (Macmillan, 2000).

18 See Schmitt and Mishel chapter 5.

19 Robert Buchele and Jens Christiansen find that job turnover rates in France were 27.6 per cent, in Italy and the US 23.7 per cent, in Germany 16.5 per cent and the UK 14.4 per cent. See their 'Do Employment and Income Security Cause Unemployment?'

20 Peter Taylor-Gooby (ed.), *Welfare States under Pressure* (Sage, 2002).

21 Figures computed from OECD *Economic Outlook*, June 2001.

22 Ibid.

23 *OECD Economic Surveys – Germany* (OECD, May 2001).

9: Siblings under the skin

1 See *OECD Economic Survey of the Euro Area* (OECD, 2001), figures 4 and 12 and table 11. The dispersion of interest rates and inflation has fallen dramatically, while members of the euro area have nearly identical budgetary stances.

2 The OECD 2001 country survey for Germany says that 44 per cent of wage agreements are set collectively and a further 20 per cent voluntarily follow the collective agreement. See *OECD Economic Surveys – Germany* (OECD, May 2001).

3 This story is told in Kathleen Thelen, 'Why German Employers Cannot Bring Themselves to Dismantle the German Model', in Torben Iversen et al. (eds), *Unions, Employers and Central Banks* (Cambridge University Press, 2000).

4 O'Sullivan, *Contests for Corporate Control*, p. 246.

5 See Ian Finlay, Stuart Niven and Stephanie Young (eds), *Changing Vocational Education and Training: An International Comparative Perspective* (Routledge, 1998).

6 Wolfgang Streeck, 'Beneficial Constraints on the Economic Limits of Rational Voluntarism', in J. Rogers Hollingsworth and Robert Boyer (eds), *Contemporary Capitalism: The Embeddedness of Institutions* (Cambridge University Press, 1997), p. 205.

7 Combined employer and employee social security contributions are for Austria 38 per cent of labour costs, for the Netherlands 37 per cent, and for Germany and Belgium 34 per cent: OECD, *Taxing Wages in OECD Countries*, 1998/9.

8 See Martin Hopner, *Corporate Governance in Transition: Ten Empirical Findings on Shareholder Value and Industrial Relations in Germany*, discussion paper 01/05 (Max Planck Institute, 2001).

9 Ibid.

10 Deeg, *Finance Capitalism Unveiled*.

11 Ibid.

12 For a useful description of East European capitalism, see Lawrence Peter King, *The Basic Features of Postcommunist Capitalism in Eastern Europe: Firms in Hungary, the Czech Republic and Slovakia* (Praeger, 2001).

13 Trade union coverage of the workforce is 95.6 per cent for Finland, 89.9 per cent for Denmark, 86.4 per cent for Sweden and 71.3 per cent for Norway. See TUC Task Force on Promoting Trade Unionism, *Reaching the Missing Millions* (TUC, Aug. 2001), p. 17.

14 Income tax as a proportion of gross wages runs at 34 per cent in Denmark, 28 per cent in Finland, 27 per cent in Sweden and 22 per cent in Norway, compared with 21 per cent in Germany, 11 per cent in Austria and 7 per cent in the Netherlands. Social security contributions, however, are lower than those in Germany, the Netherlands and Austria by a very considerable margin. See OECD, *Taxing Wages*.

15 Pal Eitrheim and Stein Kuhnle, *The Scandinavian Model: Trends and Perspectives*, EU working paper 99/7 (1999).

16 *Sweden: a Guide to Financial Management in a Global Economy* (Economist Intelligence Unit, 2001).

17 The OECD, in 'Employment Protection and Labour Market Performance', gives employment protection rankings of 3.7 to Portugal, 3.5 to Greece, 3.4 to Italy and 3.1 to Spain. By contrast, Britain ranks at 0.9. See OECD *Employment Outlook 2000*.

18 Arthur R. Pinto and Gustavo Visentini (eds), *The Legal Basis of Corporate Governance in Publicly Held Corporations: A Comparative Approach* (Kluwer Law International, 1998).

19 Peter Hall, 'The Evolution of Economic Policy', in A. Guyomarch, H. Machin, P. Hall and J. Hayward (eds), *Developments in French Politics 2* (Palgrave, 2001).

20 France's index number is 2.8: OECD *Employment Outlook 2000*.

21 Charles Grant, in his pamphlet *EU 2010: An Optimistic Vision for the Future* (Centre for European Policy Reform, 2001), looks forward to a 2010 when 'globalisation is forcing even the French to liberalise their economy'(p. 4).

22 Hall, 'Evolution of Economic Policy'.

23 *OECD Economic Surveys – France* (OECD, 1997).

24 Pinto and Visentini, *The Legal Basis of Corporate Governance*.

25 Britain's index number is 0.9; see note 17 above.

26 *British Social Attitudes; the 16th Report*.

27 Timothy Smeeding, *Financial Poverty in Developed Countries: The Evidence from the Luxembourg Income Study* (UNDP, 1997).

28 All replacement ratios from OECD, *Benefit Systems and Work Incentives* (OECD, 1999).

29   Taylor-Gooby, *Welfare States under Pressure*, ch. 8.
30   Richard Freeman, *The Politics of Health in Europe* (Manchester University Press, 2000), p. 60.
31   Frey et al., *America by the Numbers*.
32   OECD, *Health Data 1999: A Comparative Analysis of 29 Countries* (OECD).
33   Ibid.
34   Commonwealth Fund, *International Health Policy Survey* (1998).
35   See Emmanuel Paraschos, *Media Law and Regulation in the European Union: National, Transnational and US Perspectives* (Iowa State University Press, 1998).
36   Alain Supiot, quoted in Mark Freedland and Silvan Sciarra (eds), *Public Services and Citizenship in EU Law* (Clarendon, 1998), p. 139.

10: The idea of Europe

1   Bulgaria and Romania are among the ten east European countries that want to join, but will do so later than the other eight.
2   See Simon Hix's account, 'Judicial Politics', in his *The Political System of the European Union* (Macmillan, 1999).
3   For an excellent account of Europe's democratic deficit see Michael T. Greven, 'Can the European Union Finally become a Democracy?', in Michael T. Greven and Louis W. Pauly (eds), *Democracy Beyond the State: The European Dilemma and the Emerging Global Order* (Rowman and Littlefield, 2000).
4   Reynolds, *One World Divisible*, p. 129.
5   Scharpf, *Governing in Europe: Effective and Democratic?*, p. 45.
6   D. Collins, 'Social Policy', in J. Lodge (ed.), *Institutions and Policies of the European Community* (Pinter, 1983), p. 98.
7   Reynolds, *One World Divisible*.
8   Leading monetarists Tim Congdon, for example, and the City University both scorned the EMS's workability and viability. See David Cobham and George Zis (eds), *From EMS to EMU* (Macmillan, 2000), p. 53.
9   Charles Grant, *The House that Jacques Built* (Nicholas Brealey, 1994), p. 55.
10   Belen Balanya et al., *Europe Inc* (Pluto, 2000), p. 21.
11   Neil Fligstein and Iona Mara-Drita advance this argument in 'How to Make a Market: Reflections on the Attempt to Create a Single Market in the European Union', *American Journal of Sociology*, July 1996.
12   Renaud Dehousse, 'Integration vs Regulation? On the Dynamics of Regulation in the European Community', *Journal of Common Market Studies* (1992).
13   Quoted in Ruth Nielsen and Erika Szyszczak, *The Social Dimension of the European Union* (Handelshojskolens Forlag, 1997), p. 29.
14   Charles Grant, *The House that Jacques Built*, p. 119.
15   See Nicholas Jabko, 'In the Name of the Market: How the European Commission Paved the Way for Monetary Union', *Journal of European Public Policy*, Sept. 1999.
16   The rights were: to freedom of movement, to choose an occupation and be fairly remunerated, to improvement of living conditions, to freedom of association and collective bargaining, to vocational training, to equal treatment, to information, consultation and participation, to protection of health and safety at the workplace, and to the protection of children, the elderly and the disabled.

17 'From Confederacy to Federation', speech by Joschka Fischer at the Humboldt University in Berlin, 12 May 2000.
18 Charter of Fundamental Rights, article 17.
19 Wolfgang Streeck, 'Neo-voluntarism: A New European Social Policy Regime', in Gary Marks *et al.* (eds), *Governance in the European Union* (Sage, 1996).
20 Jürgen Habermas, 'Why Europe Needs a Constitution', *New Left Review*, Sept./Oct. 2001.

11: Fighting back

1 Quoted in Debra Johnson and Colin Turner, *Trans-European Networks: the Political Economy of Integrating Europe's Infrastructure* (Macmillan, 1997), p. 12.
2 Nic Isles and Marcello Palazzi (eds), *The European Model for Enterprise* (Industrial Society Learning/Capita, 2002).
3 EU background papers for the 2000 Lisbon Summit.
4 Speech by French Prime Minister Lionel Jospin on 'The Future of Europe', Paris, 28 May 2001.
5 Quoted in 'Lost in Space', *Financial Times*, 22 Dec. 2001.
6 George Zis, 'The European Monetary System: An Unexpected Success?', in Cobham and Zis (eds), *From EMS to EMU*, p. 45.
7 William Greider, *One World Ready or Not: The Manic Logic of Global Capitalism* (Simon & Schuster, 1997), p. 245.
8 Author's calculations from IMF data.
9 Chris Huhne, 'Arguments For', in James Forder and Chris Huhne, *Both Sides of the Coin* (Penguin, 2001), p. 13.
10 European Commission, *One Market, One Money: European Economy*, 44 (Luxembourg, Oct. 1990).
11 If the euro was weak from its launch in January 1999, the forces that drove it down against the dollar would have played even more havoc with national currencies.
12 Chris Huhne in Forder and Huhne, *Both Sides of the Coin*, quotes Richard Baldwin's paper, 'On the Microeconomics of EMU', in European Commission, *One Market, One Money*.
13 Both the Confederation of British Industry and the Engineering Employers' Federation use these as ballpark numbers.
14 See Georg Christopher Schweiger, *European Central Bank* (Minerva, 2000).
15 James Forder, 'Arguments Against', in Forder and Huhne, *Both Sides of the Coin*, pp. 43–78.
16 Willem Buiter, 'The UK and EMU', Willem Buiter, *EmuNet*, 8 July 1998.
17 ECB Executive Board member Ottmar Issing, quoted in Schweiger, *European Central Bank*, p. 135.
18 B. Eichengreen and C. Wyplosz, 'The Stability Pact: More than a Minor Nuisance?', in D. Begg (ed.), *EMU Prospects and Challenges* (Oxford, 1998).
19 See *OECD Survey of the Euro Area*, p. 83.
20 Quoted in *Guardian*, 24 Jan. 2002.
21 Grant, *EU 2010: An Optimistic Vision of the Future*, pp. 28–9.
22 Pierre Jacquet and Jean Pisani-Ferry, *Economic Policy Co-ordination in the Euro-zone* (Centre for European Reform, 2001).

23 No Campaign, 'The Economic Case against the Euro', *New Europe* (2001).

24 The NIESR *Quarterly Review* of Summer 2001 commented that the British and European economic cycles were already synchronised, and the April 2002 *Review* is set to say the five tests have been passed. Ray Barrel, at the CEPII/NIESR conference in London on 6 Feb. 2002, indicated that in his view the five tests had been passed.

25 A senior Bank of England official has unattributably made this point to the author.

26 It has been estimated that British seigniorage would increase by 158.8 per cent by 2010: see Andrew Fischer, Thomas Jordan and Caeser Lack, *Giving Up the Swiss Franc: Some Considerations on Seigniorage under EMU*, CEPR discussion paper DP 3156 (Dec. 2001), table 4.

27 See Peter Mair, 'Political Parties, Popular Legitimacy and Public Privilege', in Jack Hayward (ed.) *The Crisis of Representation in Europe* (Frank Cass, 1995). Mair shows that in key European states disenchantment with political parties is growing and party ties are loosening.

28 Habermas, 'Why Europe Needs a Constitution'; Larry Siedentop, *Democracy in Europe* (Penguin, 2000).

Conclusion

1 Quoted in *Financial Times*, 19 Dec. 2001.

2 Grant Aldonas, US under-secretary of commerce for international trade quoted in the *Financial Times*, 13 March. 2002.

3 Commission on Economic Development and Health, World Health Organisation, Dec. 2001.

References

Aarberge, Rolf et. al, 'Income Inequality and Income Mobility in the Scandinavian Countries Compared to the United States' (1996), paper presented at the NEF workshop on income distribution, 26–27 Sept. 1996, Aarhus, Denmark

Albert, Michel, *Capitalism against Capitalism* (Whurr, 1993)

Alesina, Alberto, di Tella, Rafael, and MacCulloch, Robert, 'Inequality and Happiness: Are Europeans Different?' (Feb. 2001)

Arendt, Hannah, *The Human Condition* (University of Chicago Press, 1958)

Arestis, Philip (ed.), *Employment, Economic Growth and the Tyranny of the Market* (Edward Elgar, 1996)

Arestis, Philip (ed.), *Keynes, Money and the Open Economy* (Edward Elgar, 1996)

Arestis, Philip, and Marshall, Mike (eds) *The Political Economy of Full Employment* (Edward Elgar, 1995)

Aristotle, *Politics*, trans. C. D. C. Reeve (Hackett, 1998)

Augar, Philip, *The Death of Gentlemanly Capitalism* (Penguin, 2001)

Autor, David H., *Outsourcing at Will: Unjust Dismissal Doctrine and the Growth of Temporary Help Employment*, NBER working paper 7557 (Feb. 2000)

Baker, G., and Smith, G., *The New Financial Capitalists* (Cambridge University Press, 1998)

Balanya, Belen, et al., *Europe Inc* (Pluto, 2000)

Barber, Benjamin R., 'How to Make Society More Civil and Democracy Strong', in Anthony Giddens (ed.), *The Global Third Way Debate* (Polity, 2001)

Barnouw, Erik *et al.*, *Conglomerates and the Media* (New Press, 1997)

Barry, Brian, *Culture and Equality: An Egalitarian Critique of Multiculturalism* (Polity, 2001)

Bauman, Zygmunt, *Globalization: The Human Consequences* (Polity, 1998)

Baun, Michael J., 'The Maastricht Treaty as High Politics: Germany, France, and European Integration', *Political Science Quarterly* (Winter 1996)

Beck, Wolfgang, van der Maesen, Laurent, and Walker, Alan (eds), *The Social Quality of Europe* (Kluwer Law International, 1997)

Beckett, Katherine, and Sasson, Theodore, *The Politics of Injustice* (Pine Forge Press, 2000)

Bedau, Hugo Adam, *The Death Penalty in America: Current Controversies* (Oxford University Press, 1997)

Begg, David (ed.) *EMU Prospects and Challenges* (Oxford University Press, 1998)

Bekier, Matthias M., Bogardus, Anna J., and Oldham, Tim, 'Is the Belief that Mergers Drive Revenue Growth an Illusion?', *McKinsey Quarterly* (2001), no. 4

Berman, Morris, *The Twilight of American Culture* (Norton, 2000)

Berman, William C., *America's Right Turn from Nixon to Clinton* (Johns Hopkins University Press, 1998)

Bernstein, Michael A., and Adler, David E. (eds), *Understanding American Economic Decline* (Cambridge University Press, 1994)

Bevan, Judi, *The Rise and Fall of Marks and Spencer* (Profile, 2001)

Birnbaum, Jeffrey H., *The Money Men: How the Media Undermine American Democracy* (Crown, 1996)

Bitsch, Marie-Thérèse, *Histoire de la construction Européenne*, 2nd edn (Editions Complexe, 1999)

Blakely, Edward J., and Snyder, Mary Gail, *Fortress America: Gated Communities in the United States* (Brookings Institution Press, 1997)

Bluestone, Barry, and Harrison, Bennett, *Growing Prosperity* (Houghton Mifflin, 2000)

Blumenthal, Sidney, *The Rise of the Counterestablishment* (Harper & Row, 1988)

Blustein, Paul, 'The Chastening: Inside the Crisis that Rocked the Global Financial System and Chastened the IMF', *Public Affairs* (2001)

Bossuat, G., and Wilkens, A. (eds), *Jean Monnet. L'Europe et les chemins de la Paix*, proceedings of a colloquium organised by Paris 1 University and the Historical German Institute, Paris, May 1997 (Publications de la Sorbonne, 1999)

Bowman, Scott R., *The Modern Corporation and American Political Thought: Law, Power and Ideology* (Pennsylvania State University, 1996)

Brock, David, *Blinded by the Right* (Crown Publishing, 2002)

Brown, Kenneth M., *Downsizing Science – Will the United States Pay a Price?* (AEI Press, 1998)

Buchele, Robert, and Christiansen, Jens, 'Do Employment and Income Security Cause Unemployment? A Comparative Study of the US and the E-4', *Cambridge Journal of Economics*, vol. 22 (1998)

Bugliosi, Vincent, *The Betrayal of America* (Nation Books, 2001)

Burkhauser, R. V., and Poupore, J. G., 'A Cross-National Comparison of Permanent Inequality in the United States and Germany during the 1980s', *Review of Economics and Statistics*, vol. 79, no. 1 (1997), pp. 10–17

Calhoun, Craig (ed.) *Habermas and the Public Sphere* (MIT Press, 1992)

Callinicos, Alex, *Against the Third Way* (Polity, 2001)

Carter, Dan T., *From George Wallace to Newt Gingrich – Race in the Conservative Counterrevolution, 1963–94* (Louisiana State University Press, 1996)

Charkham, Jonathan, *Keeping Good Company: A Study of Corporate Governance in Five Countries* (Clarendon Press, 1994)

Clayton, Richard, and Pontusson, Jonas, *New Politics of the Welfare State Revisited: Welfare Reform, Public Sector Restructuring and Inegalitarian Trends in Advanced Capitalist Societies* (European University Institute, 1998)

Cline, William R., *International Debt: Systemic Risk and Policy Response* (Institute for International Economics, 1984)

Coates, David, *Models of Capitalism: Growth and Stagnation in the Modern Era* (Polity, 2000)

Cobham, David, and Zis, George (eds), *From EMS to EMU* (Macmillan, 2000)

Cockett, Richard, *Thinking the Unthinkable: Think-Tanks and the Economic Counter-Revolution, 1931–83* (HarperCollins, 1994)

Cohen, G. A., *If You're an Egalitarian, How Come You're So Rich?* (Harvard University Press, 2000)

Coleman, James, *The Equality of Educational Opportunity* (US Government Printing Office, 1996)

Collins, D., 'Social Policy', in J. Lodge (ed.), *Institutions and Policies of the European Community* (Pinter, 1983)

Collins, James C., and Porras, Jerry I., *Built to Last: Success Habits of Visionary Companies* (Century, 1994)

Commonwealth Fund, *International Health Policy Survey* (Commonwealth Fund, 1998)

Comor, Edward A., *Communication, Commerce and Power: The Political Economy of America and the Direct Broadcasting Satellite 1960–2000* (Macmillan, 1998)

Cook, Adell, *Between Two Absolutes: Public Opinion and the Politics of Abortion* (Westview, 1992)

Council on Competitiveness, *US Competitiveness 2001* (Council on Competitiveness, 2001)

Cox, Ronald W., and Skidmore-Hess, Daniel, *US Politics and the Global Economy: Corporate Power, Conservative Shift* (Lynne Rienner, 1999)

Cram, Laura, 'The Commission as a Multi-organisation: Social Policy and IT Policy in the EU', *Journal of European Public Policy*, vol. 1, no. 2 (1994)

Critchlow, Donald, *Intended Consequences* (Oxford University Press, 1999)

Cummings, Stephen D., *The Dixification of America* (Praeger, 1998)

Curtin, Deirdre M., *Postnational Democracy: The European Union in Search of a Political Philosophy* (Kluwer Law International, 1997)

Dallek, Robert, *Ronald Reagan: The Politics of Symbolism* (Harvard University Press, 1994)

Darity, William, and Horn, Bobbie, *The Loan Pushers* (Ballinger, 1988)

Daveri, Francesco, and Tabellini, Guido, *Unemployment, Growth and Taxation in Industrial Countries* (Centre for Economic Policy Research, 1997)

Davidson, Osha Gray, *Under Fire: The NRA and the Battle for Gun Control* (University of Iowa Press, 1998)

Davis, E. Philip, and Steil, Benn, *Institutional Investors* (MIT Press, 2001)

Deeg, Richard, *Finance Capitalism Unveiled: Banks and the German Political Economy* (University of Michigan Press, 1999)

Dehousse, Renaud, 'Integration vs Regulation? On the Dynamics of Regulation in the European Community', *Journal of Common Market Studies*, vol. 30, no. 4 (1992)

DeMartino, George F., *Global Economy, Global Justice: Theoretical Objections and Policy Alternatives to Neoliberalism* (Routledge, 2000)

Denham, Andrew, *Think-Tanks of the New Right* (Dartmouth, 1996)

Diamond, Peter, 'A Model of Price Adjustment', *Journal of Economic Theory*, no. 3 (1971)

Dolowitz, David, *Learning from America: Policy Transfer and the Development of the British Workfare State* (Sussex Academic Press, 1998)

Dolowitz, David, *et al.*, *Policy Transfer and British Social Policy: Learning from the USA?* (Open University Press, 2000)

Dore, Ronald, *Stock Market Capitalism: Welfare Capitalism, Japan and Germany vs. the Anglo-Saxons* (Oxford University Press, 2000)

Drew, Elizabeth, *The Corruption of American Politics* (Overlook Press, 2000)

Drew, Elizabeth, *Whatever it Takes* (Penguin, 1997)

Drury, Shadia B., *Leo Strauss and the American Right* (Macmillan, 1997)

Durkheim, Emile, *De la division du travail social*, 5th edn (Félix Alcan, 1926; first publ. 1893)

Dworkin, Ronald, 'Does Equality Matter?', in Anthony Giddens (ed.), *The Global Third Way Debate* (Polity, 2001)

Dymski, Gary A., *The Bank Merger Wave: The Economic Causes and Social Consequences of Financial Consolidation* (M. E. Sharpe, 1999)

Easton, Nina J., *Gang of Five* (Simon & Schuster, 2000)

Eatwell, John, and Taylor, Lance, *Global Finance at Risk* (New Press, 2000)

Economic Policy Institute, *Hardship in America* (2001)

Economist Intelligence Unit, *Sweden: a Guide to Financial Management in a Global Economy* (EIU, 2001).

Edsall, Thomas Byrne, *Chain Reaction: The Impact of Race, Rights and Taxes on American Politics* (Norton, 1991)

Ehrenreich, Barbara, *Nickel and Dimed* (Metropolitan Books, 2001)

Ehrman, John, *The Rise of Neoconservatism: Intellectuals and Foreign Affairs* (Yale University Press, 1995)

Eichengreen, Barry, *Globalising Capital* (Princeton, 1996)

Eitrheim, Pal, and Kuhnle, Stein, *The Scandinavian Model: Trends and Perspectives*, EU working paper 99/7 (1999)

Enthoven, Alain, *Reflections on the Management of the NHS* (Nuffield Trust, 1985)

Erikson, Robert, and Goldthorpe, John, 'Are American Rates of Social Mobility Exceptionally High?', *European Sociological Review* (May 1985)

Esping-Andersen, Gosta, *The Three Political Economies of the Welfare State* (European University Institute, 1988)

Esping-Andersen, Gosta, 'A Welfare State for the Twenty-first Century', in Anthony Giddens (ed.), *The Global Third Way Debate* (Polity, 2001)

European Commission, *One Market, One Money: European Economy*, 44 (Luxembourg, Oct. 1990)

European Commission, *RTD Strategies of the Top 500 European Industrial Companies and their Participation in the Framework Programme and EUREKA*, report 17244 (European Commission, 1996)

Fairris, David, *Shopfloor Matters: Labor–Management Relations in Twentieth-Century American Manufacturing* (Routledge, 1997)

Fallows, James, *Breaking the News: The Real Story of Political Power in America* (Crown, 2000)

Ferrera, Maurizio, Hemerijck, Anton, and Rhodes, Martin, 'The Future of Social Europe: Recasting Work and Welfare in the New Economy', in Anthony Giddens (ed.), *The Global Third Way Debate* (Polity, 2001)

Finlay, Ian, Niven, Stuart, and Young, Stephanie (eds), *Changing Vocational Education and Training: An International Comparative Perspective* (Routledge, 1998)

Fischer, Andrew, Jordan, Thomas, and Lack, Caeser, *Giving Up the Swiss Franc: Some Considerations on Seigniorage under EMU*, CEPR discussion paper DP 3156 (Dec. 2001)

Fligstein, Neil, and Mara-Drita, Iona, 'How to Make a Market: Reflections on the Attempt to Create a Single Market in the European Union', *American Journal of Sociology* (July 1996)

Forder, James, and Chris Huhne, *Both Sides of the Coin* (Penguin, 2001)

Frank, Robert H. *Luxury Fever* (Free Press, 1999)

Frank, Robert H., and Cook, Philip J., *The Winner-Take-All Society* (Free Press, 1995)

Frank, Thomas, *One Market Under God* (Secker & Warburg, 2001)

Freedland, Mark, and Sciarra, Silvan (eds) *Public Services and Citizenship in EU Law* (Clarendon, 1998)

Freeman, Richard, *The Politics of Health in Europe* (Manchester University Press, 2000)

Freeman, Richard, *The US Economic Model at Y2K: Lodestar for Advanced Capitalism*, working paper 7757 (National Bureau for Economic Research, June 2000)

Frey, William, Abresch, Bill, and Yesting, Jonathan, *America by the Numbers* (New Press, 2001)

Friedman, Milton, *Capitalism and Freedom* (Chicago University Press, 1962)

Gabe, Jonathan, *The Americanization of British Health Care* (Royal Holloway, 1997)

Gabel, Matthew J., *Interests and Integration: Market Liberalization, Public Opinion and European Union* (University of Michigan Press, 1998)

Garry, Patrick M., *A Nation of Adversaries: How the Litigation Explosion is Reshaping America* (Plenum, 1997)

Gates, Jeff, *The Ownership Solution: Toward a Shared Capitalism for the Twenty-first Century* (Allen Lane, 1998)

Gibson, James William, *Warrior Dreams: Violence and Manhood in Post-Vietnam America* (Hill & Wang, 1994)

Giddens, Anthony, 'The Question of Inequality', in Anthony Giddens (ed.), *The Global Third Way Debate* (Polity, 2001)

Giddens, Anthony (ed.), *The Global Third Way Debate* (Polity, 2001)

Glassman, Ronald M., *Caring Capitalism: A New Middle-class Base for the Welfare State* (Macmillan, 2000)

Godley, Wynne, and Izuricta, Alex, *The Developing US Recession and Guidelines for Policy*, Levy Economics Foundation, Oct. 2001

Gordon, Robert J., 'Does the "New Economy" Measure Up to the Great Inventions of the Past?', draft paper for *Journal of Economic Perspectives* (2000)

Gowan, Peter, *The Global Gamble: Washington's Faustian Bid for World Dominance* (Verso, 1999)

Grant, Charles, *EU 2010: An Optimistic Vision for the Future* (Centre for European Policy Reform, 2001)

Grant, Charles, *The House that Jacques Built* (Nicholas Brealey, 1994)

Grantham, Dewey W., *The South in Modern America: A Region at Odds* (HarperPerennial Library, 1995)

Gray, John, *False Dawn: The Delusions of Global Capitalism* (Granta, 1998)

Greider, William, *One World Ready or Not: The Manic Logic of Global Capitalism* (Simon & Schuster, 1997)

Greven, Michael T., 'Can the European Union Finally become a Democracy?', in Michael T. Greven and Louis W. Pauly (eds), *Democracy Beyond the State: The European Dilemma and the Emerging Global Order* (Rowman and Littlefield, 2000)

Greven, Michael, and Pauly, Louis W. (eds), *Democracy beyond the State? The European Dilemma and the Emerging Global Order* (Rowman and Littlefield, 2000)

Griliches, Z., 'R&D and Productivity,' in collected papers (University of Chicago, 1998)

Guyatt, Nicholas, *Another American Century? The United States and the World after 2000* (Zed, 2000)

Habermas, Jürgen, 'The European Nation-State and the Pressures of Globalization', *New Left Review*, May–June 1999

Habermas, Jürgen, *The Structural Transformation of the Public Sphere* (Polity, 1985)

Habermas, Jürgen, 'Why Europe Needs a Constitution', *New Left Review*, Sept.–Oct. 2001

Hall, Peter, 'The Evolution of Economic Policy', in A. Guyomarch, H. Machin, P. Hall and J. Hayward (eds), *Developments in French Politics 2* (Palgrave, 2001)

Hall, Peter, and David Soskice, *Varieties of Capitalism: The Institutional Foundations of Comparative Advantage* (Oxford University Press (2001)

Hanley, D. L. (ed.), *Christian Democracy in Europe: A Comparative Perspective* (Pinter, 1993)

Hauser, Robert, *et al.*, 'Occupation Status, Education and Social Mobility in the Meritocracy', in Kenneth Arrow, Samuel Bowles and Steven Durlauf (eds), *Meritocracy and Economic Inequality* (Princeton University Press, 2000)

Hayward, Jack (ed.), *The Crisis of Representation in Europe* (Frank Cass, 1995)

Heineman, Kenneth J., *God is a Conservative* (New York University Press, 1998)

Held, David, *et al.*, *Global Transformations* (Polity, 1999)

Hendry, D. F., and Ericsson, N. R., 'An Econometric Analysis of UK Money Demand in *Monetary Trends in the United States and the United Kingdom* by Milton Friedman and Anna J. Schwartz', *American Economic Review* (1991), 8–38

Henwood, Doug, *Wall Street: How It Works and for Whom* (Verso, 1997)

Héritier, Adrienne, 'Policy-Making by Subterfuge: Interest Accommodation, Innovation and Substitute Democratic Legitimation in Europe', *Journal of European Public Policy*, vol. 4, no. 2 (1997)

Herman, Edward S., and McChesney, Robert W., *The Global Media: The New Missionaries of Global Capitalism* (Cassell, 1997)

Hernson, Paul S. (ed.), *The Clinton Presidency: The First Term* (Macmillan, 1999)

Herzenberg, Stephen A., *et al.*, *New Rules for a New Economy: Employment and Opportunity in Postindustrial America* (Cornell University Press, 1998)

Hey, Kenneth R., and Moore, Peter D., *The Caterpillar Doesn't Know* (Free Press, 1998)

Hill, Andrew D., 'Wrongful Discharge' and the Derogation of the At-Will Employment Doctrine, Labor Relations and Public Policy Series no. 3, 1 (University of Pennsylvania, 1987)

Hindley, Brian, and Howe, Martin, *Better Off Out? The Benefits or Costs of EU Membership* (Institute of Economic Affairs, 2001)

Hix, Simon, *The Political System of the European Union* (Macmillan, 1999)

Hobhouse, Dominic, and Duncan, Alan, *Saturn's Children: How the State Devours Liberty and Prosperity* (Sinclair-Stevenson, 1995)

Hoffe, Otfried, *L'Etat et la Justice : John Rawls et Robert Nozick* (Librairie Philosophique Jean Vrin, 1988)

Hollingsworth, J. Rogers, and Boyer, Robert (eds), *Contemporary Capitalism: The Embeddedness of Institutions* (Cambridge University Press, 1997)

Hooghe, Lisbet, *Territorial Politics – A Zero-sum Game? EU Cohesion Policy and Competing Models of European Capitalism*, European University Institute working paper 98/41 (1998)

Hooghe, Lisbet, and Marks, Gary, *The Making of a Polity: The Struggle over European Integration*, European University Institute working paper 97/31 (1997)

Hopner, Martin, *Corporate Governance in Transition: Ten Empirical Findings on Shareholder Value and Industrial Relations in Germany*, discussion paper 01/05 (Max Planck Institute, 2001)

Hudson, Michael (ed.), *Merchants of Misery: How Corporate America Profits from Poverty* (Common Courage Press, 1996)

Hutton, Will, *The State We're In* (Cape, 1995; pb Vintage, 1996)

Inglehart, Ronald, Basaney, Miguel, and Moreno, Alejandro, *Human Values and Beliefs: A Cross-Cultural Sourcebook. Political, Religious, Sexual and Economic Norms in 43 Countries: Findings from the 1990–93 World Value Survey* (University of Michigan Press, 1998)

Institute for Public Policy Research, *Building Better Partnerships*, (IPPR, 2001)

Isles, Nic, and Palazzi, Marcello (eds), *The European Model for Enterprise* (Industrial Society Learning/Capita, 2002)

Iversen, Torben, *et al.* (eds), *Unions, Employers and Central Banks: Macroeconomic Coordination and Institutional Change in Social Market Economies* (Cambridge University Press, 2000)

Jabko, Nicolas, 'In the Name of the Market: How the European Commission Paved the Way for Monetary Union', *Journal of European Public Policy* (Sept. 1999)

Jacquet, Pierre, and Pisani-Ferry, Jean, *Economic Policy Co-ordination in the Euro-zone* (Centre for European Reform, 2001)

Jensen, M., 'The Modern Industrial Revolution: Exit and the Failure of Internal Control Systems', *Journal of Finance* 48, no. 9 (July 1993), pp. 831–80

Jensen, M., and Ruback, R., 'The Market for Corporate Control: The Scientific Evidence', *Journal of Financial Economics* (1983), no. 11, pp. 5–50

Johnson, Chalmers, *Blowback* (Little, Brown, 2000)

Johnson, Debra, and Turner, Colin, *Trans-European Networks: The Political Economy of Integrating Europe's Infrastructure* (Macmillan, 1997)

Jones, Ci, and Williams, J. C., 'Measuring the Social Return to R&D', *Quarterly Journal of Economics* (Nov. 1998)

Johnston, Carla Brooks, *Screened Out: How the Media Control Us and What We Can Do About It* (M. E. Sharpe, 2000)

Jowell, Roger et al. (eds), *British Social Attitudes; the 16th Report. Who Shares New Labour Values?* (National Centre for Social Research, 1999)

Judis, John B., *The Paradox of American Democracy: Elites, Special Interests and the Betrayal of Public Trust* (Random House, 2000)

Judis, John B., and Teixeira, Ruy, *The Emerging Democratic Majority* (Scribner, 2001)

Kann, Mark E., *A Republic of Men* (New York University Press, 1988)

Kant, Immanuel, *Political Writings*, ed. Hans Reiss, trans. H. B. Nisbett (Cambridge University Press, 1970)

Karake Shalhoub, Zeinab A., *Organizational Down-sizing, Discrimination and Corporate Social Responsibility* (Quorum, 1994)

Katz, Harry C. (ed.), *Telecommunications: Restructuring Work and Employment Relations Worldwide* (Cornell University Press, 1997)

Kennedy, Alan, *The End of Shareholder Value: The Real Effects of the Shareholder Value Phenomenon and the Crisis it is Bringing to Business* (Orion Business, 2000)

Kersbergen, Kees van, *Social Capitalism: A Study of Christian Democracy and the Welfare State* (Routledge, 1995)

King, Lawrence Peter, *The Basic Features of Postcommunist Capitalism in Eastern Europe: Firms in Hungary, the Czech Republic and Slovakia* (Praeger, 2001)

Klein, Naomi, *No Logo* (Flamingo, 2000)

Kluth, Michael F., *The Political Economy of a Social Europe: Understanding Labour Market Integration in the European Union* (Macmillan, 1998)

Knack, S., and Keefern, P. 'Does Social Capital Have an Economic Pay-off?', *Quarterly Journal of Economics*, 1997, 4, pp. 1251–88

KPMG, *Unlocking Shareholder Value, the Key to Success* (KPMG, 2001)

Kreisky, Bruno, 'The Hidden Agenda of the Information Society', *International Studies* (1997)

Kroes, Rob, *If You've Seen One You've Seen the Mall: Europeans and American Mass Culture* (University of Illinois Press, 1996)

Krugman, Paul, *Peddling Prosperity* (Norton, 1994)

Kukathas, Chandran, and Philip Pettit, *Rawls, a Theory of Justice and its Critics* (Polity, 1990)

Kuttner, Robert, *Everything for Sale: The Virtues and Limits of Markets* (Knopf, 1996)

Kuttner, Robert, *The End of Laissez-Faire: National Purpose and the Global Economy after the Cold War* (University of Pennsylvania Press, 1991)

Lafontaine, Oskar, 'The Future of German Social Democracy', *New Left Review* 227 (Jan.–Feb. 1998)

Landesmann, Michael A., and Pichelman, Karl (eds), *Unemployment in Europe*, proceedings of a conference held by the Confederation of European Economic Associations, Vienna (Macmillan, 2000)

Lasch, Christopher, *The Culture of Narcissism* (Norton, 1979)

Leach, William, *Country of Exiles: The Destruction of Place in American Life* (Pantheon, 1999)

Lemann, Nicholas, *The Big Test: The Secret History of the American Meritocracy* (Farrar, Straus & Giroux, 1999)

Light, Donald, and May, Annabelle, *Britain's Health System: From Welfare State to Managed Markets* (Faulkner & Gray, 1993)

Link, Rosemary J., Anthony, A., *et al.*, *When Children Pay: US Welfare Reform and its Implications for UK Policy* (Child Poverty Action Group, 2000)

Lipset, Seymour Martin, *American Exceptionalism: A Double-edged Sword* (Norton, 1999)

Lipset, Seymour Martin, and Bendix, R., *Social Mobility in Industrial Society* (University of California Press, 1967)

Lipset, Seymour Martin, and Marks, Gary, *It Didn't Happen Here: Why Socialism Failed in the United States* (Norton, 2000)

Litan, Robert E., and Rauch, Jonathan, *American Finance for the 21st Century* (Brookings Institution Press, 1998)

Locke, John, *Two Treatises of Government* (Cambridge University Press, 1988)

Lodge, J. (ed.), *Institutions and Policies of the European Community* (Pinter, 1983)

Lynn, Matthew, *Birds of Prey: The War Between Boeing and Airbus* (Four Walls Eight Windows, 1997)

McAllister, Matthew P., *The Commercialisation of American Culture* (Sage, 1996)

Macfarlane, Leslie J., *Socialism, Social Ownership and Social Justice* (Macmillan, 1998)

McQuaid, Kim, *Uneasy Partners: Big Business in American Politics 1945–1990* (Johns Hopkins University Press, 1994)

Madison, James, *et al.*, *The Federalist Papers* (Penguin, 1987)

Majone, Giandomenico, *Regulating Europe* (Routledge, 1996)

Mandel, Michael, *The Coming Internet Depression* (Pearson Education, 2001)

Marchak, Patricia M., *The Integrated Circus: The New Right and the Restructuring of Global Markets* (McGill-Queen's University Press, 1991)

Marks, Gary, *et al.* (eds), *Governance in the European Union* (Sage, 1996)

Marsden, Keith, *Towards a Treaty of Commerce* (Centre for Policy Studies, 2000)

Marshall, T. H., *Citizenship and Social Class* (Cambridge University Press, 1950)

Mazower, Mark, *Dark Continent* (Penguin, 1998)

Melchionni, Maria Grazia, *Altiero Spinelli et Jean Monnet* (Fondation Jean Monnet pour l'Europe, 1993)

Mellin, Phil, and Roper, Jon, *Americanisation and the Transformation of World Cultures: Melting Pot or Cultural Chernobyl* (Edwin Mellen, 1996)

Mény, Yves, 'Five (Hypo)theses on Democracy and its Future', in Anthony Giddens (ed.), *The Global Third Way Debate* (Polity, 2001)

Micklethwait, John, and Wooldridge, Adrian, *The Witch Doctors: What the Management Gurus Are Saying, Why It Matters and How to Make Sense of It* (Heinemann, 1996)

Midgley, James, 'Growth, Redistribution and Welfare: Towards Social Investment', in Anthony Giddens (ed.), *The Global Third Way Debate* (Polity, 2001)

Miles, David, 'Testing for Short-Termism in the UK Stock Market', *Economic Journal* (Nov. 1993)

Mishel, Lawrence, Bernstein, Jared, and Schmitt, John, *The State of Working America 2000–2001* (Cornell University Press, 2001)

Misner, Paul, *Social Catholicism in Europe: From the Onset of Industrialisation to the First World War* (Darton, Longman and Todd, 1991)

Monks, Robert, *The New Global Investors* (Capstone, 2001)

Morris, Dick, *Behind the Oval Office* (Renaissance, 1997)

Mowery, David C., *US Industry in 2000: Studies in Competitive Performance* (National Academy Press, 1999)

Mowery, David, and Rosenberg, Nathan, *Paths of Innovation: Technological Change in Twentieth-Century America* (Cambridge University Press, 1998)

National Institute for Economic and Social Research, *Britain's Productivity Performance, 1990–1996* (NIESR, 1999)

Nelson, Joel L., *Post-Industrial Capitalism: Exploring Economic Inequality in America* (Sage, 1995)

Nickell, Stephen, 'The Distribution of Wages and Unemployment across Skill Groups', in Michael Landesmann and Karl Pichelman (eds), *Unemployment in Europe* (Macmillan, 2000)

Nickell, Stephen, *The Performance of Companies* (Blackwell, 1995)

Nielsen, Ruth, and Szyszczak, Erika, *The Social Dimension of the European Union* (Handelshojskolens Forlag, 1997)

No Campaign, 'The Economic Case against the Euro', *New Europe* (2001)

Nozick, Robert, *Anarchy, State and Utopia* (Harvard University Press, 1973)

Nuffield Trust, *Reflections on the Management of the NHS* (Nuffield Trust, 1985)

Nugent, Neil, *The Government and Politics of the EU*, 4th edn (Macmillan, 1999)

Nye, Joseph S., 'In Government We Don't Trust', in Anthony Giddens (ed.), *The Global Third Way Debate* (Polity, 2001)

O'Connor, Karen, *No Neutral Ground?* (Westview, 1996)

OECD, *Benefit Systems and Work Incentives* (OECD, 1999)

OECD, *Economic Outlook* no. 70 (OECD, Dec. 2001)

OECD, *Education at a Glance: OECD Indicators* (OECD, 2000)

OECD, *Growth Effects of Education and Social Capital in the OECD Countries*, working paper no. 263 (OECD, 2000)

OECD, *Health Data 1999: A Comparative Analysis of 29 Countries* (OECD, 1999)

OECD, *Human Capital Investment* (OECD, 1998)

OECD, *OECD Economic Survey of the Euro Area* (OECD, 2001)

OECD, *OECD Economic Surveys – France* (OECD, 1997)

OECD, *OECD Economic Surveys – Germany* (OECD, May 2001)

OECD, *OECD Employment Outlook 2000* (OECD, 2000)

OECD, *Taxing Wages in OECD Countries* (OECD, 1998/9)

Olufs III, Dick W., *The Making of Telecommunications Policy* (Lynne Rienner, 1999)

O'Mahoney, Mary, *Britain's Productivity Performance, 1990–1996* (NIESR, 1999)

Osterman, Paul (ed.), *Broken Ladder: Managerial Careers in the New Economy* (Oxford University Press, 1996)

O'Sullivan, Mary, *Contests for Corporate Control: Corporate Governance and Economic Performance in the United States and Germany* (Oxford University Press, 2000)

Palley, Thomas I., *Plenty of Nothing* (Princeton University Press, 1998)

Paraschos, Emmanuel E., *Media Law and Regulation in the European Union: National, Transnational and US Perspectives* (Iowa State University Press, 1998)

Parkinson, J. E., *Corporate Power and Responsibility: Issues in the Theory of Company Law* (Clarendon Press, 1993)

Paul, Ellen Frankel, and Dickman, Howard (eds), *Liberty, Property and the Foundations of the American Constitution* (State University of New York Press, 1989)

Perlstein, Rick, *Before the Storm* (Hill & Wang, 2001)

Petras, James, and Morley, Morris, *Empire or Republic?* (Routledge, 1995)

Pfeffer, Leo, *This Honourable Court: A History of the United States Supreme Court* (Beacon Press, 1965)

Pierson, Paul, 'The Path to European Integration', *Comparative Political Studies*, vol. 29, no. 2 (1996)

Pinto, Arthur R., and Visentini, Gustavo (eds), *The Legal Basis of Corporate Governance in Publicly Held Corporations: A Comparative Approach* (Kluwer Law International, 1998)

Pitt, Ivan L., and Norsworthy, John R., *Economics of the US Commercial Airline Industry: Productivity, Technology and Deregulation* (Kluwer Academic, 1999)

Pollack, Mark, 'Delegation, Agency and Agenda-Setting in the European Community', *International Organisation*, vol. 51, no. 1 (1997)

Porter, Michael E., *On Competition* (Harvard University Press, 1996)

Porter, Michael E., *The Competitive Advantage of Nations* (Macmillan, 1998)

Porter, Michael E., and van Opstal, Debra, *US Competitiveness 2001* (US Council on Competitiveness, 2001)

Postman, Neil, *Amusing Ourselves to Death: Public Discourse in the Age of Show Business* (Methuen, 1985)

Powell, Martin (ed.), *New Labour, New Welfare State: The Third Way in British Social Policy*, (Polity, 1999)

Poynter, Gavin, *Restructuring in the Service Industry: Management Reform and Workplace Relations in the UK Service Sector* (Mansell, 2000)

Pries, Ludiger, *Accelerating from a Multinational to a Transnational Carmaker: The Volkswagen Consortium in the 1990s* (Institute of Sociology, University of Erlanger-Nurnberg, 1999)

Purdey, Jebediah, *For Common Things* (Knopf, 2000)

Puttnam, Robert D., *Bowling Alone* (Simon & Schuster, 2000)

Ranade, Wendy (ed.), *Markets and Health Care: A Comparative Analysis* (Longman, 1998)

Rawls, John, *A Theory of Justice* (Oxford University Press, 1973)

Reich, Robert, *The Future of Success* (Knopf, 2001)

Reynolds, David, *One World Divisible* (Allen Lane, 2000)

Rifkin, Jeremy, *The Age of Access* (Putnam, 2000)

Roberts, Richard, and Kynaston, David, *City and State* (Profile, 2001)

Robinson, John P., and Godbey, Geoffrey, *Time for Life* (Pennsylvania University Press, 1999)

Rosanvallon, Pierre, *The New Social Question: Rethinking the Welfare State* (Princeton University Press, 2000; first publ. in French as *La Nouvelle Question Sociale: Repenser l'Etat Providence*, Seuil, 1995)

Saint-Martin, Denis, *Building the New Managerialist State: Consultants and the Politics of Public Sector Reform in Comparative Perspective* (Oxford University Press, 2000)

Sandel, Michael, *Democracy's Discontent: America in Search of a Public Philosophy* (Harvard University Press, 1996)

Sassoon, Donald, *One Hundred Years of Socialism: The West European Left in the Twentieth Century* (I. B. Tauris, 1996)

Sauter, Wolf, 'EU Competition Rules: Promoting and Policing the Internal Market', in Thomas C. Lawton (ed.), *European Industrial Policy and Competitiveness* (Macmillan, 1999)

Scharpf, Fritz, *Governing in Europe: Effective and Democratic?* (European University Institute, 1999)

Scharpf, Fritz, 'The Joint Decision Trap: Lessons from German Federalism and European Integration', *Public Administration*, vol. 66, no. 3 (1988)

Schiller, Dan, *Digital Capitalism: Networking the Global Market System* (MIT Press, 1998)

Schiller, Herbert, *Information Inequality* (Routledge, 1996)

Schiller, Robert J., *Irrational Exuberance* (Princeton University Press, 2000)

Schmitter, Philippe C., *How to Democratize the European Union . . . And Why Bother?* (Rowman & Littlefield, 2000)

Schor, Juliet (ed.), *Do Americans Shop Too Much?* (Beacon Press, 2000)

Schweiger, Georg Christopher, *European Central Bank* (Minerva, 2000)

Seabrooke, Leonard, *US Power in International Finance: The Victory of Dividends* (Palgrave, 2001)

Sennett, Richard, *The Corrosion of Character* (Norton, 1998)

Sennett, Richard, *The Fall of Public Man* (Faber, 1993)

Sfez, Lucien, *Leçons sur l'égalité* (Presses de la Fondation Nationale des Sciences Politiques, 1984)

Shahin, Jamal, and Wintle, Michael (eds), *The Idea of a United Europe: Political, Economic and Cultural Integration since the Fall of the Berlin Wall* (Macmillan, 2000)

Siedentop, Larry, *Democracy in Europe* (Allen Lane / Penguin Press, 2000)

Skidelsky, Robert, *John Maynard Keynes: Fighting for Britain* (Macmillan, 2000)

Slater, David, and Taylor, Peter S. (eds), *The American Century: Consensus and Coercion in the Projection of American Power* (Blackwell, 1999)

Slotkin, Richard, *Gunfighter Nation: The Myth of the Frontier in Twentieth-Century America* (Atheneum, 1992)

Smeeding, Timothy, *Financial Poverty in Developed Countries: The Evidence from the Luxembourg Income Study* (UNDP, 1997)

Smith, Mitchell P., 'Autonomy by the Rules: The European Commission and the Development of State Aid Policy', *Journal of Common Market Studies* (March 1998)

Solinger, Ricky (ed.), *Abortion Wars* (University of California Press, 1998)

Sorkin, Michael (ed.), *Variations on a Theme Park: The New American City and the End of Public Space* (Hill & Wang, 2000)

Soskice, David, 'Divergent Production Regimes: Coordinated and Uncoordinated Market Economies in the 1980s and 1990s', in H. Kitschelt, P. Lange, G. Marks and J. D. Stevens (eds), *Continuity and Change in Contemporary Capitalism* (Cambridge University Press, 1999)

Sparrow, Bartholomew H., *Uncertain Guardians: The News Media as a Political Institution* (Johns Hopkins University Press, 1999)

Spector, Robert, *Amazon.com: Get Big Fast* (Random House, 2000)

Steinbock, Dan, *The Nokia Revolution: The Story of an Extraordinary Company that Transformed an Industry* (Amacom, 2001)

Strauss, Leo, *Natural Rights and History* (Chicago University Press, 1953)

Streeck, Wolfgang, 'Beneficial Constraints on the Economic Limits of Rational Voluntarism', in J. Rogers Hollingsworth and Robert Boyer (eds), *Contemporary Capitalism: The Embeddedness of Institutions* (Cambridge University Press, 1997)

Streeck, Wolfgang, 'Neo-voluntarism: A New European Social Policy Regime', in Gary Marks et al. (eds), *Governance in the European Union* (Sage, 1996)

Tawney, R. H., *Equality* (Allen & Unwin, 1931; rev. 1938, 1952)

Teixeira, Ruy, and Rogers, Joel, *America's Forgotten Majority: Why the White Working Class Still Matters* (Basic Books, 2000)

Thatcher, Margaret, *Statecraft* (HarperCollins, 2002)

Thelen, Kathleen, 'Why German Employers Cannot Bring Themselves to Dismantle the German Model', in Torben Iversen et al. (eds), *Unions, Employers and Central Banks* (Cambridge University Press, 2000)

Thornley, Andy, *Urban Planning under Thatcherism: The Challenge of the Market* (Routledge, 1991)

Tocqueville, Alexis de, *Democracy in America* (Cambridge, 1864)

Treasury, *The Myners Report* (HM Treasury, 2001)

Triplett, Jack E., *Economic Statistics, the New Economy, and the Productivity Slowdown* (Brookings Institution, 1999)

TUC Task Force on Promoting Trade Unionism, *Reaching the Missing Millions* (TUC, Aug. 2001)

Turner, Adair, *Just Capital* (Macmillan, 2001)

Védrine, Hubert, and Moïsi, Dominique, *France in an Age of Globalisation* (Brookings Institution, 2001)

Von Ark, Bart, *et al.* (eds), *Productivity, Technology and Economic Growth* (Kluwer, 2000)

Wallace, William, and Smith, Julie, 'Democracy or Technocracy? European Integration and the Problem of Popular Consent', in Jack Hayward (ed.), *The Crisis of Representation in Europe* (Frank Cass, 1995)

Walter, Andrew, *World Power and World Money* (Harvester Wheatsheaf, 1993)

Watson, Justin, *The Christian Coalition* (Macmillan, 1999)

Weiler, J. H. H., *The Constitution of Europe: 'Do the New Clothes Have an Emperor?' and other Essays on European Integration* (Cambridge University Press, 1999)

Wenglinsky, Harold, *When Money Matters: How Educational Expenditures Improve Student Performance and How They Don't* (Princeton University Press, 1997)

Zepengauer, Mark, and Naiman, Arthur, *Take the Risk of Welfare* (Odonion, 1996)

Zweig, Michael, *The Working Class Majority: America's Best Kept Secret* (Cornell University Press, 2000)

Zweigenhaft, Richard L., and Domhoff, William, *Diversity in the Power Elite: Have Women and Minorities Reached the Top?* (Yale University Press, 1998)

Index

Index

American state tradition, and the public realm 80–2
American War of Independence 40, 209
  and property 52, 56–7
Anderson, Mark 147
Aquinas, St Thomas 54
Arendt, Hannah 84
aristocracy, and the concept of *noblesse oblige* 68
Aristotle 83
Ashcroft, John 81, 96
Asian economies 197, 199, 329
AT&T 200, 201, 204, 205
Augustine, St 54

Baker, George 134
banks:
  and the Basle Accord 191
  and corporate America 119, 125–7
  deregulation 113, 126–7, 169, 191
  European banking systems 247, 248
  European Central Bank (ECB) 332, 333, 334, 336, 337, 338, 339, 340, 341, 342
  German 263–4
  investment banks in Britain 36–7
  Nordic countries 265
  US Federal Reserve (the Fed) 16, 21, 27, 191, 193
Barry, Brian 77
Bartley, Robert 104
Berlusconi, Silvio 345
Bevan, Judi 227
Birnbaum, Jeffrey 172
black Americans:
  and American conservatism 99, 105, 108
  and American liberalism 92–3
  and civil rights 18, 43, 88–9, 91, 92
  and the New Deal 87
  and the underclass 213
Blair, Tony 34, 36, 208, 229
Bloomberg, Michael 171, 370
Bluestone, Barry 22
Blustein, Paul 197
Boeing 122–3, 128–33, 141, 249, 250–1
Brandts, Franz 64
Britain 268–71, 358–64
  and American conservatism 5–6, 16–17, 19, 34–42, 208–36
  Conservative Party 14, 41, 211, 228

economic performance 211, 218, 269, 331–2
  and the euro 1, 3, 331–46
  and the European Union 15, 16–17, 228, 236, 263, 294, 297, 301, 307–8, 362
    and the EMS 295, 307, 327
  inequalities in 5, 181, 218, 274–5, 358–9
  Labour government (1945) 213
  manufacturing sector 331–2
  political apathy in 2
  private schools 156–7, 181
  and the public realm 2, 5, 79, 81, 178, 218
  relationship with the United States 34–42, 209–11
  and telecoms deregulation 206
  unemployment 218, 254, 275
  see also businesses, British; New Labour
broadcasting, public service 282
Brock, David 114
Brown, Gordon 208, 221, 229, 269, 336, 343
Buchanan, Pat 110
Buckley, William 94
Buffet, Warren 153, 154–5, 157
Bugliosi, Vincent 44
Built to Last (Collins and Porras) 23, 360
Buiter, Professor William 333
Bush family 157
Bush, George, senior 34, 107, 108, 109–10, 192
Bush, George W. 87–8, 367, 369
  and American unilateralism 10, 115, 353
  anti-terrorist measures 81
  and Britain 36
  and the presidential election (2000) 30, 33, 43
  and taxation 28–9, 149, 153, 172
businesses:
  British:
    codes of corporate governance 269
    and European capitalism 268–70
    ideology of 359–61
    and New Labour 217, 230, 361–6
    productivity, innovation and shareholder value 219–28
  European attitudes to 230